Investing For Canadians For Dummies, 3rd Edition

By Eric Tyson and Tony Martin

D1533261

Cheat Sheet

Tony and Eric's 20 Immutable Investing Laws

1. **Saving is a prerequisite to investing.** Unless you have wealthy, benevolent relatives, living within your means and saving money are prerequisites to investing and building wealth.

2. **Know the three best wealth-building investments.** People of all economic means make their money grow in ownership assets — stocks, real estate, and small business — where you share in the success and profitability of the asset.

3. **Be realistic about expected returns.** Over the long term, 9 to 10 percent per year is about right for ownership investments (such as stocks and real estate). If you run a small business, you can earn higher returns and even become a multimillionaire, but years of hard work and insight are required.

4. **Think long term.** Because ownership investments are riskier (more volatile), you must keep your long-term perspective when investing in them. Don't invest money in such investments unless you plan on holding them for a minimum of five years and preferably a decade or longer.

5. **Match the time frame to the investment.** Selecting good investments for yourself involves matching the time frame you have to the riskiness of the investment. For example, for money that you expect to use within the next year, focus on safe investments, such as high-interest savings accounts or money market funds. Invest your longer-term money mostly in wealth-building investments.

6. **Diversify.** Diversification is a powerful investment concept that helps you to reduce the risk of holding more aggressive investments. Diversifying simply means that you should hold a variety of investments that don't move in tandem in different market environments. For example, if you invest in stocks, invest worldwide, not just in the Canadian or North American markets. You can further diversify by investing in real estate.

7. **Look at the big picture first.** Understand your overall financial situation and how wise investments fit within it. Before you invest, examine your debt obligations, tax situation, ability to fund retirement plans, and insurance coverage.

8. **Ignore the minutiae.** Don't feel mystified by or feel the need to follow the short-term gyrations of the financial markets. Ultimately, the prices of stocks, bonds, and other financial instruments are determined by supply and demand, which are influenced by thousands of external issues and millions of investors' expectations and fears.

9. **Allocate your assets.** How you divvy up or allocate your money among major investments greatly determines your returns. The younger you are and the more money you earmark for the long term, the greater the percentage you should devote to ownership investments.

10. **Do your homework before you invest.** You work hard for your money, and investments cost you to buy and sell. Investing is not a field where acting first and asking questions later works well. Never buy an investment based on an advertisement or a salesperson's solicitation of you.

For Dummies: Bestselling Book Series for Beginners

Investing For Canadians For Dummies, 3rd Edition

By Eric Tyson and Tony Martin

Cheat Sheet

11. **Keep an eye on taxes.** Take advantage of tax-deductible RRSPs and other retirement plans, as well as RESPs and the Tax-Free Savings Account. Understand the impact of your tax bracket when investing outside tax-sheltered retirement plans.

12. **Consider the value of your time and your investing skills and desires.** Investing in stocks and other securities via the best mutual funds is both time efficient and profitable. Real estate investing and running a small business are the most time-intensive investments.

13. **Where possible, minimize fees.** The more you pay in commissions and management fees on your investments, the greater the drag on your returns. And don't fall prey to the thinking that "you get what you pay for."

14. **Don't expect to beat the market.** If you have the interest and the right skills, your ability to do better than the investing averages is greater with real estate and small business than with stock market investing. The large number of full-time, experienced stock market professionals makes it next to impossible for you to choose individual stocks that will consistently beat a relevant market average over an extended time period.

15. **Don't bail when things look bleak.** The hardest time, psychologically, to hold on to your investments is when they're down. Even the best investments go through depressed periods, which is the worst possible time to sell. Don't sell when there's a sale going on; if anything, consider buying more.

16. **Ignore soothsayers and prognosticators.** Predicting the future is nearly impossible. Select and hold good investments for the long term. Don't try to time when to be in or out of a particular investment.

17. **Minimize your trading.** The more you trade, the more likely you are to make mistakes. You also suffer increased transaction costs and higher taxes (for investments outside a tax-deferred retirement plan).

18. **Hire advisers carefully.** Before you hire investing help, first educate yourself so you can better evaluate the competence of those you may hire. Beware of conflicts of interest when you consider advisers to hire.

19. **You are what you read and listen to.** Don't pollute your mind with bad investing strategies and philosophies. The quality of what you read and listen to is far more important than the quantity. Find out how to evaluate the quality of what you read and hear.

20. **Your personal life and health are the highest-return, lowest-risk investments.** They're far more important investments than the size of your financial portfolio.

For Dummies: Bestselling Book Series for Beginners

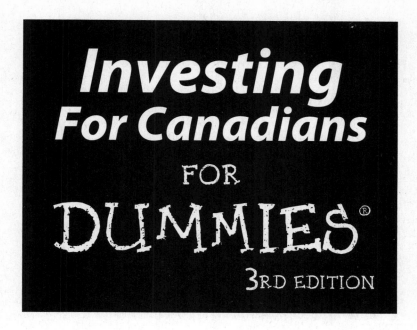

Investing
For Canadians
FOR
DUMMIES®
3RD EDITION

by Eric Tyson, MBA
Tony Martin

WILEY

John Wiley & Sons Canada, Ltd.

Investing For Canadians For Dummies®, 3rd Edition

Published by
John Wiley & Sons Canada, Ltd.
6045 Freemont Blvd.t
Mississauga, ON L5R 4J3
www.wiley.com

For general information on John Wiley & Sons Canada, Ltd., including all books published by Wiley Publishing Inc., please call our warehouse, Tel. 1-800-567-4797. For reseller information, including discounts and premium sales, please call our sales department, Tel. 416-646-7992. For press review copies, author interviews, or other publicity information, please contact our publicity department, Tel. 416-646-4582, Fax 416-236-4448.

Library and Archives Canada Cataloguing in Publication Data

Tyson, Eric (Eric Kevin)

Investing for Canadians for dummies / by Eric Tyson and Tony Martin. — 3rd ed.

Includes index.

ISBN 978-0-470-16029-9

1. Investments. 2. Investments—Canada. I. Martin, Tony (Tony M.) II. Title.

HG4521.T97 2009   332.6   C2009-901892-6

Printed in the United States

1 2 3 4 5 RRD 13 12 11 10 09

WILEY

About the Authors

Eric Tyson is an acclaimed best-selling personal finance author, lecturer, and adviser. Through his work, he is dedicated to teaching people to manage their money better and to successfully direct their own investments.

He earned a bachelor's degree in economics at Yale and an MBA at the Stanford Graduate School of Business. Despite these impediments to lucid reasoning, he came to his senses after working as a management consultant to businesses, deciding that life was too short to spend it working long hours and waiting in airports for the benefit of larger companies.

An accomplished freelance personal finance writer, Eric is the author of numerous best-selling books including *For Dummies* books on personal finance, mutual funds, taxes (co-author), and home buying (co-author) and is a syndicated columnist. His work has been featured and quoted in hundreds of U.S. national and local publications, including *Newsweek, Kiplinger's Personal Finance Magazine, The Wall Street Journal,* and on NBC's *Today Show,* ABC, CNBC, PBS's *Nightly Business Report,* CNN, National Public Radio, and Business Radio Network.

Tony Martin is a nationally recognized best-selling personal finance writer, speaker, and commentator. Tony's focus is on giving Canadians the tools they need to make sense of the world of money and investing. Through his work, he is dedicated to teaching people how to manage their money better and to successfully choose and grow their own investments.

Tony is the co-author, along with Eric, of the national best-seller *Personal Finance For Dummies For Canadians.* For many years he has also written the popular and widely read column, "Me and My Money," for the *The Globe and Mail*'s Report on Business. These columns were the focus of his book *Me and My Money: Strategies of Real-life Investors.*

A graduate in Commerce at Queen's University, his work appears regularly in leading national publications, including *The Globe and Mail, Canadian Business*, *Profit Magazine,* and *Reader's Digest.* Tony has produced television and radio programs about personal finance, and has also appeared on numerous television and radio programs, including CBC, BNN, and TVOntario.

Dedication

Actually, before we get to the thank-yous, please allow us a *really* major thank you and dedication.

This book is hereby and irrevocably dedicated to our family and friends, as well as to all those who have spoken with us over the years about investing and personal finance, who ultimately have taught us everything we know about how to explain financial terms and strategies so that all of us may benefit.

Authors' Acknowledgements

First, we'd like to thank Georgette Beatty, project editor of the US edition. Thanks as well to Elizabeth McCurdy for managing the project in Canada, and to Lisa Berland for her fine copy editing. Thanks also to all of the fine folks in Composition and Graphics for making this book and all of our charts and graphs look great! Thanks also to everyone else who contributed to getting this book done well and on time.

And last but not least, a tip of our cap to the fine lot of technical reviewers who helped to ensure that we didn't write something that wasn't quite right. For the 3rd edition, this important job was well handled by Christopher Cottier.

Publisher's Acknowledgments

We're proud of this book; please send us your comments through our online registration form located at `http://dummies.custhelp.com`

Some of the people who helped bring this book to market include the following:

Acquisitions and Editorial Development

Editor: Robert Hickey

Senior Project Editor, US Edition: Georgette Beatty

Project Manager: Elizabeth McCurdy

Project Editor: Pauline Ricablanca

Copy Editor: Lisa Berland

Technical Editor: Christopher Cottier

Cartoons: Rich Tennant (www.the5thwave.com)

Composition Services

Vice-President Publishing Services: Karen Bryan

Project Coordinator: Lynsey Stanford

Layout and Graphics: Claudia Bell, Reuben W. Davis

Proofreader: Laura L. Bowman

Indexer: Valerie Haynes Perry

John Wiley & Sons Canada, Ltd.

   Bill Zerter, Chief Operating Officer

   Jennifer Smith, Vice-President and Publisher, Professional and Trade Division

Publishing and Editorial for Consumer Dummies

   Diane Graves Steele, Vice President and Publisher, Consumer Dummies

   Kristin Ferguson-Wagstaffe, Product Development Director, Consumer Dummies

   Ensley Eikenburg, Associate Publisher, Travel

   Kelly Regan, Editorial Director, Travel

Publishing for Technology Dummies

   Andy Cummings, Vice-President and Publisher, Dummies Technology/General User

Composition Services

   Gerry Fahey, Vice-President of Production Services

   Debbie Stailey, Director of Composition Services

Contents at a Glance

Table of Contents

Introduction

The almost ten years since the first edition of this book was published have witnessed increased interest in and media coverage of the investment world. In that time, the Internet has established itself as a fixture within the home and office, along with all the investment-related stories, facts, figures, applications, and scams that reside there. You can't flip through the channels on your television without running into a stock ticker at the bottom of your screen or a pitchman claiming that folks are just waiting to pay you to buy their property. And new books are published daily that claim to possess *the* secret to investing success. With all this attention, you may think that investing times have changed. But to a large degree, things haven't changed all that much. Investments that were considered lousy years ago — products with high fees and commission — generally are still lousy today.

The best investment vehicles for building wealth — stocks, real estate, and small business — haven't changed either. And you still need money to play in the investment world. Like the first edition of *Investing For Canadians For Dummies,* this third edition includes complete coverage of these wealth-building investments as well as other common investments, such as bonds. Here are the biggest changes in this edition:

- **Completely revised and updated:** We've freshened up the data and examples in this book to provide you with the latest insights and analyses, including an explanation of the credit crisis that hit in 2008 and the stock market collapse that followed. Wondering what all the fuss is about with gold, oil, and other commodities? Seeking a way to invest in stocks without exposing yourself to tremendous risk? Curious about what an exchange-traded fund or hedge fund is and whether you should invest? Weighing whether it's too risky or difficult to invest in real estate? Wondering what the best ways are to invest globally? Having trouble making sense of various economic indicators and what they mean to your investment strategy? Confused about how tax law changes should affect your investment strategies? Wanting to invest in a Tax-Free Savings Account but don't know why, where, or how? You can find the answers to these questions and many more in this edition.

- **Investing resources:** With the continued growth in Web sites, software, publications, media outlets, and many other information sources offering investing advice and information, you're probably overwhelmed about how to choose among the numerous investing research tools and resources. Equally problematic is knowing whom you can trust and listen to — and whom you need to ignore. We explain how to evaluate the quality of current investment tools and resources, and we provide tips for whom to listen to and whom to tune out.

How Savvy Investors Build Wealth

Through our many years speaking with many hundreds of individuals of modest and immodest economic means, we know that the time-tested ways they use to increase their wealth are by doing the following:

- ✔ Living within their means and systematically saving and investing money, ideally in a tax-favoured manner
- ✔ Buying and holding a diversified portfolio of stocks
- ✔ Building their own small business or career
- ✔ Investing in real estate

That kind of investing is what this book is all about. Equally, if not more, important, we help you understand and choose investments compatible with your personal and financial goals.

You don't need a fancy university or graduate-school degree, and you don't need a rich dad (or mom), biological or adopted! What you do need is a desire to read and practice the many simple yet powerful lessons and strategies in this book.

Seriously, investing intelligently isn't rocket science. By all means, if you're dealing with a complicated, atypical issue, get quality professional help. But educate yourself first. Hiring someone is dangerous if you yourself are financially challenged. If you do finally decide to hire someone, you'll be much better prepared by educating yourself, and you'll be more focused in your questions and better able to assess that person's competence.

Conventions Used in This Book

We use the following conventions in this book to help you manoeuvre through topics:

- ✔ We *italicize* all new words and terms that are defined.
- ✔ We **boldface** keywords or the main parts of bulleted items.
- ✔ We use `monofont` for all Web addresses.

Foolish Assumptions

Every book is written with a certain reader in mind, and this book is no different:

✔ You may have some investments, but you're looking to develop a full-scale investment plan.

✔ You'd like to strengthen your portfolio.

✔ You want to evaluate your investment adviser's advice.

✔ You have a company-sponsored pension plan, and you're looking to make some decisions.

If one or more of these descriptions sound familiar, you've come to the right place.

How This Book Is Organized

This book helps you fill in the gaps in your investment knowledge. It's structured so that you can read it cover to cover or simply dive in to particular sections that most interest you. Here are the major parts.

Part I: Investing Fundamentals

Before you can confidently and intelligently choose investments, you need to be able to cut through the lingo and jargon to get to the heart of what investments are and are not, and how they differ from one another. In this part, we explain what rate of return you can reasonably expect to earn and how much risk you need to take to get it. This part also details how investments best fit your specific financial goals and situation.

Part II: Stocks, Bonds, and Bay Street

We know that you probably don't want to trade in your day job for one where you'd wear a three-piece suit and need to know on which page of *The Globe and Mail*'s daily Report on Business section you can find yield curves. But you *do* need to understand what the financial markets are and how you can participate in them without suffering too many bumps and bruises. In this part, we explain what stocks and bonds are all about and how to best buy them and build your future fortune.

Part III: Getting Rich with Real Estate

We all need places to live, work, and shop, so it makes sense that real estate can be a profitable part of your investment portfolio. Intelligently buying and managing real estate is harder than it looks, which is why this part covers lots of territory. We show you the best ways to invest in real estate and provide a crash course in mortgages, landlording, buying low, selling high, taxes, and more.

Part IV: Savouring Small Business

There's nothing small about the potential profits you can make from small business. You can choose the small-business investment option that matches your skills and time. If you aspire to be the best boss you've ever had, here you can find the right ways to start your own business or buy someone else's small business. Or maybe you'd like to try your hand at spotting up-and-comers but don't want to be on the front lines — try investing in someone else's small business.

Part V: Investing Resources

Flip through your cable television channels, crack open a magazine or newspaper, or surf the Web, and you quickly discover that you can't escape investment advice. Surprisingly, each new guru you stumble upon contradicts the one who came before. Before you know it, although you've spent an avalanche of your valuable free time on all this investment stuff, you're no closer to making an informed decision. In fact, if you're like most people, you find yourself even more confused and paralyzed. Fear not! In this important part, we explain why many experts really aren't experts and why most of them try to make the world of investing so mysterious. We highlight the best resources to use and the experts worth listening to.

Part VI: The Part of Tens

These shorter chapters build your investment knowledge further. You find advice about topics such as overcoming common psychological investment obstacles, tips for investing in a down market, and points to ponder when you sell an investment.

If you're the kind of reader who jumps around from topic to topic instead of reading from cover to cover, you'll be pleased that this book has a helpful index and that it highlights the pages where investing terms are defined.

Icons Used in This Book

Throughout this book, icons help guide you through the maze of suggestions, solutions, and cautions. We hope you find that the following images make your journey through investment strategies smoother.

In the shark-infested investing waters, you'll find creatures that feast on novice waders, ready to take a bite out of a swimmer's savings. This icon notes when and where the sharks may be circling.

If you see this icon, we're pointing out companies, products, services, and resources that have proved to be exceptional over the years — in other words, resources that we would or do use personally or would recommend to our friends and family.

We use this icon to highlight an issue that requires more detective work on your part. Don't worry, though; we prepare you for your work so you don't have to start out as a novice gumshoe.

We think the name says it all, but this icon indicates something really, really important — don't you forget it!

Skip it or read it; the choice is yours. You'll fill your head with more stuff that may prove valuable as you expand your investing know-how, but you risk overdosing on stuff that you may not need right away.

This icon denotes strategies that can enable you to build wealth faster and leap over tall obstacles in a single bound.

This icon indicates treacherous territory that has made mincemeat out of lesser mortals who have come before you. Skip this point at your own peril.

Where to Go from Here

If you have the time and desire, we encourage you to read this book in its entirety. It provides you with a detailed picture of how to maximize your returns while minimizing your risks through wealth-building investments. But you don't have to read this book from cover to cover. If you have a specific question or two that you want to focus on today, or if you want to find some additional information tomorrow, it's not a problem. *Investing For Canadians For Dummies,* 3rd Edition, makes it easy to find answers to specific questions. Just turn to the table of contents or the index to locate the information you need. You can get in and get out, just like that.

Part I

Investing Fundamentals

The 5th Wave · By Rich Tennant

In this part . . .

Like a good map or aerial photograph, this part helps you see the big picture of the investment world. Here, we explain the different types of investments, which ones are good and bad for a variety of circumstances, what returns you can expect, and how to make wise investing decisions that fit with your overall financial situation.

Chapter 1

Exploring Your Investment Choices

*I*n many parts of the world, life's basic necessities — food, clothing, shelter, and taxes — gobble the entirety of people's meagre earnings. Although some Canadians do struggle for basic necessities, the bigger problem for most Canadians is that they consider just about *everything* — eating out, driving new cars, hopping on an airplane for vacation — to be a necessity. We've taken it upon ourselves (using this book as our tool) to help you recognize that investing — that is, putting your money to work for you — is *also* a necessity. If you want to accomplish important personal and financial goals, such as owning a home, starting your own business, helping your kids through university (and spending more time with them when they're young), retiring comfortably, and so on, you must know how to invest well.

It has been said, and too often quoted, that the only certainties in life are death and taxes. To these two certainties we add one more: being confused by and ignorant about investing. Because investing is a confounding activity, you may be tempted to look with envious eyes at those people in the world who appear to be savvy with money and investing. Remember that all of us start with the same level of financial knowledge — none! *No one* is born knowing this stuff! The only difference between those who know and those who don't is that those who know have invested their time and energy acquiring knowledge about the investment world.

Getting Started with Investing

Before we discuss the major investing alternatives in the rest of this chapter, we want to start with something that's quite basic, yet important. What exactly do we mean when we say "investing"? Simply stated, *investing* means you have money put away for future use.

There are thousands of stocks, bonds, mutual funds, and other investments. Unfortunately for the novice, and even for experts who are honest with you, knowing the name of the investment is just the tip of the iceberg. Underneath each of these investments lurks a veritable mountain of details.

If you wanted to and had the ability, you could make a full-time endeavour out of analyzing economic trends and financial statements and talking to business employees, customers, suppliers, and so on. However, we don't want to scare you away from investing just because some people do it on a full-time basis. Making wise investments need not take a lot of your time. If you know where to get high-quality information, and you purchase well-managed investments, you can leave the investment management to the best experts. Then you can do the work that you're best at and have more free time for fun stuff.

An important part of making wise investments is knowing when you have enough information to do things well on your own versus when you should hire others to help you. For example, the foreign stock markets is generally more difficult to research and understand compared with domestic markets. Thus, hiring a good money manager, such as through a mutual fund, makes more sense when investing overseas than going to all the time, trouble, and expense of trying to pick your own individual stocks.

We're here to give you the information you need to make your way through the complex investment world. In the rest of this chapter, we clear a path so that you can identify the major investments and understand what each is good for.

Building Wealth with Ownership Investments

If you want your money to grow, and you don't mind a bit of a roller-coaster ride from time to time in your investment's values, ownership investments are for you. *Ownership investments* are those where you own a piece of some company or other asset (such as stock, real estate, or a small business) that has the ability to generate revenue and, potentially, profits.

If you want to build wealth, observing how the world's richest have built their wealth is enlightening. Not surprisingly, the champions of wealth around the globe gained their fortunes largely through owning a piece (or all) of a successful company that they (or others) have built. Take the case of Steve Jobs, co-founder and chief executive officer of Apple Inc. Apple, of course, makes the iPod portable digital music player, computers, mobile communication devices (specifically, the iPhone), and software, among other products.

Every time we, or millions of other people, buy an Apple iPod, computer, or iPhone, Apple makes more money. As an owner of more than 5 million shares of stock, each of which was valued at around US$100 per share in late 2008 — after soaring to over US$200 — Jobs makes more money as increasing sales and profits drive up the stock's price, which was less than US$10 per share as recently as 2004.

In addition to owning their own businesses, many well-to-do people have built their nest eggs by investing in real estate and the stock market. With softening housing prices in many regions in recent years, some folks newer to the real estate world incorrectly believe that real estate is a loser, not a long-term winner. Likewise, the stock market goes through down periods but does well over the long-term. (See Chapter 2 for the straight scoop on investment risks and returns.)

And of course, some people come into wealth the old-fashioned way — they inherit it. Even if your parents are among the rare wealthy ones and you expect them to pass on big bucks to you, you need to know how to invest money intelligently.

If you understand and are comfortable with the risks and take sensible steps to diversify (don't put all your eggs in the same basket), ownership investments are the key to building wealth. To accomplish typical longer-term financial goals, such as retiring, the money you save and invest needs to grow at a healthy clip. If you dump all your money in bank accounts that pay little if any interest, you're likely to fall short of your goals.

Not everyone needs to make his or her money grow, of course. Suppose that you inherit a significant sum and/or maintain a restrained standard of living and work your whole life simply because you enjoy doing so. In this situation, you may not need to take the risks involved with a potentially faster-growth investment. You may be more comfortable with *safer* investments, such as paying off your mortgage faster than necessary. Chapter 3 helps you think through such issues.

The stock market

Stocks are an example of an ownership investment because they represent shares of ownership in a company.

If you want to share in the growth and profits of companies like Apple, you can! You simply buy shares of their stock through a brokerage firm. However, just because Apple makes money in the future, there's no guarantee that the value of its stock will increase.

Some companies today sell their stock directly to investors, allowing you to bypass brokers. You can also invest in stocks via a stock mutual fund, where a fund manager decides which individual stocks to include in the fund. (We discuss the various methods for buying stock in Chapter 6.)

You don't need a BA, MBA, MD, or PhD to make money in the stock market. If you can practice some simple lessons, such as making regular and systematic investments and investing in proven companies and funds while minimizing your investment expenses and taxes, you'll be a winner.

However, we don't believe that you can "beat the markets," and you certainly can't beat the best professional money managers at their own full-time game. This book shows you time-proven, non-gimmicky methods to make your money grow in the stock market as well as in other financial markets. (We explain how in Part II.)

Real estate

Another method that people of varying economic means use to build wealth is to invest in real estate. Owning and managing real estate is like running a small business. You need to satisfy customers (tenants), manage your costs, keep an eye on the competition, and so on. Some methods of real estate investing require more time than others, but many are proven ways to build wealth.

John, who works for a city government, and his wife, Linda, a computer analyst, have built several million dollars in investment real estate *equity* (the difference between the property's market value and debts owed) over the past three decades. "Our parents owned rental property, and we could see what it could do for you by providing income and building wealth," says John. Investing in real estate also appealed to John and Linda because they didn't know anything about the stock market, so they wanted to stay away from it. The idea of *leverage* — making money with borrowed money — on real estate also appealed to them.

John and Linda bought their first property, a duplex, when their combined income was $20,000 per year. Every time they moved to a new home, they kept the prior one and converted it to a rental. Now in their 50s, John and Linda own seven pieces of investment real estate and are multimillionaires. "It's like a second retirement, having thousands in monthly income from the real estate," says John.

John readily admits that rental real estate has its hassles. "We haven't enjoyed getting calls in the middle of the night, but now we have a property manager who can help with this when we're not available. It's also sometimes a pain finding new tenants," he says.

Who wants to invest like a millionaire?

Having a million dollars isn't nearly as rare as it used to be. In fact, according to Investor Economics, a firm that conducts research on wealth, in 2008 482,000 Canadian households had at least $1 million in wealth (excluding the value of any real estate they owned as well as any pensions). Nearly 70,000 households had $5 million or more in wealth. (Note that these figures come from before the major drop in the stock market in the fall of 2008!) Interestingly, one Investor Economics study found that 64 percent of those households with wealth of at least $1 million used full-service brokers, and only one in four used the services of a financial planner.

As in past surveys, recent wealth surveys show that affluent investors achieved and built upon their wealth with ownership investments, such as their own small businesses, real estate, and stocks.

Overall, John and Linda figure that they've been well rewarded for the time they spent and the money they invested. The income from John and Linda's rental properties allows them to live in a nicer home.

Ultimately, to make your money grow much faster than inflation and taxes, you must absolutely, positively do at least one thing — take some risk. Any investment that has real growth potential also has shrinkage potential! You may not want to take the risk or have the stomach for it. Don't despair: We discuss lower-risk investments in this book as well. You can find out about risks and returns in Chapter 2.

Small business

We know people who have hit investing home runs by owning or buying a business. Unlike the part-time nature of investing in the stock market, most people work at running their business full time, increasing their chances of doing something big financially with it. If you try to invest in individual stocks, by contrast, you're likely to work at it part time, competing against professionals who invest practically around the clock. Even if you devote almost all of your time to managing your stock portfolio, you're still a passive bystander in a business run by someone else. When you invest in your own small business, you're the boss, for better or worse.

A decade ago, Calvin set out to develop a corporate publishing firm. Because he took the risk of starting his business and has been successful in slowly building it, today, in his 50s, he enjoys a net worth of more than $10 million and can retire if he wants. Even more important to many business owners —

and the reason that financially successful entrepreneurs such as Calvin don't call it quits after they've amassed a lot of cash — are the non-financial rewards of investing, including the challenge and fulfillment of operating a successful business.

Sandra has worked on her own as an interior designer for more than two decades. She previously worked in fashion as a model, and then as a retail store manager. Her first taste of interior design was redesigning rooms at a condominium project. "I knew when I did that first building and turned it into something wonderful and profitable that I loved doing this kind of work," says Sandra. Today, Sandra's firm specializes in the restoration of landmark hotels, and her work has been written up in numerous magazines. "The money is not of primary importance to me . . . my work is driven by a passion . . . but obviously it has to be profitable," she says. Sandra has also experienced the fun and enjoyment of designing hotels in many parts of the world, including one in Japan.

Most small-business owners (ourselves included) quickly point out that the entrepreneurial life is not a walk through the rose garden (although it does have its share of thorns). Emotionally and financially, entrepreneurship is sometimes a roller coaster. In addition to the financial rewards, however, small-business owners can enjoy seeing the impact of their work and knowing that it makes a difference. Combined, Calvin and Sandra's firms created dozens of new jobs.

Not everyone needs to be sparked by the desire to start her own company to profit from small business. You can share in the economic rewards of the entrepreneurial world through buying an existing business or investing in someone else's budding enterprise. We talk more about evaluating and buying a business in Part IV of this book.

Generating Income from Lending Investments

The other major types of investment include those in which you lend your money. Suppose that, like most people, you keep some money in your local bank — most likely in a chequing account, but perhaps also in a savings account or *guaranteed investment certificate* (GIC). No matter what type of account you place your money in, you're lending your money to the bank or credit union.

The double whammy of inflation and taxes

Bank accounts and bonds that pay a decent return are reassuring to many investors. Earning a small amount of interest sure beats losing some or all of your money in a risky investment.

The problem is that money in a savings account, for example, that pays 3 percent isn't actually yielding you 3 percent. It's not that the bank is lying — it's just that your investment bucket contains some not-so-obvious holes.

The first hole is taxes. When you earn interest, you must pay taxes on it (unless you invest the money in a tax-deferred retirement plan or a Tax-Free Savings Account). If you're a moderate-income earner, you end up losing about a third of your interest to taxes. Your 3 percent return is now down to 2 percent.

But the second hole in your investment bucket can be even bigger than taxes: inflation. Although a few products become cheaper over time (computers, for example), most goods and services increase in price. Inflation in Canada has recently been running at around 3 percent per year. Inflation depresses the purchasing power of your investment's returns. If you subtract the 3 percent "cost" of inflation from the remaining 2 percent after payment of taxes, we're sorry to say that you lost 1 percent on your investment.

To recap: For every dollar you invested in the bank a year ago, despite the fact that the bank paid you your 3 pennies of interest, you're left with only 99 cents in real purchasing power for every dollar you had a year ago. In other words, thanks to the inflation and tax holes in your investment bucket, you can buy less with your money now compared to what you could have a year ago, even though you've invested your money for a year.

For how long and under what conditions you lend money to your bank depend on the specific bank and account that you use. With a GIC, you commit to lending your money to the bank for a specific length of time — perhaps six months or even a year. In return, the bank probably pays you a higher rate of interest than if you put your money in a bank account offering you immediate access to the money. (You may be able to demand termination of the GIC early; however, you'll typically be penalized.)

As we discuss in more detail in Chapter 7, you can also invest your money in bonds — another type of lending investment. When you purchase a bond that has been issued by the government or a company, you agree to lend your money for a predetermined period of time and receive a particular rate of interest. A bond may pay you 6 percent interest over the next five years, for example.

An investor's return from lending investments is typically limited to the original investment plus interest payments. If you lend your money to Rogers Communications — the cable and cell phone giant — through one of its bonds that matures, say, in ten years, and Rogers triples in size over the next decade, you won't share in its growth. Rogers stockholders and — to a much lesser degree — employees reap the rewards of the company's success, but as a bondholder, you don't (you simply get interest and the face value of the bond back at maturity).

Many people keep too much of their money in lending investments, thus allowing others to reap the rewards of economic growth. Although lending investments appear safer because you know in advance what return you'll receive, they aren't that safe. The long-term risk of these seemingly safe money investments is that your money will grow too slowly to enable you to accomplish your personal financial goals. In the worst cases, the company or other institution to which you're lending money can go under and stiff you for your loan.

Considering Cash Equivalents

Cash equivalents are any investments that you can quickly convert to cash without cost to you. With most chequing accounts, for example, you can write a cheque or withdraw cash by visiting a teller — either the live or the automated type.

Money market mutual funds are another type of cash equivalent. Investors, both large and small, invest hundreds of billions of dollars in money market mutual funds because the best money market funds produce higher yields than bank savings accounts. The yield advantage of a money market fund almost always widens when interest rates increase because banks move about as fast as molasses on a cold winter day to raise savings account rates.

Why shouldn't you take advantage of an extra 1 or 2 percent yield? Many bank savers sacrifice this yield because they think that money market funds are risky — but they're not. Money market mutual funds generally invest in ultrasafe things such as GICs, government-issued Treasury bills, and commercial paper (short-term bonds) that the most creditworthy corporations issue.

Another reason people keep too much money in traditional bank accounts is that the local bank branch office makes the cash seem more accessible. Money market mutual funds and high-interest savings accounts, however, offer many quick ways to get your cash. You can generally call or write and request that your money be mailed or wired to you, or have it transferred to your bank account.

By all means, keep your chequing account at the local bank so that you can write smaller cheques to pay your cable television, phone, and utility bills. But with that done, move any extra money that's dozing away in your bank savings account into a higher-yielding money market mutual fund or high-interest savings account! Even if you have just a few thousand dollars, the extra yield more than pays for the cost of this book. (See Chapter 8 to find out more about money market funds.)

Steering Clear of Futures and Options

Suppose you think that the stock of Research in Motion (RIM) — maker of the BlackBerry — is a good investment. The direction that the management team is taking impresses you, and you like the products and services that the company offers. Profits seem to be on a positive trend; everything's looking up.

You can go out and buy the stock — suppose that it's currently trading at around $100 per share. If the price rises to $150 in the next six months, you've made yourself a 50 percent profit ($150 – $100 = $50) on your original $100 investment. (Of course, you have to pay some brokerage fees to buy and then sell the stock.)

But instead of buying the stock outright, you can buy what are known as call options on RIM. A *call option* gives you the right to buy shares of RIM under specified terms from the person who sells you the call option. You may be able to purchase a call option that allows you to exercise your right to buy RIM stock at, say, $120 per share in the next six months. For this privilege, you may pay $2 per share.

If RIM's stock price skyrockets to, say, $150 in the next few months, the value of your options that allow you to buy the stock at $120 will be worth a lot — at least $30. You can then simply sell your options, which you bought for $2 in this example, at a huge profit — you've multiplied your money 15-fold!

Although this talk of fat profits sounds much more exciting than simply buying the stock directly and making far less money from a stock price increase, options have two big problems:

- ✔ If RIM's stock price goes nowhere or rises only a little during the six-month period when you hold the call option, the option expires as worthless, and you lose all — that is, 100 percent — of your investment. In fact, in our example, if RIM's stock trades at $120 or less at the time the option expires, the option is worthless.

- ✔ A call option represents a short-term *gamble* (in this example, over the next six months) on RIM's stock price — not an *investment* in RIM. RIM could expand its business and profits greatly in the years and decades ahead, but the value of the call option hinges on the ups and downs of RIM's stock price over a relatively short period of time. If the stock market happens to dip in the next six months, RIM may get pulled down as well, despite the company's improving financial health.

Get rich with oil and gold?

During the global economic expansion of the 2000s, oil and other commodities increased significantly in value. The surge in oil prices certainly garnered plenty of headlines when it surged past US$100 per barrel. So too did the price of gold as it surged past US$1,000 in 2008, setting a new all-time high. These prices represented tremendous increases over the past decade, with the price of oil having increased more than 600 percent (from less than US$20 per barrel) and gold more than tripling in value (from less than US$300 per ounce).

However, despite these seemingly major moves, when considering the increases in the cost of living, at US$100-plus per barrel, oil prices were just reaching the levels attained in late 1979!

(To underscore just how volatile prices can be, oil went to over US$140 in July of 2008, and by the end of the year was trading at just US$40!) And when gold hit a new high in early 2008, it was still far, far from the inflation-adjusted levels it reached nearly three decades earlier. To reach those levels, gold would have to more than double from its current high levels to more than US$2,000 an ounce!

So although the price increases in gold and oil (as well as some other commodities) were dramatic during the past decade, over the past 30 years, oil and gold increased in value less than the overall low rate of inflation. So, one would hardly have gotten rich investing in oil and gold over the long-term.

Futures are similar to options in that both can be used as gambling instruments. Futures deal mainly with the value of commodities such as heating oil, corn, wheat, gold, silver, and pork bellies. Futures have a delivery date that's in the not-too-distant future. (Do you really want bushels of wheat delivered to your home? Or worse yet, pork bellies?) You can place a small down payment — around 10 percent — toward the purchase of futures, thereby greatly leveraging your "investment." If prices fall, you need to put up more money to keep from having your position sold.

Our advice: Don't gamble with futures and options.

The only real use that you may (if ever) have for these *derivatives* (so called because their value is "derived" from the price of other securities) is to hedge. Suppose that you hold a lot of a stock that has greatly appreciated, and you don't want to sell now because of the tax bite. Perhaps you want to postpone selling the stock until next year because you plan on not working, and you can then benefit from the lower, long-term capital gains tax rate. You can buy what's called a *put option,* which increases in value when a stock's price falls (because the put option grants you the right to sell your stock to the purchaser of the put option at a preset stock price). Thus, if the stock price does fall, the rising put option value offsets some of your losses on the stock you still hold. Using put options allows you to postpone selling your stock without exposing yourself to the risk of a falling stock price.

Passing Up Precious Metals

Over the millennia, gold and silver have served as mediums of exchange or currency because they have intrinsic value and can't be debased the way that paper currencies can (by printing more money). These precious metals are used in jewellery and manufacturing.

As investments, gold and silver perform well during bouts of inflation. For example, from 1972 to 1980, when inflation zoomed into the double-digit range in Canada and the United States and stocks and bonds went into the tank, gold and silver prices skyrocketed more than 500 percent. With precious metals prices zooming skyward again in the 2000s, some have feared the return of inflation, but the surging prices seem to have been driven by the global economic boom, not inflation.

Over the long term, precious metals are lousy investments. They don't pay any dividends, and their price increases at best may just keep up with, but not ahead of, increases in the cost of living. Although investing in precious metals is better than keeping cash in a piggy bank or stuffing it in a mattress, the investment returns aren't nearly as good as bonds, stocks, and real estate. One way to earn better long-term returns than what investing in simple precious metals provides is to invest in a mutual fund of stocks of gold and precious metals companies (see Chapter 8 for more information).

Counting Out Collectibles

The term *collectibles* is a catchall category for antiques, art, autographs, hockey cards, clocks, coins, comic books, diamonds, dolls, gems, photographs, rare books, rugs, stamps, vintage wine, writing utensils, and a whole host of other items. Although connoisseurs of fine art, antiques, and vintage wine wouldn't like the comparison of their pastime with buying old playing cards or chamber pots, the bottom line is that collectibles are all objects with little intrinsic value. Wine is just a bunch of old mushed-up grapes. A painting is simply a canvas and some paint that at retail would set you back a few bucks. Stamps are small pieces of paper, just a few square centimeters. Hockey cards — heck, when we were young, we used to stick these between our bike spokes!

We're not trying to diminish contributions that artists and others make to our culture. And we know that some people place a high value on some of these collectibles. But true investments that can make your money grow, such as stocks, real estate, or a small business, are assets that can produce income and profits. Collectibles have little intrinsic value and are thus subject to the whims and speculations of buyers and sellers.

Here are some other major problems with collectibles:

- **Markups are huge.** The spread between the price that a dealer pays for an object and the price that the dealer sells the same exact object for is often around 100 percent. Sometimes the difference is even greater, particularly if a dealer is the second or third middleman in the chain of purchase. So at a minimum, your purchase must typically double in value just to get you back to even. And that may take 10 to 20 years or more!

- **Lots of other costs add up.** If the markups aren't bad enough, with some collectibles you incur all sorts of other costs. If you buy more-expensive pieces, you may need to have them appraised. You may have to pay storage and insurance costs as well. And unlike the markup, you pay some of these fees year after year after year of ownership.

- **You can get stuck with a pig in a poke.** Sometimes, you may overpay even more for a collectible because you don't realize some imperfection or inferiority of an item. Worse, you may buy a forgery. Even reputable dealers have been duped by forgeries.

- **Your pride and joy can deteriorate over time.** Damage from sunlight, humidity, temperatures that are too high or too low, and a whole host of vagaries can ruin the quality of your collectible. Insurance doesn't cover this type of damage or negligence on your part.

- **The returns stink.** Even if you ignore the substantial costs of buying, holding, and selling, the average returns that investors earn from collectibles rarely keep ahead of inflation and are generally inferior to stock market, real estate, and small-business investing. Objective collectible return data are hard to come by. Never, ever trust "data" that dealers or the many collectible trade publications provide.

The best returns that collectible investors reap come from the ability to identify, years in advance, items that will *become* popular. Do you think you can do that? You may be the smartest person in the world, but you should know that most dealers can't tell what's going to rocket to popularity in the coming decades. Dealers make their profits the same way as other retailers, from the spread or markup on the merchandise that they sell. The public and collectors have fickle, quirky tastes that no one can predict. Did you know that Beanie Babies, Furbies, Pet Rocks, or Cabbage Patch Kids were going to be such hits?

You can find out enough about a specific type of collectible to become a better investor than the average person, but you're going to have to be among the best — perhaps the top 10 percent of such collectors — to have a shot at earning decent returns. To get to this level of expertise, you need to invest hundreds if not thousands of hours reading, researching, and educating yourself about your specific type of collectible.

Nothing is wrong with *spending* money on collectibles, but we don't want you to fool yourself into thinking that they're investments. You can sink lots of your money into these non-income-producing, poor-return "investments." At their best as investments, collectibles give the wealthy a way to buy quality stuff that doesn't depreciate.

If you must buy collectibles, here are some tips to keep in mind:

- ✔ Collect for your love of the collectible, your desire to enjoy it, or your interest in finding out about or mastering a subject, not because you expect high investment returns, because you probably won't get them.

- ✔ Keep quality items that you and your family have purchased and hope will be worth something someday. Keeping these quality items is the simplest way to break into the collectible business. The complete sets of baseball cards Eric gathered as a youngster are now (30-plus years later) worth hundreds of dollars — in one case, $1,000!

- ✔ Buy from the source and cut out the middlemen whenever possible. In some cases, you may be able to buy from the artist. (Tony's wife purchases much of her pottery and paintings directly from the artists.)

- ✔ Check collectibles that are comparable to the one you have your eye on, shop around, and don't be afraid to negotiate. An effective way to negotiate, after you decide what you like, is to make your offer to the dealer or artist by phone. Because the seller isn't standing right next to you, you don't feel pressure to decide immediately.

- ✔ Ask the dealer who thinks that the item is such a great investment for a written guarantee to buy back the item from you, if you opt to sell, for at least the same price you paid or higher within five years.

- ✔ Use a comprehensive resource to research, buy, sell, maintain, and improve your collectible, such as the books by Ralph and Terry Kovel or their Web site at www.kovels.com.

Chapter 2

Weighing Risks and Returns

. . . .

In This Chapter

▶ Determining risks

▶ Reducing risk while earning decent returns

▶ Figuring out expected investment returns

▶ Determining how much you need your investments to return

. . . .

A woman passes up eating a hamburger at a picnic because she heard that she could contract a deadly *E. coli* infection from eating improperly cooked meat. The next week, that same woman hops in the passenger seat of her friend's car without buckling her seat belt.

A mother covers her young daughter in sunscreen and makes sure she's wearing a wide-brimmed hat before going outside in the summertime. That same mother leaves the child — fully protected from the sun's rays — to play unwatched with a relative's dog that then bites the child.

We're not trying to depress or frighten anyone. However, we are trying to make an important point about risk — something that we all deal with on a daily basis. Risk is in the eye of the beholder. Many of us base our perception of risk, in large part, on our experiences and what we've been exposed to. Many people fret about relatively small risks while overlooking much larger risks.

Sure, a risk of an *E. coli* infection from eating poorly cooked meat exists, so the woman who was leery of eating the hamburger at the picnic had a legitimate concern. However, by getting into the friend's car without doing up her seat belt, that same woman placed herself at far greater risk of dying than if she had eaten the hamburger. Annually in Canada, about 3,500 people die in automobile accidents, and not wearing a seat belt greatly increases the odds of serious or even fatal injuries should you crash.

Likewise, the odds of developing skin cancer are greater if you're regularly exposed to the sun's rays without protection, so it's logical for the mother to clothe her child in protective clothing and regularly apply sunscreen. However, the mother completely overlooked the significant risk posed by allowing a small child to play with a dog.

Evaluating Risks

Everywhere you turn, risks exist; some are just more apparent than others. Many people misunderstand risks. With increased knowledge, you may be able to reduce or conquer some of your fears and make more sensible decisions about reducing risks. For example, some people who fear flying don't understand that, statistically, flying is much safer than driving a car. You're approximately 40 times more likely to die in a motor vehicle than in an airplane. But when a plane goes down, it's big news because dozens and sometimes hundreds of people, who weren't engaging in reckless behaviour, perish. Meanwhile, the media seem to pay less attention to the seven-plus people, on average, who die on the road in Canada every day.

This doesn't mean that you shouldn't drive or fly, or that you shouldn't drive to the airport. However, you may consider taking steps to reduce the significant risks you expose yourself to in a car. For example, you can get a car with more safety features, or you may bypass riding with reckless taxi drivers whose cars lack seat belts.

Although some of us like to live life to its fullest and take "fun" risks (how else can you explain extreme skiers, parachutists, and bungee jumpers?), most people seek to minimize risk and maximize enjoyment in their lives. But most people also understand that they'd be a lot less happy living a life that sought to eliminate all risks, and they likely wouldn't be able to anyway.

Likewise, if you attempt to avoid all the risks that investing involves, you won't succeed, and you likely won't be happy with your investment results and lifestyle. In the investment world, some people don't go near stocks or any investment that they perceive to be volatile. As a result, such investors often end up with lousy long-term returns, and they expose themselves to some high risks that they overlooked, such as the risk of inflation and taxes eroding the purchasing power of their money.

You can't live without taking risks. Risk-free activities or ways of living don't exist. You can minimize, but never eliminate, risks. Some methods of risk reduction aren't palatable because they reduce your quality of life. Risks are also composed of several factors. In the sections that follow, we discuss the various types of investment risks and methods that you can use to sensibly reduce these risks while not missing out on the upside that growth investments offer.

Market-value risk

Although the stock market can help you build wealth, most people recognize that it can also plunge quite a bit — 10, 20, or 30 percent or more in no time. Consider what happened in 2008. After peaking in October 2007, Canadian and

U.S. stocks, as measured by the major indexes representing the value of large companies (for Canada, the TSX composite index, and for the United States, the S&P 500 index), dropped about 42 percent over the next 12 months.

In the fall of 2008, in fact, these stocks dropped over 30 percent in just over a single month! If you had invested $5,000 during this time period, your investment may have shrunk to $3,500 or less. Similarly, those who invested $50,000 saw it shrink to $35,000 or less. Although that loss doesn't feel good, it's the reality of risk. Your investment can — and sometimes will — shrink in value.

The drop in 2008 echoed what happened at the beginning of the decade. After soaring to new highs in 2000 due to the dot.com bubble of the late 1990s, large-cap Canadian and U.S. stocks — again, using the TSX composite index for Canada and the S&P 500 index for the U.S. — dropped about 50 percent by 2002. Stocks on the NASDAQ, which is heavily weighted toward technology stocks, plunged more than 76 percent from 2000 through 2002.

A few years earlier, it took just a mere six weeks (from mid-July 1998 to early September 1998) for large-company Canadian and U.S. stocks to plummet by about 20 percent. In just under three months, a broad measurement of companies traded on the Toronto Stock Exchange fell by almost 27 percent. During the same period, an index of smaller-company U.S. stocks plunged 33 percent.

True, the stock market crash that occurred in the fall of 2008 was a hard, fast one (the market plunged 30 percent in a matter of weeks). But take a look at Tables 2-1 and 2-2, which show other massive plunges in the Canadian and U.S. stock markets, respectively, over the past several decades.

Table 2-1	Most Depressing Canadian Stock Market Declines*
Period	*Size of Fall*
1929–1932	80% (ouch!)
1937–1942	56%
2000–2002	50%
1980–1982	44%
2007–2008	42%
1973–1974	38%
1987–1987	31%
1956–1957	30%
1969–1970	28%

*As measured by changes in the TSE/TSX composite index

Table 2-2	Largest U.S. Stock Market Declines*
Period	*Size of Fall*
1929–1932	89% (ouch!)
1937–1942	52%
1906–1907	49%
1890–1896	47%
1919–1921	47%
1901–1903	46%
1973–1974	45%
2007–2008	43%
1916–1917	40%
2000–2002	39%

*As measured by changes in the Dow Jones Industrial Average

Real estate exhibits similar unruly, annoying tendencies. Although real estate (like stocks) has been a terrific long-term investment, various real estate markets get clobbered from time to time.

When the oil industry collapsed in Alberta in the early 1980s, real estate prices in the province dropped by 25 percent. And after a massive run-up in prices in the mid-1980s, house prices in the Toronto area plummeted by nearly 28 percent over the next few years. U.S. housing prices took a 25 percent tumble from the late 1920s to the mid-1930s. Later in the 1980s and early 1990s, the northeastern United States became mired in a severe recession, and real estate prices fell by 20-plus percent in many areas. After peaking near 1990, many of the West Coast housing markets, especially those in California, experienced falling prices — dropping 20 percent or more in most areas by the mid-1990s. The Japanese real estate market crash also began around the time of the California market fall. Property prices in Japan collapsed more than 60 percent.

Declining U.S. housing prices in the mid- to late 2000s garnered unprecedented attention. Some folks and pundits acted like this was the worst housing market ever. To date, it seems comparable to the decline of the early 1990s. After hitting their peak in the summer of 2006, housing prices had fallen by almost 20 percent by the fall of 2008, with some areas seeing prices drop by 30 percent. Foreclosures increased in part due to buyers financing their home's purchase with risky mortgages. (This became known as *subprime lending,* hence the term "subprime crisis.") We must note here that housing market conditions vary by area. For example, some portions of the

U.S. Pacific Northwest and South actually appreciated during the mid- to late 2000s, while other markets experienced declines.

After reading this section, you may want to keep all your money in the bank — after all, you know you won't lose your money, and you won't have to be a non-stop worrier. No one has ever lost 20, 40, 60, or 80 percent of a bank-held savings vehicle in a few years! But just letting your money sit around would be a mistake.

If you pass up the stock and real estate markets simply because of the potential market value risk, you miss out on a historic, time-tested method of building substantial wealth. Instead of seeing declines and market corrections as a horrible thing, view them as the markets having a sale. If you're considering buying stocks or real estate, a decline in prices presents opportunities, but human emotions often scare us away from buying something that seemingly others are shunning.

Later in this chapter, we show you the generous returns that stocks and real estate as well as other investments have historically provided. The following sections suggest some simple things you can do to lower your investing risk and help prevent your portfolio from suffering a huge fall.

Diversify for a gentler ride

Individual stock markets may crash. However, the various stock markets around the world don't always crash at the same time, as they did in 2008. For example, when the Canadian and U.S. stock markets collapsed in the fall of 1987, some overseas stock markets dropped far less or not at all. So if you had spread your money across the many different stock markets, your portfolio wouldn't have suffered nearly as much as it would have if you held all your stocks in North America.

You can invest outside of Canada to reduce your investment risk if you worry about the health of the Canadian economy, the government, and the dollar. Most large Canadian companies do business in the United States and overseas, so when you invest in larger Canadian company stocks, you get some international investment exposure. You can also invest in international company stocks, ideally via mutual funds (which we discuss in Chapter 8).

Of course, investing overseas can't totally protect you. You can't do much about a global economic catastrophe. If you worry about the risk of such a calamity, you should probably also worry about a huge meteor crashing into Earth. Maybe there's a way to colonize outer space. . . .

Diversifying your investments can involve more than just your stock portfolio, however. You can also hold some real estate investments to diversify your investment portfolio. Many real estate markets actually appreciated in the early 2000s while North American stock markets were in the doghouse.

Conversely, while real estate in many regions began a multi-year slump in the mid-2000s, stocks performed well for the next few years leading up to the 2008 crash.

Consider your time horizon

Investors who worry that the stock market may take a dive and take their money down with it should first consider the length of time that they plan to invest. In a one-year period in the stock and bond markets, anything can happen (as shown in Figure 2-1). History shows that about once in every three years that you invest in the stock and bond markets, you lose money. However, stock market investors have made money (sometimes substantial amounts) approximately two-thirds of the time over a one-year period. (Bond investors made money about two-thirds of the time, too, although they made a good deal less on average.)

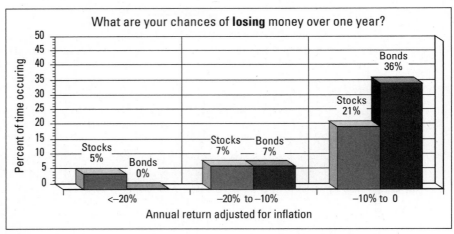

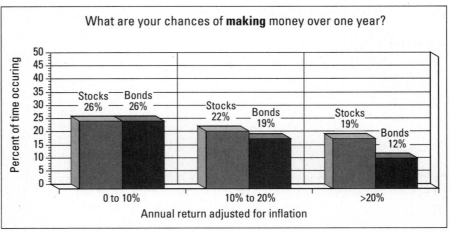

Figure 2-1: What are the odds of making or losing money in the Canadian market? Anything can happen, but you win far more often (and bigger) than you lose with stocks.

Although the stock market is more volatile than the bond market in the short term, stock market investors have earned far better long-term returns than bond investors have. (See the "Stock returns" section, later in this chapter.) Why? Because stock investors bear risks that bond investors don't bear, and it's a reasonable expectation they will be compensated for it. Remember, however, that bonds generally outperform a boring old bank account.

History has shown that the risk of a stock or bond market fall becomes less of a concern the longer the period that you plan to invest. As Figure 2-2 shows, as the holding period during which you own stocks increases from 1 year to 3 years to 5 years to 10 years, and then to 20 years, your likelihood of making a profit increases. In fact, over any 20-year time span, U.S. stock market investors have *never* lost money, even after you subtract for the effects of inflation.

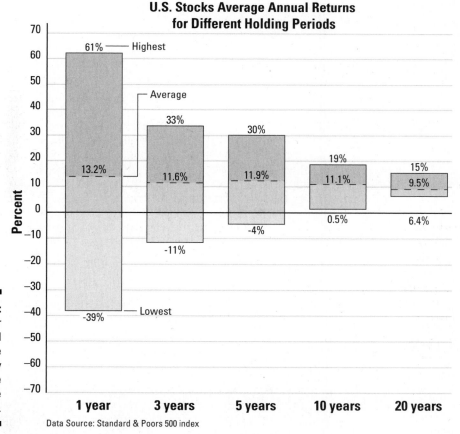

Figure 2-2: The longer you hold stocks, the more likely you are to make money.

We've used U.S. data in Figure 2-2 above simply because several more decades of market data are available, giving us a better view of the market's long-term behaviour. However, the same essential point holds true for Canada. Since 1957, only one 5-year period has had a negative return. In other words, if you had invested in the broad market (meaning your returns were similar to the composite index) and held on for five years, in only one period would you have had less after five years than you started with. And if you had invested and stayed invested for *ten* years, you would always have come out ahead. To put it another way, starting in 1957, if you had invested in any year and held those investments for a minimum of ten years, you would have ended up with a profit, assuming your returns matched those of the index.

Most stock market investors we know are concerned about the risk of losing money. What Figure 2-2 clearly shows is that the key to minimizing the probability that you'll lose money in stocks is to hold them for the longer term. Don't invest in stocks unless you plan to hold them for at least five years — and preferably a decade or longer. Please see Part II of this book for more on using stocks as a long-term investment.

Pare down holdings in bloated markets

Perhaps you've heard the expression "Buy low, sell high." Although we don't believe that you can *time the markets* (that is, predict the most profitable time to buy and sell), spotting a greatly overpriced market isn't too difficult. For example, in the first edition of this book, published in 2000, we warned readers about the grossly inflated prices of many Internet and technology stocks (see Chapter 5). Throughout this book, we explain some simple yet powerful methods you can use to measure whether a particular investment market is of fair value, of good value, or overpriced. You should avoid overpriced investments for two important reasons:

- ✔ If and when these overpriced investments fall, they usually fall farther and faster than more fairly priced investments.
- ✔ You can always find other investments that offer higher potential returns.

Ideally, you want to avoid having a lot of your money in markets that appear to be overpriced (see Chapter 5 for how to spot pricey markets). Practically speaking, avoiding overpriced markets doesn't mean that you should try to sell all your holdings in such markets with the vain hope of buying them back at a much lower price. However, you may benefit from the following strategies:

- ✔ **Invest new money elsewhere.** Focus investment of new money somewhere other than the overpriced market; put it into investments that offer you better values. Thus, without selling any of your seemingly expensive investments, they become a smaller portion of your total holdings. If you hold investments outside tax-sheltered retirement plans, focusing your money elsewhere also offers the benefit of allowing you to avoid incurring taxes from selling appreciated investments.

> ✔ **If you *have* to sell, sell the expensive stuff.** If you need to raise money to live on, such as for retirement or for a major purchase, sell the big-ticket items. As long as the taxes aren't too troublesome, it's better to sell high and lock in your profits. Chapter 21 discusses issues to weigh when you contemplate selling an investment.

Individual investment risk

A downdraft can put an entire investment market on a roller-coaster ride, but healthy markets also have their share of individual losers. For example, from the early 1980s through the late 1990s, North American stock markets had one of the greatest periods of appreciation in history. You'd never know it, though, if you held one of the great losers of that period.

Consider a company now called Navistar, which has undergone enormous transformations in the past two decades. This company used to be called International Harvester and manufactured farm equipment, trucks, and construction and other industrial equipment. Today, Navistar makes mostly trucks.

In late 1983, this company's stock traded at more than US$140 per share. It then plunged more than 90 percent over the ensuing decade (as shown in Figure 2-3). Even with a rally in recent years, Navistar stock still trades at under US$50 per share (after dipping below US$10 per share). Lest you think that's a big drop, this company's stock traded as high as US$455 per share in the late 1970s! If a worker retired from this company in the late 1970s with $200,000 invested in the company stock, the retiree's investment would be worth about $25,000 today! On the other hand, if the retiree had simply swapped his stock at retirement for a diversified portfolio of stocks, which I explain how to build in Part II, his $200,000 nest egg would've instead grown to more than $2,800,000!

Figure 2-3: Even the bull market of the 1990s wasn't kind to every company.

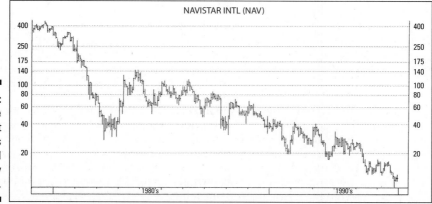

Like most other markets, the Canadian stock market paled by comparison with the U.S. juggernaut in the 1990s, but this country has had its share of stocks that have plummeted in value. How about Dylex, which through its many brand name outlets, such as Suzy Shier, at one time took in one out of every ten dollars consumers spent in retail clothing outlets? The stock, which began the 1990s at $24, ended the decade languishing beneath the $10 mark, dwindling lower and lower until the company eventually went under in 2001.

And then, of course, there's Nortel. In the late 1990s, many of the investors Tony profiled in his *Globe and Mail* column "Me and My Money" happily recounted how well they'd done by buying Nortel, making two, three, even ten times or more on their original investment. Nortel, or so we were told, just couldn't keep up with the Internet-driven demand for its products. The stock peaked at over $120 in August 2000. And then, in a matter of months, the company's cheerleaders were proven to be completely, hopelessly wrong. Nortel crumbled, and by October 2002 it had literally turned into a penny stock, trading at under a buck. Tony soon found that many of the investors he profiled in his column were calling Nortel one of their "worst moves," and by the end of the decade, it was still in the basement!

Just as individual stock prices can plummet, so can individual real estate property prices. In California during the 1990s, for example, earthquakes rocked the prices of properties built on landfill. These quakes highlighted the dangers of building on poor soil. (Ultimately, many property owners in these areas were compensated for their losses by the U.S. government, as well as by some real estate agencies that didn't disclose these known contaminants.)

Here are some simple steps you can take to lower the risk of individual investments that can upset your goals:

- ✔ **Do your homework.** When you purchase real estate, a whole host of inspections can save you from buying a money pit. With stocks, you can examine some measures of value and the company's financial condition and business strategy to reduce your chances of buying into an over-priced company or one on the verge of major problems. Parts II, III, and IV of this book give you more information on researching your investment.

- ✔ **Diversify.** Investors who seek growth invest in securities such as stocks. Placing significant amounts of your capital in one or a handful of securities is risky, particularly if the stocks are in the same industry or closely related industries. To reduce this risk, purchase stocks in a variety of industries and companies within each industry. (See Part II for details.)

- ✔ **Hire someone to invest for you.** The best mutual funds (see Chapter 8) offer low-cost, professional management and oversight, as well as diversification. Stock mutual funds typically own 25 or more securities in a variety of companies in different industries. The best exchange-traded funds offer similar benefits at low cost. In Part III, we explain how you can invest in real estate in a similar way (that is, by leaving the driving to someone else).

Liquidity

The term *liquidity* refers to how long it takes and how much it costs to convert an investment into cash. The money in your wallet is considered perfectly liquid — it's already cash.

Suppose that you invested money in a handful of stocks. Although you can't easily sell these stocks on a Saturday night, you can sell most stocks quickly through a broker for a nominal fee any day that the financial markets are open (normal working days). You pay a higher percentage to sell your stocks if you use a high-cost broker or if you have a small amount of stock to sell.

Real estate is generally much less liquid than stock. Preparing your property for sale takes time, and if you want to get fair market value for your property, finding a buyer may take weeks or months. Selling costs (agent commissions, fix-up expenses, and closing costs) can easily approach 10 percent of the home's value.

A privately run small business is among the least liquid of the better growth investments that you can make. Selling such a business typically takes longer than selling most real estate.

So that you're not forced to sell one of your investments that you intend to hold for long-term purposes, keep an emergency reserve of three to six months' worth of living expenses in a money market account or high-interest savings account. Also consider investing some money in bonds (see Chapter 8), which pay higher than money market yields without the high risk or volatility that comes with the stock market.

Purchasing-power risk

Increases in the cost of living (that is, inflation) can erode the value of your retirement resources and what you can buy with that money — also known as its *purchasing power*. When Ethel retired at the age of 60, she was pleased with her retirement income. She was receiving an $800-per-month pension and $1,200 per month from money that she had invested in long-term bonds. Her monthly expenditures amounted to about $1,500, so she was able to save a little money for an occasional trip.

Fast-forward 15 years. Ethel still receives $800 per month from her pension, but now she gets only $900 per month of investment income, which comes from some GICs *(guaranteed investment certificates)*. Ethel bailed out of bonds after she lost sleep over the sometimes roller-coaster-like price movements in the bond market. Her monthly expenditures now amount to approximately $2,400, and she uses some of her investment principal (original investment). She's terrified of outliving her money.

Ethel has reason to worry. She has 100 percent of her money invested without protection against increases in the cost of living. Although her income felt comfortable in the beginning of her retirement, it doesn't at age 75, and Ethel may easily live another 15 or more years.

The erosion of the purchasing power of your investment dollar can, over longer time periods, be as bad as or worse than the effect of a major market crash. Table 2-3 shows the effective loss in purchasing power of your money at various rates of inflation and over differing time periods.

Table 2-3	Inflation's Corrosive Effect on Your Money's Purchasing Power			
Inflation Rate	10 Years	15 Years	25 Years	40 Years
2%	−18%	−26%	−39%	−55%
4%	−32%	−44%	−62%	−81%
6%	−44%	−58%	−77%	−90%
8%	−54%	−68%	−85%	−95%
10%	−61%	−76%	−91%	−98%

We often see skittish investors keep their money in bonds and money market accounts, thinking they are playing it safe. The risk in this strategy is that your money won't grow enough over the years in order for you to accomplish your financial goals. In other words, the lower the return that you earn, the more you need to save to reach a particular financial goal.

A 40-year-old wanting to accumulate $500,000 by age 65 would need to save $722 per month if she earns a 6 percent average annual return, but needs to save only $377 per month if she earns 10 percent average return per year. Younger investors need to pay the most attention to the risk of generating low returns, but so should younger senior citizens. At the age of 65, seniors need to recognize that a portion of their assets may not be used for a decade or more from the present.

Career risk

Your ability to earn money is most likely your single biggest asset, or at least one of your biggest assets. Most people achieve what they do in the working world through education and hard work. By education, we're not simply talking about what one learns in formal schooling. Education is a lifelong process. We've learned far more about business from our own front-line experiences and those of others than we've learned in educational settings. We also read a lot. (In Part V, we recommend books and other resources that we've found most useful.)

Inflation ragin' outta control

You think 6, 8, or 10 percent annual inflation rates are bad? How would you like to live in a country that experienced that rate of inflation in a day?! As we discuss in Chapter 4, too much money in circulation chasing after too few goods causes high rates of inflation.

A government that runs amok with the nation's currency and money supply usually causes excessive rates of inflation — dubbed *hyperinflation*. Over the decades and centuries, hyperinflation has wreaked havoc in more than a few countries.

What happened in Germany in the late 1910s and early 1920s demonstrates how bad hyperinflation can get. Consider that during this time period, prices increased nearly one billionfold! What cost 1 reichsmark (the German currency in those days) at the beginning of this mess eventually cost nearly 1,000,000,000 reichsmarks. People had to cart around so much

currency that at times they needed wheelbarrows to haul it! Ultimately, this inflationary burden was too much for German society, creating a social climate that fuelled the rise of the Nazi party and Adolf Hitler.

During the 1990s, a number of countries, especially many that made up the former U.S.S.R. and others such as Brazil and Lithuania, got themselves into a hyperinflationary mess with inflation rates of several hundred percent per year. In the mid-1980s, Bolivia's yearly inflation rate exceeded 10,000 percent. In 2008, Zimbabwe's annual inflation rate was 231 million percent, and growing.

Governments often try to slap on price controls to prevent runaway inflation (Pierre Trudeau did this in Canada in the 1970s, as did Richard Nixon in the United States), but the underground economy, known as the *black market,* usually prevails.

If you don't continually invest in your education, you risk losing your competitive edge. Your skills and perspectives can become dated and obsolete. Although that doesn't mean you should work 80 hours a week and never do anything fun, it does mean that part of your "work" time should involve upgrading your skills.

The best organizations are those that recognize the need for continual knowledge and invest in their workforce through training and career development. Just remember to look at your own career objectives, which may not be the same as your company's.

Analyzing Returns

When you make investments, you have the potential to make money in a variety of ways. Each type of investment has its own mix of associated risks that you take when you part with your investment dollar, and, likewise, offers a different potential rate of return. In this section, we cover the returns you can expect with each of the common investing avenues, but first, we walk you through the different components of calculating the total return on an investment.

The components of total return

To figure out exactly how much money you've made (or lost) on your investment, you need to calculate the *total return*. To come up with this figure, you need to determine how much money you originally invested and then factor in the other components, such as interest, dividends, and appreciation (or depreciation).

If you've ever had money in a bank account that pays *interest,* you know that the bank pays you a small amount of interest when you allow it to keep your money. The bank then turns around and lends your money to some other person or organization at a much higher rate of interest. The rate of interest is also known as the *yield.* So if a bank tells you that its savings account pays 2 percent interest, the bank may also say that the account yields 2 percent. Banks usually quote interest rates or yields on an annual basis. Interest that you receive is one component of the return you receive on your investment.

If a bank pays monthly interest, for example, the bank also likely quotes a *compounded effective annual yield.* After the first month's interest is credited to your account, that *interest* starts earning interest as well. So the bank may say that the account pays 2 percent, which compounds to an effective annual yield of 2.04 percent.

When you lend your money directly to a company — which is what you do when you invest in a bond that a corporation issues — you also receive interest. Bonds, as well as stocks (which are shares of ownership in a company), fluctuate in value after they're issued.

When you invest in a company's stock, you hope that the stock increases *(appreciates)* in value. Of course, a stock can also decline, or *depreciate,* in value. This change in market value is part of your return from a stock or bond investment:

$$\frac{\text{Current investment value} - \text{Original investment}}{\text{Original investment}} = \text{Appreciation or depreciation}$$

For example, if one year ago you invested $10,000 in a stock (you bought 1,000 shares at $10 per share), and the investment is now worth $11,000 (each share is worth $11), your investment's appreciation is

$$\frac{\$11,000 - \$10,000}{\$10,000} = 10\%$$

Stocks can also pay *dividends,* which are the company's sharing of some of its profits with you as a stockholder. Some companies, particularly those that are small or growing rapidly, choose to reinvest all of their profits back into the company. (Of course, some companies don't turn a profit, so there's nothing to pay out!) You need to factor these dividends into your return as well.

Suppose that in the previous example, in addition to your stock appreciating $1,000 to $11,000, it paid you a dividend of $100 ($1 per share). Here's how you calculate your total return:

$$\frac{(\text{Current investment value} - \text{Original investment}) + \text{Dividends}}{\text{Original investment}} = \text{Total return}$$

Or, to apply it to the example:

$$\frac{(\$11,000 - \$10,000) + \$100}{\$10,000} = 11\%$$

After-tax returns

Although you may be happy that your stock has given you an 11 percent return on your invested dollars, *remember:* Unless you held your investment in a tax-sheltered retirement plan or Tax-Free Savings Account, you owe taxes on your return. Specifically, the dividends and investment appreciation that you realize upon selling are taxed, although often at relatively low rates. The tax rates on so-called long-term capital gains and stock dividends are lower than the tax rates on other income. In Chapter 3, we discuss the different tax rates that affect your investments and explain how to make tax-wise investment decisions that fit with your overall personal financial situation and goals.

(If you're talking about savings accounts, money market accounts, or bonds, you owe the Canada Revenue Agency taxes on the interest.)

Often, people make investing decisions without considering the tax consequences of their moves. This is a big mistake. What good is making money if the government takes away a substantial portion of it?

If you're in a moderate tax bracket, taxes on your investments probably run in the neighbourhood of 30 percent. So if your investment returned 7 percent before taxes, you're left with a return of 4.9 percent after taxes.

Psychological returns

Profits and tax avoidance can powerfully motivate your investment selections. However, as with other life decisions, you need to consider more than the bottom line. Some people want to have fun with their investments. Of course, they don't want to lose money or sacrifice a lot of potential returns — less expensive ways to have fun do exist!

Psychological rewards compel some investors to choose particular investment vehicles such as individual stocks, real estate, or a small business. Why? Because compared with other investments, such as managed mutual funds, they see these investments as more tangible and . . . well, more fun.

Be honest with yourself about why you choose the investments that you do. Allowing your ego to get in the way can be dangerous. Do you invest in individual stocks because you really believe that you will do better than the best full-time professional money managers? Chances are high that you won't. (See Chapter 6 for the details.) Do you like investing in real estate more because of the gratification from driving by and showing off your properties to others than because of the investment rewards? Such questions are worth considering as you contemplate what investments you want to make.

Savings, high-interest, and money market account returns

You need to keep your extra cash that awaits investment (or an emergency) in a safe place, preferably one that doesn't get hammered by the sea of changes in the financial markets. By default and for convenience, many people keep their extra cash in a bank savings account. Banks also offer the backing of the Canadian Deposit Insurance Corporation, a federal Crown corporation that protects certain holdings at each bank up to $100,000. (Credit unions in some provinces have unlimited deposit guarantees.) However, most banks and credit unions pay a low interest rate on their savings accounts.

A far better place to keep your liquid savings are the growing number of high-interest savings accounts offered by companies such as President's Choice Financial, ING Direct, and even some mutual fund companies. These accounts typically offer rates anywhere from 4 to 40 — yes, *40* — times the rate on savings accounts.

Another good choice is to keep your liquid savings in a money market mutual fund. These are the safest types of mutual funds around; for all intents and purposes, they equal a bank savings account's safety. However, the best money market funds pay higher yields than most bank savings accounts. Unlike a bank, money market mutual funds tell you how much they deduct for the service of managing your money. See Chapter 8 for more on money market funds.

If you don't need immediate access to your money, consider using Treasury bills (T-bills) or guaranteed investment certificates (GICs), which are usually issued for terms of anywhere from three months to five years. Your money will surely earn more in one of these vehicles than in a bank savings account. The drawback to GICs and T-bills is that you incur a penalty (with GICs) or a transaction fee (with T-bills) if you withdraw your investment before the term expires (see Chapter 7).

Bond returns

When you buy a bond, you lend your money to the issuer of that bond (borrower), which is generally the federal government, a provincial government, or a corporation, for a specific period of time. When you buy a bond, you expect to earn a higher yield than you can with a money market or savings account. You're taking more risk, after all. Companies can and do go bankrupt, in which case you may lose some or all of your investment.

Generally, you can expect to earn a higher yield when you buy bonds that

- ✔ **Are issued for a longer term:** The bond issuer is tying up your money at a fixed rate for a longer period of time.
- ✔ **Have lower credit quality:** The bond issuer may not be able to repay the principal.

Wharton School of Business professor Jeremy Siegel has tracked the performance of U.S. bonds and stocks all the way back to 1802. Although you may say that what happened in the 19th century has little relevance to the financial markets and economy of today, the decades since the Great Depression, which most other return data track, are a relatively small slice of time. Figure 2-4 presents the data, so if you'd like to give more emphasis to the recent numbers, you may.

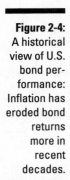

Figure 2-4:
A historical
view of U.S.
bond per-
formance:
Inflation has
eroded bond
returns
more in
recent
decades.

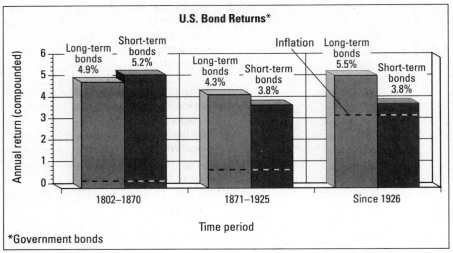

Note that although the rate of inflation has increased since the Great
Depression, bond returns have not increased over the decades. Long-term
bonds maintain slightly higher returns in recent years than short-term bonds.
The bottom line: Bond investors typically earn about 4 to 5 percent per year.

Stock returns

Investors expect — indeed, they demand — a fair return on investment. And
if one investment doesn't offer a high enough rate of return, investors can
choose to move their money into other investments that they believe will
perform better. Instead of buying a diversified basket of stocks and holding,
some investors frequently buy and sell, hoping to cash in on the latest hot
investment. This tactic seldom works in the long run.

Unfortunately, some of these investors use a rearview mirror when they purchase their stocks, chasing after investments that have recently performed
strongly on the assumption (and the hope) that those investments will continue to earn strong returns. But chasing after the strongest performing investments can be dangerous if you catch the stock at its peak, ready to begin a
downward spiral. You may have heard that the goal of investing is to buy low
and sell high. Chasing high-flying investments can lead you to buy high, with
the prospect of having to sell low if the stock runs out of steam. Even though
stocks as a whole have proved to be a good long-term investment, picking
individual stocks is a risky endeavour. See Chapters 5 and 6 for advice on
making sound stock investment decisions.

A tremendous amount of data exists regarding stock market returns. In fact, in the U.S. markets, data going back more than two centuries documents the fact that stocks have been a terrific long-term investment. The long-term returns from stocks that investors have enjoyed, and continue to enjoy, have been remarkably constant from one generation to the next.

Going all the way back to 1802, the U.S. stock market has produced an annual return of 8.3 percent, while inflation has grown at 1.4 percent per year. Thus, after subtracting for inflation, stocks have appreciated about 6.9 percent faster annually than the rate of inflation. The U.S. stock market returns have consistently and substantially beaten the rate of inflation over the years (see Figure 2-5).

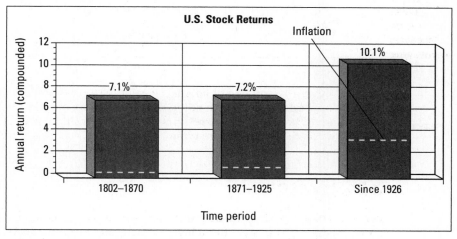

Figure 2-5:
History
tells us
that stocks
have been
a consistent
long-term
winner.

Stocks don't exist only in Canada and the United States, of course (see Figure 2-6). More than a few investors seem to forget this fact, especially during periods when North American stock markets sizzle like they did during the late 1990s. As we discuss in the earlier section "Diversify for a gentler ride," one advantage of buying and holding overseas stocks is that they don't always fall when Canadian and U.S. stocks drop. In other words, overseas stocks help diversify your portfolio.

Total Value of Stocks Worldwide

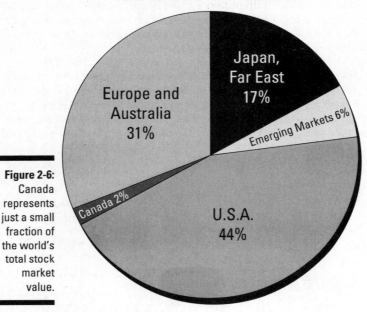

Figure 2-6:
Canada
represents
just a small
fraction of
the world's
total stock
market
value.

In addition to enabling investors to diversify, investing overseas has proved to be profitable. The investment banking firm Morgan Stanley tracks the performance of stocks in both economically established countries and so-called emerging economies. As the name suggests, countries with *emerging economies* (for example, Brazil, China, India, Malaysia, Mexico, Russia, South Korea, and Taiwan) are "behind" economically but show high rates of growth and progress. Faster-growing countries tend to have fast-rising and more volatile stock prices.

Real estate returns

Like investing in the stock market, real estate has proved to be lucrative over the years. Whenever there's a big real estate downturn, folks question this historic fact (see Chapter 11 for more details). However, just as stock prices have down periods, so too do real estate markets.

The fact that real estate offers solid long-term returns makes sense because ultimately, growth in the economy, in jobs, and in population fuels the demand for real estate.

Consider what has happened to the Canadian population over the past two centuries. In 1867 a mere 3.5 million people lived within our borders. In 1900 that figure grew to over 5 million, and by 1929 it had doubled to over 10 million. Today it's over 33 million. All these people need a place to live, and as long as jobs exist, the income from them largely fuels the demand for housing. Businesses and people have an understandable tendency to cluster in major cities and suburban towns. Although some people commute, most people and businesses locate near airports and major highways. Thus, real estate prices in and near major metropolises and suburbs generally appreciate the most. Consider the areas of the world that have the most expensive real estate prices: London, Paris, Tokyo, Moscow, Singapore, New York, and Hong Kong. Here at home, our most expensive cities are Vancouver and Toronto. What these areas have in common are lots of businesses and people and limited land.

Contrast these areas with the many rural parts of the country where the price of real estate is relatively low because of the abundant supply of buildable land and the relatively lower demand for housing.

Small-business returns

As we discuss in Part IV of this book, you have several choices for tapping into the exciting potential of the small-business world. If you have the drive and determination, you can start your own small business. Or perhaps you have what it takes to buy an existing small business. If you obtain the necessary capital and skills to assess opportunities and risk, you can invest in someone else's small business.

What potential returns can you get from small business? Small-business owners like us who do something they really enjoy will tell you that the non-financial returns can be huge! The financial rewards can be handsome as well.

Every year, *Forbes* magazine publishes a list of the world's wealthiest individuals. Perusing this list shows that most of these people built their wealth through a significant ownership stake from starting a small business that became large. These individuals achieved extraordinarily high effective returns (often in excess of hundreds of percent per year) on the amounts they invested to get their companies off the ground.

You may also achieve potentially high returns from buying and improving an existing small business. As we discuss in Part IV, such small-business investment returns may be a good deal lower than the returns you may gain from starting a business from scratch.

TECHNICAL STUFF

Are smaller-company stock returns higher?

Stocks are generally classified by the size of the company. Small company stocks aren't stocks that physically small companies issue — they're simply stocks issued by companies that haven't reached the size of corporate behemoths like the big banks, Bombardier, and Barrick, or U.S. giants like IBM, AT&T, and Coca-Cola. The S&P/TSX SmallCap Index tracks the smallest companies that qualify for the TSX compound index, while the S&P/TSX Venture Composite Index measures the performance of the larger and more actively traded companies listed on the TSX Venture Exchange, where smaller or more speculative companies are listed. (In the United States, the Standard & Poor's 500 index tracks the performance of 500 large-company stocks in the United States. The Russell 2000 index tracks the performance of 2,000 smaller-company U.S. stocks.

Small-company stocks have outperformed larger-company stocks during the past seven decades. Historically, small-company stocks have produced slightly higher compounded annual returns (1.9 percent) than large-company stocks. However, nearly all of this extra performance occurred in just one high-performance time period, from the mid-1970s to the early 1980s. If you eliminate this time period from the data, small-company stocks have had virtually identical returns to those of larger-company stocks.

Also, be aware that small-company stocks can get hammered in down markets. For example, during the Great Depression, small-company stocks plunged more than 85 percent between 1929 and 1932, while the S&P 500 fell 64 percent. In 1937, small-company stocks plummeted 58 percent; the S&P 500 fell 35 percent. And in 1969 to 1970, small-company stocks fell 38 percent, while the S&P 500 fell just 5 percent. (In the bear market of the early 2000s, small-company stocks fell less than large-company stocks). During the steep market drop in the fall of 2008, small-company stocks lost 53 percent while large-company stocks lost just over 42 percent.

Unlike the stock market, where plenty of historic rate-of-return data exists, data on the success, or lack thereof, that investors have had with investing in small, private companies is harder to come by. Smart venture capitalist firms operate a fun and lucrative business: They identify and invest money in smaller start-up companies that they hope will grow rapidly and eventually go public. Venture capitalists allow outsiders to invest with them via limited partnerships. To gain entry, you generally need $1 million to invest. (We never said this was an equal-opportunity investment club!)

Venture capitalists, also known as general partners, typically skim off 20 percent of the profits and also charge limited partnership investors a hefty 2 to 3 percent annual fee on the amount that they've invested. The return that's left over for the limited partnership investors isn't stupendous. According to Venture Economics, a U.S. firm that tracks limited partners' returns, venture funds have averaged comparable annual returns to what stock market investors have earned on average over this same period. The general partners that run venture capital funds make more than the limited partners do.

You can attempt to do what the general partners do in venture capital firms and invest directly in small, private companies. You're quite likely to be investing in much smaller and simpler companies. Earning venture capitalist returns isn't easy to do. If you think that you're up to the challenge, we explain the best ways to invest in small business in Chapter 15.

Considering Your Goals

How much do you need or want to earn? That may seem like an extraordinarily stupid question for us to ask you! Who *doesn't* want to earn a high return? However, although investing in stocks, real estate, or small business can produce high long-term returns, you invest in these vehicles with greater risk, especially over the short term.

Some people can't stomach the risk. Others are at a time in their lives when they can't afford to take great risk. If you're near or in retirement, your portfolio and nerves may not be able to wait a decade for your riskier investments to recover after a major stumble. Perhaps you have sufficient assets to accomplish your financial goals and are concerned with preserving what you do have, rather than risking it to grow more wealth.

If you work for a living, odds are that you need and want to make your investments grow at a healthy clip. If your investments grow slowly, you may fall short of your goals of owning a home or retiring or changing careers.

Chapter 3

Getting Your House in Order before You Invest

*B*efore you make any great, wealth-building investments, we recommend that you get your financial house in order. The truth is that understanding and implementing some simple personal financial management concepts will pay off big for you in the decades ahead.

You want to know how to earn healthy returns on your investments without getting clobbered, right? Who doesn't? Although you generally must accept greater risk to have the potential for earning higher returns (see Chapter 2), in this chapter we tell you about some free lunches in the world of investing. You have a right to be skeptical about free lunches — but this chapter points out some easy-to-tap opportunities for managing your money you likely have overlooked.

Establishing an Emergency Reserve

You never know what life will bring, so it makes good financial sense to have a readily accessible reserve of cash to meet unexpected expenses. If you have a sister who works on Bay Street as an investment banker or have wealthy and understanding parents, you may be able to use them as your emergency reserve. (Although you should ask them how they feel about that before you count on receiving funding from them!) If not, the ball's in your court to establish a reserve.

Make sure you have quick access to at least three months' to as much as six months' worth of living expenses. Keep this emergency money in a high-interest savings account or a high-yielding money market fund (see Chapter 8). You may also be able to borrow against the equity you've built up in your home should you find yourself in a bind, but this option is much less desirable.

If you don't have a financial safety net, you may be forced into selling an investment that you've worked hard for. Consider the case of Warren, who owned his home as well as an investment property. He felt, and appeared to be, financially successful. But then Warren lost his job, accumulated sizable medical expenses, and had to sell his investment property to come up with the cash to tide himself over. Warren didn't have enough equity in his home to borrow. He didn't have other sources — a wealthy relative, for example — to borrow from either, so he was stuck selling his investment property.

Selling some investments, such as real estate, costs big money (transaction costs, taxes, and so on). Warren wasn't able to purchase another investment property and missed out on the large appreciation the property earned over the subsequent two decades. Between the costs of selling and taxes, getting rid of the investment property cost Warren about 15 percent of its sales price. Ouch!

Introducing a New Investment Option: The Tax-Free Savings Account

A good place to stash your emergency cash is in a *Tax-Free Savings Account* (TFSA). A TFSA is also a good choice if you are already contributing the maximum allowed to your Registered Retirement Savings Plan (RRSP) and Registered Education Savings Plan (RESP), and still have savings left over.

You can put up to a maximum of $5,000 a year into a TFSA. The $5,000 limit on annual contributions will be indexed to inflation — in $500 increments — starting in 2010. If you don't contribute the maximum allowed in any one year, you can carry forward that unused amount and contribute it in the future without any limitations.

Should you invest emergency money in stocks?

As interest rates drifted lower during the 1990s, keeping emergency money in money market accounts became less and less rewarding. When interest rates were 8 or 10 percent, fewer people questioned the wisdom of an emergency reserve. However, in the late 1990s, with money market interest rates of 5 percent or less and stock market returns of 20 percent per year, more investors balked at keeping a low-interest stash of cash.

We began reading articles that suggested you simply keep your emergency reserve in stocks. After all, you can easily sell stocks (especially those of larger companies) any day the financial markets are open. Why not treat yourself to the 20 percent annual returns that stock market investors enjoyed during the 1990s rather than earning a paltry 5 percent?

As we discuss in Chapter 2, stocks historically have returned about 9 to 10 percent per year. But in some years — in fact, about one-third of the time — stocks decline in value, sometimes substantially.

Stocks can drop and have dropped 20, 30, or 50 percent or more over relatively short periods of time. Witness what happened to stock prices in 2008. Suppose that such a drop coincides with an emergency — such as the loss of your job, major medical bills, and so on. Your situation may force you to sell at a loss, perhaps a substantial one.

Another reason not to keep emergency money in stocks is that if your stocks appreciate and you need to sell some of them for emergency cash, you get stuck paying taxes on your gains.

We suggest that you invest your emergency money in stocks (ideally through well-diversified mutual funds) only if you have a relative or some other resource to tap for money in an emergency. Having a backup resource for money minimizes your need to sell your stock holdings on short notice. As we discuss in Chapter 5, stocks are intended to be a longer-term investment, not an investment that you expect (or need) to sell in the near future.

Unlike an RRSP, you don't earn a tax deduction for your contribution. However, any interest you earn on the money after it's inside this special account is tax-free. You can also invest money inside your TFSA into most of the same investments that qualify for RRSPs. This includes most mutual funds, as well as bonds and individual stocks.

No tax is payable when you take money out of a TFSA. In addition, any amount you withdraw is added back to your contribution room. This means you can choose to recontribute that amount in future years.

Evaluating Your Debts

Yes, paying down debts is boring, but it makes your investment decisions less difficult. Rather than spending so much of your time investigating specific investments, paying off your debts (if you have them) may be your best high-return, low-risk investment. Consider the interest rate you pay and your investing alternatives to determine which debts you should pay off.

Conquering consumer debt

Many folks have credit card or other consumer debt, such as auto loans, that costs 8, 10, 12, or as much as 18-plus percent per year in interest (some credit cards whack you with interest rates exceeding 20 percent if you make a late payment). Reducing and eventually eliminating this debt with your savings is like putting your money in an investment with a guaranteed *tax-free* return equal to the rate that you pay on your debt.

For example, if you have outstanding credit card debt at 15 percent interest, paying off that debt is the same as putting your money to work in an investment with a guaranteed 15 percent tax-free annual return. Because the interest on consumer debt isn't tax-deductible, you would need to earn more than 15 percent investing your money elsewhere in order to net 15 percent after paying taxes. Earning such high investing returns is highly unlikely, and in order to earn those returns, you'd be forced to take great risk.

Consumer debt is hazardous to your long-term financial health (not to mention the damage it can do to your credit rating and future ability to borrow for a home or other wise investments) because it encourages you to borrow against your future earnings. Consider what happened to many Americans in the 2000s who borrowed most if not the full value of their home in the form of a mortgage. It was common for these homebuyers — who in normal times wouldn't have been able to get a mortgage — to then turn around and use the short-term increase in the value of their property to borrow even more money thanks to the aggressiveness of lenders to do business with just about anybody. When housing prices fell and the cost of the interest on their mortgages rose, some were unable to pay the interest on their homes, much less their other debts, and lost most if not all they had.

We often hear people say such things as "I can't afford to buy most new cars for cash — look at how expensive they are!" That's true, new cars *are* expensive, so set your sights lower and buy a good used car that you *can* afford. You can then invest the money that you'd otherwise spend on your auto loan.

Borrowing via credit cards, auto loans, and the like is also one of the most expensive ways to borrow. Banks and other lenders charge higher interest rates for consumer debt than for debt for investments, such as real estate and business. The reason: Consumer loans are the riskiest type of loan for a lender.

However, using consumer debt may make sense if you're financing a business. If you haven't built up extra equity in your home, personal loans (through a credit card or auto loan) may actually be your lowest-cost source of small-business financing. (See Chapter 14 for more details.)

Mitigating your mortgage

Paying off your mortgage quicker is an "investment" for your spare cash that may make sense for your financial situation. However, the wisdom of making this financial move isn't as clear as is paying off high-interest consumer debt, because mortgage interest rates are generally lower. When used properly, debt can help you accomplish your goals — such as buying a home or starting a business — and make you money in the long run. Borrowing to buy a home also generally makes sense. Over the long term, homes usually appreciate in value.

If your financial situation has changed or improved since you first needed to borrow mortgage money, you need to reconsider how much mortgage debt you need or want. Even if your income hasn't escalated or you haven't inherited vast wealth, your frugality may allow you to pay down some of your debt sooner than the lender requires. Whether paying down your debt sooner makes sense for you depends on a number of factors, including your other investment options and goals.

When evaluating whether to pay down your mortgage faster, you need to compare your mortgage interest rate versus your investments' rates of return (which we define in Chapter 2). Suppose that you have a fixed-rate mortgage with an interest rate of 7 percent. If you decide to make investments instead of paying down your mortgage more quickly, your investments need to produce an average annual rate of return, after taxes, of about 7 percent to come out ahead financially.

Besides the most common reason of lacking the money to do so, other good reasons *not* to pay off your mortgage any quicker than necessary include the following:

> ✔ **You instead contribute to your RRSP or other retirement plans, especially if your employer offers matching money.** Paying off your mortgage faster has no tax benefit. By contrast, putting additional money into a retirement plan can immediately reduce your income tax burden. The more years you have until retirement, the greater the benefit you receive if you invest in your retirement plans. Thanks to the compounding of your retirement plan investments without the drain of taxes, you can actually earn a lower rate of return on your investments than you pay on your mortgage and still come out ahead. (We discuss RRSPs in detail in the "Funding Your RRSP" section, later in this chapter.)

✔ **You're willing to invest in growth-oriented, volatile investments, such as stocks and real estate.** For you to have a reasonable chance of earning more on your investments than it costs you to borrow on your mortgage, you must be aggressive with your investments. As we discuss in Chapter 2, stocks and real estate have produced annual average rates of return of about 8 to 10 percent. You can earn even more with your own small business or by investing in others' businesses. Paying down a mortgage ties up more of your capital, reducing your ability to make other attractive investments. To more aggressive investors, paying off the house seems downright boring — the financial equivalent of watching paint dry.

Remember that you have no guarantee of earning high returns from growth-type investments, which can easily drop 20 percent or more in value over a year or two. The Toronto market lost more than 50 percent of its value between the summer of 2008 and March of 2009.

✔ **Paying down the mortgage depletes your emergency reserves.** Psychologically, some people feel uncomfortable paying off debt more quickly if it diminishes their savings and investments. You probably don't want to pay down your debt if doing so depletes your financial safety cushion. Make sure that you have access — through a money market fund or other source (a family member, for example) — to at least three months' living expenses (as we explain in the earlier section "Establishing an Emergency Reserve").

Finally, don't be tripped up by the misconception that somehow a real estate market downturn, such as many areas experienced in the mid- to late 2000s, will harm you more if you pay down your mortgage. Your home is worth what it's worth — its value has *nothing* to do with your debt load. Unless you're willing to walk away from your home and send the keys to the bank (also known as *default*), you suffer the full effect of a price decline, regardless of your mortgage size, if real estate prices collapse.

Establishing Your Financial Goals

You may want to invest money for different purposes simultaneously. For example, when you're in your 20s, you may want to put some money away toward retirement, but also save a stash so you could hit the eject button from your job. Perhaps you know that one day you want to pursue an entrepreneurial path, and realize that in the early years of starting your own business, you can't count on an income as stable or as large as what you get from your job.

In this case, you should invest your two "pots" of money — one for retirement, the other for your small-business cushion — quite differently. As we discuss in the section "Choosing the Right Investment Mix," later in this chapter, you can afford to take more risk with the money you plan on using longer term. As a result, you could invest the bulk of your retirement nest egg in stock mutual funds.

With the money you save for the start-up of your small business, consider taking an entirely different track. None of this money should go into risky stocks — what if the market plummets just as you're ready to leave the security of your full-time job? Keep this money safely invested in a high-interest savings account or a money market fund that pays a healthy rate of interest but doesn't put your savings — your *principal* — at risk.

Tracking your savings rate

To accomplish your financial and some personal goals, you need to save money, and you need to know your savings rate. Your savings rate is the percentage of your past year's income that you saved and didn't spend. You may already know that your rate of savings is low, non-existent, or negative, and that you need to save more.

Part of being a smart investor involves figuring out how much you need to save to reach your goals. Not knowing what you want to do a decade or more from now is perfectly normal — after all, your goals and needs evolve over the years. But that doesn't mean that you should just throw your hands in the air and not make an effort to see where you stand today and think about where you want to be in the future.

An important benefit of knowing your savings rate is that you'll know better how much risk you need to take to accomplish your goals. Seeing how much you need to save to achieve your dreams may encourage you to take more risk with your investments.

If you consistently save about 10 percent of your income during your working years, you're probably saving enough to meet your goals unless you want to retire at a relatively young age. On average, most people need about 75 percent of their pre-retirement income throughout their retirement to maintain their standard of living.

If you're one of the many people who don't save enough, you need to do some homework. To save more, you need to reduce your spending, increase your income, or both.

For most people, reducing spending is the more feasible way to save. But where do you begin? First, figure out where your money goes. You may have some general idea, but you need to have facts. Get out your chequebook register, examine your online bill-paying records, and review your credit card bills and any other documentation you have of your spending history. Tally up how much you spend on dining out, operating your car(s), paying your taxes, and everything else. After you have this information, you can begin to prioritize and make the necessary trade-offs to reduce your spending and increase your savings rate. Earning more income may help boost your savings rate as well. Perhaps you can get a higher-paying job or increase the number of hours you work. But if you already work a lot, reining in your spending is usually better for your emotional and economic well-being.

If you don't know how to evaluate and reduce your spending or haven't thought about your retirement goals, looked into what you can expect from the Canada Pension Plan or Quebec Pension Plan, or calculated how much you should save for retirement, now's the time to do it. Pick up the latest edition of our book *Personal Finance For Canadians For Dummies* (published by Wiley), and find out all the necessary details for retirement planning and much more.

Determining your investment tastes

Many good investing choices exist — you can invest in real estate, the stock market, mutual funds, exchange-traded funds, or your own business or someone else's, or you can pay down mortgage debt more quickly. What makes sense for you depends on your goals as well as your personal preferences. If you detest risk-taking and volatile investments, paying down your mortgage, as recommended earlier in this chapter, may make better sense than investing in the stock market.

How would you deal with an investment that plunges 20 percent, 40 percent, or more in a few years or less? Some aggressive investments can fall fast. Sometimes stocks in general collapse, as they did in 2008, with some markets falling more than 40 percent. (See Chapter 2 for examples.) You shouldn't invest in the stock market, real estate, or a small business if such a drop is likely to cause you to sell low or make you a miserable wreck. If you haven't tried riskier investments yet, you may want to experiment a bit to see how you feel with your money invested in them.

A simple way to "mask" the risk of volatile investments is to *diversify* your portfolio — that is, to put your money into different investments. Not watching prices too closely helps, too — that's one of the reasons real estate investors are less likely to bail out when the market declines. Stock market investors, unfortunately from our perspective, can get daily and even minute-by-minute price updates. Add that fact to the quick phone call or click of your computer mouse that it takes to dump a stock in a flash, and you have all the ingredients for short-sighted investing — and financial disaster.

Investing as couples

You've probably learned over the years how challenging it is just for you to navigate the investment maze and make sound investing decisions. When you have someone else to consider, dealing with these issues becomes doubly hard, given the typically different money personalities and emotions that come into play.

In most couples, usually one person takes primary responsibility for managing the household finances, including investments. As with most marital issues, the couples that do the best job with their investments are those who communicate well, plan ahead, and compromise.

Here are a couple of examples to illustrate our point. Martha and Alex scheduled meetings with each other every three to six months to discuss financial issues. With investments, Martha came prepared with a list of ideas, and Alex would listen and explain what he liked or disliked about each option. Alex would tend toward more aggressive, growth-oriented investments, whereas Martha preferred conservative, less volatile investments. Inevitably, they would compromise and develop a diversified portfolio that was moderately aggressive. Martha and Alex worked as a team, discussed options, compromised, and made decisions they were both comfortable with. Ideas that made one of them very uncomfortable were nixed.

Henry and Melissa didn't do so well. The only times they managed to discuss investments were in heated arguments. Melissa often criticized what Henry was doing with their money. Henry got defensive and counter-criticized Melissa for other issues. Much of their money lay dormant in a low-interest bank account, and they did little long-term planning and decision making. Melissa and Henry saw each other as adversaries, argued and criticized rather than discussed, and were plagued with inaction because they couldn't agree and compromise. They needed a motivation to change their behaviour toward each other, and they needed some counselling (or a few advice guides for couples) to make progress with investing their money.

Aren't your long-term financial health and marital harmony important? Don't allow your problems to fester!

Often, one of the most valuable (and difficult) things couples stuck in unproductive patterns of behaviour can do to help themselves is get the issue out on the table. When it comes to money, often the biggest step for couples is to make an appointment with an adviser to discuss their financial management. Once they do, it's usually relatively easy to get them to explain their different points of view, which then enables the adviser to offer some compromises. *Remember:* You can't change something if you don't first acknowledge it.

Funding Your RRSP

Saving money for the future is difficult for most people. Don't make a tough job impossible by forsaking the terrific tax benefits that come from contri-buting money to — and investing inside — an RRSP.

Gaining tax benefits

Registered retirement savings plans (RRSPs) should be called tax-reduction plans — if they were, people might be more jazzed about contributing to them. Contributions to these plans are tax-deductible. Suppose that you pay about 35 percent between federal and provincial income taxes on your last dollars of income. (See the section "Determining your tax bracket," later in this chapter.) With an RRSP, you can save yourself about $350 in taxes for every $1,000 that you contribute in the year that you make your contribution.

After your money is in an RRSP, any interest, dividends, and appreciation grow inside the account without taxation. You defer taxes on all the accumulating gains and profits until you withdraw your money down the road. In the meantime, more of your money works for you over a long period of time.

Understanding RRSPs

You can contribute to an RRSP as long as you have what the government dubs *earned income.* For most people, their earned income is their salary, along with any bonuses or commissions. If you're self-employed or an active partner in a business, it includes any net income from your business. Earned income also includes any taxable alimony and maintenance payments as well as any research grants, royalties, and net rental income.

As long as you have earned income in a year, you can contribute 18 percent of that amount to your RRSP in the following year. However, two restrictions may cap the total amount you can contribute for that year:

- There is a maximum amount you'll be able to contribute for any one year. The limit is scheduled to rise to $21,000 for 2009, and $22,000 for 2010. After 2010, the maximum will be *indexed,* meaning it will increase at the rate of inflation.

- The maximum amount you are allowed to contribute may be further reduced if you belong to a company pension plan. The government calculates the value of contributions made to your employer-sponsored pension plan, called a pension adjustment (PA), and deducts this from whichever is less — the absolute dollar maximum allowed for the year or 18 percent of your earned income — to arrive at your allowable contribution.

Your pension adjustment for a given year should appear in that year's T4 slip that you receive from your employer. (It should also be stated on the Notice of Assessment you receive in the spring after you file your tax return for the previous year.)

Note that when we talk about the maximum contribution per year, we're referring to how much you can contribute *for* each year. There's no limit on how much you can contribute *in* any one given year. All that's required is that you've built up that amount of allowable contributions. Say that based on your last year's salary, your new allowable contribution is $5,000, but you only contribute $2,000. Next year, your new allowable contribution is another $5,000, based on your income this year. This means that the amount you can put into your RRSP will then be the sum of $5,000 and the $3,000 of allowable contribution you didn't use this year, for a total of $8,000.

One nice feature of RRSPs is they're not a case of "Use it or lose it." If you don't put in the full amount you're allowed to in any given year, you can carry forward that amount — your *RRSP deduction limit* — and use it in the future. Think of it as having an ongoing allowable contribution account. Any time you have earned income, the next year you can add to your allowable contribution account the difference between the amount that year's earned income gave you the right to contribute and what you actually put into your RRSP.

Delaying increases your pain

The common mistake that investors make is neglecting to take advantage of retirement plans because of their enthusiasm to spend or invest in "non-retirement" plans. Not investing inside tax-sheltered retirement plans can cost you hundreds, perhaps thousands, of dollars per year in lost tax savings. Add that loss up over the many years that you work and save, and not taking advantage of these tax reduction accounts can easily cost you tens of thousands to hundreds of thousands of dollars in the long term. Ouch!

To take advantage of retirement savings plans and the tax savings that accompany them, you must first spend less than you earn. Only after you spend less than you earn can you afford to contribute to these retirement savings plans (unless you already happen to have a stash of cash from previous savings or inheritance).

The sooner you start to save, the less painful it is each year to save enough to reach your goals because your contributions have more years to compound.

Each decade you delay saving approximately doubles the percentage of your earnings that you need to save to meet your goals. For example, if saving 5 percent per year in your early 20s gets you to your retirement goal, waiting until your 30s to start may mean socking away 10 percent to reach that same goal; waiting until your 40s, 20 percent. Beyond that, the numbers get truly daunting.

Choosing RRSP and other tax-deferred investments

When you establish an RRSP, RESP, or TFSA, you may not realize that you're simply putting your money into a shell or shield that keeps the government from taxing your investment earnings each year. You still must choose what investments you want to hold inside your retirement plan shell.

You may invest money inside your tax-deferred plans in stocks, bonds, and mutual funds.

Mutual funds (offered in most employer-based plans), which we cover in detail in Chapter 8, are an ideal choice because they offer diversification and professional management. After you decide which financial institution you want to invest through, simply obtain and complete the appropriate paperwork for establishing the specific type of account you want.

If you enjoy spending money and living for today, you should be more motivated to start saving sooner. The longer you wait to save, the more you ultimately need to save and, therefore, the less you can spend today!

Investing for University

From paying for diapers to having to buy a heck of a lot more groceries when your kids become teenagers, having children is a costly affair. But it can feel downright punitive when you start thinking about what it will cost to get them a post-secondary education.

That's not exactly welcome news for those already trying to pay off their mortgage and save for retirement. But one of the best approaches is often to simply pay attention to your first two goals and ignore the third. If you work hard and knock down your mortgage, you'll have a good chance of being able to reduce or even eliminate your mortgage payments by the time the little ones are ready to go to university. If you've knocked a good deal off of your mortgage, you'll also be in the position to borrow against the equity you've built up in your home to pay for educational expenses.

By working hard to grow your RRSP, hopefully you'll accumulate a good-sized sum that has built up some compounding steam. If you're accustomed to "paying yourself first" — regularly diverting a portion of your income to your RRSP — you can turn your financial sights away from your old age and toward your children's educational bills while they're at school, and resume your RRSP contributions after they graduate.

We understand the feeling some have that education is so important they don't feel comfortable unless they're putting away some dollars specifically earmarked for that purpose. Others may be in the enviable position of being able to set aside savings for future educational costs while also taking care of their mortgage and building up their RRSP. If you want to start an education savings program, you have two basic ways to do it, each with some distinct benefits and drawbacks you need to consider. The approach that works best for you will be determined by your family circumstances, your outlook, and your sense of where your children are heading.

Looking at Registered Education Savings Plans

Registered Education Savings Plans (RESPs) sound similar to Registered Retirement Savings Plans (RRSPs), and they are, with a few important differences.

RESPs are a way to set money aside and defer tax on the earnings on that money. Although you don't get a tax deduction for your contributions — as you do with an RRSP — you're not taxed on any gains inside the plan. Similar to an RRSP, the money is treated as income and taxed accordingly only when it's withdrawn. However, as long as it's used to pay for your child's education, the proceeds of the contributions are treated as if they are your child's income. In most cases, because your child will have little or no other income, the funds will be able to come out of the RESP tax-free.

You can set up an RESP for each of your children, with a lifetime maximum contribution ceiling of $50,000. When RESPs were first introduced, there was also an annual limit on how much you could contribute, but that has been eliminated.

What makes RESPs financially friendly is that the government tops up your contributions. Under the Canada Education Savings Grant (CESG), the federal government will put in another 20 percent of any contribution you make, to a maximum of $500 a year. The grant is available every year the beneficiary of the RESP is under the age of 18, up to a maximum of $7,200. (The grant amounts aren't included when calculating your contribution limits.)

If you don't make the most use of the CESG in any one year by contributing $2,500 and receiving the maximum annual grant of $500, don't worry. If you put in less in any one year, you can earn the untapped grant in future years. However, in any one single year, the CESG grant per beneficiary is limited to the lesser of $1,000 or 20 percent of the unused CESG room.

How to pay for university or college

If you keep stashing away money in an RRSP, it's reasonable for you to wonder how you'll actually pay for your child's education expenses when the momentous occasion arises. In most cases, even if you have some liquid assets that can be directed to your child's university or college bill, you will, in all likelihood, need to borrow some money. Only the affluent can truly afford to pay for university or college with cash.

One good source of money is your home's equity. You can borrow against your home at a relatively low interest rate. Another place to look is the Canada Student Loans Program, which the federal government runs in conjunction with the various provinces. (Quebec and the Northwest Territories run their programs independently from Ottawa.) To apply, contact your provincial ministry of education. While your child is at school, the federal government pays the interest, but your child will have to start repaying the loan six months after he or she graduates.

In addition to loans, a number of grant programs are available through schools and the government, as well as through independent sources. A good starting point is your child's guidance counselling office. Most schools have lists of local government and private bursaries, grants and awards, and scholarships. You should also consider your family's various employers. A surprising number of companies have student grants available for their employees or children of employees. Contact the university or college your child is considering to see what other sources of funding are available. You can find easy links to their financial resources page by visiting www.canadian-universities.net/index.html and clicking on Financial Aid & Scholarships. You can then choose a province, and you'll get a page listing links to the financial aid page of each school.

Also, contact the Canada Millennium Scholarships Foundation. The federal government plans to distribute 100,000 scholarships to low- and middle-income students. The scholarships will average $3,000 a year, and may be awarded for four years. You can find out more at www.millennium scholarships.ca.

Other lists of funding sources are available online. Visit the sites of the universities or colleges your child is considering attending. You can find links to all the provincial and territorial student assistance offices at www.canlearn.ca. Another good source for information on grants and scholarships is www.scholarshipscanada.com. Your child can also work and save money for university during high school. Besides giving your gangly teen a stake in his or her own future, this training encourages sound personal financial management down the road.

Like RRSPs, you can invest money inside an RESP in a wide choice of investments, including the many types of mutual funds and even individual stocks. (Be sure to opt for a self-directed RESP, not one of the group plans that have higher fees and more restrictions.)

If your child does not pursue a further education that allows him or her to use the money inside the plan, you can take out the original contributions without any penalty. However, you'll have to return any grants you've received under the CESG. In addition, the money you've made on any grants as well as on your own contributions may be taxable.

If the beneficiary is not a post-secondary student by age 21 and the plan has been running for at least ten years, you can transfer up to $50,000 of the plan's profits to your own or your spouse's RRSP. However, you must have sufficient unused RRSP deduction limit available. (The result is that the RRSP deduction you receive will offset any taxes including the RESP's earnings in your income). Any of the plan's profits that don't get sheltered in this way are taxed at your full marginal tax rate. In addition, you pay an extra 20 percent penalty. On top of your tax bill, that could mean giving up as much as 65 percent of the profits. Ouch!

Allocating university investments

If you keep up to 80 percent of your university investment money in stocks (diversified worldwide) with the remainder in bonds when your child is young, you can maximize the money's growth potential without taking extraordinary risk. As your child makes his way through the later years of elementary school, you need to begin to make the mix more conservative — scale back the stock percentage to 50 or 60 percent. Finally, in the years just before he enters college, whittle the stock portion down to no more than 20 percent or so.

Diversified mutual funds (which invest in stocks in Canada and internationally) and bonds are ideal vehicles to use when you invest for college. Be sure to choose funds that fit your tax situation if you invest your funds in non-retirement plans. See Chapter 8 for more information.

Taming Your Taxes

When you invest outside of tax-sheltered retirement plans and accounts, the profits and distributions on your money are subject to taxation. So the type of non-sheltered plan investments that makes sense for you depends (at least partly) on your tax situation.

If you have money to invest, or if you're considering selling current investments you hold, taxes should factor into your decision. But tax considerations alone shouldn't dictate how and where you invest your money. You should also weigh investment choices, your desire and the necessity to take risk, personal likes and dislikes, and the number of years you plan to hold the investment (see the "Choosing the Right Investment Mix" section, later in the chapter, for more information on these other factors).

Determining your tax bracket

You may not know it, but the government charges you different tax rates for different parts of your annual income. You pay less tax on the *first* dollars of your earnings and more tax on the *last* dollars of your earnings. For example, suppose your taxable income totalled $60,000 during 2009. The first $9,600 of income is essentially tax-free, because the tax you would otherwise pay on that amount is offset by a federal tax credit of $1,440, the *basic personal amount.* After that, the approximate tax rate (the combined federal and provincial rates) you would pay would be 24 percent on the income between $9,600 and $37,885, and 36 percent on the income from $37,885 to $75,770. Income from 75,770 to $123,185 is taxed at 42 percent, and income over $123,185 is taxed at 46 percent.

Your *marginal tax rate* is the rate of tax that you pay on your *last* (or your most recent) dollar(s) of income. In the example of a person with taxable income of $60,000, that person's marginal tax rate is 36 percent. In other words, he effectively pays a 36 percent federal tax on his last dollars of income — those dollars earned between $37,885 and $60,000. Knowing your marginal tax rate allows you to quickly calculate the following:

✔ Any additional taxes that you would pay on additional income

✔ The amount of taxes that you save if you contribute more money into retirement plans or reduce your taxable income

Table 3-1 shows the approximate marginal tax bracket, including federal and provincial taxes and surtaxes.

Table 3-1	2009 Combined Federal and Provincial Income Tax Rates
Approximate Taxable Income	*Approximate Tax Rate*
Less than $10,320	0%
$10,320 to $40,726	20% to 24%
Over $40,726 to $81,452	30% to 35%
Over $81,452 to $126,264	36% to 43%
More than $126,264	39% to 46%

Knowing what's taxed and when to worry

Interest you receive from bank accounts, GICs, and bonds is generally taxable. It's treated just like your regular income, and taxed at the same rate.

Taxation on your *capital gains,* which is the *profit* (sales minus adjusted cost base) on an investment, works under a unique system. When you make a profit on an investment, defined as selling it for more than its cost to you, you have to include half of your gain in your income, which is then taxed at your marginal tax rate. The result is that the current tax rate you effectively pay on capital gains — your effective tax rate — will be half of your marginal tax rate.

If you're in the lowest marginal tax bracket of 24 percent — remember that exact tax rates and marginal tax brackets vary from province to province — your effective capital gains tax rate will be 12 percent. If you are in the next tax bracket, where your salary is taxed at 36 percent, your effective tax rate on capital gains is 18 percent, while those in the 42 percent marginal tax bracket will have an effective capital gains tax rate of 21 percent. Finally, those in the top 46 percent marginal tax bracket will have capital gains taxed at 23 percent. See Table 3-2 for a look at the effective tax rates on capital gains.

Table 3-2	2009 Income Tax Rates
Taxable Income	*Approximate Effective Tax Rate on Capital Gains*
$10,320 to $40,726	10% to 12%
$40,726 to $81,452	15% to 20%
$81,452 to $126,264	20% to 22%
$126,264 and higher	21% to 24%

Any *dividends* you receive from Canadian corporations are taxed at the lowest effective rate. (Dividends from foreign corporations are treated and taxed just like your regular income.) A rather strange formula is used to determine the tax rate on dividends. This is because dividends are the distribution of a company's after-tax profits, so you receive a special tax credit to prevent the same profits being taxed twice.

First, the amount of the dividend actually received is increased by 45 percent — *grossed up* — to reflect what the corporation is assumed to have made pre-tax. This inflated number is what you show on your tax return as the amount of your dividend income. To offset this, you then get a federal tax credit of 19 percent of the grossed-up dividends, or 27.5 percent of the actual dividend you received.

In addition, your dividend is eligible for a corresponding provincial tax credit. The levels of the provincial tax credits for dividends range widely, as do the levels of income at which they apply. That said, in most provinces you can receive just shy of $40,000 in income from eligible dividends before you have to pay any tax on that income. Table 3-3 shows the approximate tax rates for dividends.

Table 3-3	2009 Dividend Income Tax Rates
Taxable Income	**Approximate Tax Rate on Eligible Dividends**
$9,600 to $37,885	0% to 7%
$37,885 to $75,770	2% to 19%
$75,770 to $123,185	11% to 26%
$123,185 and higher	17% to 29%

The lower your overall income level, the lower the tax rate for any dividends you receive. But there's more. In most provinces, if your income is below certain levels, not only is your dividend income not taxed, the tax you owe on income from other sources, including your regular job, is reduced. How? For lower-income earners, the marginal tax rate for dividends is actually negative. (In British Columbia, the most favourable province to receive dividend income in, the rate is negative 15.5 percent!) When there is a negative marginal tax rate for dividends, the dividend tax credit you earn not only offsets any tax due on the dividend income, but also reduces tax payable on other income. If your marginal tax rate for dividends is –10 percent, for example, a dollar of dividend income would mean you'd pay $0.10 less overall in taxes than you would without the dollar of dividend income.

Use these strategies to reduce the taxes on investments exposed to taxation:

✔ **Invest in tax-friendly stock funds.** *Index funds* are mutual funds that invest in a relatively static portfolio of securities, such as stocks and bonds. They don't attempt to beat the market. Rather, they invest in the securities to mirror or match the performance of an underlying index, such as the TSX Composite Index or Standard & Poor's 500 index (which we discuss in Chapter 5). Although index funds can't beat the market, the typical actively managed fund doesn't either, and index funds have several advantages over actively managed funds. Because index funds trade less, they tend to produce lower capital gains distributions. For mutual funds held outside tax-sheltered plans, this reduced trading effectively increases an investor's total rate of return. See Chapter 8 to find out more about tax-friendly stock mutual funds.

✔ **Invest in tax-friendly stocks.** Companies that pay little in the way of dividends reinvest more of their profits back into the company. If you invest outside of a retirement plan, unless you need income to live on, minimize your exposure to stocks with dividends. Be aware that low-dividend stocks tend to be more volatile.

✔ **Invest in small business and real estate.** The growth in value of a business and real estate asset isn't taxed until you sell the asset. However, the current income that a small business and real estate produce is taxed as ordinary income. (If you sell the home you live in — your *principal residence* — for a profit, all those gains are tax-free.)

Choosing the Right Investment Mix

Diversifying your investments helps buffer your portfolio from being sunk by one or two poor performers. In this section, we explain how to mix up a great recipe of investments.

Considering your age

When you're younger and have more years until you plan to use your money, you should keep larger amounts of your long-term investment money in *growth* (ownership) vehicles, such as stocks, real estate, and small business. As we discuss in Chapter 2, the attraction of these types of investments is the potential to really grow your money. The risk: The value of your portfolio can fall from time to time.

The younger you are, the more time your investments have to recover from a bad fall. In this respect, investments are a bit like people. If a 30-year-old and an 80-year-old fall on a concrete sidewalk, odds are higher that the younger person will fully recover. Such falls sometimes disable older people.

A long-held guiding principle says to subtract your age from 110 and invest the resulting number as a percentage of money to place in growth (ownership) investments. So if you're 35 years old,

110 – 35 = 75 percent of your investment money can be in growth investments.

If you want to be more aggressive, subtract your age from 120:

120 – 35 = 85 percent of your investment money can be in growth investments.

Note that even retired people should generally still have a healthy chunk of their investment dollars in growth vehicles like stocks. A 70-year-old person may want to totally avoid risk, but doing so is generally a mistake. Such a person can live another two or three decades. If you live longer than anticipated, you can run out of money if it doesn't continue to grow.

These tips are only general guidelines and apply to money that you invest for the long term (ideally for ten years or more). For money that you need to use in the shorter term, such as within the next several years, more-aggressive growth investments aren't appropriate. See Chapters 7 and 8 for more ideas.

Making the most of your investment options

No hard-and-fast rules dictate how to allocate the percentage you've earmarked for growth investments among specific investments, like stocks and real estate. Part of how you decide to allocate your investments depends, for example, on the types of investments you want to focus on. As we discuss in Chapter 5, diversifying in stocks worldwide can be prudent as well as profitable.

Here are some general guidelines to keep in mind:

- ✔ Maximize contributions to **retirement plans.** Unless you need accessible money for shorter-term non-retirement goals, why pass up the free extra returns from the tax benefits of retirement plans?

- ✔ **Take advantage of a Tax-Free Savings Account** (TFSA). The capital gains, dividends, and interest you earn on money inside these accounts are tax-free, as are any withdrawals. Put short-term money such as your emergency funds into a TFSA. Also consider sheltering savings in a TFSA if you're already contributing the maximum to your RRSP.

- ✔ **Don't pile into investments that gain lots of attention.** Many investors make this mistake, especially those who lack a thought-out plan to buy stocks. In Chapter 5, we provide numerous illustrations of the perils of buying attention-grabbing stocks.

✔ **Have the courage to be a contrarian.** No one wants to jump on board a sinking ship or support a losing cause. However, just like shopping for something at retail stores, the best time to buy something is when its price is reduced.

✔ **Diversify.** As we discuss in Chapter 2, the values of different investments don't move in tandem. So when you invest in growth investments, such as stocks or real estate, your portfolio's value will have a smoother ride if you diversify properly.

✔ **Invest more in what you know.** Over the years, we've met successful investors who have built substantial wealth without spending gobs of their free time researching, selecting, and monitoring investments. Some investors, for example, concentrate more on real estate because that's what they best understand and feel comfortable with. Others put more money in stocks for the same reason. No one-size-fits-all code exists for successful investors. Just be careful that you don't put all your investing eggs in the same basket (for example, don't load up on stocks in the same industry that you believe you know a lot about).

✔ **Don't invest in too many different things.** Diversification is good to a point. If you purchase so many investments that you can't perform a basic annual review of them (for example, reading the annual report from your mutual fund), you have too many investments.

✔ **Be more aggressive inside retirement plans.** When you hit your retirement years, you'll probably begin to live off your non-retirement plan investments first. Why? For the simple reason that allowing your retirement plans to continue growing will save you tax dollars. Therefore, you should be relatively less aggressive with investments outside of retirement plans because that money will be invested for a shorter time period.

Easing into risk: Dollar cost averaging

Dollar cost averaging (DCA) is the practice of investing a regular amount of money at set time intervals, such as monthly or quarterly, into volatile investments, such as stocks and stock mutual funds. If you've ever deducted money from a paycheque and pumped it into a retirement savings plan investment account that holds stocks and bonds, you've done DCA.

Most of us invest a portion of our employment compensation as we earn it, but if you have extra cash sitting around, you can choose to invest that money in one fell swoop or to invest it gradually via DCA. The biggest appeal of gradually feeding money into the market via DCA is that you don't dump all of your money into a potentially overheated investment just before a major drop. Thus, DCA helps shy investors to psychologically ease into riskier investments.

DCA is made to order for skittish investors with a large lump sum of money sitting in safe investments like GICs or a savings account. For example, using DCA, an investor with $100,000 to invest in stock funds can feed her money into investments gradually — say, at the rate of $12,500 or so quarterly over two years — instead of investing her entire $100,000 in stocks at once and possibly buying all of her shares at a market peak. Most large investment companies, especially mutual fund companies, allow investors to establish automatic investment plans so the DCA occurs without an investor's ongoing involvement.

Of course, like any risk-reducing investment strategy, DCA has drawbacks. If growth investments appreciate (as they're supposed to), a DCA investor misses out on earning higher returns on his money awaiting investment. Finance professors Richard E. Williams and Peter W. Bacon found that approximately two-thirds of the time, a lump-sum stock market investor earned higher first-year returns than an investor who fed the money in monthly over the first year. (They studied data from the U.S. market over the past seven decades.)

York University business professor Moshe Arye Milevsky came to the same conclusion in his book *Money Logic*. According to Milevsky's research, if you invested a $10,000 lump sum in a Canadian equity mutual fund, you would likely have $11,000 after a year had passed. In short, his research showed that two-thirds of the time, your initial investment would be worth between $9,500 and $12,500. In contrast, if you invested the money in equal amounts over 12 months, by the end of that year your initial investment would likely be worth $10,748. More specifically, two-thirds of the time you could anticipate having somewhere between $9,898 and $11,598.

However, knowing that you'll probably be ahead most of the time if you dump a lump sum into the stock market is little solace if you happen to invest just before a major plunge in the stock market. In the fall of 2008, the Canadian stock market, as measured by the TSX composite index, plummeted 30 percent in just over four weeks. From late 2007 to the fall of 2008, the market shed 42 percent of its value.

So investors who fear that stocks are due for such a major correction should practice DCA, right? Well, not so fast. Apprehensive investors who shun lump-sum investments and use DCA are more likely to stop the DCA investment process if prices plunge, thereby defeating the benefit of doing DCA during a declining market.

So what's an investor with a lump sum of money to do?

- ✔ **First, weigh the significance of the lump sum to you.** Although $100,000 is a big chunk of most people's net worth, it's only 10 percent if your net worth is $1,000,000. It's not worth a millionaire's time to use DCA. If the cash that you have to invest is less than a quarter of your net worth, you may not want to bother with DCA.

- ✔ **Second, consider how aggressively you invest (or invested) your money.** For example, if you aggressively invested your money through an employer's retirement plan that you roll over, don't waste your time on DCA.

DCA makes sense for investors with a large chunk of their net worth in cash who want to minimize the risk of transferring that cash to riskier investments, such as stocks. If you fancy yourself a market prognosticator, you can also assess the current valuation of stocks. Thinking that stocks are pricey (and thus riper for a fall) increases the appeal of DCA.

Over how long a time period should you practice DCA? If you use DCA too quickly, you may not give the market sufficient time for a correction to unfold, during and after which some of the DCA purchases may take place. If you practice DCA over too long of a period of time, you may miss a major upswing in stock prices. We suggest using DCA over one to two years to strike a balance.

As for the times of the year that you should use DCA, mutual fund investors should use DCA quarterly early in each calendar quarter because mutual funds that make taxable distributions tend to do so late in the quarter. Your money that awaits investment should have a suitable parking place. Select a high-yielding money market fund or high-interest savings account.

One last critical point: When you use DCA, establish an automatic investment plan so you're less likely to chicken out. And for the more courageous, you may want to try an alternative strategy to DCA — *value averaging,* which allows you to invest more if prices are falling and invest less if prices are rising.

Suppose that you want to value average $500 per quarter into an aggressive stock mutual fund. After your first quarterly $500 investment, the fund drops 10 percent, reducing your account balance to $450. Value averaging has you invest $500 the next quarter plus another $50 to make up the shortfall. (Conversely, if the fund value had increased to $550 after your first investment, you would invest only $450 in the second round.) Increasing the amount that you invest requires confidence when prices fall, but doing so magnifies your returns when prices ultimately turn around.

Protecting Your Assets

You may be at risk of making a catastrophic investing mistake: not protecting your assets properly due to a lack of various insurance coverages. That's the error that Manny, a successful entrepreneur, made. Starting from scratch, he built up a successful million-dollar manufacturing operation. He invested a lot of his own personal money and sweat into building the business over 15 years.

One day, catastrophe struck: An explosion ripped through his building, and the ensuing fire destroyed virtually all the firm's equipment and inventory, none of which was insured. The explosion also seriously injured several workers, including Manny, who didn't carry disability insurance. Ultimately, Manny had to file for bankruptcy.

Decisions regarding what amount of insurance you need to carry are, to some extent, a matter of your desire and ability to accept financial risk. But some risks aren't worth taking. Don't overestimate your ability to predict what accidents and other bad luck may befall you. Here's what you need to protect yourself and your assets: .

- ✔ **Adequate liability insurance on your home and car to guard your assets against lawsuits:** You should have at least enough liability insurance to protect your *net worth* (assets minus your liabilities/debts) or, ideally, twice your net worth. If you run your own business, get insurance for your business assets if they're substantial, such as in Manny's case. Also consider professional liability insurance to protect against a lawsuit. You may also want to consider incorporating your business (which we discuss more in Chapter 14).

- ✔ **Long-term disability insurance:** What would you (and your family) do to replace your income if a major disability prevents you from working? Even if you don't have dependents, odds are that *you* are dependent on you. Most larger employers offer group plans that have good benefits and are much less expensive than coverage you'd buy on your own. Also, check with your professional association for a competitive group plan.

- ✔ **Life insurance if others are dependent on your income:** If you're single or your loved ones can live without your income, skip life insurance. If you need coverage, buy term insurance that, like your auto and home insurance, is pure insurance protection. The amount of term insurance you need to buy largely depends on how much of your income you want to replace.

✔ **Estate planning:** At a minimum, most people need a simple will to delineate to whom they would like to leave all their worldly possessions. If you hold significant assets outside retirement plans, you may also benefit from establishing a living trust, which keeps your money from filtering through the hands of probate lawyers. Living wills and medical powers of attorney are useful to have in case you're ever in a medically incapacitated situation. If you have substantial assets, doing more involved estate planning is wise to minimize taxes and ensure the orderly passing of your assets to your heirs.

In our experience, we've seen that although many people lack particular types of insurance, others possess unnecessary policies. Many people also keep very low deductibles. Remember to insure against potential losses that would be financially catastrophic for you — don't waste your money to protect against smaller losses. (See the latest edition of our book *Personal Finance For Canadians For Dummies,* published by Wiley, to discover the right and wrong ways to buy insurance, what to look for in policies, and where to get good policies.)

Part II
Stocks, Bonds, and Bay Street

The 5th Wave   By Rich Tennant

"Oh Martin, you scared me half to death! Next time let me know when you're picking a new stock."

In this part . . .

Stocks, bonds, and mutual funds are the core financial market instruments that investors play with these days. But what the heck *are* these devices, and how can you invest in them, make some decent money, and not lose your shirt? Here, you find out how and where to evaluate and buy these securities and how to comprehend the mind-numbing jargon the money pros use.

Chapter 4

The Workings of Stock and Bond Markets

*T*o buy and enjoy a watch, you don't need to understand the details of how it's put together and works. Ditto for investing in stocks and bonds. However, spending some time understanding how and why the financial markets function will make you more comfortable with investing and make you a better investor.

This is especially true after events such as the stock market collapse in the fall of 2008 and spring of 2009. Most people saw the value of their investments drop dramatically from the fall-out of something they knew little about, namely the subprime mortgage market. (Later in this chapter we explain how the implosion of this type of security hampered the economy and took a big chunk out of most people's savings.)

In this chapter, we tell you the ways that companies raise capital, and we give you a brief primer on financial markets and economics so you can understand and be comfortable with investing in the financial markets.

How Companies Raise Money through the Financial Markets

All businesses start small — often in a garage, a spare bedroom, or a rented office. As companies begin to grow, they often need more money (known as *capital* in the financial world) to expand and afford their growing needs, such as hiring more employees, buying computer systems, and purchasing manufacturing equipment. Companies can choose between two major options for raising money when they go into the financial markets: issuing stocks or issuing bonds.

Deciding whether to issue stocks or bonds

A world of difference exists between stocks and bonds, two major types of securities, both from the perspective of the investor and from that of the issuing company, as the following explanations illustrate:

- **Bonds are loans that a company must pay back.** Rather than borrowing money from a bank, many companies elect to sell *bonds,* which are IOUs to investors. The primary disadvantage of issuing bonds compared with issuing stock, from a company's perspective, is that the company must pay this money back with interest. On the other hand, the business doesn't have to relinquish ownership when it borrows money. Companies are also more likely to issue bonds if the stock market is depressed, meaning that companies can't fetch as much for their stock.

- **Stocks are shares of ownership in a company.** Some companies choose to issue stock to raise money. Unlike bonds, the money that the company raises through a stock issue isn't paid back, because it's not a loan. When the public (people like you and us) buys stocks, these outside investors continue to hold and trade it. (Although companies may occasionally choose to buy their own stock back, usually because they think it's a good investment, they're under no obligation to do so. If a company does a *stock buyback,* the price that the company pays is simply the price that the stock currently trades for.)

When a company issues stock, it makes it much easier for the founders and owners to sell some of their part of the business and reap the rewards of their successful venture. (It's extremely difficult to sell off part of a private company, since valuing what a certain percentage is worth is a daunting challenge. This drastically reduces the number of potential buyers, which in turn makes selling even more challenging, since they know the difficulty they'll face should they want to later sell their share. When an investment is difficult to purchase or sell, and has few potential buyers, its known as an *illiquid investment.*) Many growing companies also favour issuing stock because they don't want the cash drain that comes from paying loans (bonds) back.

Although many companies' owners like to take their companies public (selling shares of the business) to cash in on their stake of the company, not all owners want to go public, and not all who do go public are happy that they did. One of the numerous drawbacks of selling shares that can be traded on the stock market is that you have to let others in on the workings of your business. Deciding to sell shares of a company that has been completely privately owned to the general public — "going public" — includes burdensome financial reporting requirements, such as the production of quarterly earnings statements and annual reports. These documents not only take lots of time and money to produce, but they can also reveal competitive secrets. Some companies also harm their long-term planning ability because of the pressure and focus on short-term corporate performance that comes with being a public company.

Ultimately, companies seek to raise capital in the lowest-cost way they can, so they'll elect to sell stocks or bonds— or borrow — based on what the finance folks tell them is the cheapest option. For example, if the stock market is booming and new stock can be sold at a premium price, companies usually opt to sell more stock.

From your perspective as a potential investor, you can usually make more money in stocks than bonds, but as we saw in the collapse of stock markets in 2008, stocks are generally more volatile in the short term (see Chapter 2).

Taking a company public: Understanding IPOs

Suppose that The Capitalist Company (TCC) wants to issue stock for the first time, which is called an *initial public offering (IPO)*. If TCC decides to go public, the company's management team works with *investment bankers,* who help companies decide when and at what price to sell stock.

Suppose further that, based upon their analysis of the value of TCC, the investment bankers believe that TCC can raise $20 million by issuing stock, which represents a specific percentage of the company. When a company issues stock, the price they set per share of the stock is somewhat arbitrary. The amount that a prospective investor will pay for a particular portion of the company's stock should depend on the company's profits and future growth prospects. Companies that produce higher levels of profits and grow faster can generally command a higher sales price for a given portion of the company.

Suppose that the investment bankers valued TCC's total business at $40 million, and the company wanted to raise $20 million by selling half the business to the public. Consider the following ways that investment bankers can structure the IPO for TCC:

Price of Stock	Number of Shares Issued
$5	4 million
$10	2 million
$2	1 million

In fact, TCC can raise the $20 million in an infinite number of ways, thanks to varying stock prices. If the company wants to issue the stock at a higher price, the company sells fewer shares.

A stock's price per share by itself is meaningless in evaluating whether to buy a stock. Ultimately, the amount that investors will pay for a company's stock should depend greatly on the company's growth and profitability prospects.

$$\frac{\text{The value of a company's stock}}{\text{Relative to (divided by) its earnings}} = \text{Its } price/earnings \ ratio$$

In the case of TCC, supposing that its stock outstanding in the marketplace has a total value of $30 million and that it earned $3 per share in the past year, here are the numbers:

$$\frac{\$30 \text{ million}}{\$3 \text{ million}} = 10$$

In Chapter 5, we talk more about price/earnings ratios and the factors that influence stock prices.

Understanding Financial Markets and Economics

Tens of thousands of books, millions of articles, and enough PhD dissertations to pack a major landfill explore the topics of how the financial markets and economy will perform in the years ahead. You can spend the rest of your life reading all this stuff, and you still won't get through it. In this section, we cut to the chase and explain what you need to know about the factors that make the financial markets and economy work so you can make informed investing decisions.

Uncovering the roots: Capitalism

In Canada, we live in a *capitalistic* (also known as free-market) society. Have you ever stopped to think what that term means? Capitalism means that you have a tremendous (although not unlimited) amount of economic freedom.

If you want to start your own business, you can. However, that's not to say that you don't have to deal with obstacles, such as affording the start-up stages of your business and dealing with regulatory red tape. Most Canadian entrepreneurs will tell you that one of their greatest business frustrations is dealing with all the various government agencies that regulate and tax businesses. In addition to the long lists of licences you need to obtain for certain businesses, you may have to deal with zoning and planning offices regarding the use of the location of your business. You may also have to work with other provincial and local agencies if you decide to incorporate, and with still more government folks to comply with the myriad tax laws of the land.

Whine, whine, whine. Go to a socialist country if you want to see tape that's *really* red and a lack of economic opportunity and mobility. *Socialism,* in contrast to capitalism, is an economic system that its 19th-century promoters, Karl Marx and Friedrich Engels, best sum up: "Abolish all private property."

Vladimir Lenin transformed the socialist theory of Marx and Engels into a political system known as communism. In *communism,* the government largely controls and owns the organizations that provide what people need. Over time, various countries in Europe, the former Soviet Union (Russia), and China have tried to make communism work. However, most of these parts of the world continue to become more capitalistic. The low standard of living in communist countries, long waits in lines to purchase goods, and poor health care all contributed to the downfall of communist systems.

Driving stock prices through earnings

The goal of most companies is to make money, or earnings (also called *profits*). *Earnings* result from the difference between what a company takes in *(revenue)* and what it spends *(costs).* We say *most* companies because some organizations' primary purpose is not to maximize profits. Non-profit organizations, such as charities and universities, are a good example. But even non-profits can't thrive and prosper without a steady flow of money coming in.

Companies that trade publicly on the stock exchanges are supposed to maximize their profit — that's what their shareholders want. Higher profits generally make stock prices rise. Most private companies seek to maximize their profits as well, but they retain much more latitude to pursue other goals.

The following are the major ways that successful companies increase profits:

- ✔ **Build a better mousetrap.** Some companies develop or promote an invention or innovation that better meets customer needs. For example, many consumers welcomed the invention of the digital camera, which eliminated the need for costly and time-consuming development of film.

The digital camera also made transferring and working with pictures much easier, allowing you to turn your pictures into cards and send them via e-mail.

✔ **Sell their products to new markets.** Many successful companies based in Canada have been stampeding into foreign countries to sell their products. Although some product adaptation is usually required to sell overseas, selling an already proven and developed product or service to new markets generally increases a company's chances for success.

✔ **Be in related businesses.** Consider the hugely successful Walt Disney Company, which was started in the 1920s as a small studio that made cartoons. Over the years, it expanded into many new but related businesses, including theme parks and resorts, movie studios, radio and television programs, toys, children's books, and video games.

✔ **Build a brand name.** Coca-Cola, for example, and many types of well-known beers often aren't rated any higher in blind taste tests than many generic colas and beers that are far less expensive. Yet consumers (perhaps you) fork over more of their hard-earned loot because of the name and packaging. Companies build brand names largely through advertising and other promotions. (*For Dummies* is a brand name, but *For Dummies* books cost about the same as lower-quality and smaller books on similar subjects!)

✔ **Manage costs and prices.** Smart companies control costs. Lowering the cost of manufacturing their products or providing their services allows companies to offer their products and services more cheaply. Managing costs may help fatten the bottom line (profit). Sometimes, though, companies try to cut too many corners, and their cost-cutting ways come back to haunt them in the form of dissatisfied customers — or even lawsuits based on a faulty or dangerous product.

✔ **Watch the competition.** Successful companies don't follow the herd, but they do keep an eye on what their competition is up to. If lots of competitors target one part of the market, some companies target a less-pursued segment that, if they can capture it, may produce higher profits thanks to reduced competition.

Weighing whether markets are efficient

Companies generally seek to maximize profits and maintain a healthy financial condition. Ultimately, the financial markets judge the worth of a company's stock or bond. Trying to predict what happens to the stock and bond markets and to individual securities consumes many a market prognosticator.

In the 1960s, somewhat to the chagrin of market soothsayers, academic scholars developed a theory called the *efficient market hypothesis.* This theory basically maintains the following logic: Lots of investors collect and analyze all sorts of information about companies and their securities. If investors think that a security, such as a stock, is overpriced, they sell it or don't buy it. Conversely, if the investors believe that a security is underpriced, they buy it or hold what they already own. Because of the competition among all these investors, the price that a security trades at generally reflects what many (supposedly informed) people think it's worth.

Therefore, the efficient market theory implies that trading in and out of securities and the overall market in an attempt to obtain the right stocks at the right time is a futile endeavour. Buying or selling a security because of "new" news is also fruitless because the stock price adjusts so quickly to this news that investors can't profit by acting on it. As Burton Malkiel so eloquently said in his classic book *A Random Walk Down Wall Street*, this theory, "Taken to its logical extreme . . . means that a blindfolded monkey throwing darts at a newspaper's financial pages could select a portfolio that would do just as well as one carefully selected by the experts." Malkiel added, "Financial analysts in pin-striped suits don't like being compared with bare-assed apes."

Some money managers have beaten the markets. In fact, beating the market over a year or three years isn't difficult, but few can beat the market over a decade or more. Efficient market supporters argue that some of those who beat the markets, even over a ten-year period, do so because of luck. Consider that if you flip a coin five times, on some occasions you get five consecutive heads. This coincidence actually happens, on average, once every 32 times you do 5 coin-flip sequences. And the results are due to random luck, not skill. Consistently identifying in advance which particular sequence will give you five consecutive heads isn't possible.

Strict believers in the efficient market hypothesis say that it's equally impossible to identify the best money managers in advance. Some money managers, such as those who manage mutual funds, possess publicly available track records. Inspecting those track records (and understanding the level of risk taken for the achieved returns) and doing other common-sense things, such as investing in funds that have lower expenses, improve your odds of performing a bit better than the market.

Various investment markets differ in how efficient they are. *Efficiency* means that the current price of an investment accurately reflects its true value. Although the stock market is reasonably efficient, many consider the bond market to be even more efficient. The real estate market is less efficient because properties are unique, and sometimes less competition and access to information exist. If you can locate a seller who really needs to sell, you may be able to buy property at a discount from what it's really worth. Small business is also less efficient. Entrepreneurs with innovative ideas and approaches can sometimes earn enormous returns.

Moving the market: Interest rates, inflation, and the Bank of Canada

For decades, economists, investment managers, and other (often self-anointed) gurus have attempted to understand the course of interest rates, inflation, and the monetary policies set forth by the Federal Reserve and, to a lesser degree, the Bank of Canada. Millions of investors follow these economic factors. Why? Because interest rates, inflation, and monetary policy seem to move the world's financial markets and the economy.

Realizing that high interest rates are generally bad

Many businesses borrow money to expand. People like you and us, who are affectionately referred to as consumers, also borrow money to finance home and auto purchases and education.

Interest rate increases tend to slow the economy. Businesses scale back on expansion plans because it's too expensive to borrow money to grow, and some debt-laden businesses can't afford the cost of higher interest rates and go under. Most individuals possess limited budgets as well and have to scale back some purchases because of higher interest rates. For example, the higher interest rates are, the larger mortgage payments are for homebuyers.

If high interest rates choke business expansion and consumer spending, then economic growth slows or the economy actually shrinks — and possibly ends up in a recession. The definition of a *recession* is two consecutive quarters (six months) of contracting economic activity.

The stock market usually develops a case of the queasies as corporate profits shrink. High interest rates may depress investors' appetites for stocks as the yields increase on guaranteed investment certificates (GICs), Treasury bills, and other bonds.

Higher interest rates actually make some people happy. If you locked in a fixed-rate mortgage on your home or on a business loan, your loan looks much better than if you had a variable-rate mortgage. Some retirees and others who live off the interest income on their investments are happy with interest rate increases as well. Consider back in the early 1980s, for example, when a retiree received $10,000 per year in interest for each $100,000 invested in guaranteed investment certificates that paid 10 percent.

Fast-forward to the early 2000s: A retiree purchasing the same GICs saw interest income slashed by about 80 percent, because many GIC rates were just 3 percent. So for every $100,000 invested, only $3,000 in interest income was paid.

If you try to live off the income that your investments produce, an 80 percent drop in that income is likely to cramp your lifestyle. So higher interest rates are better if you're living off your investment income, right? Not necessarily.

Discovering the inflation and interest rate connection

Consider what happened to interest rates in the late 1970s and early 1980s. After Canada and the United States successfully emerged from a terrible recession in the mid-1970s, their economies seemed to be on the right track. But within just a few years, they were in turmoil again. The annual increase in the cost of living (known as the *rate of inflation*) burst through 10 percent on its way to 14 percent. Interest rates, which are what bondholders receive when they lend their money to corporations and governments, followed inflation skyward.

Inflation and interest rates usually move in tandem. The primary driver of interest rates is the rate of inflation. Interest rates were much higher in the 1980s because Canada and the United States had double-digit inflation. If the cost of living increases at the rate of 10 percent per year, why would you, as an investor, lend your money (which is what you do when you purchase a bond or GIC) at 5 percent? Interest rates were so much higher in the early 1980s because you would never do such a thing.

In recent years, interest rates have been low because inflation has declined significantly since the early 1980s. Therefore, the rate of interest that investors could earn lending their money dropped accordingly. Although low interest rates reduce the interest income that comes in, the corresponding low rate of inflation doesn't devour the purchasing power of your principal balance. That's why lower interest rates aren't necessarily worse and higher interest rates aren't necessarily better as you try to live off your investment income.

So what are investors to do when they're living off the income they receive from their investments but don't receive enough because of low interest rates? Some retirees have woken up to the risk of keeping all or too much of their money in short-term GIC and bond investments. (Please review the sections in Chapter 3 dealing with asset allocation and investment mix.) A simple but psychologically difficult solution is to use up some of your principal to supplement your interest and dividend income. Using up your principal to supplement your income is what effectively happens anyway when inflation is higher — the purchasing power of your principal erodes more quickly. You may also find that you haven't saved enough money to achieve your desired standard of living — that's why you may want to run a retirement analysis (see Chapter 3) before you retire.

Exploring the U.S. Federal Reserve

Much of the direction of interest rates in Canada is dictated by interest rates in the United States. And those rates are set by the *Federal Reserve Board*. When the chairman of the "Fed" speaks, an extraordinary number of people listen. Most financial market watchers and the media — in Canada and other countries, as well as in the United States — want to know what the Federal Reserve has decided to do about monetary policy. (The Federal Reserve is the central bank of the United States. The Federal Reserve Board is comprised of the 12 presidents from the respective Federal Reserve district banks and the 7 Federal Reserve governors, including the chairman who conducts the Federal Open Market Committee meetings behind closed doors eight times a year.)

Much like the Bank of Canada does here, the Federal Reserve sets monetary policy. To do so, the Fed raises or lowers short-term interest rates, primarily by buying and selling U.S. Treasury bills on the open market. Through this trading activity, known as open market operations, the Fed is able to target the Federal funds rate, the rate banks charge each other for overnight borrowing.

Over the years, the Fed has come under attack for various reasons. Various pundits have accused former Fed Chairman Alan Greenspan of causing speculative bubbles (see Chapter 5), such as the boom in technology stock prices in the late 1990s or in housing in the early 2000s.

Greenspan came under even more criticism after the stock market crash of 2008. The staunch believer in free markets, who often awed lawmakers, called the chaos in the banking and housing markets a "once-in-a-lifetime credit tsunami" that had left him in a state of "shocked disbelief." Yet he admitted that the flaw in his anti-regulatory philosophy was the belief that self-interest would mean the banks would do what was necessary to protect their shareholders and institutions. Unfortunately, he and his ilk missed the key, and we'd say kind of obvious, fact that, left uncontrolled, the bank (as well as mortgage and insurance company) executives' overriding interest would be lining their own pockets with massive bonuses. And, of course, this would come at the expense of everybody from the shareholders to the taxpayers and consumers faced with the economic cost of cleaning up the subprime mess. As one pundit so nicely put it, would you want to drink milk from a dairy that "self-regulates"? Fly in an airplane given safety clearance through "self-regulation"? Or how about drink water downstream from a "self-regulating" chemical plant?

In addition, some economists have argued that the Federal Reserve has, with a nudge of encouragement from the president, goosed the economy. The Fed gooses the economy by loosening up on the money supply, which leads to a growth spurt in the economy and a booming stock market, just in time to make El Presidente look good prior to an election. Conveniently, the consequences of inflation take longer to show up — not until after the election. In recent years, others have questioned the Fed's ability to largely do what it wants without accountability.

The role of the Bank of Canada

What exactly is the "Bank of Canada," and what does it do? The Bank of Canada sets monetary policy. In other (perhaps *clearer*) words, the Bank of Canada influences interest rate levels and the amount of money or currency in circulation, known as the *money supply,* in an attempt to maintain a stable rate of inflation and growth in the Canadian economy.

Buying money is no different from buying lettuce, computers, or sneakers. All these products and goods cost you dollars when you buy them. The cost of money is the interest rate that you must pay to borrow it. And the cost or interest rate of money is determined by many factors that ultimately influence the supply of and demand for money.

The Bank of Canada, from time to time and in different ways, attempts to influence the supply and demand for money and the cost of money. To this end, the Bank of Canada raises or lowers short-term interest rates, primarily by managing its target for the overnight rate — the rate at which banks borrow from one another overnight.

The senior officials at the Bank of Canada readily admit that the economy is quite complex and affected by many things, so it's difficult to predict where the economy is heading. If forecasting and influencing markets are such difficult undertakings, why does the Bank of Canada exist? Well, the officials believe that they can have a positive influence in creating a healthy overall economic environment — one in which inflation is low and growth proceeds at a modest pace

Many factors influence the course of stock prices. Never, ever make a trade or investment based upon what someone at, say, the Federal Reserve says or what someone in the media or some market pundit reads into the interest rate comments. You need to make your investment plans based on your needs and goals, not based on what those supposedly steering the economy do or don't do.

Chapter 5

Building Wealth with Stocks

Some people liken investing in the stock market to gambling. A real casino structures its games — slot machines, blackjack, roulette, and so on — so that in aggregate, the casino owners siphon off a healthy slab (40 percent) of the money that people bring with them. The vast majority of casino patrons lose money, in some cases all of it. The few who leave with more money than they came with are usually people who are lucky and smart enough to quit while they're ahead.

We can understand why some individual investors feel that the stock market resembles legalized gambling. So why bother with the stock market if it's so confusing and filled with people who are eager to separate you from your money? In Chapter 2, we discuss the potential risks and rewards of different investments. Shares of stock, which represent portions of ownership in companies, offer a way for people of modest and wealthy means, and everybody in between, to invest in companies and build wealth.

Fortunately, the stock market isn't a casino — far from it. History shows that nearly all long-term investors can win in the stock market because it appreciates over the years. We say *nearly* because even some people who remain active in the market over many years manage to lose some money because of easily avoidable mistakes, which we can keep you from making in the future.

R. Foster Winans, a former writer for *Newsweek* and *The Wall Street Journal*, said, "The only reason to invest in the market is because you think you know something others don't." Mr. Winans, who was later convicted of insider trading, was wrong in more ways than one. You don't need inside information to profit from stock investments. You simply need to understand this basic concept: The increasing profits that expanding companies produce ultimately propel stock prices higher. The trajectory path isn't a straight line up, but more like the path that a small bird takes when it fights to gain altitude in a headwind. Although the bird sometimes hits an air pocket or spot of bad weather and loses some altitude, the bird's aerodynamics win out. How many birds have you seen crash to the ground?

The same theory applies with corporate profits. Corporate profits also tend to trend up, but sometimes the economy hits a bad patch, and profits fall. As with the bird, economies don't usually get completely decimated. Yes, it's possible that if a huge meteor smashes into Earth or a horrible, contagious virus spreads like wildfire, society may be done for — people and companies may cease to exist. In the meantime, why not share in the expansion of the economy and keep an optimistic view on life?

Taking Stock of How You Make Money

When you purchase a share of a company's stock, you can profit from your ownership in two ways:

- **Dividends:** Many stocks pay dividends. Companies ideally make some profits during the year. Some high-growth companies reinvest most or all of their profits right back into the business. Other companies, however, pay out some of their profits to shareholders in the form of *dividends*.

- **Appreciation:** When the price per share of your stock rises to a level greater than you originally paid for it, you make money. This profit, however, is only on paper until you sell the stock, at which time you realize a *capital gain*. Of course, the stock price per share can fall below what you originally paid (in which case you have a loss on paper unless you realize that loss by selling at a lower price than you paid for the stock).

If you add together dividends and appreciation, you arrive at your total return. Stocks differ in the dimensions of these possible returns, particularly with respect to dividends. Utility companies, for example, tend to pay out more of their profits as dividends. But don't buy utility stocks thinking that you'll make more money because of the heftier dividends. Utilities and other companies paying high dividends tend not to appreciate as much over time because they don't reinvest as much in their businesses, and they're not growing as fast as other businesses.

Defining "The Market"

So you invest in stocks to share in the rewards of capitalistic economies. When you invest in stocks, you do so through the stock market. What is the stock market? Everybody refers to "The Market" the same way they refer to the largest city nearby as "The City":

The Market is down 137 points today.

With The Market hitting new highs, isn't now a bad time to invest?

The Market seems ready for a fall.

When people talk about The Market, they're usually referring to the U.S. stock market. Even more specifically, they're speaking about the *Dow Jones Industrial Average,* created by Charles Dow and Eddie Jones, which is a famously known index or measure of the performance of the U.S. stock market. Dow and Jones, two reporters in their 30s, started publishing a paper that you may have heard of — *The Wall Street Journal* — in 1889. Like its modern-day version, the 19th-century *Wall Street Journal* reported current financial news. Dow and Jones also compiled stock prices of larger, important companies and created and calculated indexes to track the performance of the U.S. stock market.

The Dow Jones Industrial Average (DJIA) market index tracks the performance of 30 large companies that are headquartered in the United States. The Dow 30 includes companies such as telecommunications giant Verizon Communications; airplane manufacturer Boeing; beverage maker Coca-Cola; oil giant Exxon Mobil; automaker General Motors; technology behemoths IBM, Intel, and Microsoft; drug makers Merck and Pfizer; fast-food king McDonald's; and retailers Home Depot and Wal-Mart.

Some criticize the Dow index for encompassing so few companies and for lacking diversity. The 30 stocks that make up the Dow aren't the 30 largest or the 30 best companies in America. They just so happen to be the 30 companies that senior staff members at *The Wall Street Journal* think reflect the diversity of the economy in the United States (although utility and transportation stocks are excluded and tracked in other Dow indexes). The 30 stocks in the Dow change over time as companies merge, decline, and rise in importance.

Depending on whom you're speaking to — or listening to on TV or the radio — "The Market" may also be short for the Toronto Stock Exchange, or the *TSX.* The TSX is where the largest and most well-known Canadian companies trade.

Looking at major stock market indexes

Just as Toronto and New York City aren't the only cities to visit or live in, the stocks in the TSX Composite and the Dow Jones Industrial Average are far from representative of all the different types of stocks that you can invest in. Here are some other important market indexes and the types of stocks they track:

- **Standard & Poor's 500:** Like the Dow Jones Industrial Average, the S&P 500 tracks the price of 500 larger-company U.S. stocks. These 500 big companies account for more than 70 percent of the total market value of the tens of thousands of stocks traded in the United States. Thus, the S&P 500 is a much broader and more representative index of the larger-company stocks in the United States than is the Dow Jones Industrial Average.

- Unlike the Dow index, which is primarily calculated by adding the current share price of each of its component stocks, the S&P 500 index is calculated by adding the total market value (capitalization) of its component stocks

- **S&P/TSX 60:** This index replaced the older TSE 35 and TSE 100 indexes. It was developed by the TSX in conjunction with Standard & Poor's Corp. of New York. To be considered for the index, a company must be part of the TSX Composite Index, but those with poor liquidity don't make the grade. An index committee chooses 60 of the largest companies that offer a representation of the major industries. There's also a capped version of this index, which limits the weighting of any one stock to a maximum of 10 percent of the total market capitalization of all the stocks in the index. This was done to prevent situations where one company whose stock has soared (as

Nortel's did in the late 1990s) dominates the index and gives an unbalanced reading of the market's overall performance.

- **S&P/TSX Venture Composite Index:** This index is a broad measure of the performance of the TSX Venture Exchange, home to Canada's smaller and often much more speculative companies. The index has a somewhat confusing past. When the Vancouver Stock Exchange and the Alberta Stock Exchange merged, the two exchanges were replaced by the new Canadian Venture Exchange, or *CDNX,* and a new index — the Canadian Venture Exchange Index — was created. But that index was short-lived, and was replaced by the new S&P/TSX Venture Composite Index in 2001. However, the new Venture index isn't a continuation of the old Canadian Venture Exchange index, but an entirely new index based on different rules and requirements. The Canadian Venture Exchange index was simply closed down, and the new index began on a different — and completely unconnected — level than its predecessor. The new index looks at market capitalization when determining eligibility, and the number of companies it includes is typically in the low 500 range.

- **Russell 2000:** This index tracks the market value of 2,000 smaller U.S. company stocks of various industries. Although small-company stocks tend to move in tandem with larger-company stocks over the longer term, it's not unusual for one to rise or fall more than the other or for one index to fall while the other rises in a given year. For example, in 2001, the Russell 2000 actually rose 2.5 percent while the S&P 500 fell 11.9 percent. In 2007, the Russell 2000 lost 1.6 percent versus a gain of 5.5 percent for the S&P 500. Be aware that smaller-company stocks tend to be more volatile. (We discuss this in more detail in Chapter 2.)

✔ **Wilshire 5000:** Despite its name, the Wilshire 5000 index actually tracks the prices of more than 6,500 stocks of U.S. companies of all sizes — small, medium, and large. Thus, many consider this index the broadest and most representative of the overall U.S. stock market.

✔ **Morgan Stanley EAFE:** Stocks don't exist only in North America. Morgan Stanley's EAFE index (EAFE stands for Europe, Australasia, and Far East) tracks the prices

of stocks in the other major developed countries of the world.

✔ **Morgan Stanley Emerging Markets:** This index follows the value of stocks in the less economically developed but "emerging" countries such as Korea, Brazil, China, Russia, Taiwan, India, South Africa, Mexico, and so on. These stock markets tend to be more volatile than those in established economies. During good economic times, emerging markets usually reward investors with higher returns, but stocks can fall farther and faster than stocks in developed markets.

When people talk about how "Toronto" fared, they're usually talking about performance of the S&P/TSX Composite Index. Similar to the Dow Jones Industrial Average, the S&P/TSX Composite tracks the performance of larger-company Canadian stocks. In general, the index is made up of the companies with the largest market capitalization — their stock price multiplied by the number of shares outstanding. To be included in the index, companies must meet a number of other criteria. The most important is liquidity, which is measure by looking at the number of shares traded, the number of transactions, and the total value.

(The index used to be called the TSE 300, but that ended in 2002. That year, all the indexes were revamped when the administration of the indexes was taken over by Standard & Poor's, which revamped and became involved in administering the index. The number of companies included can now vary depending on how many meet the requirements. Recently, the number has been running in the low 200s.)

Conspicuously absent from this list of major stock market indexes is the NASDAQ index. With the boom in technology stock prices in the late 1990s, CNBC and other financial media started broadcasting movements in the technology-laden NASDAQ index, thereby increasing investor interest and the frenzy surrounding technology stocks. (See the section later in this chapter titled "The Internet and technology bubble.") We're not fans of sector-(industry-) specific investing; it undermines diversification and places you in the role of a professional money manager in having to determine when and how much to invest in specific industry groups. We suggest ignoring the NASDAQ as well as other industry-concentrated indexes.

Counting reasons to use indexes

Indexes serve several purposes. First, they can quickly give you an idea of how particular types of stocks fare and perform in comparison with other types of stocks. In 1998, for example, the S&P 500 was up 28.6 percent, whereas the small-company Russell 2000 index was down 2.5 percent. That same year, the Morgan Stanley foreign stock EAFE index rose 20.3 percent. In 2001, by contrast, the S&P 500 fell 11.9 percent, and the EAFE foreign stock index had an even worse year — falling 21.4 percent.

Indexes also allow you to compare or benchmark the performance of your stock market investments. If you invest primarily in large-company Canadian stocks, for example, you should compare the overall return of the stocks in your portfolio to a comparable index — in this case, the S&P/TSX composite index. (As we discuss in Chapter 8, index mutual funds, which invest to match a major stock market index, offer a cost-effective, proven way to build wealth by investing in stocks.)

As we explain in the sidebar "Looking at major stock market indexes," earlier in this chapter, you may also hear about some other types of more narrowly focused indexes, including those that track the performance of stocks in particular industries, such as advertising, banking, computers, pharmaceuticals, restaurants, semiconductors, textiles, and utilities. Other indexes cover the stock markets of other countries, such as the United Kingdom, Germany, France, Hong Kong, and China. Focusing on your investments in the stocks of just one or two industries or smaller countries is dangerous due to the lack of diversification and your likely lack of expertise in making the difficult decision about what to invest in and when. As a result, we suggest that you ignore these narrower indexes. Many companies, largely out of desire for publicity, develop their own indexes. If the news media report on these indexes, the index developer effectively obtains free advertising. (In Chapter 8, we discuss investing strategies, such as those that focus on value stocks or growth stocks, which also have market indexes.)

Stock-Buying Methods

When it comes to investing in stocks, many (perhaps too many) choices exist. Besides the tens of thousands of stocks among which you can select, you can hire a mutual fund manager, invest in exchange-traded funds (ETFs), put your money into hedge funds, or have an investment adviser select for you.

Recognizing bull and bear markets

If you read magazines or newspapers or listen to people talk about the stock market, you often hear references to bull markets and bear markets. You may know which term means a good market and which term means a bad market for investors, but even if you do, you may wonder where these silly terms came from.

It's hard to find agreement on the origin of these terms, but our favourite description comes from Robert Claiborne's *Loose Cannons and Red Herrings — A Book of Lost Metaphors*. The term *bear,* according to Claiborne, originates from a proverb that mocks a man who "sells the bearskin before catching the bear." This is the connection to the stock market: When dealers in the stock market thought that the market became too pricey and speculative, these dealers sold stock that they hadn't yet "caught" (bought). These dealers were labelled "bearskin jobbers" and, later, "bears."

The practice that these bearish dealers engaged in is *short selling*. They hoped that when they ultimately bought the stock that they had first sold, they could buy it back at a lower price. Their profit was the difference between the price that they originally sold it for and what

they later bought it for. Short selling is simply investing in reverse: You sell first and buy back later. The worst situation for a bear is if prices go up, and she must buy back the stock at a high price. As Claiborne said, "He who sells what isn't his'n, must buy it back or go to prison."

The bulls, according to Claiborne, are those who work the "other side" of the street. Bulls buy stocks with the hope and expectation that they will rise in value. Ben Travato, a man whom Claiborne describes as one prone to inventing colourful, but often inaccurate, etymologies, said that bulls toss stocks up in the air with their horns.

An alternative explanation for these terms comes from the research of economic and investment strategist Don Luskin. He says that the terms were in use in the early 1700s in the financial markets in England, and that they derive from the staged fights between wild animals that were offered as cruel public amusements at the time. When bulls were pitted against bears, the bull fought with an upward motion of its horns; the bear fought with a downward motion of its paws.

Buying stocks via mutual funds

If you're busy and suffer no delusions about your expertise, you'll love the best stock mutual funds. Investing in stocks through mutual funds can be as simple as dialing a toll-free phone number or logging on to a fund company's Web site, completing some application forms, and zapping them some money.

Mutual funds take money invested by people like you, your neighbours, and your Aunt Cathy, pool that money, and invest it in a single portfolio of securities, such as stocks or bonds, that is professionally managed. Stock mutual funds, as the name suggests, invest primarily or exclusively in stocks (some "stock" funds sometimes invest a bit in other stuff, such as bonds).

Stock mutual funds offer many advantages:

- **Diversification:** No matter how little you invest in a mutual fund, your money is automatically spread out over the dozens if not hundreds of individual investments the fund holds. Buying individual stocks on your own is relatively costly unless you buy reasonable chunks (100 shares or so) of each stock. But in order to buy 100 shares each in, say, a dozen companies' stocks to ensure diversification, you need about $60,000 if the stocks that you buy average $50 per share.

- **Professional management:** Even if you have big bucks to invest, mutual funds offer something that you can't deliver: professional, full-time management. Mutual fund managers peruse a company's financial statements and otherwise track and analyze a company's business strategy and market position. The best managers put in long hours and possess lots of expertise and experience in the field. (If you've been misled into believing that with minimal effort you can rack up market-beating returns by selecting your own stocks, please be sure to read the rest of this chapter.)

  Look at it this way: Mutual funds are a huge timesaver. It's Friday night — would you rather do some research on semiconductor and toilet paper manufacturers, or enjoy dinner or a movie with family and friends? (Of course, the answer to that question may depend on who your family and friends are!)

- **Low costs — if you pick 'em right:** To convince you that mutual funds aren't a good way for you to invest, those with a vested interest, such as stock-picking newsletter pundits, may point out the high fees that some funds charge. An element of truth rings here: Some funds are expensive, charging you 2 percent or more per year in operating expenses on top of hefty sales commissions.

  But just as you wouldn't want to invest in a fund that a novice with no track record manages, you wouldn't want to invest in a high-cost fund. Contrary to the "You get what you pay for" notion often trumpeted by those trying to sell you something at an inflated price, some of the best managers are the cheapest to hire. Through a *no-load* (commission-free) mutual fund, you can hire a professional, full-time money manager to invest your $10,000 for a mere $50 to $150 per year. And if you have far less than this to invest, they'll still invest your money at a low cost: $5 to $15 per year if you invest $1,000.

As with all investments, mutual funds have drawbacks.

- ✔ **Control is a problem for some investors.** If you're a controlaholic, turning over your investment dollars to a seemingly black-box process where others decide when and in what to invest your money may unnerve you. However, you need to be more concerned about the potential blunders that you may make investing in individual stocks of your own choosing or, even worse, those stocks pitched to you by an investment adviser.

- ✔ **Taxes are another concern when you invest in mutual funds outside retirement plans.** Because the fund manager, not you, decides when to sell specific stock holdings, some funds may produce relatively high levels of taxable distributions. Fear not — simply select tax-friendly funds if taxes concern you.

In Chapter 8, we discuss investing in the best mutual funds that offer a time- and cost-efficient, high-quality way to invest in stocks worldwide.

Using exchange-traded funds

Exchange-trade funds (ETFs) are the new kid on the block, certainly in comparison to mutual funds. ETFs are similar to mutual funds, specifically index funds (see Chapter 8), in many ways, except that they trade on a stock exchange. The chief attraction is those ETFs that offer investors the potential for even lower operating expenses than comparable mutual funds. We expand on ETFs and explain which ones to consider using in Chapter 8.

Using hedge funds

Like mutual funds, *hedge funds* are pools of money invested by a manager or managers on behalf of investors. But that's where the similarities end. Much less regulated, hedge funds face nowhere near the same amount of rules and oversight mutual funds must comply with. Securities regulators also allow hedge funds to undertake a much wider range of investing activities. This includes the use of leverage, as well as trying to profit from the fall in value of investments through *short-selling*. As a result, in order to invest in a hedge fund, investors typically are required to make a large initial investment. What's more, investors may have to have a net worth of $1 million or more, and may have to make a certain amount in income each year. However, hedge funds typically charge steep fees — a 1.0 to 1.5 percent annual management fee plus a 20 percent cut of the annual fund returns. More importantly, there's no proof that hedge funds as a group perform any better than mutual funds. In fact, a number of objective studies that we've reviewed show inferior hedge fund returns, which makes sense. Those high hedge fund fees depress their returns.

Selecting individual stocks

More than a few investment books suggest and enthusiastically encourage people like you to do their own stock picking. However, the vast majority of people are better off *not* picking their own stocks.

We've long been advocates of people educating themselves and taking responsibility for their own financial affairs, but taking responsibility for your own finances doesn't mean that you should do *everything* yourself. Table 5-1 includes some thoughts to consider about choosing your own stocks.

Table 5-1	The Pros and Cons of Buying Your Own Stocks
Good Reasons to Pick Your Own Stocks	*Bad Reasons to Pick Your Own Stocks*
You enjoy the challenge.	You think you can beat the best money managers. (If you can, you're in the wrong profession!)
You want to learn more about business.	You want more control over your investments, which you think may happen if you understand the companies that you invest in.
You possess a substantial amount of money to invest.	You think that mutual funds are for people who aren't smart enough to choose their own stocks.
You're a buy-and-hold investor.	You're attracted to the ability to trade your stocks any time you want.

Some popular investing books try to convince investors that they can do a *better* job than the professionals at picking their own stocks. Amateur investors, however, need to devote a lot of study to become proficient at stock selection. Many professional investors work 60, 70, or even 80 hours a week at investing. It's unlikely that you're willing to spend that much time on it. Don't let the popularity of those do-it-yourself stock-picking books lead you astray.

Choosing a stock isn't as simple as visiting a restaurant chain (or buying a pair of shoes or an iGadget), liking it, buying its stock, and then sitting back and getting rich watching your stock zoom to the moon.

If you invest in stocks, we think you know by now that guarantees don't exist. But as in many of life's endeavours, you can buy individual stocks in good and not-so-good ways. In Chapter 6, we explain how to research and trade individual stocks.

Spotting the Best Times to Buy and Sell

Now that you know about the different types of stock markets and ways to invest in stocks, you may wonder how you can build wealth with stocks and not lose your shirt. Nobody wants to buy stocks before the markets take a big drop (which we discuss in Chapter 2). Thousands of books have been written about how to get rich in the stock market by buying the best stocks cheaply and selling them when they become expensive.

As we discuss in Chapter 4, the stock market is reasonably efficient. A company's stock price normally reflects many smart people's assessments as to what is a fair price. Thus, it's not realistic for an investor to expect to discover a system for how to "buy low and sell high."

A few rare professional investors may obtain an ability for spotting good times to buy and sell particular stocks, but consistently doing so is enormously difficult. In fact, the investing public doesn't possess a great track record with buying low and selling high. Smaller investors tend to sell heavily *after* major declines and step up buying *after* major price increases.

The simplest and best way to make money in the stock market is to consistently and regularly feed new money into building a diversified and larger portfolio. If the market drops, you can use your new investment dollars to buy more shares. The danger of trying to time the market is that you may be "out" of the market when it appreciates greatly and "in" the market when it plummets.

Calculating price/earnings ratios

Suppose we tell you that Liz's Distinctive Jewellery's stock sells for $50 per share, and another stock in the same industry, The Jazzy Jeweller, sells for $100. Which would you rather buy?

If you answer, "I don't have a clue because you didn't give me enough information," go to the head of the class! On its own, the price per share of stock is meaningless.

Although The Jazzy Jeweller sells for twice as much per share, its profits might also be twice as much per share — in which case, The Jazzy Jeweller stock price may not be out of line given its profitability. The level of a company's stock price relative to its earnings or profits per share helps you calibrate how expensively, cheaply, or fairly a stock price is valued.

$$\frac{\text{Stock price per share}}{\text{Annual earnings per share}} = \text{Price/earnings (P/E) ratio}$$

Over the long term, stock prices and corporate profits tend to move in sync, like good dance partners. The *price/earnings (P/E) ratio* (say "P E" — the "/" isn't pronounced) compares the level of stock prices to the level of corporate profits, giving you a good sense of the stock's value. Over shorter periods of time, investors' emotions as well as fundamentals move stocks, but over longer terms, fundamentals possess a far greater influence on stock prices. P/E ratios can be calculated for individual stocks as well as for entire stock indexes, portfolios, or funds.

A particular price level in and of itself is meaningless, like a given stock (such as RIM) that rises above a specific price (such as $100 per share). The level of a stock's price, or a stock market index, is important and meaningful when you compare it with earnings for the company or companies in the stock market index.

Over the past 100-plus years, the P/E ratio of stocks has averaged around 15. During times of low inflation, the ratio has tended to be higher — in the high teens to low 20s. As we cautioned in the first edition of this book, published in 2000, the P/E ratio for stocks got into the 30s, well above historic norms even for a period of low inflation. Thus, the down market that began that year wasn't surprising, especially given the fall in corporate profits that put even more pressure on stock prices.

Just because stocks have historically averaged P/E ratios of about 15 doesn't mean that every individual stock will trade at such a P/E. Here's why: Suppose that you have a choice between investing in two companies, Superb Software, which makes computer software, and Tortoise Technologies, which makes typewriters. If both companies' stocks sell at a P/E of 15 and Superb Software's business and profits grow 40 percent per year and Tortoise's business and profits remain flat, which would you buy?

Because both stocks trade at a P/E of 15, Superb Software appears to be the better buy. Even if Superb's stock continues to sell at 15 times the earnings, its stock price should increase 40 percent per year as its profits increase. Faster-growing companies usually command higher price/earnings ratios.

Just because a stock price or an entire stock market seems to be at a high price level doesn't necessarily mean that the stock or market is overpriced. Always compare the price of a stock to that company's profits per share or the overall market's price level to overall corporate profits. The price/earnings ratio captures this comparison. Faster-growing and more-profitable companies generally sell for a premium — higher P/E ratios. Also remember that future earnings, which are difficult to predict, influence stock prices more than current earnings, which are old news.

Citing times of speculative excess

Because the financial markets move on the financial realities of the economy as well as people's expectations and emotions (particularly fear and greed), we don't believe that you should try to time the markets. Knowing when to buy and sell is much harder than you think.

Be careful that you don't get sucked into investing lots of your money in aggressive investments that seem to be in a hyped state. In fact, many people don't become aware of an investment until it receives lots of attention. By the time everyone else talks about an investment, it's often nearing or at its peak. In the sections that follow, we walk you through some of the biggest speculative bubbles. Although some of these examples are from prior decades and even centuries, we chose these examples because we find that they best teach the warning signs and dangers of speculative fever times.

The Internet and technology bubble

Unless you've isolated yourself from what we call civilization, you've surely heard about the explosive growth in the Internet . . . and the Internet stock bubble. In the mid-1990s, a number of Internet-based companies launched initial public offerings of stock. (We discuss IPOs in Chapter 4.) Most of the early Internet company stock offerings failed to really catch fire. By the late 1990s, however, some of these stocks began meteoric rises.

The bigger-name Internet stocks included companies such as Internet service provider America Online, bookseller and online retailer Amazon.com, Internet auctioneer eBay, and Internet portal Yahoo! As with the leading new consumer product manufacturers of the 1920s that we discuss in "The 1920s' consumer spending binge" section later in this chapter, many of the leading Internet companies' stocks zoomed to the moon. Note that in the late 1990s, the absolute stock price per share of these companies was meaningless — the P/E ratio is what mattered. Valuing Internet stocks based on earnings posed a challenge because many of these companies were losing money or just beginning to make money. Some Wall Street analysts, therefore, valued Internet stocks based on revenue and not profits.

Valuing a stock based on revenue and not profits can be highly dangerous. Revenues don't necessarily translate into high profits — or any profits at all.

In the case of Amazon.com, its stock price soared in early 1999 to $221 per share, which gave the company's stock a total market valuation in excess of $35 billion, or more than 12 times that of competing bookseller Barnes & Noble. B&N had prior-year sales of nearly $3 billion compared with Amazon.com's approximate $400 million in sales as it was losing money! At its low in 2001, Amazon's market value had fallen nearly 95 percent to less than $2 billion, very nearly the same valuation that Barnes & Noble had at that time. (Since its low in 2001, Amazon's stock value has bounced back — but it was recently valued at $18 billion, which still represents almost a 50 percent decline since its 1999 peak.)

Amazon.com, eBay, and other current leading Internet companies may go on to become some of the great companies and stocks of future decades. However, consider this perspective from veteran money manager David Dreman. "The Internet stocks are getting hundredfold more attention from investors than, say, a Ford Motor in chat rooms online and elsewhere. People are fascinated with the Internet — many individual investors have accounts on margin. Back in the early 1900s, there were hundreds of auto manufacturers, and it was hard to know who the long-term survivors would be. The current leaders won't probably be long-term winners."

Internet stocks weren't the only stocks being swept to excessive prices relative to their earnings at the dawn of the new millennium. Various traditional retailers announced the opening of Internet sites to sell their goods, and within days their stock prices doubled or tripled. Also, leading name-brand technology companies, such as Dell Computer, Cisco Systems, Lucent, and PeopleSoft, traded at P/E ratios in excess of 100. Companies in other industries, like investment brokerage firm Charles Schwab, which expanded to offer Internet services, saw their stock price balloon to push their P/E ratio over 100. As during the 1960s and 1920s, name-brand growth companies soared to high P/E valuations. For example, coffee purveyor Starbucks at times had a P/E near 100.

What we find troubling about the way investors piled into the leading name-brand stocks, especially in Internet and technology-related fields, is that many of these investors didn't even know what a price/earnings ratio was and why it was important. Before you invest in any individual stock, no matter how great a company you think it is, you need to understand the company's line of business, strategies, competitors, financial statements, and price/earnings ratio versus the competition, among many other issues. Selecting and monitoring good companies take lots of research, time, and discipline.

Also, remember that if a company taps into a product line or way of doing business that proves highly successful, that company's success invites lots of competition. So you need to understand the barriers to entry that a leading company has erected and how difficult or easy it is for competitors to join the fray. Also, be wary of analysts' predictions about earnings and stock prices. As more and more investment banking analysts initiated coverage of Internet companies and issued buy ratings on their stocks, investors bought more shares. Analysts, who are too optimistic (as shown in numerous independent studies), have a conflict of interest: The investment banks they work for seek to cultivate the business (new stock and bond issues) of the very companies they purport to rate and analyze. The analysts who say "Buy, buy, buy all the current market leaders" are the same analysts who generate much new business for their investment banks and get the lucrative job offers and multi-million-dollar annual salaries.

Simply buying today's rising and analyst-recommended stocks often leads to future investor disappointment. If the company's growth slows or the profits don't materialize as expected, the underlying stock price can nose-dive. This happened to investors who piled into the stock of computer disk-drive maker Iomega back in early 1996. After a spectacular rise to about $27½ per share, the company fell on tough times. Iomega stock subsequently plunged to less than $3 per share. This stock probably won't recover to its early 1996 price levels for many more years.

Presstek, a company that uses computer technology for so-called direct imaging systems, rose from less than $10 per share in mid-1994 to nearly $100 per share just two years later — another example of supposed can't-lose technology that crashed and burned. As was the case with Iomega, herds of novice investors jumped on the Presstek bandwagon simply because they believed the stock price would keep rising. By 1999, less than three years after hitting nearly $100 per share, the stock plunged more than 90 percent to about $5 per share. It's been recently trading at around $10 per share.

ATC Communications, which was similar to Iomega, plunged by more than 80 percent in a matter of months before the Fools recommended selling.

The Japanese stock market juggernaut

Lest you think that the United States cornered the market on manias, overseas examples abound. A rather extraordinary mania happened not so long ago in the Japanese stock market.

After Japan's crushing defeat in World War II, its economy was in shambles. Two major cities — Hiroshima and Nagasaki — were destroyed, and more than 200,000 died when the United States dropped atomic bombs.

Out of the rubble, Japan emerged a strengthened nation that became an economic powerhouse. Over the course of 22 years, from 1967 to 1989, Japanese stock prices rose an amazing 30-fold (3,000 percent) as the economy boomed. From 1983 to 1989 alone, Japanese stocks soared more than 500 percent.

In terms of the U.S. dollar, the Japanese stock market rise was all the more stunning, as the dollar lost value versus Japan's currency, the yen. The dollar lost about 65 percent of its value during the big run-up in Japanese stocks. In dollar terms, the Japanese stock market rose an astonishing 8,300 percent from 1967 to 1989.

Many considered an investment in Japanese stocks to be close to a sure thing. Increasing numbers of people became full-time stock market investors in Japan. Many of these folks were actually speculators because they relied heavily on borrowed funds. As the Japanese real estate market boomed in tandem with the stock market, real estate investors borrowed from their winnings to invest in stocks and vice versa.

Borrowing heavily was easy to do; Japan's banks were awash in cash, and it was cheap, cheap, cheap to borrow. Investors could borrow money for an interest rate of a mere few percent. "Established investors" could make property purchases with no money down. Cash abounded from real estate as the price of land in Tokyo, for example, soared 500 percent from 1985 to 1990. Despite the fact that Japan has only $^{@@bf1}/_{25}$ as much land as the United States, Japan's total land values at the close of the 1980s were four times that of all the land in the United States.

Speculators also used futures and options (discussed in Chapter 1) to gamble on higher short-term Japanese stock market prices. (Interestingly, Japan doesn't allow selling short.)

Price/earnings ratios? Forget about it. To justify the high prices they paid for stocks, Japanese market speculators pointed out that the real estate that many companies owned was soaring to the moon and making companies more valuable.

Price/earnings ratios on the Japanese market soared during the early 1980s and ballooned to more than 60 times earnings by 1987. As we point out elsewhere in this chapter, such lofty P/E ratios were sometimes awarded beloved stocks in Canada and the United States. But the *entire* Japanese stock market, which included many mediocre and not-so-hot companies, possessed P/E ratios of 60-plus!

When Japan's Nippon Telegraph and Telephone went public in February 1987, it met such frenzied enthusiasm that its stock price was soon bid up to a stratospheric 300-plus price/earnings ratio. At the close of 1989, Japan's stock market, for the first time in history, unseated the U.S. stock market in total market value of all stocks. And this feat happened despite the fact that the total output of the Japanese economy was less than half that of the U.S. economy.

Even some North American observers began to lose sight of the big picture and added to the rationalizations for why the high levels of Japanese stocks were justified. After all, it was reasoned, Japanese companies and executives were a tightly knit and closed circle, investing heavily in the stocks of other companies that they did business with. The supply of stock for outside buyers was thus limited as companies sat on their shares.

Corporate stock ownership went further, though, as stock prices were sometimes manipulated. Speculators gobbled up the bulk of outstanding shares of small companies and traded shares back and forth with others whom they partnered with to drive up prices. Company pension plans began to place all (as in 100 percent) of their employees' retirement money in stocks with the expectation that stock prices would always keep going up.

The collapse of the Japanese stock market was swift. After peaking at the end of 1989, the Tokyo market fell nearly 50 percent in the first nine months of 1990 alone. By the middle of 1992, the worst of the damage was over, with Japanese stocks down nearly 65 percent — a drop that the U.S. market hasn't experienced since the Great Depression. However, prices stagnated during the rest of the 1990s and then fell again in the early 2000s, finally reaching a bottom in 2003 that was more than 80 percent lower than the peak reached nearly 15 years prior. Japanese investors who borrowed lost everything and sometimes more. The total loss in stock market value was about $3 trillion, about the size of the entire Japanese annual output.

Several factors finally led to the pricking of the Japanese stock market bubble. Japanese monetary authorities tightened credit as inflation started to creep upward and concern increased over real estate market speculation. As interest rates began to rise, investors soon realized that they could earn 15 times more interest from a safe bond versus the paltry yield on stocks.

As interest rates rose and credit tightened, speculators were squeezed first. Real estate and stock market speculators began to sell their investments to pay off mounting debts. Higher interest rates, less-available credit, and the already grossly inflated prices greatly limited the pool of potential stock buyers. The falling stock and real estate markets fed off each other. Investor losses in one market triggered more selling and price drops in the other. The real estate price drop was equally severe — registering 50 to 60 percent or more in most parts of Japan after the late 1980s.

The 1960s weren't just about sex, drugs, and rock 'n' roll

North American stock markets mirrored the cultural climate during this decade of change and upheaval. There were good years and bad years, but overall, the stock market gained. Unfortunately, most investors who were old enough to remember what happened to the stock market during the

Great Depression were retired or had passed away. The majority of investors during the 1960s were born after the go-go years of the 1920s or were still sucking on a pacifier in the 1920s.

During the 1960s, consumer product companies' stocks were quite popular and were bid up to stratospheric valuations. When we say "stratospheric valuations," we mean that some stock prices were high relative to the companies' earnings — our old friend, the price/earnings (P/E) ratio. Investors had seen such stock prices rise for many years and thought that the good times would never end.

Take the case of Avon Products, which sells cosmetics door to door, primarily with an army of women. During the late 1960s, Avon's stock regularly sold at a P/E of 50 to 70 times earnings. (Remember, the market average is about 15.) After trading as high as $140 per share in the early 1970s, Avon's stock took more than two decades to return to that price level. Remember that during this time period the overall U.S. stock market rose more than tenfold!

When a stock such as Avon's sells at such a high multiple of earnings, two factors can lead to a bloodletting:

- ✔ First, the company's profits may continue to grow, but investors may decide that the stock isn't such a great long-term investment after all and not worth, say, a P/E of 60. Consider that if investors decide it's worth only a P/E of 30 (still a hefty P/E), the stock price would drop 50 percent to cut the P/E in half.

- ✔ The second shoe that can drop is the company's profits or earnings. If profits fall, say, 20 percent, as Avon's did during the 1974–1975 recession, the stock price will fall 20 percent, even if it continued to sell for 60 times its earnings. But when earnings drop, investors' willingness to pay an inflated P/E plummets along with the earnings. So when Avon's profits finally did drop, the P/E that investors were willing to pay plunged to 9 — in less than two years, Avon's stock price thus dropped nearly 87 percent!

Avon wasn't alone in its stock price soaring to a rather high multiple of its earnings in the 1960s and early 1970s. Well-known companies such as Black & Decker, Eastman Kodak, Kmart (used to be called S.S. Kresge in those days), and Polaroid sold for 60 to as much as 100 times earnings. All these companies, like Avon, sell today at about the same or at a lower price than they achieved decades ago. Many other well-known and smaller companies sold at similar and even more outrageous premiums to earnings.

The 1920s' consumer spending binge

The Dow Jones Industrial Average soared nearly 500 percent in a mere eight years (from 1921 to 1929, one of the best bull market runs for the U.S. stock market). The country and investors had good reason for economic optimism. "New" devices — telephones, cars, radios, and all sorts of electric appliances —

were making their way into the mass market. The stock price of RCA, the radio manufacturer, for example, ballooned 5,700 percent during this eight-year stretch.

Speculation in the stock market moved from Wall Street to Main Street. Investors during the 1920s were able to borrow lots of money to buy stock through *margin borrowing.* You can still margin borrow today — for every dollar that you put up, you may borrow an additional dollar to buy stock. At times during the 1920s, investors were able to borrow up to nine dollars for every dollar that they had in hand. The amount of margin loans outstanding swelled from $1 billion in the early 1920s to more than $8 billion in 1929. When the market plunged, *margin calls* forced margin borrowers to sell their stock, thus exacerbating the decline.

The steep run-up in stock prices was also due in part to market manipulation. Investment pools used to buy stock from and sell stock to one another, thus generating high trading volume in a stock, which made it appear that interest in the stock was great. Also in cahoots with pool operators were writers who dispensed enthusiastic prognostications about said stock. (Reforms later passed by the U.S. Securities and Exchange Commission addressed these problems.)

Not only were members of the public largely enthusiastic, so too were the supposed experts. After a small decline in September 1929, economist Irving Fisher said in mid-October, "Stock prices have reached what looks like a permanently high plateau." High? Yes! Permanent plateau? Investors wish!

On October 25, 1929, just days before all heck began breaking loose, President Herbert Hoover said, "The fundamental business of the country . . . is on a sound and prosperous basis." Days later, multimillionaire oil tycoon John D. Rockefeller said, "Believing that fundamental conditions of the country are sound . . . my son and I have for some days been purchasing sound common stocks."

By December of that same year, the stock market had dropped by more than 35 percent. General Electric President Owen D. Young said at that time, "Those who voluntarily sell stocks at current prices are extremely foolish."

Well, actually not. By the time the crash had run its course, the market had plunged 89 percent in value in less than three years.

The economy went into a tailspin. Unemployment soared to more than 25 percent of the labour force. Companies entered this period with excess inventories, which mushroomed further when people slashed their spending. Tariffs stifled exports. Thousands of banks failed, because early bank failures triggered "runs" on other banks. (Government insurance on financial institutions didn't exist in those days.)

Manias in prior centuries

We could fill an entire book with modern-day stock market manias. But bear with us as we roll back the clocks a couple of centuries to observe other market manias, the first being England's so-called South Seas bubble of 1719. South Seas wasn't the kind of company that would've met today's socially responsible investor's needs. Initially, the South Seas Company focused on the African slave trade, but too many slaves died in transit, so it wasn't a lucrative business.

If you think government corruption is a problem today, consider what politicians of those days did without the scrutiny of a widely read press. King George backed the South Seas Company and acted as its governor. Politicos in Parliament bought tons of stock in the South Seas Company and even rammed through Parliament a provision that allowed investors to buy stock on borrowed money. The stock of the South Seas Company soared from about £120 to more than £1,000 in just the first six months of 1720.

After such an enormous run-up, insiders realized that the stock price was greatly inflated and quietly bailed. Citizens fell all over themselves to get into this surefire moneymaker.

Other seafaring companies pursued the South Seas trade business, so the greedy politicians passed a law that allowed only government-approved companies to pursue trade. The stocks of these other companies tumbled, and investor losses led to a chain reaction that prompted selling of the South Seas Company stock, which plunged more than 80 percent by the autumn of that same year.

Unfortunately, England wasn't the only European country that was swept up in an investment mania. Probably the most famous mania of them all was the tulip bulb (yes, those flowers that you can plant in your own home garden). A botany professor introduced tulips into Holland from Turkey in the late 1500s. A fascination with these bulbs among residents turned into an investment feeding frenzy.

At their speculative peak, the price of a single tulip bulb was the equivalent of more than $10,000 in today's dollars. Many people sold their land holdings to buy more. Documented cases show that people traded a bulb for a dozen acres of land! Labourers cut back on their work to invest. Eventually, tulip bulb prices came crashing back to earth. A trip to your local nursery shows you what a bulb sells for today.

Psychologically, it's easier for many people to buy stocks *after* the stocks have had a huge increase in price. Just as you shouldn't attempt to drive your car looking solely through your rearview mirror, basing investments solely on past performance usually leads novice investors into overpriced investments. If many people talk about the stunning rise in the market, and new investors pile in based on the expectation of hefty profits, tread carefully.

We're not saying that you need to sell your current stock holdings if you see an investment market getting frothy and speculative. As long as you diversify your stocks worldwide and hold other investments, such as real estate and bonds, the stocks that you hold in one market need to be only a fraction of your total holdings. Timing the markets is difficult: You can never know how high is high and when it's time to sell, and then how low is low and when it's time to buy. And if you sell non-retirement plan investments at a profit, you end up sacrificing some of the profit to taxes.

Buy more when stocks are "on sale"

Along with speculative buying frenzies come valleys of pessimism when stock prices fall sharply. Having the courage to buy when stock prices are "on sale" can pay big returns.

The 1970s' stock sale

In the early 1970s, interest rates and inflation escalated. Oil prices shot up as the oil embargo choked off supplies, and Americans had to wait in long lines for gas. Gold prices soared, and the U.S. dollar plunged in value on foreign currency markets. Canada was coping with the kidnappings of the October Crisis.

If the economic problems weren't enough to make most everyone gloomy, the U.S. political system hit an all-time low during this period as well. Vice President Spiro Agnew resigned in disgrace under a cloud of tax-evasion charges; then Watergate led to President Richard Nixon's August 1974 resignation, the first presidential resignation in our history.

When all was sold and done, the Dow Jones Industrial Average plummeted more than 45 percent from early 1973 until late 1974. The Toronto Stock Exchange dropped alongside the U.S. markets, falling 38 percent. Among the stocks that fell the hardest were those that had been most popular and selling at extreme multiples of earnings in the late 1960s and early 1970s. (See the section "The 1960s weren't just about sex, drugs, and rock 'n' roll," earlier in this chapter.)

Take a gander at Table 5-2 to see the drops in some well-known companies and how cheaply these stocks were valued relative to corporate profits (look at the P/E ratios) after the worst market drop since the Great Depression.

Table 5-2	Stock Bargains Galore in the Mid-1970s		
Company	*Industry*	*Stock Price Fall from Peak*	*1974 P/E*
Abbott Laboratories	Drugs	66%	8
AIG	Insurance	67%	10
Chemical Bank	Banking	64%	4
Coca-Cola	Beverages	70%	12

(continued)

Table 5-2 *(continued)*

Company	Industry	Stock Price Fall from Peak	1974 P/E
Disney	Entertainment	75%	11
Dun & Bradstreet	Business information	68%	9
General Dynamics	Military	81%	3
H&R Block	Tax preparation	83%	6
Hilton Hotels	Hotels	87%	4
Humana	Hospitals	91%	3
Intel	Semiconductors	76%	6
Kimberly-Clark	Consumer products	63%	4
McGraw-Hill	Publishing	90%	4
Mobil	Oil	60%	3
PepsiCo	Beverages	67%	8
Pitney Bowes	Postage meters	84%	6
PPG Industries	Glass	60%	4
Quaker Oats	Packaged food	76%	6
Rite Aid	Drug stores	95%	4
Scientific-Atlanta	Communications equipment	82%	4
Sprint	Telephone	67%	7

Those who were too terrified to buy stocks in the mid-1970s actually had plenty of time to get on board and take advantage of the buying opportunities. The U.S. stock market did have a powerful rally and, from its 1974 low, rose nearly 80 percent over the next two years. But over the next half-dozen years, the market backpedalled, losing much of its gains. The mid- to late 1970s was also a good time to take advantage of bargain prices on many Canadian stocks. From a low in late 1974, the TSE 300 climbed steadily to the end of the decade, rising 193 percent.

In the late 1970s and early 1980s, inflation continued to escalate well into double digits. Corporate profits declined further, and unemployment rose higher than in the 1974 recession. Although some stocks dropped, others simply treaded water and went sideways for years after major declines in the mid-1970s. As some companies' profits increased, P/E bargains abounded (as shown in Table 5-3).

Table 5-3	More Stock Bargains in the Late 1970s and Early 1980s		
Company	*Industry*	*Stock Price Fall from Peak*	*P/E Late '70s/ Early '80s*
Anheuser-Busch	Beer	75%	8
Campbell Soup	Canned foods	36%	6
Coca-Cola	Beverages	61%	8
Colgate-Palmolive	Personal care	69%	6
General Electric	Consumer/industrial products	44%	7
General Mills	Food	44%	6
Gillette	Shaving products	74%	5
J.C. Penney	Department stores	80%	6
McDonald's	Fast food	46%	9
MMM	Consumer/industrial products	50%	8
Pacific Gas & Electric	Utility	52%	6
Procter & Gamble	Consumer products	46%	8
Ralston Purina	Pet food	49%	6
Rubbermaid	Rubber products	60%	7
Sara Lee	Food	60%	5
Schering Plough	Drugs	71%	7
Wells Fargo	Banking	50%	3
Whirlpool	Household appliances	63%	5

When bad news and pessimism abound and the stock market has dropped, it's actually a much safer and better time to buy stocks. You may even consider shifting some of your money out of your safer investments, such as bonds, and invest more aggressively in stocks. Most investors understandably feel — and worry — during these times that prices can drop further, but if you buy and wait, you'll be amply rewarded. Most of the stocks listed in the last several pages appreciated 500 to 2,500-plus percent over the next couple of decades.

The 2008 subprime crisis

At the time this book was going to the printers, stock markets worldwide had plummeted due to the lending and banking crisis in the United States. Rewarded by ever-increasing fees — and huge bonuses to the head honchos — lenders went crazy offering money to American consumers. Mortgages covering the full amount of their home purchases were regularly made available to homebuyers who only a few years earlier wouldn't have qualified to borrow 75 percent of the value. When house prices rose, consumers used that new equity in their property to borrow even more. Wall Street, meanwhile, got in on the action, and began turning those mortgages into tradeable investment securities. Along the way, the finance whizzes somehow decreed that these bundles of shaky mortgages were now low-risk investments.

The end of this sorry mess came quickly and painfully. When house prices fell instead of rose, many homeowners found they could no longer afford their mortgage payments and defaulted on their loans. (Some homeowners had bought at peak prices, and borrowed the full cost of their home. But when housing prices dropped, they found themselves unable to refinance.) Overnight, it seemed, the associated bundles of mortgages that insurance companies and investment dealerships were busy trading and marketing turned sour. In a matter of weeks, previously major-league players in the insurance, mortgage, and brokerage worlds had collapsed or were desperately looking for bailouts.

The larger economy soon hit the ropes. Lenders, once so anxious to lend money to just about anybody who asked, were suddenly terrified, unsure about who really had the financial stability to be a safe bet for a loan. Credit is the oil that keeps businesses chugging along, and when that dried up, so too did the economies around the world.

By the fall of 2008, North American markets had fallen by over 40 percent. The Japanese market had dropped 46 percent, while the Hong Kong market had lost 65 percent of its value. The London stock exchange was down 45 percent, and the German market had dropped by almost 50 percent.

The events of 2008 posed very serious challenges. The financial industry managed to blow itself up and sideswipe the economy with it. But stock markets typically overshoot the mark, driven by the two extreme emotions of investors: fear and greed. It's impossible to tell in the short term what will happen to the markets, and 2008 was no different. At the time of writing, we wouldn't dream of hazarding a guess as to whether the lows reached late in 2008 were setting the stage for more stable markets and possibly a recovery, or if many more violent drops are still ahead. But selling most or all of your stocks after dramatic market plunges has largely proved to be a bad idea.

Table 5-4 and Table 5-5 show just how far some large and well-known U.S. and Canadian companies had fallen by late 2008. The charts also show how relatively inexpensive these stocks were in terms of their price/earnings ratios. It's highly likely that a few years after 2008, investors will once again look back and realize that it was a good time to go shopping for stocks on the cheap.

Table 5-4	Cheap U.S. Stocks in Late 2008		
Company	*Industry*	*Stock Price Fall from Peak*	*Late 2008 P/E*
Abercrombie & Fitch	Retail	71%	5
AT&T	Communications	48%	9
Archer Daniels Midland	Agriculture	71%	6
Boeing	Aerospace	65%	9
Caterpillar	Heavy machinery	63%	6
CBS	Broadcasting	74%	4
Chesapeake Energy	Oil and gas	84%	5
Coca-Cola	Beverages	70%	7
Corning	Fibre optics	64%	6
Del Monte	Processed foods	70%	3
General Electric	Conglomerate	57%	9
Goodyear Tire	Manufacturing	70%	3
Halliburton	Construction	72%	7
Honeywell	Technology and manufacturing	58%	7
Ingersoll-Rand	Industrial products	70%	6
Macy's	Retail	82%	4.5
MGM Mirage	Hotels	90%	6
National Semiconductor	Electronics	60%	9
Newell Rubbermaid	Consumer products	60%	9
Radio Shack	Retail	58%	7
Royal Caribbean Cruises	Tourism	70%	5
Schering Plough	Pharmaceuticals	62%	8
Thomson Reuters	Information	57%	4
United States Steel	Steel	84%	3

Table 5-5	Cheap Canadian Stocks in Late 2008		
Company	**Industry**	**Stock Price Fall from Peak**	**Late 2008 P/E**
Agrium	Agriculture	70%	5
Barrick	Gold mining	58%	11
Bombardier	Transport	61%	9
CAE	Aerospace	56%	9
CP	Railways	41%	9
Petro-Canada	Oil and Gas	63%	3
Potash	Fertilizers	68%	8
Sun Life	Financial	56%	7
Talisman Energy	Oil and Gas	62%	5
Teck Resources	Mining	73%	4
TD Bank	Banking	33%	10

Avoiding Problematic Stock Buying Practices

You may be curious about other ways to buy individual stocks, but if we list those methods in this section, it's because we *don't* recommend using them. You can greatly increase your chances of success and earn higher returns if you avoid the commonly made stock investing mistakes that we present in this section.

Beware of investment advisers' conflicts of interest

Some investors invest in individual stocks through an investment adviser who earns a living from commissions. The standard pitch of these firms and their investment advisers is that they maintain research departments that monitor and report on stocks. Their advisers, using this research, tell you when to buy, sell, or hold. Sounds good in theory, but this system has significant problems.

Many investment dealers happen to be in another business that creates enormous conflicts of interest in producing objective company reviews. You see, these investment firms also solicit companies to help them sell new stock and bond issues. To gain this business, the investment dealers need to demonstrate enthusiasm and optimism for the company's future prospects.

Investment analysts who, with the best of intentions, write negative reports about a company, find their careers hindered in a variety of ways. Some firms fire such analysts. Companies that the analysts criticize sometimes exclude the analysts from analyst meetings about the company. Analysts who know what's good for their careers and their investment dealers don't write disapproving reports.

Although investment insiders know that analysts are overly optimistic, little documented proof about this fact exists, and few people are willing to talk on the record about it. One firm got caught encouraging its analysts via a memo not to say negative things about companies. As uncovered by *Wall Street Journal* reporter Michael Siconolfi, Morgan Stanley's head of new stock issues stated in a memo that the firm's policy needed to include "no negative comments about our clients." The memo also stated that any analyst's changes in a stock's rating or investment opinion, "which might be viewed negatively" by the firm's clients, had to be cleared through the company's corporate finance department head!

Various studies of the investment dealer's stock ratings have conclusively demonstrated that from a predictive perspective, most of its research is barely worth the cost of the paper it's printed on. In Chapter 6, we recommend independent research reports that beat the investment dealer industry track record hands down. In Chapter 9, we cover the important issues you need to consider when you select a good investment adviser.

Don't day trade or short-term trade

Unfortunately (for themselves), some investors track their stock investments closely and believe that they need to sell after short holding periods —months, weeks, or even days. With the growth of Internet and computerized trading, such shortsightedness took a turn for the worse with more investors engaging in a foolish process known as *day trading,* where you buy and sell a stock within the same day!

If you hold a stock only for a few hours or a few months, you're not investing; you're gambling. Specifically, the numerous drawbacks that we see to short-term trading include the following:

✔ **Higher trading costs:** Although the commission that you pay to trade stocks has declined greatly in recent years, especially through online trading (which we discuss in Chapter 9), the more you trade, the more of your investment dollars go into an investment adviser's wallet. Commissions are like taxes — once collected, your dollars are forever gone, and your return is reduced. Similarly, the spread between what you pay to purchase a stock and the price you would receive to sell the same stock (known as the bid-ask spread) can be a significant drag on your investment return.

✔ **More taxes (and tax headaches):** When you invest outside of tax-sheltered retirement plans, you must track and report every time that you buy and then sell a stock on your annual income tax return. And if you make a profit, you must part with a good portion of it through the *capital gains* tax that you owe on your profits when you sell your stock. The return that you keep (after taxes) is more important than the return that you make (before taxes).

✔ **Lower returns:** If stocks increase in value over time, long-term buy-and-hold investors will enjoy the fruits of the stock's appreciation. However, when you jump in and out of stocks, your money spends a good deal of time *not* invested in stocks. The overall level of stock prices in general, and individual stock prices in particular, sometimes rises sharply during short periods of time. Thus, day traders and other short-term traders inevitably miss some stock run-ups. The best professional investors we know don't engage in short-term trading for this reason (as well as because of the increased transaction costs and taxes that such trading inevitably generates).

✔ **Lost opportunities:** Most of the short-term traders we've met over the years spend inordinate amounts of time researching and monitoring their investments. During the late 1990s, we began to hear of more and more people who quit their jobs so they could manage their investment portfolio full time! Some of the firms that sell day-trading seminars tell you that you can make a living trading stocks. Your time is clearly worth something. Put your valuable time into working a little more on building your own business or career instead of using all those extra hours each day and week to watch your investments like a hawk, which usually hampers rather than enhances your returns.

✔ **Poorer relationships:** Time is our most precious commodity. In addition to the financial opportunities you lose when you indulge in unproductive trading, you need to consider the personal consequences. Like drinking, smoking, and gambling, short-term trading is often an addictive behaviour. Spouses of day traders and other short-term traders report unhappiness over how much more time and attention their mates spend on their investments than their families. And what about the lack of attention that day traders and short-term traders give friends and other relatives? (See the sidebar "Recognizing an investment-gambling problem" in this chapter to help determine whether you or a loved one has a gambling addiction.)

How a given stock performs in the next few hours, days, weeks, or even months may have little to do with the underlying financial health and vitality of the company's business. In addition to short-term swings in investor emotions, unpredictable events (the emergence of a new technology or competitor, analyst predictions, changes in government regulation, and so on) push stocks one way or another for short periods of time.

As we say throughout this part of the book, stocks are intended to be long-term holdings. You shouldn't buy stocks if you don't plan on holding them for at least five years or more — and preferably seven to ten. When stocks suffer a setback, it may take months or even years for them to come back.

Don't buy penny stocks

Even worse than buying stocks through an investment adviser whose compensation depends on what you buy and how often you trade is purchasing penny stocks through investment advisers that specialize in such stocks. Tens of thousands of smaller-company stocks trade on the over-the-counter market. Some of these companies are quite small and sport low prices per share that range from pennies to several dollars, hence the name *penny stocks*.

Here's how penny-stock investment advisers typically work. Many of these firms purchase prospect lists of people who have demonstrated a propensity for buying other lousy investments by phone. Advisers are taught to first introduce themselves by phone and then call back shortly thereafter with a tremendous sense of urgency about a great opportunity to get in on the "ground floor" of a small but soon-to-be stellar company. Not all of these companies and stocks have terrible prospects, but many do.

The biggest problem with buying penny stocks through such advisers is that the stocks are grossly overpriced. Just as you don't make good investment returns by purchasing jewellery that's marked up 100 percent, you don't have a fighting chance of making decent money on penny stocks that the adviser may flog with similar markups. The individual adviser who cons you into "investing" in such cheap stocks gains a big commission, which is why he continues to call you with "opportunities" until you send him a cheque. Many advisers in this business who possess records of securities violations also possess an ability to sell, so they have no problem gaining employment with other penny-stock peddlers.

Recognizing an investment-gambling problem

Some gamblers spend their time at the racetrack, and you can find others in casinos. Increasingly, though, you can find gamblers at their personal computers, tracking and trading stocks.

More investors than ever are myopically focused on stocks' short-term price movements. Several factors contribute to this troubling activity: the continued growth of the Internet, the increased responsibility more folks have in managing their own retirement investments, and increased media coverage (including stock market channels). Also, companies touting themselves as educational institutions suck legions of novice investors into dangerous practices. Masquerading under such pompous names as "institutes" or "academies," these firms purport to teach you how to get rich by day trading stocks. Perhaps you've heard their ads on the radio or seen them on stock market television channels or on the Internet for "seminars" or other "training" methods. All you have to do is part with several thousands of dollars for the training, but the only people getting rich are the owners of such seminar companies.

The non-profit organization Gamblers Anonymous developed the following 20 questions to help you figure out whether you or someone you know is a compulsive gambler who needs help. According to Gamblers Anonymous, compulsive gamblers typically answer yes to seven or more of these questions:

1. Did you ever lose time from work or school due to gambling?

2. Has gambling ever made your home life unhappy?

3. Did gambling affect your reputation?

4. Have you ever felt remorse after gambling?

5. Did you ever gamble to get money with which to pay debts or otherwise solve financial difficulties?

6. Did gambling cause a decrease in your ambition or efficiency?

7. After losing, did you feel you must return as soon as possible and win back your losses?

8. After a win, did you have a strong urge to return and win more?

9. Did you often gamble until your last dollar was gone?

10. Did you ever borrow money to finance your gambling?

11. Have you ever sold anything to finance gambling?

12. Were you reluctant to use "gambling money" for normal expenditures?

13. Did gambling make you careless of the welfare of your family?

14. Did you ever gamble longer than you had planned?

15. Have you ever gambled to escape worry or trouble?

16. Have you ever committed, or considered committing, an illegal act to finance gambling?

17. Did gambling cause you to have difficulty in sleeping?

18. Do arguments, disappointments, or frustrations create within you an urge to gamble?

19. Did you ever have an urge to celebrate any good fortune with a few hours of gambling?

20. Have you ever considered self-destruction as a result of your gambling?

A number of penny-stock investment dealerships are known for engaging in manipulation of stock prices, driving up prices of selected shares to suck in gullible investors, and then leaving the public holding the bag. These firms may also encourage companies to issue new overpriced stock that their advisers can then sell to people like you.

If you remember a fellow by the name of Robert Brennan, you know that he is the granddaddy of this reptilian business. We won't bore you with all the details except to say that after more than a decade of financial shenanigans, Brennan was ordered by a judge to pay investors more than $70 million for all the bad stuff that he did. And Brennan was sentenced to nearly a decade of prison time.

Brennan used to run infamous "Come Grow with Us" television ads, in which he hopped out of a helicopter. Brennan was always nicely dressed and maintained a polished image. It's interesting to note that in addition to being in the penny-stock business, Brennan owned a horse racetrack and wanted to get into the casino business. All Brennan's businesses share the same characteristics — they don't involve investments, and they stack the deck against the gullible members of the public whom they hoodwink.

The Keys to Stock Market Success

Anybody, no matter what his or her educational background, IQ, occupation, income, or assets, can make good money through stock investments. Over long periods of time, based on historic performance, you can expect to earn an average of 9 to 10 percent per year total return by investing in stocks.

To maximize your chances of stock market investment success, do the following:

- ✔ **Don't try to time the markets.** Anticipating where the stock market and specific stocks are heading is next to impossible, especially over the short term. Consider that in 2008, the overwhelming majority of analysts, commentators, on-air "experts," and columnists completely failed to offer any advance warning that the stock markets were headed for a massive collapse. Economic factors, which are influenced by thousands of elements, as well as human emotions, determine stock market prices. Be a regular buyer of stocks with new savings. As we discuss earlier in this chapter, buy more stocks when they're on sale and when market pessimism is running high.

- ✔ **Diversify.** Invest in the stocks of different-size companies in varying industries around the world. When you assess the performance of your investments, look at your whole portfolio at least once a year, and calculate your total return after expenses and trading fees.

✔ **Keep trading costs, management fees, and commissions to a minimum.** These represent a big drain on your returns. If you invest through an individual investment adviser who earns a living on commissions, odds are high that you're paying far more than you need to, and you're likely receiving biased advice.

✔ **Pay attention to taxes.** Like commissions and fees, taxes are a major investment "expense" that you can minimize. Contribute most of your money to your RRSP and other tax-advantaged retirement plans. You can invest your money outside of tax-deferred savings plans, but keep an eye on taxes (see Chapter 3). Calculate your annual returns on an *after*-tax basis.

✔ **Don't overestimate your ability to pick the big winning stocks.** One of the best ways to invest in stocks is through mutual funds (see Chapter 8), where you can use an experienced, full-time money manager at a low cost to perform all the investing grunt work for you.

Chapter 6

Investigating and Purchasing Individual Stocks

This chapter provides a crash course in researching individual companies and their stocks. Be sure that you consider your reasons for taking this approach before you head down the path of picking and choosing your own stocks. If you haven't already done so, please read Chapter 5 to better understand the process of purchasing stocks on your own.

If you decide to tackle the task of researching your own stocks, you don't need to worry about finding enough information: The problem to worry about is information overload. You can literally spend hundreds of hours researching and reading information on one company alone. Therefore, unless you're financially independent and want to spend nearly all your productive time investing, you need to focus on where you can get the best bang for your buck and time.

Building on Others' Research

If you were going to build a house, we'd bet that you wouldn't actually try to do it on your own. At the very least, you'd probably find some sort of kit or a set of plans drawn up by others who have built many houses. You can do the same when it comes to picking individual stocks. In this section, we highlight useful resources that allow you to hit the ground running when trying to pick the best stocks. In addition to the resources we cover here, please see Chapter 19 for a list and description of numerous other useful resources for researching individual stocks.

Checking out ShareOwner

ShareOwner Education Inc. is a Canadian company that helps educate individual investors. (ShareOwner evolved out of The Canadian Shareowners Association, a non-profit organization.) Through its mentorship program, ShareOwner's online seminars help you develop a portfolio, and a ShareOwner "mentor" provides you with written feedback on your plan. Students can then try out their proposed portfolio without having to commit a lot of money, buying anywhere from $1 to $100 worth of up to 20 different stocks. The maximum allowable amount to invest at this stage is $2,000. At the end of nine months, students can choose to cash out or remain with ShareOwner and switch over to a regular ShareOwner account.

Memberships in the mentorship program are available for three months for around $500. A six-month membership costs about $700, and a nine-month membership goes for about $900. A membership includes a monthly tutorial and a monthly case study.

ShareOwner's focus is on helping individual investors research and invest in high-quality growth stocks and exchange-traded funds (ETFs) for the long term. To help investors do that, ShareOwner has an easy-to-understand methodology. To locate what it calls "Great Stocks," it suggests looking for companies with a track record of consistently increasing both their revenues and their earnings per share at high rates. ShareOwner also looks for companies with a stable price/earnings ratio (refer to Chapter 5).

To help investors assess how companies are doing on these fronts, Share Owner produces a software program as well as digital data on some 6,000 companies, including just under 2,000 Canadian companies. The stock assessment software — included as part of the mentorship program — is also available without the membership service for around $200 as a download, and slightly more if you want it mailed out on a disk. The data on the companies — which is sold separately from the program — costs about $230 a year for unlimited downloads. You can also choose to have the database mailed out to you on disk every two months for a slightly higher price.

Discovering the Value Line Investment Survey

Value Line's securities analysts have tracked and researched stocks since the Great Depression. Their analysis and recommendation track record is quite good, and their analysts are beholden to no one. Many professional money managers use Value Line as a reference because of its comprehensiveness.

TIP

How to minimize commissions with ShareOwner's portfolio-building services

To maximize your returns, you must keep investment fees and other costs to a minimum. Staying diversified is also key. If one of your investments collapses, the other healthy securities you hold will limit the overall damage.

For investors who want to buy their own stocks, these two goals often conflict. Without a substantial sum to invest, purchasing shares of enough different companies to ensure proper diversification usually means paying a significant amount in commissions and other costs. This is why we recommend mutual funds and exchange-traded funds (ETFs). By buying these efficient investments, investors get immediate broad diversification at a low cost.

For those who want to pick their own stocks, ShareOwner offers a second way to purchase shares and accomplish these two goals. Through its pooled-buying service, individual investors can make small purchases of numerous stocks and keep commissions low. ShareOwner charges commissions based on the number of different companies you

purchase shares in, not the number of shares or the dollar amount. What's more, you can purchase fractions of shares (up to four decimal points!). Your purchase order for shares of a particular company will be added to those of other investors buying the same stock, and the orders for each company are processed on a regular basis, usually every two weeks or once a month.

If your purchase order is for shares in anywhere from one to four different companies, the charge is $9 per company. But what makes ShareOwner's service appealing is the maximum order cost: $36. You can divide your purchase between many more companies, and the order cost remains capped at $36. You can choose from 180 large Canadian and U.S. companies, and 30 exchange-traded funds. These stocks and ETFs have been selected by ShareOwner because they qualify as good-quality growth investments according to its assessment methodology.

The beauty of Value Line's service is that it condenses the key information and statistics about a stock (and the company behind the stock) to a single page. Suppose that you're interested in investing in Starbucks, the retail coffeehouse operator. You've seen all its stores, and you figure that if you're going to shell out more than $3 for a cup of its flavoured hot water, you may as well participate in the profits and growth of the company. You look up the recent stock price (we explain how to do that later in this chapter) and see that it's $19 per share.

Let's take a look at the important elements of a Value Line page for Starbucks, shown in Figure 6-1.

The information in Value Line reports is in no way inside information. Look at these reports the same way that you review a history book — as useful background information that can keep you from repeating common mistakes.

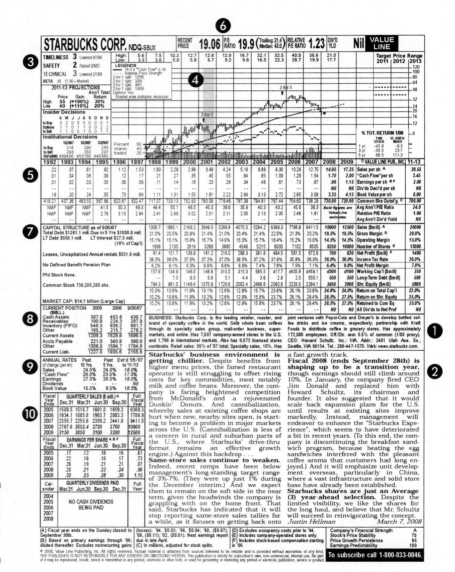

Figure 6-1:
Value Line's
report on
Starbucks.

1. Business

This section describes the business(es) that Starbucks participates in. You can see that Starbucks is the largest retailer of specialty coffee in the world. Although 85 percent of the company's sales come from retail, note that 15 percent come from other avenues — such as mail order and supermarket sales. You also find details about joint ventures, such as the partnership of Starbucks and Pepsi to develop and sell a bottled coffee drink. In this section, you also can see that the senior executives and directors of the company own a sizable stake (5.5 percent) of the stock — it's good to see these folks have a financial stake in the success of the company and stock.

2. Analyst assessment

Securities analysts (in Starbucks' case, a fellow called Justin Hellman) follow each Value Line stock. An analyst focuses on specific industries and follows a few dozen stocks. This section provides the analyst's summary and commentary of the company's current situation and future plans.

Hellman notes that although the company and stock are facing some near-term challenges, the shares are attractive over the longer term.

3. Value Line's rating

Value Line provides a numerical ranking for each stock's timeliness (expected performance) over the next year. A rating of 1 is highest and 5 is lowest, but only about 5 percent of all stocks receive these extreme ratings. A 2 rating is above average and a 4 rating is below average, and about one-sixth of the ranked stocks receive each of these ratings. All remaining stocks, a little more than half the total ranked, get the average 3 rating.

The safety rank works the same way as the timeliness rating, with 1 representing the best and least volatile stocks and the most financially stable companies. Five is the worst safety ranking and is given to the most volatile stocks and least financially stable companies.

We've never been fans of predictions and short-term thinking. One year is a very short period of time for the stock market. Consider that at the time he wrote this analysis of Starbucks — early March 2008 — the stock was trading at around US$19. And while Hellman outlined the numerous challenges the company was facing, nothing in the report suggests that just over six months later, the stock would be trading for half that amount due to the collapse of stock markets in general.

That said, historically, Value Line's system holds one of the best overall track records according to the *Hulbert Financial Digest,* which tracks the actual performance of investment newsletter recommendations. However, you shouldn't necessarily run out and buy any stock that Value Line gives a high ranking to. Just keep in mind that higher-ranked stocks within Value Line have historically outperformed those without such ratings.

4. Stock price performance

This graph shows you the stock price's performance over the past decade or so. The highest and lowest points of the line on the graph indicate the high and low stock prices for each month. At the top of the graph you see the year's high and low prices. Starbucks stock has steadily risen since it first issued stock in 1992, but the company certainly has experienced some down periods. (The small box in the lower-right corner of the graph shows you the total return that an investor in this stock earned over the previous one, three, and five years and how those returns compare with the average stock. This graph shows you that Starbucks declined significantly over the past one to three years but has increased over the past five years.)

The graph also shows how the price of the stock moves with changes in the company's *cash flow* (money coming in minus money going out). Over time, just as stock prices tend to track corporate profits, so too should they generally follow cash flow. Cash flow is an important measure of a company's financial success and health — it's different from *net profits,* which the company reports for tax purposes. For example, the tax laws allow companies to take a tax deduction each year for the *depreciation* (devaluation) of the company's equipment and other assets. Although depreciation is good because it helps lower a company's tax bill, subtracting it from the company's revenue gives an untrue picture of the company's cash flow. Thus, in calculating a company's cash flow, depreciation isn't subtracted from revenue.

5. Historic financials

This section shows you 12 to 18 years of financial information on the company (in the case of Starbucks, you get information going back to just 1992 because that's when the company went public). The two most helpful pieces of information in this section are

- ✔ **Book value per share:** This indicates the value of the company's assets, including equipment, manufacturing plants, and real estate, minus any liabilities. Book value gives you somewhat of a handle on the amount that the company can sell for if it has a "going-out-of-business sale." We say "somewhat" because the value of some assets on a company's books isn't correct. For example, some companies own real estate, bought long ago, that is worth far more than the company's current financial statements indicate. Conversely, some manufacturers with equipment find that if they have to dump some equipment in a hurry, they need to sell the equipment at a discount to entice a buyer.

The book value of a bank, for example, can mislead you if the bank makes loans that won't be paid back, and the bank's financial statements don't document this fact. (This could be seen in action during the collapse of mortgage companies, insurers, and investment dealers during the 2008 subprime lending crisis.) All these complications with book value are why full-time, professional money managers exist. (If you want to delve more into a company's book value, you need to look at other financial statements, such as the company's annual report, which we discuss in the "Understanding Annual Reports" section, later in this chapter.)

✔ **Market share:** For some companies (not Starbucks), Value Line also provides another useful number in this section — the *market share,* which indicates the portions of the industry that the company has captured in a given year. A sustained decline in a company's market share is a dangerous sign that may indicate its customers are leaving for other companies that presumably offer better products at lower prices. But that doesn't mean that you should avoid investing in a company that has such problems. You can produce big returns if you can identify companies that reposition and strengthen their product offerings to reverse a market share decrease.

6. P/E ratio

This tells you that Starbucks sells at a *P/E* (price-to-earnings) ratio of 19.9 because of its recent stock price and earnings. This P/E ratio is higher than that of the overall market. (You can see that Starbucks' P/E ratio is 1.23 times that of the overall market.) To understand the importance of the P/E ratio in evaluating a stock, please refer to Chapter 5.

7. Capital structure

This section summarizes the amount of outstanding stocks and bonds the company possesses. Remember that when a company issues these securities, it receives *capital* (money). What is most useful to examine in this section is the company's debt. If a company accumulates a lot of debt, the burden of interest payments can create a real drag on profits. If profits stay down for too long, debt can even push some companies into bankruptcy.

Figure 6-1 shows you that Starbucks has outstanding debt of $4 million. This section delineates between two types of debt:

✔ **Short-term debt:** Debt due within one year

✔ **Long-term debt:** Debt that has to be paid back in more than a year

So how do you know if this is a lot, a little, or just the right amount of debt? You can calculate *long-term interest earned,* which compares a company's annual profits to the yearly interest payments on its long-term debt. For example, if a company has long-term interest earned of 4.5x, that means that the company's most recent yearly profits can cover the interest payments on its long-term debt for about 4¹/₂ years. Starbucks has little debt — the company's most recent annual profits of $392 million dwarf its long-term interest payments of $0.1 million.

Possessing a larger cushion to cover debt is more important when the company's business is volatile. *Total interest coverage* represents a similar comparison of profits to interest owed for all the debt that a company owes, not just long-term debt. This number tells you the number of years that the company's most recent annual profits can cover interest on all the company's debt. Warning signs for total interest coverage numbers include a steep decline in this number over time and profits that cover less than one year's worth of interest.

8. Current position

This section provides a quick look at how the company's *current assets* (*current* meaning an asset that can be sold and converted into cash within a year relatively easily) compare with its *current liabilities* (debts due within the year). Trouble may be brewing if a company's current liabilities exceed or are approaching its current assets.

Some financial analysts calculate the *quick ratio,* which ignores inventory when comparing current assets to current liabilities. A company may have to dump inventory at a relatively low price if it needs to raise cash quickly. Thus, some analysts argue, you need to ignore inventory as a current asset.

9. Annual rates

This nifty section can save wear and tear on your calculator. The good folks at Value Line calculate rates of growth (or shrinkage) on important financial indicators, such as *sales* (revenues) and *earnings* (profits) over the past five and ten years. Value Line also lists its projections for the next five years.

Projections can prove highly unreliable, even from a research firm as good as Value Line. In most cases, the projections assume that the company will continue as it has in the most recent couple years.

10. Quarterly financials

For the most recent years, Value Line shows you an even more detailed quarterly breakout of sales and profits, which may disclose changes that annual totals mask. You can also see the seasonality of some businesses. Starbucks, for example, tends to have its slowest quarter in the winter (quarter ending March 31). This makes sense if you figure that many of the customers who frequent Starbucks' coffee shops do so as they walk around town, which people tend to do less of on a blustery winter day.

Getting your hands on Value Line reports

The least costly way to obtain Value Line pages on stocks that interest you is to visit your local library. Many libraries that have decent business sections subscribe to it.

If you want your own copy of Value Line to read in the comfort of your home, Value Line (800-634-3583) offers a 13-week trial subscription to its *Value Line Investment Survey* for US$95. An annual subscription costs US$680. At the start of your subscription, you receive a rather large binder, divided into 13 sections, that includes the most recent reports on the 1,700-plus larger-company stocks that this publication tracks. Every week, you receive a new packet of reports that replaces one of the 13 sections. Thus, at the end of 13 weeks, you have new reports on all the stocks. (If you prefer, an

electronic edition is available for US$65 for the 13-week trial; US$538 yearly.)

The trial subscription is a great place to start your research because you receive all the current reports plus three months' worth of updates for a reasonable fee. You can also see how much use you get out of the reports. The trial offer is available to each household only once every three years.

Value Line also offers a *Small and Mid-Cap Edition* that contains reports on about 1,800 additional smaller companies. Unlike traditional Value Line pages, these pages include no analyst commentary or projections. A one-year subscription to this publication costs US$249.

Considering independent investment dealer research

If you're going to invest in individual stocks, you need an investment dealer account. In addition to low trading fees, the best investment dealers allow you to easily tap into useful research, especially through the firm's Web site, that will assist you with your investing decisions.

Because discount brokers aren't in the investment banking business of working with companies to sell new issues of stock, discount brokers sometimes have a level of objectivity in their research reports that too often is absent among traditional advisers. Please see Chapter 9 for how to select a top-notch investment dealer.

Examining successful money managers' stock picks

To make money in stocks, you certainly don't need an original idea. In fact, it makes sense to examine what the best money managers are buying for their portfolios. Don't worry; we're not suggesting that you invade their privacy or ask rude questions!

Mutual fund managers, for example, are required to disclose at least twice a year what stocks they hold in their portfolio. You can call the best fund companies and ask them to send their most recent semi-annual reports that detail their stock holdings; you can also view those reports on many fund company's Web sites. (See Chapter 8 for more information on the best stock mutual funds.)

Through its Web site, Morningstar (www.morningstar.ca) allows you to see which mutual funds hold large portions of a given stock that you may be researching and what the success or lack thereof is of the funds buying a given stock.

Finally, you can follow what investment legend Warren Buffett is buying through his holding company, Berkshire Hathaway. If you'd like to review Berkshire's complete corporate filings on your own, visit the U.S. Securities and Exchange Commission Web site at www.sec.gov.

Reviewing financial publications and Web sites

Many publications and Web sites cover the world of stocks. Be careful. Just because a columnist or publication advocates particular stocks or investing strategies doesn't mean you'll achieve success by following her advice.

The following publications offer useful columns and commentary, sometimes written by professional money managers, on individual stocks: *Barron's, Business Week, Canadian Business, Forbes, Kiplinger's, Report on Business Magazine,* and *The Wall Street Journal.* In addition, hundreds of Web sites are devoted to stock picking. We name our favourite investing sites in Chapter 19.

Understanding Annual Reports

After you review the Value Line page on a company and want to dig further into financial documents, the next step is to ask yourself why. Why do you want to torture yourself so?

We both have business degrees from what are supposedly better business schools, and we have taken more than our fair share of accounting and finance courses. Over the years, we've gotten to know investment managers and financial analysts who research companies. Although some financial documents aren't that difficult to read (we show you how in this section), interpreting what they mean in respect to a company's future isn't easy.

All publicly traded companies must annually file certain financial documents. Consider reviewing these documents to enhance your understanding of a company's businesses and strategies rather than for the predictive value that you may hope they provide.

The first of such useful documents that companies produce is the *annual report*. This yearly report provides standardized financial statements as well as management's discussion about how the company has performed and how it plans to improve its performance in the future. If you're a bit of the skeptical sort, like we are, you may think, "Aren't the company's officials going to make everything sound rosy and wonderful?"

To a certain extent, yes, but not as badly as you may think, especially with companies that adhere to sound accounting principles and good old-fashioned ethics. First, a large portion of an annual report includes the company's financial statements, which an accounting firm must audit. However, audits don't mean that companies and their accounting firms can't (often legally) structure the company's books to make them look rosier than they really are. And some companies have pulled the wool over the eyes of their auditors, who then became unwitting accomplices in producing false financial figures.

You've surely heard of the accounting scandals at companies such as Enron and WorldCom. These companies manipulated their financial books, with the blessing of supposedly blue-chip corporate auditors, to mislead investors into believing that they were more profitable than they really were. (Identifying trouble *before* other investors do is a skill that many professional investors haven't mastered — if you can identify trouble early, go manage other people's money!)

Also keep in mind that more than a few companies have been sued for misleading shareholders with inflated forecasts or lack of disclosure of problems. Responsible companies try to present a balanced and, of course, hopeful perspective in their annual reports. Most companies' annual reports are written by non-techno geeks, so you have a decent chance of understanding them.

Financial and business highlights

The first section of most annual reports presents a description of a company's recent financial highlights and business strategies. You can use this information to find out about the businesses that the company is in and where the company is heading. For example, in Figure 6-1, Value Line mentioned that Starbucks is also in the specialty sales business. The annual report can provide more detail about Starbucks' specialty business.

Okay, enough about the coffee business — we want to expose you to another industry. Sears is one of Canada's best-known retailers. In Figure 6-2, you can see Sears Canada's discussion of its business activity in 2007.

FINANCIAL HIGHLIGHTS

For the 57-week period ended February 2, 2008 and the 52-week period ended December 30, 2006	Fiscal 2007	Fiscal 2006
Results for the year (in millions)		
Total revenues	$ 6,326	$ 5,933
Interest expense, net	13	48
Earnings before unusual items and income taxes	380	264
Unusual items – expense/(gain)	(82)	25
Income taxes	154	87
Net earnings	308	153
Year end position (in millions)		
Inventories	$ 855	$ 805
Working capital	777	373
Total assets	3,003	3,060
Shareholders' equity	1,093	785
Per share of capital stock		
Net earnings (basic)	$ 2.87	$ 1.42
Dividends declared	–	0.12
Shareholders' equity	10.16	7.29

Figure 6-2: Sears Canada's annual report discusses the past year's business highlights.

Balance sheet

You can find a company's hard-core financials in the back portion of most annual reports. You can find many of these same numbers in Value Line reports, except you get more specific details in the company's annual report. All annual reports contain a *balance sheet,* which is a snapshot summary of all the company's *assets* (what the company owns) and *liabilities* (what the company owes). The balance sheet covers the company's assets and liabilities from the beginning of the year to the last day of the company's year-end, which is typically December 31. Some companies use a fiscal year that ends at other times of the year.

A company's balance sheet resembles a personal balance sheet. The entries, of course, look a little different because you likely don't own things like manufacturing equipment. Figure 6-3 shows a typical corporate balance sheet.

Assets

The assets section lists the following items that the company holds or owns that are of significant value:

- ✔ **Cash:** We suspect that you know what cash is. Lest you think that stacks of bills sit around in corporate vaults, rest assured that companies invest this money to earn interest. Many items are explained in more detail in explanatory notes that follow these financial statements.

- ✔ **Accounts receivable:** This is money that is owed to the company, such as invoices that customers haven't paid yet.

  As companies grow, their accounts receivable usually do, too. Watch out for cases where the receivables grow faster than the sales (revenue). This growth may indicate that the company is having problems with its products' quality or pricing. Unhappy customers pay more slowly or demand bigger price discounts.

- ✔ **Inventories:** Manufacturing and retail companies (such as Sears) also track and report *inventory* (the products that haven't yet been sold) as an asset. Generally speaking, as a business grows, so too does its inventory. If inventory grows more quickly than revenue, such growth may be a warning sign. This growth can indicate that customers are scaling back purchases and that the company miscalculated and overproduced or overbought. It can also be a leading indicator of an obsolete or inferior product offering.

- ✔ **Investments:** In addition to cash, some companies may invest in other securities, such as bonds and stocks. Just as with your own personal situation, companies usually invest money that they don't expect to use in the near future. Sears, for example, details in an explanatory note how its investments are divvied up, with different amounts invested in unsecured debentures, subordinated loans, and so on.

CONSOLIDATED STATEMENTS OF FINANCIAL POSITION

(in millions)	As at February 2, 2008	As at December 30, 2006
ASSETS		
Current Assets		
Cash and short-term investments	$ 871.6	$ 722.9
Restricted cash (Note 11)	5.2	10.1
Accounts receivable	118.4	135.9
Income taxes recoverable	0.4	0.6
Inventories	855.4	804.5
Prepaid expenses and other assets	115.4	120.0
Current portion of future income tax assets (Note 2)	30.6	121.2
	1,997.0	1,915.2
Capital assets (Note 3)	742.0	874.3
Deferred charges (Note 4)	205.0	220.2
Future income tax assets (Note 2)	24.9	15.2
Other long-term assets	34.2	35.4
	$ 3,003.1	$ 3,060.3
LIABILITIES		
Current Liabilities		
Accounts payable	$ 683.6	$ 810.1
Accrued liabilities	439.0	480.0
Income and other taxes payable	81.5	105.1
Principal payments on long-term obligations due within one year (Note 6)	16.1	146.7
Future income tax liabilities (Note 2)	–	0.1
	1,220.2	1,542.0
Long-term obligations (Note 6)	356.0	395.6
Accrued benefit liability (Note 5)	164.1	167.7
Other long-term liabilities	169.7	170.0
	1,910.0	2,275.3
SHAREHOLDERS' EQUITY		
Capital stock (Note 7)	15.7	15.7
Retained earnings	1,077.4	769.3
Accumulated other comprehensive income (Note 15)	–	–
	1,093.1	785.0
	$ 3,003.1	$ 3,060.3

Figure 6-3: The balance sheet from the Sears annual report.

Source: T. Rowe Price Associates, Inc. 2007 Annual Report

✔ **Property and equipment:** All companies need equipment to run their businesses. This equipment can include office furniture, computers, real estate they own, and manufacturing machinery that the company uses to make its products. Equipment — sometimes called *fixed assets,* or, as Sears does, *capital assets* — becomes less valuable over time, so the company considers this depreciation as a cost of doing business each year. Therefore, if a company ceases buying new equipment, this entry on the balance sheet gradually decreases because the depreciation is subtracted from the value of the equipment.

✔ **Goodwill:** One of the assets that doesn't show up on most companies' balance sheets is their *goodwill.* Companies work hard through advertising, product development, and service to attract and retain customers. *Name-brand recognition* is a term that you sometimes hear thrown around. Companies can't put a value on the goodwill that they've generated, but when they purchase (acquire) another firm, some of the purchase price is considered goodwill. Specifically, if a company is acquired for $100 million but has a *net worth* (assets minus liabilities) of just $50 million, the extra $50 million goes to goodwill. The goodwill then becomes an asset on the acquiring company's balance sheet.

✔ **Other assets:** This is a catch-all category that may include some stuff that can make your eyes glaze over. For example, companies keep a different set of books for tax purposes (yes, this is legal). Not surprisingly, companies do this because the tax authorities allow, in some cases, more deductions than what the company is required to show from an accounting standpoint on their financial statements. (If you were a company, wouldn't you want your shareholders, but not the tax collectors, to see gobs of profits?) Companies treat tax deferment as an asset until the tax department receives more of its share down the road.

Liabilities

This section summarizes all the money that the company owes to others:

✔ **Accounts payable:** When a company places orders to purchase things for its business, it sometimes has a lag between receiving a bill and paying it; the money owed is called *accounts payable.* As with inventory and accounts receivable, accounts payable generally increases with a company's increasing revenue.

If accounts payable increases faster than revenue, it can indicate a problem. On the other hand, that increase can also be a sign of good financial management. The longer you take to pay your bills, the longer you have the money in your pocket working for you.

✔ **Accrued liabilities:** This line tallies money that the company must someday pay its employees. For example, many larger firms maintain pension plans. These plans promise workers who retire with at least five years of service a monthly income cheque in retirement. Thus, the company must reserve this money that it owes and list it as a liability or debt that it must someday pay. This is sometimes called *accrued compensation*.

✔ **Income taxes payable:** Companies are in business to make a profit, and as they earn those profits, they need to reserve a portion to pay income taxes. As we explain in the previous section, some of the taxes that the company owes can be caused by accounting differences between the company's financial statements and those filed with the tax authorities.

✔ **Dividends payable:** Not all companies pay dividends (see Chapter 4) to their shareholders. But those companies that do pay dividends typically declare the dividend several weeks in advance of when they actually owe the dividend. During this interim period, the company lists the not-yet-paid dividends as a liability.

Stockholders' equity

The difference between a company's assets and liabilities is known as *stockholders' equity*. Stockholders' equity is what makes balance sheets always balance.

When companies issue stock, they receive cash, which they then list as an asset. Companies divide stock proceeds between *par value* and *capital in excess of par value*. Par values are arcane — and largely meaningless.

Income statement

The other big financial statement in an annual report is the income statement (see Figure 6-4).

Revenue

Revenue is simply the money that the company receives from its customers as compensation for its products or services. Just as you can earn income from your job(s) as well as investments and other sources, a company can make money from a variety of sources. Sears, of course, makes its money from retail sales, along with other ventures, including its travel division and its credit card operations.

Ideally, you want to see a steady or accelerating rate of growth in a company's revenue. If a company's revenue grows more slowly, you need to inquire why. Is it because of poor service or product performance, better competitor offerings, ineffective marketing, or all of the above?

CONSOLIDATED STATEMENTS OF EARNINGS AND COMPREHENSIVE INCOME

For the 57-week period ended February 2, 2008 and the 52-week period ended December 30, 2006 (in millions, except per share amounts)	2007	2006
Total revenues	$ 6,326.4	$ 5,932.8
Cost of merchandise sold, operating, administrative and selling expenses	5,783.8	5,468.3
Depreciation and amortization	150.1	152.1
Interest expense, net	12.7	48.0
Unusual items – expense (gain) (Note 9)	(82.2)	25.2
Earnings before income taxes	462.0	239.2
Income tax expense (Note 2)		
Current	75.7	35.5
Future	77.8	51.1
	153.5	86.6
Net earnings	$ 308.5	$ 152.6
Other comprehensive income (Note 15)	–	–
Total comprehensive income	$ 308.5	$ 152.6
Net earnings per share (Note 16)	$ 2.87	$ 1.42
Diluted net earnings per share (Note 16)	2.87	1.42

Figure 6-4:
The Sears income statement.

For companies with multiple divisions or product lines, the annual report may detail the revenue of each product line in a later section. If it doesn't, check out some of the other financial statements that the next section, "Exploring Other Useful Corporate Reports," recommends. Examine what spurs or holds back the company's overall growth and what different businesses the company operates in. Look for businesses that were acquired but don't really fit with the company's other business units, and mark these as red flags. Large companies that have experienced stalled revenue growth sometimes try to "enter" new businesses through acquisition but then don't manage them well because they don't understand the keys to their success.

When researching department stores (such as Sears), restaurant chains (for example, McDonald's), or clothing stores (such as The Gap), examine the revenue changes that come from opening new locations versus the revenue changes at existing locations, sometimes referred to as *same stores*. Be concerned if you find that a company's revenue growth comes from opening new locations rather than growth at existing locations. This may indicate that weakness in the company's business is being masked by simply opening more locations.

Expenses

Just as personal income taxes, housing, food, and clothing expenses gobble up much of your personal income, company expenses use up much and sometimes all of a company's revenue.

Even healthy, growing businesses can get into trouble if their expenses grow faster than their revenues. Well-managed companies stay on top of their expenses during good and bad times. Unfortunately, it's easy for companies to get sloppy during good times.

Examine each category of expenses relative to (in other words, as a percentage of) the company's revenue to see which categories grow and which shrink. As a well-managed and financially healthy company grows, expenses as a percentage of revenue should decrease. As this happens, profits as a percentage of revenue increase. (Not all expense categories necessarily decrease.)

Net income calculations

The net result of expenses increasing slower than revenues is a fatter bottom line. In the case of Sears, net income increased from 4.03 percent to 7.30 percent of revenue between 2006 and 2007. (To help you better see any trends, companies typically will include financial information for the previous two years alongside the current year's results. Although Sears only provides the preceding year's numbers, elsewhere in its annual report the company summarizes its financial record for the last 11 years.) When you examine how a company's profits change relative to total revenue received, focus on operating income. Sometimes companies experience one-time events, such as the sale of a division, that can change profits temporarily. Companies usually list these one-time events in the section under expenses.

We also encourage you to review a company's statement of cash flows included in its annual report. Cash can flow into and out of a company from normal business operations, investment activities, and financing activities. Sometimes a company may report higher profits but actually be facing decreased cash flow from operations, for example, if its customers are getting slower with paying bills (which could indicate that its customers are having financial problems or they're unhappy with the product or service being provided).

Earnings per share

Last but not least, and of great importance to shareholders, is the calculation of earnings per share. Higher profits per share generally help fuel a higher stock price, and declining profits feed falling stock prices. Remember, though, that smart financial market participants are looking ahead, so if you run out to buy stock in a company that is reporting higher profits, it's old news and likely already priced into the company's current market value.

Exploring Other Useful Corporate Reports

In addition to annual reports, companies produce other financial statements that you may want to peruse. You can generally obtain these from the company for free from their Web sites, or by contacting a company's investor relations department. You can also obtain financial statements from the SEDAR site (www.sedar.com) for Canadian companies, and from the U.S. Securities and Exchange Commission site (www.sec.gov) for U.S. companies. (See Chapter 19 for more on these sites.)

10-Ks

Filed by U.S.-based companies, *10-K*s are expanded versions of an annual report. Most investment professionals read the 10-K instead of the annual report because the 10-K contains additional data and information, especially for a company's various divisions and product lines. Also, 10-Ks contain little of the verbal hype that you find in most annual reports. The 10-K is probably one of the most objective reports that a company publishes. If you're not intimidated by annual reports, or you want more company meat, go for it!

Quarterly reports

Quarterly reports (called *10-Q*s in the United States) provide information on a quarterly basis. These reports are worthwhile if you like to read a reasonably detailed discussion by management of the latest business and financial developments at the company. However, we recommend leaving the research to folks like Value Line's analysts.

The financial data in these reports is unaudited and not of great use for the long-term investor. If you want to watch your investments like a hawk and try to be among the first to detect indications of financial problems (easier said than done), these reports are required reading.

Many companies go back to restate their quarterly financials. Remember that the accountants haven't approved these numbers. Sometimes companies take their financial lump in one quarter to get problems behind them, so one bad quarter doesn't necessarily indicate a harmful long-term trend.

Fundamental versus technical analysis

Throughout this chapter and Chapter 5, we talk a lot about the financial statements and analysis of a company — balance sheets, revenues, expenses, earnings, price/earnings ratios, and so on. Analyzing financial statements and making investing decisions based on them is known as *fundamental analysis.*

Another school of stock market analysis, known as *technical analysis,* exists. Folks who employ technical analysis like to examine chart patterns, volume, and all sorts of indicators that have little if anything to do with the underlying stock.

Technicians say things like "Stock XYZ has a major support area at $20 per share" and "Stock ABC has broken out above $30 per share." Although it may be a bit extreme to say that all the technicians who have ever existed have never produced anything of value, you can safely ignore this school of thinking. In fact,

ignoring the technicians will likely increase your stock market profits. Why? Because technical analysis thinking encourages a trader's, not an investor's, mindset.

Not surprisingly, most technicians come from one of two camps. Many technical analysts work for investment dealers and write daily, weekly, or monthly assessments of the entire stock market and some individual stocks. Recommendations and advice change over time, and the result is that you trade more. Not coincidentally, these investment dealers make more money the more you trade! Investment newsletter writers are the other big advocates of this Ouija-board approach to investment management. Again, it's a great system for the newsletter writers who hook you on a $200-per-year newsletter.

Proxy forms and information circulars

The final corporate documents that you may want to review are the annual *proxy form and information circular.* (In the United States, the two together are collectively called the *proxy statement.*) These are sent out in advance of a company's annual meeting. These documents contain important financial information and discussions, and also contain information on other corporate matters, such as the election of the board of directors. *Directors* — who are usually corporate executives, lawyers, accountants, and other supposedly knowledgeable luminaries — serve as sounding boards, counsellors, and sometimes overseers to the management team of a company.

A *proxy* is a power of attorney that transfers a shareholder's right to vote at a shareholders' meeting to someone else, typically the company's management. The information circular tells you who serves on the board of directors as well as how much they and the executives of the company are paid. It also must contain information on any important matters that will be under discussion, and the interest of management in these issues.

At annual meetings, where the board of directors discusses proxy statements, shareholders sometimes get angry and ask why the executives are paid so much when the company's stock price and business underperform. The proxy statement becomes much more important when a company faces a takeover or some other controversial corporate matter, such as the election of an alternative board of directors. As a shareholder, you get to vote on proposed board members and on select other corporate issues.

Getting Ready to Invest in Stocks

Especially during the tech boom of the late 1990s, amid the chorus of self-anointed gurus saying that you can make fat profits if you pick your own stocks, we sometimes thought that we were a lone voice urging caution and sensible thinking.

Unless you're extraordinarily lucky or unusually gifted at analyzing company and investor behaviour, you won't earn above-average returns if you select your own stocks.

For most people, it's wise to keep to a minimum — ideally, no more than 20 percent of your invested dollars — the amount that you dedicate to individual stock investments. We encourage you to do such investing for the educational value and enjoyment that you derive from it, not because you smugly think you're as skilled as the best professional money managers. (If you want to find out more about analyzing companies, read the chapters in Part IV on small business as well as the chapters about investing resources in Part V.)

Understanding stock prices

Just about every major financial and news site on the Internet offers stock quotes, usually for free as a lure to get you to visit the site. To view a stock price quote online, all you need is the security's trading symbol (which you obtain by using the stock symbol lookup feature universally offered with online quote services). Many major newspapers print a listing of the prior day's stock prices, while some — notably *The Globe and Mail* — have stopped this practice given how readily available the information is online. Cable business channels such as BNN, Bloomberg, CNBC, and Fox Business have stock quotes streaming across the bottom of the screen. You can stop by a local investment dealer office and see the current stock quotes whizzing by on a long, narrow screen on a wall. Many investment dealers also maintain publicly accessible terminals (that look a lot like a personal computer) on which you can obtain current quotes.

The following table is a typical example of the kinds of information that you can find in daily price quotes in papers and online — in this case, for Canadian National Railway (also known as CNR). After the name of the company, you see the trading symbol, CNR, which is the code that you and investment advisers use to look up the price on computer-based quotation systems.

Stock:	Canadian National Railway (CNR)
52-wk High	$58.44
52-wk Low	$42.51
Last Traded	15:32
Last Trade	$52.67
Net Change	$0.72
% Change	1.25%
Open	50.00
Day High	54.04
Day Low	49.15
Volume	2,184,562
P/E	11.70
Mkt Cap	$24,341 ($Mil)
Div/Shr	0.84
Yield	1.68

Here's a breakdown of what this information means:

- ✔ **52-Week Range:** These two numbers indicate the low ($42.51) and high ($58.44) trading prices for CNR during the past 52 weeks.

- ✔ **Last Trade:** This line indicates the most recent price that the stock traded at (you can see that we happened to get this CNR quote at 15:32, or 3:32 p.m. eastern standard time).

- ✔ **Change:** This entry indicates how that price differs from the previous day's close. In this case, you can see that the stock was up $0.72, (1.25 percent) from the prior day's close.

- ✔ **Day Range:** These two numbers are lowest and highest prices that the stock has traded at during the day.

- ✔ **Open:** This line tells you the first trade of the day.

- ✔ **Volume:** This number indicates the number of shares that traded up to this point in the trading day. (To conserve space, many newspapers indicate the volume in hundreds of shares — in other words, you must add two zeros to the end of the number to arrive at the actual number of shares.)

- ✔ **The P/E ratio:** As we explain in Chapters 4 and 5, the P/E ratio measures the price of CNR's stock relative to the company's earnings or profits.

- ✔ **Market capitalization:** This tells you the current market value of all of CNR's stock, which in this case is $24.3 billion. It is arrived at by multiplying the current price per share by the total number of shares outstanding. (See Chapter 8 for an explanation of so-called market caps as they apply to stocks and stock funds.)

- ✔ **Dividends/share:** This shows you the current dividend, which in this case is $0.84 per share, that the company pays yearly to shareholders. Most companies actually pay out one-quarter of their total annual dividend every three months.

- ✔ **Yield:** This number indicates the effective percentage yield that the stock's dividend produces. To calculate the effective yield, divide the dividend by the current stock price. Thus, CNR shareholders can expect to receive a dividend worth about 1.7 percent of the current stock price.

Now you know how to read stock quotes!

Purchasing stock "direct" from companies

Over the years, increasing numbers of companies have begun to sell their stock directly to the public. Proponents of these direct stock purchase plans say that you can invest in stocks without paying any commissions. However, some plans do charge fees, and may also require that your initial purchase be several hundred dollars.

Investing in such plans poses other challenges. In particular, you typically have to own shares in the company, and those shares must be registered in your name. These plans also typically allow you to have any dividends automatically reinvested and used to buy you more shares in the company. However, many discount brokers also allow you to reinvest dividends at no cost.

Some direct stock purchase plans entail even more hassle and cost, forcing you to buy your initial shares through an investment adviser and then transfer your shares to the issuing company in order to buy more!

Every time that you want to set up a stock purchase plan with a company, you must request and complete the company's application forms. If you go through the headache of doing so, say, a dozen times, you're rewarded with a dozen statements on a regular basis from each individual company. Frankly, because of this drawback alone, we prefer to buy stock through a discount brokerage account that allows centralized purchasing and holding of various stocks as well as consolidated tax-reporting statements.

Placing your trade through an investment adviser

Unless you decide to buy stock directly, you generally need an investment adviser. As we explain in Chapter 9, discount brokers are the best way to go — they take your orders and charge far less than conventional investment dealers, which pay their advisers on commission.

After you decide which discount broker you want to use (again, we provide all the info you need to make this decision in Chapter 9), request (by phone or via the Internet) an account application package for the type of account that you desire (non-retirement, RRSP, TFSA, RESP, and so on). Complete the forms (call the firm's toll-free number or visit a branch office if you get stuck) and mail or take them back to the discounter. Many institutions also allow you to apply online.

When it comes time to place your order, simply go online (or call the discount broker). You have two options:

- **Market order:** Our advice is to place what's known as a market order. Such an order instructs your investment adviser to buy you the amount of stock that you desire (100 shares, for example) at the current and best (lowest) price available.

- **Limit order:** Alternatively, you can try to buy a desired stock at a specific price — for example, you can place a purchase order at $32 per share when the stock's last trade was $33 per share. This type of order is known as a *limit order* and is good until you cancel it. (You can also make it a *day* order, meaning it will expire if it isn't filled at your requested price by the end of that day's trading.) We don't recommend that you try this tactic because it requires you to hope and gamble that the stock drops a little before it rises. If the stock simply rises from its current price of $33 per share or drops to $32.10 before it makes a big move higher, you may kick yourself. If you think that the stock is a good buy for the long haul, go buy it with a market order. If you don't think it's a good buy, don't buy it.

One final word of advice: Try to buy stock in good-size chunks, such as 100 shares. Otherwise, commissions gobble a larger percentage of the small dollar amount that you invest. If you don't have enough money to build a diversified portfolio all at once, don't sweat it. Diversify over time. Purchase a chunk of one stock after you have enough money accumulated and then wait to buy the next stock until you've saved another chunk to invest.

Chapter 7

Exploring Bonds and Other Lending Investments

L *ending investments* are those in which you lend your money to an organization, a bank, credit union, company, or government, which typically pays you a set or fixed rate of interest. (*Ownership investments,* by contrast, provide partial ownership of a company or some other asset, such as real estate, that has the ability to generate revenue and potential profits.)

If you really want to make your money grow, lending investments aren't for you. However, even the most aggressive investors should consider placing some of their money into lending investments. Table 7-1 shows when such investments do make sense and when they don't.

Table 7-1	Lending and Ownership Investments Compared
Consider Lending Investments If . . .	*Consider Ownership Investments When . . .*
You need current income from your savings.	You don't need or want much current income from your savings.
You expect to sell the investments within five years.	You're investing for the long term (seven to ten-plus years).
Investment volatility makes you a wreck or you just want to cushion some of the volatility of your other investments.	You don't mind or can ignore significant ups and downs.
You don't need to make your money grow after inflation and taxes.	You need more growth to reach your goals.

Lending investments are available everywhere — from banks, credit unions, investment dealers, insurance companies, and mutual fund companies. Lending investments that you may have heard of include regular bank savings accounts, high-interest savings accounts, guaranteed investment certificates *(GICs)*, treasury bills and other bonds, bond mutual funds (and now exchange-traded bond funds), and mortgages.

In this chapter, we walk you through these investments and explain what's good and bad about each of them and when you should and shouldn't use them. We also tell you what to look for (and look out for) when comparing them.

Banks: The Cost of Feeling Secure

Putting your money in a bank may make you feel safe for a variety of reasons. If you're like most people, your first investing experience was at your neighbourhood bank where you opened up a chequing or savings account.

Part of the comfort of keeping money in the bank stems from the fact that the bank is where many of our parents first steered us financially. Also, at a local branch, often within walking distance of your home or office, you find vaults, security-monitoring cameras, and sometimes security guards. Most of these latter accoutrements shouldn't make you feel safer about leaving your money with the bank — they're needed because of the risk of bank robberies. Consider that the next time you pay a visit to your local bank.

Bank branches cost a lot of money to operate. Guess where that money comes from? From bank depositors, of course! That's one of the reasons why the interest rates that banks pay often pale in comparison to other equally secure alternatives.

The realities of bank insurance

Some people are consoled by the Canada Deposit Insurance Corporation (CDIC) insurance that comes with bank accounts. It's true that if your bank fails, certain deposits — generally the savings accounts, chequing accounts, and GICs that mature in five years or less — you have with a member institution of the CDIC are insured up to a total of $100,000. So what, we say. Any Treasury bill is issued and backed by the federal government. Plenty of other equally safe lending investments yield higher returns.

Many credit unions offer unlimited deposit insurance!

Just because a bank is a member of the CDIC — a Crown corporation — doesn't mean that your money is 100 percent safe in the event of a bank failure. Although you're insured for $100,000 in a bank, if the bank crashes, you may wait quite a while to get your money back — and you may well get less interest than you thought you would.

Any investment that involves lending your money to someone else or to some organization carries risk. That includes putting your money in a bank or buying a Treasury bill (T-Bill) that the federal government issues. Although we're not doomsayers, any student of history knows that even governments and civilizations fail.

The overused guaranteed investment certificate (GIC)

Other than savings accounts, banks also sell guaranteed investment certificates (GICs). GICs are without a doubt the most overused bank investment around. The attraction is that you usually get a higher rate of return on a GIC than on a regular bank savings account or money market fund. And, unlike a bond, which we discuss in the "Why Bother with Bonds?" section, later in this chapter, a GIC's principal value doesn't fluctuate. GICs, if you meet the requirements, also give you the peace of mind — up to $100,000 — afforded by the CDIC insurance program.

The reason that GICs pay higher interest rates than savings accounts is that you commit to tie up your money for a period of time, such as 6, 12, or 24 months. The bank pays you 2 to 3 percent and then turns around and lends your money to people through credit cards, auto loans, and the like, and charges the borrower an interest rate of 6 to 16 percent. Not a bad business, eh?

When you tie up your money in a GIC, and later you decide you want it back before the GIC matures, a hefty penalty is shaved from your return. With other lending investments, such as bonds and bond mutual funds (discussed in the section "Why Bother with Bonds?" later in this chapter), you can access your money without penalty and generally at little or no cost.

In addition to penalties for early withdrawal, GICs yield less than a high-quality bond with a comparable maturity (for example, two, three, or five years). Often, the yield difference is 1 percent or more, especially if you don't shop around and simply buy GICs from the local bank where you keep your chequing account.

You can earn higher returns and have better access to your money in bonds than in GICs. GICs make the most sense when you know, for example, that you want to invest your money for one year, after which you need the money for some purchase that you expect to make. Just make sure that you shop around to get the best interest rate. Begin by simply asking for a better rate than the posted rate at your bank or trust company. If you do a reasonable amount of other business with your financial institution, or are simply a good bargainer, you may be able to get an increase of half a percent or even more. To get a sense of what the competition is offering, you'll find sample GIC rates in the financial section of many newspapers. A number of sites, including www.money sense.ca and money.canoe.ca/rates, offer extensive lists of up-to-date GIC rates. If having the CDIC insurance gives you peace of mind, take a look at Government of Canada bonds, which we discuss later in this chapter. These bonds usually pay as much interest as the vast majority of GICs available.

The money market fund alternative to savings accounts

You likely have a chequing account at a local bank that you use to pay household bills and to access cash through bank machines. But beyond keeping enough money in your chequing account to pay the bills, it doesn't pay to keep extra savings in the bank.

Keep your chequing account at one of the big banks or a credit union, but not your extra savings, including your emergency funds. Because bank savings accounts generally pay pretty crummy interest rates, you're better off stashing any extra cash elsewhere. Two good choices are a money market mutual fund and a high-interest savings account.

Money market funds, which are a type of mutual fund (other funds focus on bonds or stocks), are a great place to keep your extra savings. Money market funds offer a higher-yielding alternative to bank savings and bank money market deposit accounts.

Money market fund advantages

The best money market mutual funds offer several significant benefits over bank savings accounts. The biggest advantage is higher yields. Money market mutual funds pay higher yields because they don't have the high overhead that banks do. The most efficient mutual fund companies (we discuss them in Chapter 8) don't have scads of branch offices. Another reason that banks can get away with paying lower yields is that they know that many depositors believe that the CDIC insurance that comes with a bank savings account makes it safer than a money market mutual fund. Also, the CDIC insurance is an expense that banks ultimately pass on to their customers.

Another useful feature of money market mutual funds is that some allow you to write cheques, without charge, against your account. Most mutual fund companies require that the cheques that you write be for larger amounts — typically at least $250. They don't want you using these accounts to pay all of your small household bills because cheques cost money to process.

Money market funds are a good place to keep your emergency cash reserve of at least three to six months' living expenses. They're also a great place to keep money awaiting investment elsewhere in the near future. If you're saving money for a home that you expect to purchase soon (in the next year or so), a money market fund can be a safe place to accumulate and grow the down payment. You don't want to risk placing such money in the stock market, because the market can plunge in a relatively short period of time.

Money market funds, which are offered by mutual fund companies (see Chapter 8), are unique among mutual funds because they don't fluctuate in value and maintain a fixed $10-per-share price. As with a bank savings account, your principal investment in a money market fund doesn't change in value. If you invest your money in a money market fund, it earns *dividends* (which is just another name for the interest you would receive in a bank account).

Money market funds lack insurance

So what's the catch? Good money market funds actually don't have any, but you need to know about one difference between bank accounts and money market mutual funds: Money market funds aren't insured. As we discuss earlier in this chapter, bank accounts and GIC deposits come with CDIC insurance that protects your deposited money up to $100,000 per person for each separate financial institution you deal with. So if a bank fails because it lends too much money to people and companies that go bankrupt or abscond with the funds, you should get your money back from the CDIC.

The lack of CDIC insurance on a money market fund shouldn't trouble you. Mutual fund companies can't fail because they have a dollar invested in securities for every dollar that you deposit in their money funds. By contrast, banks are required to have available just a fraction of every dollar that you hand over to them.

A money market fund's investments can decline slightly in value, which can cause the money market fund's share price to fall below a dollar. In a few cases, money market funds have bought some bad investments. However, in each and every case except one, the parent company running the money market fund infused cash into the affected fund, thus enabling it to maintain the $1-per-share price.

One U.S. money market fund did "break the buck." It didn't take money in from people like you or us but was run by a bunch of small banks for themselves. This money market fund made some boneheaded investments. The share price of the fund declined by 6 percent, and the fund owners decided to disband the fund; they didn't bail it out because they would only have been repaying themselves.

Stick with bigger mutual fund companies if you're worried about the lack of CDIC insurance. They have the financial wherewithal and the largest incentive to save a foundering money market fund. Fortunately, the bigger fund companies have the best money funds anyway. You can find more details about money market funds in Chapter 8.

High-interest savings accounts

In many cases, you may be looking for a place where you can simply keep some money on stash. Perhaps you know you'll need to tap into it in the short term. Or maybe you want a place to put your emergency funds that will ensure your capital is protected but still earn you a decent return. High-interest savings accounts offer a great, and in some ways superior, alternative to money market funds.

High-interest savings accounts are typically made available by institutions that don't have — and don't have plans to build — a nationwide string of bricks-and-mortar branches. This saves them substantially on staffing and other overhead. As a result, they're able to offer interest rates that equal and even surpass those offered by money market funds. They generally have no minimum balance requirements, and offer other benefits not available with money market mutual funds. These benefits can include the convenience of telephone and online transactions, as well as access to your money through bank machines, often with no fees attached.

Although the idea of dealing at arm's length with a company that doesn't have a branch on your local street corner may seem a little unsettling, you need not worry. These accounts are not fly-by-night operations. President's Choice Financial, for example, is a co-venture between Loblaw Ltd. and Canadian Imperial Bank of Commerce, while ING Direct Bank is a division of International Nederlanden Groep, a Dutch bank. They also come with CDIC insurance, which protects you up to $100,000. Other institutions that offer high-interest savings accounts are Achieva Financial, Canadian Tire Financial, Citizens Bank, HSBC, ICICI Bank, Manulife Bank, Outlook Financial, RBC, and Vancity. The discount brokerage Scotia iTrade also offers a high-interest savings account, as does Altamira, the fund company.

To open an account, you need to fill out an application and send in a cheque. You can then set up your account so that money can be electronically moved back and forth between your regular bank or trust account and your high-interest account. You arrange deposits and withdrawals over the telephone or on the Internet. The transaction in most cases is completed by midnight of the next business day after you place your order. You can even arrange to have your paycheque deposited directly.

Profiting from a Tax-Free Savings Account

As long as you don't need to regularly access the money, consider a high-interest savings account or money market account that is inside a *Tax-Free Savings Account* (TFSA) wrapper. This saves you the tax you would have to otherwise pay on the interest you earn, which if earned outside a tax-deferred account or plan is taxed at your marginal tax rate.

You can put up to a maximum of $5,000 into a TFSA each year. If you put in less in any year, the unused portion gets added on to what you can contribute in the future. TFSAs came into being at the beginning of 2009, and most of the high-interest savings account choices we've listed offer the option to earn these higher rates inside a TFSA. (For more about TFSAs, refer to Chapter 3.)

Why Bother with Bonds?

Conservative investors (that is, conservative when it comes to taking risk, not when professing their political orientation) prefer bonds. Otherwise-aggressive investors who seek diversification or investments for shorter-term financial goals also prefer bonds. The reason: Bonds offer higher yields than bank accounts, usually without as much volatility as the stock market.

Bonds are similar to GICs, except that bonds are securities that trade in the market with a fluctuating value. For example, you can purchase a bond, scheduled to mature five years from now, that a company such as Bombardier, the maker of moving things from snowmobiles to planes and trains, issues. A Bombardier five-year bond may pay you 6 percent interest. The company sends you interest payments on the bond for five years. And as long as Bombardier doesn't have a financial catastrophe, the company returns your original investment to you after the five years is up. So in effect, you're lending your money to Bombardier (instead of the bank when you deposit money in a bank account).

The worst that can happen to your bond investment is that Bombardier's business goes into a tailspin and the company ends up in financial ruin — also known as bankruptcy. If that happens, you may lose all of your original investment and miss out on the remaining interest payments you were supposed to receive.

But bonds that high-quality companies such as Bombardier issue are quite safe — they rarely default. Besides, you don't have to invest all of your money in just one or two bonds. If you own bonds in many companies and one bond unexpectedly takes a hit, it affects only a small portion of your portfolio. And unlike GICs, you can generally sell your bonds any time you desire at minimal cost. (Selling and buying most bond mutual funds costs nothing, as we explain in Chapter 8.)

Bond investors accept the risk of default because bonds generally pay you more than bank savings and money market mutual funds, but there's a catch. As we discuss later in this chapter, bonds are riskier than money market funds and savings accounts because their value can fall if interest rates rise. Plus you're forgoing the security of CDIC insurance as compared to bank accounts. However, bonds tend to be more stable in value than stocks. (We cover the risks and returns of bonds and stocks in Chapter 2.)

Investing in bonds is a time-honoured way to earn a better rate of return on money that you don't plan to use within the next couple of years or more. As with stocks, bonds can generally be sold any day that the financial markets are open. Because their value fluctuates, though, you're more likely to lose money if you're forced to sell your bonds sooner rather than later. In the short term, if the bond market happens to fall and you need to sell, you could lose money. In the longer term, as is the case with stocks, you're far less likely to lose money.

Don't put your emergency cash reserve into bonds — that's what a money market fund or bank savings account is for. And don't put too much of your longer-term investment money into bonds, either. As we explain in Chapter 2, bonds are generally inferior investments for making your money grow. Growth-oriented investments, such as stocks, real estate, and your own business, hold the greatest potential to build real wealth.

The following list provides some common financial goals and reasons why investing some money in bonds can make sense:

- **A major purchase:** This purchase, such as buying a home or some other major expenditure, should be one that won't happen for at least two years. Shorter-term bonds may work for you as a higher-yielding and slightly riskier alternative to money market funds.

✔ **Diversification:** Bonds don't move in tandem with the performance of other types of investments, such as stocks. In fact, in a terrible economic environment (such as during the Great Depression and 2008–2009), bonds may appreciate in value while riskier investments such as stocks plunge.

✔ **Retirement investments:** You may invest some of your money in bonds as part of a longer-term investment strategy, such as for retirement. You should have an overall plan for how you want to invest your money, sometimes referred to as an *asset allocation strategy* (see Chapter 8). Aggressive, younger investors should keep less of their retirement money in bonds than older folks who are nearing retirement.

✔ **Income-producing investments:** If you're retired or not working, bonds can be useful because they're better at producing current income than many other investments.

Assessing the Different Types of Bonds

Bonds aren't as complicated and unique as people, but they're certainly more complex than a bank savings account. And thanks to shady marketing practices by some investing companies and salespeople who sell bonds, you can have your work cut out for you while trying to get a handle on what many bonds really are and how they differ from their peers.

Bonds differ from one another according to a number of factors — length of time to maturity, interest rate, credit quality, and the entities that issue the bonds. After you have a handle on these issues, you're ready to consider investing in individual bonds and bond mutual funds.

Determining when you get your money back: Maturity matters

Maturity simply means the time at which the bond promises to pay back your principal — next year, in 5 years, in 30 years, and so on. You need to care how long it takes a bond to mature because a bond's maturity gives you a good (although far-from-perfect) sense of how volatile a bond may be if interest rates change. If interest rates fall, bond prices rise; if interest rates rise, bond prices fall. Longer-term bonds drop more in price when the overall level of interest rates rises.

Suppose you're considering investing in two bonds that the same organization issues and that both yield 7 percent. The bonds differ from one another only in when they will mature: One is a 2-year bond; the other, a 20-year bond. If interest rates were to rise just 1 percent (from 7 percent to 8 percent), the 2-year bond might decline about 2 percent in value, whereas the 20-year bond could fall approximately five times as much — 10 percent.

If you hold a bond until it matures, you get your principal back unless the issuer defaults. In the meantime, however, if interest rates rise, bond prices fall. The reason is simple: If the bond that you hold is issued at, say, 7 percent, and interest rates on similar bonds rise to 8 percent, no one (unless they don't know any better) wants to purchase your 7 percent bond. The value of your bond has to decrease enough so that it effectively yields 8 percent.

Bonds are generally classified by the length of time until maturity:

- **Short-term bonds** mature in the next few years.

- **Intermediate-term bonds** come due within three to ten years.

- **Long-term bonds** mature in more than 10 years and generally up to 30 years. Although rare, a number of companies issue 100-year bonds! A number of railroads did, as well as Coca-Cola, Disney, Nova Scotia Power, IBM, the New York Port Authority, and the government of China! Such bonds are quite dangerous to purchase, especially if they're issued during a period of relatively low interest rates.

Most of the time, longer-term bonds pay higher yields than short-term bonds. You can look at a chart of the current yield of similar bonds plotted against when they mature — such a chart is known as a *yield curve*. At most times, this curve slopes upward. Investors generally demand a higher rate of interest for taking the risk of holding longer-term bonds. Most financial newspapers, magazines, and Web sites carry a current chart of the yield curve.

Weighing the likelihood of default

In addition to being issued for various lengths of time, bonds differ from one another in the creditworthiness of the issuer. Every year, billions of dollars' worth of bonds default (that sounds like a lot, but it's a small fraction of the multi-trillion-dollar bond market). To minimize investing in bonds that default, purchase highly rated bonds. Credit rating agencies such as Moody's, Standard & Poor's, Fitch, and Duff & Phelps rate the credit quality and likelihood of default of bonds.

The *credit rating* of a bond depends on the issuer's (company or government) ability to pay back its debt. Bond credit ratings are usually done on some sort of a letter-grade scale, for example, where AAA is the highest rating, with ratings descending through AA and A, followed by BBB, BB, B, CCC, CC, C, and so on.

- ✔ **AAA- and AA-rated bonds** are considered *high-grade* or *high-credit quality bonds*. Such bonds possess little chance — a fraction of 1 percent — of default.

- ✔ **A- and BBB-rated bonds** are considered *investment-grade* or *general-quality bonds*.

- ✔ **BB- or lower-rated bonds** are known as *junk bonds* (or by their marketed name, *high-yield bonds*). Junk bonds, also known as *non-investment grade,* are more likely to default — perhaps as many as a couple of percent per year actually default.

You may ask yourself why any right-minded investor would buy a bond with a low credit rating. That's because companies pay a higher interest rate on lower-quality bonds to attract investors. The lower a bond's credit rating and quality, the higher the yield you can and should expect from such a bond. Poorer-quality bonds, though, aren't for the faint of heart because they're generally more volatile in value.

We don't recommend buying individual junk bonds — consider investing in these only through a well-run junk-bond fund.

Examining the issuers

Bonds also differ from one another according to the type of organization that issues them — in other words, what kind of organization you lend your money to. The following sections go over the major options and let you know when each option may make sense for you.

Treasury bills

Treasury bills, or T-bills, are short-term government bonds available for terms of 3, 6, and 12 months. The federal government as well as some provinces issue T-bills in large denominations, but many financial institutions repackage them and make them available to the public in amounts as small as $1,000.

T-bills don't pay any actual interest. Instead, you purchase them at a discount to their face value. Your return — in effect, the interest you make — is the difference between your purchase price and the face value, which you receive at maturity. You'll usually see this return displayed as an interest rate by most financial institutions. This is done simply as a way to help you assess the return you'll make.

Government of Canada bonds

In addition to Treasury bills, the federal government — Canada's biggest debtor of them all — issues marketable bonds. These can be bought in denominations as low as $1,000. Government of Canada marketable bonds — like most bonds — are usually quoted as a price per $100 of the value at maturity of the bond. Interest on Government of Canada bonds is paid twice a year.

The best use of T-bills and Government of Canada Bonds is in place of bank GICs. If you feel secure with the CDIC insurance that a bank GIC provides (up to $100,000 of your investments in qualifying accounts and GICs with any one financial institution), check out a T-bill or federal marketable bond. Government of Canada bonds sometimes pay the same or better interest rate as a GIC that matures in the same length of time. If you hunt around, you may stumble upon a bank that pays a slightly higher interest rate than a comparable marketable bond. Unless you really shop around for a GIC, you'll likely earn a lower return on a GIC than on a marketable bond. No commission is charged for buying or selling these securities. Instead, brokers make their money by building a commission into the price of the bond.

Canada Savings Bonds

Buying Canada Savings Bonds (CSBs) every year used to be an almost patriotic habit to keep. Their name and image may leave you feeling slightly warm and fuzzy, but in most cases, you are better off with a high-interest savings account or a GIC.

If you cash in CSBs within three months of the issue date, you get only your original investment back. You can get the same easy access to your money with a high-interest savings account, which also offers much better returns.

CSBs are often thought of as a good choice for a short-term investment when you want to earn a decent return on your money while having the option to cash out at any time. When you cash them in you get back your original investment, known as the face amount, as well as the interest that has been earned up to the end of the previous month. (If you cash in your CSBs before they mature, try to do it at the beginning rather than the end of a month to maximize your interest.)

The interest rate on CSBs is guaranteed for at least one year. When interest rates are climbing, the government sometimes also guarantees minimum rates for a set period. Because they can be cashed in at any time, CSBs offer another useful feature: If interest rates rise, the government often resets their rates to keep them attractive and prevent large-scale redemptions.

You have to pay tax each year on the interest earned on CSBs issued from 1990 onwards. This applies even if you choose the compound-interest option. For compound-interest CSBs purchased before 1990, you can choose to declare earned interest once every three years.

Canada Savings Bonds: The details

Unlike other bonds, Canada Savings Bonds (CSBs) are registered in your name. You can't sell them to others, including your investment adviser, or on the bond market. CSBs go on sale every fall, when they're made available for several weeks up to several months, depending on anticipated demand. You can buy them from almost all financial institutions, including banks, trust companies, and credit unions. You can also buy them from most investment dealers and discount brokers.

Two basic types of Canada Savings Bonds are available: regular-interest bonds and compound-interest bonds. Regular-interest bonds pay interest annually until they mature on the anniversary of the issue date or when you redeem them. You can have the interest sent to you by cheque or deposited directly into your bank account. Regular-interest bonds come in denominations of $300, $500, $1,000, $5,000, and $10,000.

With the second type of CSBs, compound-interest bonds, instead of paying out the interest, it is automatically reinvested and added to your original principal until your bonds mature or you cash them in. Compound-interest bonds can be bought in denominations of $100, $300, $1,000, $5,000, and $10,000. Many companies set up purchase plans so that you can buy them through automatic deductions from your paycheque. Compound-interest CSBs issued since 1990 require that you pay tax on the interest earned each year, even though you don't actually receive the money.

Compound-interest bonds, unlike regular-interest bonds, also give you the option of holding them inside a self-directed RRSP or RRIF. If you don't have a self-directed RRSP, you can designate that you want to hold your CSBs in an RRSP when you make your purchase. The government will create what's called The Canada RSP — a no-fee plan in which you can hold your CSBs and benefit from tax-free growth. You can also contribute other CSBs you may have into this account. CSBs can also be held inside a Tax-Free Savings Account.

A new type of CSB was introduced in 1998 called the *Canada Premium Bond*, or CPB. You can buy a CPB for as little as $100. Unlike regular CSBs, Canada Premium Bonds can only be redeemed for a short period each year — on the anniversary of the issue date and for the following 30 days. In return for this lack of liquidity compared with regular CSBs, Canada Premium Bonds come with a slightly higher rate of interest. If you hold CSBs inside a Canada RRIF — a registered retirement income fund set up with the government to hold your CSBs — you can cash them in order to meet your minimum mandatory RRIF withdrawals without paying a penalty. Canada Premium bonds are available as both regular-interest bonds and compound-interest bonds.

CSBs are often seen as a good choice for a short-term investment when you want to earn a decent return on your money while having the option to cash out at any time. However, you'll usually earn more with a high-interest savings account, which we discuss earlier on in this section. You can generally get close to double the interest rate available on CSBs with a high-interest savings account or a GIC. The rate of return on CSBs offered in the fall of 2008, for example, was just 2 percent. Inflation at the time was pegged at 3.5 percent. Meanwhile, high-interest savings accounts were offering 3 to 4 percent, about what GICs were paying.

Municipal bonds

Municipal bonds are city and regional government bonds that pay interest. The rate is typically better than what you'd receive from other bonds with a similar maturity. They also usually offer a better rate than that paid by GICs with a comparable term. Unlike a GIC, though, you're not locked in, and you can sell them when you want.

Corporate bonds

Companies such as Bell, Domtar, and SunLife issue corporate bonds. In the section "Understanding bond prices," later in this chapter, we show you how to read the newspaper listings for such bonds. If you buy corporate bonds through a well-managed mutual fund, an approach we advocate, you don't need to read the newspaper listings.

Mortgage bonds

Remember that mortgage you took out when you purchased your home? Well, you can actually purchase a bond to invest in a portfolio of mortgages just like yours! Many banks actually sell their mortgages as bonds in the financial markets, which allows other investors to invest in them. The mortgages are bundled together and sold as mortgage-backed securities, or MBSs. The Canada Mortgage and Housing Corporation, a government agency, usually guarantees repayment of principal on MBSs at the bond's maturity. MBSs are sometimes referred to as Cannie Maes, a play on *Ginnie Maes,* the nickname for the U.S. mortgage-backed securities called Government National Mortgage Associations certificates.

The majority of mortgage bonds are quite safe to invest in. The risky ones that were in the news in the late 2000s for defaulting were so-called subprime mortgages, which lacked government agency backing.

Convertible bonds

Convertible bonds are hybrid securities — they're bonds that you can convert under specified circumstances into a preset number of shares in the company that issued the bond. Although these bonds do pay interest, their yield is lower than nonconvertible bonds because convertibles offer you the upside potential of being able to make more money if the underlying stock rises.

Stripped bonds

You can also buy marketable bonds that don't pay any interest. These bonds have had their interest coupons removed, or stripped off, thus the name *stripped bonds,* or *strips.* Stripped bonds are sold at a discount to the face value. The difference between the price you pay to buy a stripped bond and its value when it matures is expressed as an annual yield.

One benefit of strips is that they save you from having to reinvest the twice-yearly interest payments if you aren't using the bond as a source of regular income. This same feature makes their market price respond much more dramatically to changes in general interest rate levels. If interest rates rise, for example, someone who is receiving semi-annual interest payments has a chance to put that income back to work at the higher available rates. An investor who holds a stripped bond, however, has all her money locked in at the lower rates that were available when she purchased the bond.

Similarly, if interest rates fall, the value of the stripped bond will rise higher than that of regular bonds. With a regular bond, some of the interest is being paid out that, if reinvested, will earn a lower rate of return than the original rate at which the stripped bond was sold. As a result, strip bonds are highly sensitive to interest rate changes, which is why we don't recommend them unless you plan on holding them until they mature.

If you hold stripped bonds until they mature, you don't have to worry about how their value fluctuates along the way. You know exactly what your yield will be when you purchase them, and you can simply tuck them away knowing your return is guaranteed.

One drawback to stripped bonds is that you have to declare the accrued interest each year as income, even though you don't actually receive any ongoing payments. As a result, they generally should be purchased only inside an RRSP, RESP, or TFSA, where you don't have to pay any tax on the accrued interest. Shopping around is important when buying strips.

Inflation-protected bonds

Bonds called Government of Canada Real Return Bonds, with an interest rate that fluctuates with the rate of inflation, are also available. Unlike the standard *fixed-coupon* marketable bonds that pay out a fixed amount of interest, the interest paid on Real Return Bonds is adjusted according to the cost of living, measured by the consumer price index.

Compared with traditional Government of Canada bonds, the inflation-indexed bonds carry a lower interest rate. The reason is that the other portion of your return with these inflation-indexed bonds comes from the inflation adjustment to the principal you invest, which gets added back into principal. For example, if inflation were 3 percent the first year you hold your inflation-indexed bond into which you invested $10,000, your principal would increase to $10,300 at the end of the first year.

International bonds

You can buy bonds outside the country that you call home. If you live in Canada, for example, you can buy most of the bonds that we describe in this chapter from foreign issuers as well. International bonds are riskier to you because their interest payments can be offset by currency price changes.

The prices of foreign bonds tend not to move in tandem with Canadian bonds. Foreign bond

values benefit from, and thus protect against, a declining Canadian dollar and, therefore, offer some diversification value. That said, foreign bonds aren't a vital holding for a diversified portfolio. Foreign bonds are generally more expensive to purchase and hold than comparable domestic bonds.

What's appealing about these bonds is that no matter what happens with the rate of inflation, investors who buy inflation-indexed bonds will always earn some return (the yield or interest rate paid) above and beyond the rate of inflation. Thus, holders of inflation-indexed Government of Canada bonds won't have the purchasing power of their principal or interest eroded by high inflation.

Because inflation-indexed bonds protect the investor from the ravages of inflation, they represent a less risky security. As we discuss in Chapter 2, lower risk usually translates into lower returns.

Buying Bonds

You can invest in bonds in one of two major ways: You can purchase individual bonds, or you can invest in a professionally selected and managed portfolio of bonds via a bond mutual fund (newer exchange-traded funds are a twist on mutual funds). In this section, we help you make that decision and promptly send you to Chapter 8 should you fall on the side of mutual funds. If you want to take the individual-bond route, we cover that path here, where we explain how to decipher bond listings, which you find in financial newspapers or online, and the purchasing process.

Deciding between individual bonds and bond mutual funds

Unless the bonds you're considering purchasing are easy to analyze and homogeneous (such as Government of Canada bonds), you're generally better off investing in bonds through a mutual fund. The first reason is diversification. You shouldn't put your money into a small number of bonds that companies in the same industry issue or that mature at the same time. It's difficult to cost-effectively build a diversified bond portfolio with individual issues unless you have a substantial amount of money ($50,000) that you want to invest in bonds.

If you purchase individual bonds through an investment dealer, you're going to pay a commission. In most cases, the commission cost is hidden — the dealer quotes you a price for the bond that includes the commission. Even if you use a discount broker, these fees take a healthy bite out of your investment. The smaller the amount that you invest, the bigger the bite — on a $1,000 bond, the commission fee can equal up to 5 percent. Commissions take a smaller bite out of larger bonds — perhaps less than 0.5 percent if you use discount brokers.

The best reason to invest in bond funds instead of individual bonds is that you've got better things to do with your time. Do you really want to research bonds and go bond shopping? Bonds are boring! And bonds and the companies that stand behind them aren't that simple to understand. For example, did you know that some bonds can be called before their maturity date? Companies often *call* bonds (which means they repay the principal before maturity) to save money if interest rates drop significantly. After you purchase a bond, you need to do the same things that a good bond mutual fund portfolio manager needs to do, such as track the issuer's creditworthiness and monitor other important financial developments.

A final reason to invest in bonds through a mutual fund is that it's cost effective. Great bond funds are yours for less than 1 percent per year in operating expenses. Selecting good bond funds isn't hard, as we explain in Chapter 8.

Understanding bond prices

Business-focused publications, such as *The Wall Street Journal,* provide daily bond pricing. For Canadian bonds you'll need to speak with an investment adviser or access your investment dealer account online. Most Canadian newspapers no longer regularly carry bond quotes, and unlike stock quotes, bond quotes aren't generally available for free online. The following steps walk you through the bond listing for PhilEl (Philadelphia Electric), shown in Figure 7-1:

1. **Bond name:** This tells you who issued the bond. In this case, the issuer is a large utility company, Philadelphia Electric.
2. **Funny numbers after company name:** The first part of the numerical sequence here — 7⅛ — refers to the original interest rate (7.125 percent) that this bond paid when it was issued. This interest rate is known as the *coupon rate,* which is a percentage of the maturity value of the bond. The second part of the numerical sequence — 23 — refers to the year that the bond matures (2023, in this case).
3. **Current yield:** Divide the interest paid, 7.125, by the current price per bond, $93, to arrive at the current yield. In this case, it equals (rounded off) 7.7 percent.
4. **Volume:** Indicates the number of bonds that traded on this day.
5. **Close:** Shows the last price the bond traded at.
6. **Change:** Indicates how this day's close compares with the previous day's close. In this case, this bond rose 2⅛ points. Some bonds don't trade all that often. Notice that some bonds were up and others were down on this particular day. The demand of new buyers and the supply of interested sellers influence the price movement of a given bond.

REMEMBER

In addition to the direction of overall interest rates, changes in the financial health of the company that stands behind the bond strongly affect the price of an individual bond.

Bonds	Cur Yld	Vol	Close	Net Chg.
PacTT 7¼08	7.3	30	100	...
ParCm 7s03A	7.5	30	93⅛	− ¾
ParCm 7s03B	7.5	5	93⅞	+ ⅞
Pathmk zr03	...	20	66½	− ⅜
Paten 8¼12	cv	69	88½	+ 2
PaylCsh 9⅛03	12.1	1128	75¾	− 1
PennTr 9⅝05	11.6	291	82¾	− ⅛
Pennzl 6½03	5.5	15	119¼	...
Pepsic 7⅝98	7.4	5	103⅝	− ⅛
PhilEl 7⅛23	7.7	15	93	+ 2⅛ — Philadelphia Electric
PhilPt 7.92s23	8.0	75	99½	+ 1
Pier1 6⅞02	cv	80	104	+ 2½
PionFn 8s00	cv	10	128½	+ ¼
PotEl 5s02	cv	57	90	...
Primark 8¾00	8.6	15	101⅞	+ 1
PSEG 6½04	6.7	25	97¼	− ½
PSEG 7½23	7.6	102	99	+ 1⅜
RJR Nb 8s00	7.8	47	102½	+ ¾
RJR Nb 8⅝02	8.4	25	103⅛	...
RJR Nb 7⅝03	7.9	224	96¾	+ ¼
RJR Nb 8¾05	8.6	5	101⅞	+ ½
RJR Nb 8⅞07	8.7	52	101½	+ ½
RJR Nb 9¼13	9.1	84	101⅞	+ ½
RJR Nb 8.3s99	8.1	34	103	...
RJR Nb 8¾04	8.5	43	102½	+ ¼
Rallys 9⅞00	16.7	395	59	− 1
RalsP 9½16	9.1	34	103⅞	+ ⅛
RalsP 9⅜16	9.0	10	103¾	− ⅝
RalsP 8⅝22	8.0	40	108⅜	+ ⅞

Figure 7-1: Sample bond listings.

Buying individual bonds

With the exception of Government of Canada bonds, purchasing most types of individual bonds, such as corporate and mortgage bonds, is a treacherous and time-consuming undertaking. Here's our advice for doing it right and minimizing the chance of a catastrophic mistake:

- ✔ **Don't be suckered into high yields — buy quality.** Yes, junk bonds pay higher yields, but they also have a much higher chance of default. And did you know what a subprime mortgage was before reporters were all over the news in 2007 and 2008 saying that defaults were on the rise? *Subprime mortgages* are mortgage loans made to borrowers with lower credit ratings who pay higher interest rates because of their higher risk of default. Nothing personal, but you're not going to do as good a job as a professional money manager at spotting problems and red flags. Stick with highly rated bonds so you don't have to worry about and suffer through these unfortunate consequences.

- ✔ **Understand that bonds may be called.** Many bonds, especially corporate bonds, can legally be called before maturity. This means that the bond issuer pays you back early, because it doesn't need to borrow as much money or because interest rates have fallen and the borrower wants to reissue new bonds at a lower interest rate. Be especially careful about purchasing bonds that were issued at higher interest rates than those that currently prevail. Borrowers pay off such bonds first.

- ✔ **Diversify.** Invest and hold bonds from a variety of companies in different industries to buffer changes in the economy that adversely affect one industry or a few industries more than others. Of the money that you want to invest in bonds, don't put more than 5 percent into any one bond. That means that you need to hold at least 20 bonds. Diversification requires a good chunk of change to invest given the size of most bonds and because high fees erode your investment balance if you invest too little. If you can't achieve this level of diversification, use a bond mutual fund.

- ✔ **Shop around.** Just like when you buy a car, shop around for good prices on the bonds that you have in mind. The hard part is doing an apples-to-apples comparison because different investment dealers may not be able to offer the same exact bond as other dealers. Remember that the two biggest determinants of what a bond should yield are its maturity date and its credit rating (both of which we discuss earlier in this chapter).

Unless you invest in boring, simple-to-understand bonds such as Government of Canada bonds, you're better off investing in bonds via the best bond mutual funds. One exception is if you absolutely, positively must receive your principal back on a certain date. Because bond funds don't mature, individual bonds with the correct maturity for you may best suit your needs. Consider Government of Canada bonds because they carry such low default risk. Otherwise, you need a lot of time, money, and patience to invest well in individual bonds.

Out of sight: Fluctuations of mortgages, GICs, and T-bills

One of the allures of non-bond lending investments, such as private mortgages, GICs, and T-bills, is that they don't fluctuate in value — at least not that you can see. Such investments appear safer and less volatile. You can't watch your principal fluctuate in value because you can't look up the value daily, the way you can with bonds and stocks.

But the principal values of your mortgage, GIC, and T-bill investments really do fluctuate; you just don't see the fluctuations! As we explain in the section "Determining when you get your money back: Maturity matters," earlier in this chapter, just as the market value of a bond

drops when interest rates rise, so does the market value of these investments, and for the same reasons. At higher interest rates, investors expect a discounted price on your fixed-interest rate investment because they always have the alternative of purchasing a new mortgage, GIC, or T-bill at the higher prevailing rates. Some of these investments are actually bought and sold (and behave just like bonds) among investors on what's known as a secondary market.

If the normal volatility of a bond's principal value makes you queasy, try not to follow your investments so closely!

Being Wary of Private Mortgages

In the section "Mortgage bonds," earlier in this chapter, we discuss investing in mortgages that resemble the ones that you take out to purchase a home. To directly invest in mortgages, you can lend your money to people who need money to buy or refinance real estate. Such loans are known as *mortgages* or *second mortgages,* in the case where your loan is second in line behind someone's primary mortgage.

Private mortgage investments appeal to investors who don't like the volatility of the stock and bond markets and aren't satisfied with the seemingly low returns on bonds or other common lending investments. Private mortgages sometimes seem to offer the best of both worlds — stock-market-like 10-plus percent returns without volatility.

Mortgage and real estate agents often arrange mortgage investments, so you must tread carefully because these people have a vested interest in seeing the deal done. Otherwise, the mortgage broker doesn't get paid for closing the loan, and the real estate broker doesn't get a commission for selling a property.

One broker who also happens to write about real estate wrote a newspaper column describing mortgages as the "perfect real estate investment" and added that mortgages are a "high-yield, low-risk investment." If that wasn't enough to get you to whip out your chequebook, the writer/broker further gushed that mortgages are great investments because you have "little or no management, no physical labour."

You know by now that a low-risk, high-yield investment doesn't exist. Earning a relatively high interest rate goes hand in hand with accepting relatively high risk. The risk is that the borrower can default — which leaves you holding the bag. (In the mid- to late 2000s, mortgage defaults escalated significantly.) More specifically, you can get stuck with a property that you may need to foreclose on, and if you don't hold the first mortgage, you're not first in line with a claim on the property.

The fact that private mortgages are high risk should be obvious when you consider why the borrower elects to obtain needed funds privately rather than through a bank. Put yourself in the borrower's shoes. As a property buyer or owner, if you can obtain a mortgage through a conventional lender, such as a bank, wouldn't you do so? After all, banks generally give better interest rates. If a mortgage broker offers you a deal where you can, for example, borrow money at 10 percent when the going bank rate is, say, 6 percent, the deal must carry a fair amount of risk.

We would avoid these investments. If you really want to invest in such mortgages, you must do some time-consuming homework on the borrower's financial situation. A banker doesn't lend someone money without examining a borrower's assets, liabilities, and monthly expenses, and you shouldn't either. Be careful to check the borrower's credit, and get a large down payment (at least 20 percent). The best circumstance in which to be a lender is if you sell some of your own real estate and you're willing to act as the bank and provide the financing to the buyer in the form of a first mortgage.

Also recognize that your mortgage investment carries interest rate risk: If you need to "sell" it early, you'd have to discount it, perhaps substantially if interest rates have increased since you purchased it. Try not to lend so much money on one mortgage that it represents more than 5 percent of your total investments.

If you're willing to lend your money to borrowers who carry a relatively high risk of defaulting, consider investing in high-yield (junk) bond mutual funds instead. With these funds, you can at least diversify your money across many borrowers, and you benefit from the professional review and due diligence of the fund management team. You can also consider lending money to family members.

Chapter 8

Mastering Mutual Funds

In This Chapter

▶ Looking at reasons to invest in mutual funds

▶ Uncovering the secrets of successful fund investing

▶ Deciding how to allocate your assets

▶ Finding the best stock, bond, hybrid, and money market funds

A mutual fund is simply a big pool of money collected from lots of typical investors. The mutual fund manager uses this pool of money to buy a bunch of investments. These can be stocks, bonds, or other assets — or a combination of these types of different investments — that meet the particular fund's investment criteria.

The better funds enable you to easily and cost-effectively *diversify your investments* — that is, invest in many different industries and companies. (In the earlier chapters of this part of the book, we explain all about stocks, bonds, and other common securities. If you understand these securities, you can understand mutual funds.)

When you invest in a fund, you buy shares and become a shareholder of the fund. Good mutual funds enable you to have some of the best money managers in the world direct the investment of your money. Because efficient funds take most of the hassle and cost out of figuring out which companies to invest in, they're among the finest investment vehicles available today. Different types of mutual funds can help you meet various financial goals — that's one reason that Canadians have close to $497 billion invested in funds! You can use money market funds for something most everybody needs — an emergency savings stash of three to six months' living expenses. Or perhaps you're thinking about saving for a home purchase, retirement, or future educational costs. If so, you can consider some stock and bond mutual funds.

Too many people plunge in to mutual funds without looking at their overall financial situation and, in their haste, often end up paying more taxes and overlooking other valuable financial strategies. If you haven't taken a comprehensive look at your personal finances, read Chapter 3 to begin this important process.

Discovering the Benefits of the Best Funds

The best mutual funds are superior investment vehicles for people of all economic means and for accomplishing many financial objectives. The following sections go over the main reasons for investing in mutual funds rather than individual securities.

Professional management

The mutual fund investment company hires a portfolio manager and researchers whose full-time jobs are to research and purchase suitable investments for the fund. These people screen the universe of investments for those that meet the fund's stated objectives.

Typically, fund managers are graduates of the top business and finance schools, where they learned portfolio management and securities valuation and selection. Many have additional investing credentials, such as the Chartered Financial Analyst's (CFA) degree. In addition to their educational training, the best fund managers typically possess ten or more years of experience in analyzing and selecting investments.

For most fund managers and researchers, finding the best investments is more than a full-time job. Fund managers do tons of analysis that you probably lack the time or expertise to perform. For example, fund managers assess company financial statements; interview a company's managers to get a sense of the company's business strategies and vision; examine competitor strategies; speak with a company's customers, suppliers, and industry consultants; and attend trade shows and read industry periodicals.

In short, a mutual fund management team does more research, number crunching, and due diligence than you could ever have the energy or expertise to do in what little free time you have. Investing in mutual funds frees up time for friendships, family relationships, and maybe even your sex life — don't miss the terrific timesaving benefits of fund investing!

Cost efficiency

Mutual funds are a cheaper, more communal way of getting your investment work done. When you invest your money in an efficiently managed mutual fund, it likely costs you less than trading individual securities on your own. Fund managers can buy and sell securities for a fraction of the cost that you pay.

Funds also spread the cost of research over thousands of investors. The most efficiently managed stock mutual funds cost less than 2 percent per year in fees. (Bonds and money market funds cost much less — in the neighbourhood of 1 percent per year or less.) Funds that simply try to mirror the performance of a specific market such as the Toronto Stock Exchange charge annual fees of less than 0.75 percent per year — that's less than a $7.50 annual charge per $1,000 you invest. Newer exchange-traded funds (ETFs) are like index mutual funds (see the section "Buy index funds" later in this chapter), except that they trade on a stock exchange and, in the best cases, may have a slightly lower management fee than their sibling index mutual funds.

Diversification

Diversification is a big attraction for many investors who choose mutual funds. Most funds own stocks or bonds from dozens of companies, thus diversifying against the risk of bad news from any single company or sector. Achieving such diversification on your own is difficult and expensive unless you have a few hundred thousand dollars and a great deal of time to invest.

Mutual funds typically invest in 25 to 100 securities or more. Proper diversification increases the chances of the fund earning higher returns with less risk.

Although most mutual funds are diversified, some aren't. For example, some stock funds invest exclusively in stocks of a single industry (for example, health care) or country (such as Japan). We're not fans of these funds because of the narrowness of their investments and their typically higher operating fees.

Reasonable investment minimums

Most funds have low minimum investment requirements. Many funds have minimums of $500 or less. Retirement plan investors can often invest with even less. Some funds even offer monthly investment plans, so you can start with as little as $50 per month.

Even if you have lots of money to invest, you should consider mutual funds. Increasing numbers of fund companies offer higher-balance customers special funds with lower annual operating expenses and thus even better returns (more on these funds later in this chapter).

Different funds for different folks

Some people think that mutual funds = stock market investing = risky. That's wrong. The majority of money in mutual funds isn't in the stock market. You may select the funds that take on the kinds of risks that you're comfortable with and that meet your financial goals. Following is a list of the three major types of mutual funds:

- **Stock funds:** If you want your money to grow over a long period of time (and you can handle down as well as up years), choose funds that invest more heavily in stocks.

- **Bond funds:** If you need current income and don't want investments that fluctuate as widely in value as stocks do, consider some bond funds.

- **Money market funds:** If you want to be sure that your invested principal doesn't decline in value because you may need to use your money in the short term, select a money market fund.

Most investors (ourselves included) choose a combination of these three types of funds to diversify and help accomplish different financial goals. (We cover each type of fund in depth later in this chapter.)

High financial safety

In 2008 and 2009, many banks and insurance companies collapsed due to the *subprime mortgage* crisis. Very simply, they owned too many investments whose value was based on homeowners who were poor credit risks in terms of being able to continue to make their mortgage payments. When interest rates moved up and property values fell, many homeowners couldn't make those payments. This meant that the assets of many insurance companies and banks weren't anywhere near what had been believed, which led to their collapse or need to be bailed out. But this round of high-profile financial institutions collapsing won't be the last, nor was it the first.

In the U.S., thousands of banks and insurance companies have failed over the years. Banks and insurers can fail because their *liabilities* (the money that customers give them to invest, which they can be called upon to return on short notice) can exceed their *assets* (the money that they've invested or lent). For example, when big chunks of a bank's loans go sour at the same time that its depositors want their money, the bank fails, because banks typically have less than 15 cents on deposit for every dollar that you and others place with them. (This is exactly what happened to Washington Mutual, which in 2008 was the largest bank failure in U.S. history.) Likewise, if an insurance company makes several poor investments or underestimates the number of insurance policyholder claims, it too can fail.

Such failures can't happen with a mutual fund because the value of the fund's shares fluctuates as the securities in the fund fluctuate in value. For every dollar of securities they hold for their customers, mutual funds have a dollar's worth of securities. The worst that can happen with a fund is that if you want your money, you may get less cash than you originally put into the fund because the value of the investments the fund holds have declined — but you won't lose all your investment.

For added security, the specific stocks, bonds, and other securities that a mutual fund buys are held at a *custodian,* a separate organization independent of the mutual fund company. A custodian ensures that the fund management company can't embezzle your funds or use assets from a better-performing fund to subsidize a poor performer.

Accessibility

Mutual funds are set up for people who value their time and don't like going to a local branch office and standing in long lines. With funds, you can fill out a simple form (often online, if you wish) and write a cheque in the comfort of your home (or authorize electronic transfers from your bank or other accounts) to make your initial investment. You can then typically make subsequent investments by mailing in a cheque or zapping in money electronically.

Additionally, some money market funds offer cheque-writing privileges. Many mutual fund companies also allow you to electronically transfer money back and forth from your local bank account; you can access your money almost as quickly through a money market fund as you can through your local bank.

Selling your shares of a mutual fund is usually simple. Generally, all you need to do is call the fund company's toll-free number or visit its Web site. Some companies have representatives available around the clock, year-round. Most fund companies also offer online account access and trading capabilities as well (although as we discuss in Chapter 19, some people are prone to over-trading online).

The Keys to Successful Fund Investing

This chapter helps explain why funds are a good investment vehicle to use, but not all funds are worthy of your investment dollars. Would you, for example, invest in a mutual fund run by an inexperienced and unproven 18-year-old? How about a fund that charges high fees and produces inferior returns in comparison to other similar funds? You don't have to be an investing wizard to know the correct answers. When you select a fund, you can use a number of simple, commonsense criteria to greatly increase your chances of investment success. The criteria presented in this section have been scientifically proven to dramatically increase your fund investing returns.

Minimize costs

For any particular type of mutual fund (larger-company, Canadian stock funds, for example), hundreds of choices are available. The charges that you pay to buy or sell a fund, as well as the ongoing fund operating expenses, can have a big impact on the rate of return that you earn on your investments.

Fund costs are an important factor in the return that you earn from a mutual fund because fees are deducted from your investment returns and can attack a fund from many angles. All other things being equal, high fees and other charges depress your returns.

Stick with funds that maintain low total operating expenses and that don't charge *sales loads* (commissions). Both types of fees come out of your pocket and reduce your rate of return. Plenty of excellent funds are available at reasonable annual operating expense ratios (less than 2 percent for stock funds; less than 1 percent for bond funds). See our recommendations in the respective sections on the best stock mutual funds, bond funds, and money market funds, later in this chapter.

Avoid load funds

The first such fee that you need to minimize is the *sales load*, which is a commission paid to investment advisers and "financial planners" who work on commission and sell mutual funds. Commissions, or *loads*, can range up to 6 percent or more of the amount that you invest. Sales loads are an additional and unnecessary cost that is deducted from your investment money. You can find plenty of outstanding *no-load* (commission-free) funds.

Investment advisers sing the praises of buying a load fund, warn against no-loads, and even sometimes try to obscure the load. For example, advisers may tell you that the commission doesn't cost you because the mutual fund company pays it. Remember that the commission always comes out of your investment dollars, regardless of how cleverly some load funds and brokers disguise the commission.

Investment advisers also may say that load funds perform better than no-load funds. One reason, advisers claim, is that load funds supposedly hire better fund managers. Absolutely no relationship exists between paying a sales charge to buy a fund and gaining access to better investment managers.

Remember that the sales commission goes to the selling broker, not to the fund managers. Objective studies demonstrate time and again that load funds not only don't outperform but, in fact, underperform no-loads. Common sense suggests why — when you factor in the higher commission and the higher average ongoing operating expenses charged on load funds, you pay more to own a load fund, so your returns are less.

Another problem with commission-driven load fund sellers is the power of self-interest. This issue is rarely talked about, but it's even more important than the extra costs that you pay with load funds. When you buy a load fund through a salesperson, you miss out on the chance to get holistic advice on other personal finance strategies. For example, you may be better off paying down your debts or investing in something entirely different from a mutual fund. But in our experience, salespeople almost never advise you to pay off your credit cards or your mortgage — or to invest through your company's retirement plan or in real estate — instead of buying an investment through them.

Some mutual fund companies try to play it both ways (because they sell their funds through investment advisers as well as directly to consumers): They sell load as well as no-load funds.

Get what you pay for

For many people, the main reason for choosing load funds is to compensate an adviser who's providing them with help in assembling a fund portfolio. At the very minimum, if you're a new customer, request a written financial plan that examines your wider financial circumstances, not just your investment needs. Remember, too, that the commissions in mutual fund prospectuses and so forth are simply the maximum allowed by the fund company. You can and should negotiate those fees down.

There's also no reason why an adviser who's compensated through sales commissions shouldn't include some no-load funds in your portfolio. Financial advisers, whether they charge fees or commissions, are making a living at what they do. Just make sure that, whichever route you choose, you get what you pay for.

A good adviser should act as a sober second opinion that comes between you and your desire to trade, buy, or sell. Discount brokers, instant access to information, and the ease of executing trades over the phone or on the Internet all make it very easy and hassle-free to buy and sell mutual funds and other investments. Many people have a tough time fighting the desire to trade in and out of investments in a never-ending search for a better return. For some investors, an adviser can more than earn back his keep by serving as a hand-holder when the markets take a tumble or when an investment doesn't immediately pan out like you hoped it would.

Hiding loads

Unfortunately, fund companies have come up with craftier ways of hiding sales loads. Increasing numbers of investment advisers and "financial planners" sell funds that they call no-loads, but these funds aren't no-loads.

In *back-end* or *deferred sales* load funds, the commission is hidden. Salespeople tell you that as long as you stay in a fund for five to seven years, you need not pay the back-end sales charge that applies when you sell the investment. This claim may be true, but it's also true that these funds pay investment salespeople a hefty commission.

The salespeople can receive their commissions because the fund company charges you exorbitant continuing operating expenses (which are usually at least 1 percent more per year than the best funds). So one way or another, they get their commissions from your investment dollars.

Back-end loads are also an unfair arrangement that's tilted in the fund company's favour. You offer to lock up your money with a fund for a set number of years in return for them decreasing or eliminating the commission. The problem is that the fund can change the rules of the game, but you still aren't allowed to get out of the contract. The manager may leave or be fired, the fund may change its investing focus, or the results may simply turn out to be much worse than the fund's history suggested.

A good adviser will be open and forthcoming about commissions. Beware those who only sing the praises of buying a load fund, warn against the pitfalls of no-loads, or even try to obscure the load altogether. Some investment advisers and planners may even encourage you to regularly switch out of some funds and into other funds in order to earn themselves more money.

Beware of high operating expenses

In addition to loads, the other costs of owning funds are the ongoing *operating expenses*. All mutual funds charge fees as long as you keep your money in the fund. The fees pay for the costs of running a fund, such as employees' salaries, marketing, toll-free phone lines, printing and mailing *prospectuses* (legal disclosure of the fund's operations and fees), and so on.

A mutual fund's operating expenses are essentially invisible to you because they're deducted from the fund's share price. Companies charge operating expenses on a daily basis, so you don't need to worry about trying to get out of a fund at a particular time of the year before the company deducts these fees.

Although expenses are invisible to you, their impact on your returns is quite real. Expenses are critical for money market mutual funds and bond funds; these funds buy securities that are so similar and so efficiently priced in the financial markets that most fund managers in a given type of money market or bond fund earn quite similar returns before expenses.

With stock funds, expenses may play less of an important role in your fund decision. However, don't forget that over time, stocks have averaged returns of about 10 percent per year. So if one stock fund charges 1.5 percent more in operating expenses than another, you give up an extra 15 percent of your expected (pre-tax) annual returns (and an even greater portion of your after-tax returns).

All types of funds with higher operating expenses tend to produce lower rates of return on average. Conversely, funds with lower operating costs can more easily produce higher returns for you than a comparable type of fund with high costs. This effect makes sense because companies deduct operating expenses from the returns that your fund generates. Higher expenses mean a lower return to you.

Fund companies quote a fund's operating expenses as a percentage of your investment. The percentage represents an annual fee or charge, and is typically called the *management expense ratio,* or *MER.* You can find this number in a fund's prospectus, in the fund expenses section, usually in a line that says something like "Total Fund Operating Expenses." Or you can call the mutual fund's toll-free phone number and ask a representative, or try to find the information at the fund company's Web site. Make sure that a fund doesn't appear to have low expenses simply because it's temporarily waiving them. (You can ask the fund representative or look at the fees in the fund's prospectus to find this information.)

Consider performance and risk

A fund's historic rate of return or performance is another important factor to weigh when you select a mutual fund. Keep in mind, however, as all mutual fund materials must tell you, that past performance is no guarantee of future results. In fact, many former high-return funds achieved their results only by taking on high risk or simply by short-term luck. Funds that assume higher risk should produce higher rates of return. But high-risk funds usually decline in price faster during major market declines. Thus, a good fund should consistently deliver a favourable rate of return given the level of risk it takes.

A big mistake that many investors make when they choose a mutual fund is overemphasizing the importance of past performance numbers. The shorter the time period, the greater the danger of misusing high performance as an indicator for a good future fund.

Although past performance *can* be a good sign, high returns for a fund, relative to its peers, are largely possible only if a fund takes more risk (or if a fund manager's particular investment style happens by luck to come into favour for a few years). The danger of taking more risk is that it doesn't always work the way you'd like. The odds are high that you won't be able to pick the next star before it vaults to prominence in the investing sky. You have a far greater chance of boarding that star when it's ready to plummet back to Earth.

In fact, one U.S. study found that if you had invested in the annual, number-one, top-performing stock and bond funds over the last 15 years, the majority (more than 75 percent) of those top performers subsequently performed worse, over the next 3 to 10 years, than the average funds in their peer groups!

One clever way that mutual funds make themselves look better than other comparable funds is to compare themselves to funds that aren't really comparable. The most common ploy is for a fund to invest in riskier types of securities and then compare its performance to funds that invest in less risky securities. Examine the types of securities that a fund invests in, and make sure that the comparison funds or indexes invest in similar securities.

Stick with experience

A great deal of emphasis is placed on who manages a specific mutual fund. Although the individual fund manager is important, a manager isn't an island unto himself. The resources and capabilities of the parent company are equally, if not more, important. Managers come and go, but fund companies don't.

Different companies maintain different capabilities and levels of expertise with different types of funds. Phillips, Hager & North, for example, is terrific at money market, bond, and dividend stock funds, thanks in part to its low operating expenses. Fidelity and Templeton have significant experience with investing in international stocks.

A fund company gains more or less experience than others, not only from the direct management of certain fund types, but also through hiring out. For example, some fund families contract with private money management firms that possess significant experience. In other cases, private money management firms with long histories in private money management, such as Mawer Investment Management and Sceptre Investment Counsel, offer mutual funds.

Buy index funds

Unlike other mutual funds, in which the portfolio manager and a team of analysts scour the market for the best securities, an index fund manager simply invests to match the makeup, and thus also the performance, of a particular *index* — a basket of stocks representing the performance of a stock market — such as the S&P/TSX Composite Index of the largest companies on the Toronto Stock Exchange. Index funds are funds that are mostly managed by a computer.

Index funds deliver relatively good returns by keeping expenses low, staying invested, and not trying to jump around. Over ten years or more, index funds typically outperform about three-quarters of funds that invest in the same types of companies but try to pick winners! Most so-called *actively managed funds* can't overcome the handicap of high operating expenses that pull down their rates of return. Index funds can run with far lower operating expenses because significant ongoing research need not be conducted to identify companies to invest in.

The average Canadian stock mutual fund, for example, has an operating expense ratio of 2.33 percent per year. (Some funds charge expenses as high as 3 percent or more per year.) That being the case, a Canadian stock index fund with an expense ratio of just 0.7 percent per year has an advantage of 1.6 percent per year over the average fund. A 1.6 percent difference may not seem like much, but in fact it is a significant difference. Because stocks tend to return about 10 percent per year, you end up throwing away about 16 percent of your expected (pre-tax) stock fund returns with an "average fund" in terms of expenses (and an even greater portion of your post-tax returns).

With actively managed stock funds, a fund manager can make costly mistakes, such as not being invested when the market goes up, being too aggressive when the market plummets, or just being in the wrong stocks. Many actively managed funds can and do underperform the overall market index that they're competing against. For example, only 20 to 30 percent of actively managed Canadian equity funds beat the index.

Don't overestimate your own ability to pick *in advance* the few elite money managers who manage to beat the market averages by a few percentage points per year in the long run. Also, don't overestimate the pros' ability to consistently pick the right stocks. Index funds make sense for a portion of your investments, especially when you invest in bonds and larger, more conservative stocks, where beating the market is difficult for portfolio managers.

In addition to lower operating expenses, which help boost your returns, index mutual funds are tax-friendlier to invest in when you invest outside retirement plans. Mutual fund managers of actively managed portfolios, in their attempts to increase returns, buy and sell securities more frequently. However, this trading increases a fund's taxable capital gains distributions and reduces a fund's after-tax return.

Consider exchange-traded funds

Exchange-traded funds (ETFs) are relatively new. Although the first one was created back in 1993, they've gained some traction in recent years.

ETFs are similar to mutual funds, with the most significant difference being that in order to invest, you must buy into an ETF through a stock exchange where ETFs trade, just as individual stocks do. Thus, you need a brokerage account to invest in ETFs. (See Chapter 9 for general information on selecting a brokerage firm.)

ETFs are like index mutual funds in that each ETF generally tracks a major market index. (Be aware that more and more ETFs are being issued that track more narrowly focused indexes such as an industry group or small country.) The best ETFs may also have slightly lower operating expenses than the lowest-cost index funds. However, you must pay a commission to buy and sell an ETF, and the current market value of the ETF may deviate slightly from the underlying market value of the securities in its portfolio.

A number of financial advisers are cheerleading for ETFs. In our observation, in some cases this advocacy is sometimes self-serving because such advisers have established investment management businesses built around ETFs. In one case, Ric Edelman, author of *The Lies About Money,* tells his readers the following:

> The retail mutual fund industry is ripping you off . . . You need to sell all your retail mutual funds . . . the fact is that the retail mutual fund industry is now flush with liars, crooks, and charlatans. Daily business activities include deceit, hidden costs, undisclosed risks, deceptive trade practices, conflicts of interest, and fundamental violations of trust — all at your expense. Since September 2003, the retail mutual fund industry has paid out more than $5 billion in fines.

That sounds pretty awful, doesn't it? Well, in the United States, US$5 billion in fines is a pittance. Consider that the fund industry averaged about $8 trillion under management per year in America, and these fines spanned about a decade's worth of activity in the U.S. fund industry. So the US$5 billion amounts to just 0.00625 percent of the fund industry's assets under management. The mutual fund industry, like any other business or industry (brokerage firms, dentists, insurance firms, financial advisers), isn't perfect. Unlike many industries, the mutual fund industry actually returned the US$5 billion to investors, thanks to government oversight.

Creating Your Fund Portfolio

The portion of the overall pool of your investment money that you decide to put into any particular type of investment is known as *asset allocation.* Asset allocation simply means choosing what percentage of your investments you place — or *allocate* — into bonds and cash versus stocks, and into international versus Canadian stocks. (Asset allocation can also include other assets, such as real estate and small business, which are discussed throughout this book.)

When you invest money for the longer term, such as for retirement, you can choose from the various types of funds that we discuss in this chapter. Most people get a big headache when they try to decide how to spread their money across the choices. This section helps you begin cutting through the clutter. (We discuss recommended funds for shorter-term goals later in this chapter as well.)

Allocating for the long term

Many working folks have time on their side, and they need to use that time to make their money grow. You may have two or more decades before you need to draw on some portion of your retirement plan assets. If some of your investments drop a bit over a year or two — or even over five years — the value of your investments has plenty of time to recover before you spend the money in retirement.

Your current age and the number of years until you retire should be the biggest factors in your allocation decision. The younger you are and the more years you have before retirement, the more comfortable you should be with growth-oriented (and more volatile) investments, such as stock funds. (See Chapter 2 for the risks and historic returns of different investments.)

Table 8-1 lists guidelines for allocating mutual fund money that you've earmarked for long-term purposes, such as retirement. You don't need an MBA or PhD to decide your asset allocation — all you need to know is how old you are and the level of risk that you desire!

Table 8-1	**Mutual Fund Asset Allocation for the Long Haul**	
Your Investment Attitude	*Bond Fund Allocation (%)*	*Stock Fund Allocation (%)*
Play it safe	= Age	= 100 – age
Middle of the road	= Age – 10	= 110 – age
Aggressive	= Age – 20	= 120 – age

What's it all mean, you ask? Consider this example: If you're a conservative sort who doesn't like a lot of risk, but you recognize the value of striving for some growth to make your money work harder, you're a middle-of-the-road type. Using Table 8-1, if you're 35 years old, you may consider putting 25 percent (35 – 10) into bond funds and 75 percent (110 – 35) into stock funds.

Now divvy up your stock investment money between Canadian and international funds. Here's what portion of your "stock allocation" we recommend investing in overseas stocks:

- 20 percent (for play it safe)
- 35 percent (for middle-of-the-road)
- 50 percent (for aggressive)

If, for example, in Table 8-1, the 35-year-old, middle-of-the-road type invests 75 percent in stocks, she can then invest about 35 percent of the stock fund investments (which works out to be around 25 percent of the total) in international stock funds.

So here's what the 35-year-old, middle-of-the-road investor's portfolio asset allocation looks like so far:

Bonds	25%
Canadian stocks	50%
International stocks	25%

Diversifying your stock fund investments

Suppose your investment allocation decisions suggest that you invest 50 percent in Canadian stock funds. Which ones do you choose? As we explain in the section "Exploring different types of stock funds," later in this chapter, stock funds differ on a number of levels. Some stocks and funds are growth oriented, and some focus on value stocks. Small-, medium-, and large-company stocks and funds also invest in such stocks. We explain these types of stocks and funds later in this chapter. You also need to decide what portion you want to invest in index funds (which we discuss in the "Buy index funds" section, earlier in the chapter) versus actively managed funds that try to beat the market.

Generally, it's a good idea to diversify into different types of funds. You can diversify in one of two ways:

- **Purchase several individual funds, each of which focuses on a different style.** For example, you can invest in a large-company value stock fund and in a small-company growth fund. We find this approach somewhat tedious. Granted, it does allow a fund manager to specialize and gain greater knowledge about a particular type of stock. But many of the best managers invest in more than one narrow range of security.

> ✓ **Invest in a handful of funds (five to ten), each of which covers several bases and that together cover them all.** Remember, the investment delineations are somewhat arbitrary, and most funds do more than just one type of investment. For example, a fund may focus on small-company value stocks but also invest in medium-company stocks, as well as in some that are more growth oriented.

As for how much you should use index versus actively managed funds, it's really a matter of personal taste. If you're happy knowing that you'll get the market rate of return and that you can't underperform the market, index your entire portfolio. On the other hand, if you enjoy the challenge of trying to pick the better managers and want the potential to earn better than the market level of returns, don't use index funds at all. A happy medium is to do both. (John Bogle, founder of the U.S. company Vanguard and pioneer of index mutual funds, has about half of his money invested in index funds.)

If you haven't experienced the sometimes significant plummets in stock prices that occur — like the big drop investors had to live through in the fall of 2008 — you may feel queasy when it next happens and you've got a chunk of your nest egg in stocks. Be sure to read Chapters 2 and 5 to understand the risk in stocks and what you can and can't do to reduce the volatility of your stock holdings.

The Best Stock Mutual Funds

In Chapters 2 and 5, we make the case for investing in stocks (also known as equities) to make your money grow. However, stocks sometimes plummet or otherwise remain depressed for a few years. Thus, stock mutual funds (also known as equity funds), which, as their name suggests, invest in stocks, aren't a place for money that you know you may need to protect in the next few years.

Stock funds are excellent investment vehicles that reduce your risk — compared to purchasing individual stocks — because they

> ✓ **Invest in dozens of stocks:** Unless you possess a lot of money to invest, you're likely to buy only a handful of stocks. If you end up with a lemon in your portfolio, it can devastate your other good choices. If such a stock represents 20 percent of your holdings, the rest of your stock selections need to increase about 25 percent in value just to get you back to even. Stock funds mitigate this risk. For example, if a fund holds equal amounts of 50 stocks, and one goes to zero, you lose only 2 percent of the fund value if the stock was an average holding. Similarly, if the fund holds 100 stocks, you lose just 1 percent. Remember that a good fund manager is more likely than you to sidestep disasters (see the earlier section "Professional management" for details).

- **Invest in different types of stocks:** Some funds invest in stocks of different sizes of companies in a variety of industries. Others may hold Canadian and international stocks. Different types of stocks (which are explained in the upcoming section titled "Exploring different types of stock funds") don't move in tandem. So if smaller-company stocks get beat up, larger-company stocks may fare better. If Canadian stocks are in the tank, international stocks may be faring better.

Making money with stock funds

When you invest in stock mutual funds, you can make money in three ways:

- **Dividends:** As a mutual fund investor, you can choose to receive your share of the dividends paid out to the fund as cash or reinvest them in purchasing more shares in the fund. Higher-growth companies tend to pay lower dividends.

   Unless you need the income to live on (if, for example, you're already retired), reinvest your dividends into buying more shares in the fund. If you do this outside of a retirement plan, keep a record of those reinvestments because you need to factor those additional purchases into the tax calculations you make when you sell your shares.

- **Capital gains distributions:** When a fund manager sells stocks for more than he paid, the resulting profits, known as *capital gains,* must be netted against losses and paid out to the fund's shareholders. Just as with dividends, you can reinvest your capital gains distributions in the fund.

- **Appreciation:** The fund manager isn't going to sell all the stocks that have gone up in value. Thus, the price per share of the fund increases to reflect the gains in its stock holdings. For you, these profits are on paper until you sell the fund and lock them in. Of course, if a fund's stocks decline in value, the share price depreciates.

If you add together dividends, capital gains distributions, and appreciation, you arrive at the *total return* of a fund. Stocks, and the funds that invest in them, differ in the dimensions of these three possible returns, particularly with respect to dividends, as we explain in Chapter 5.

Exploring different types of stock funds

Stock funds and the stocks they invest in are usually pigeonholed into particular categories, based on the types of stocks that they focus on. Categorizing stock funds is often tidier in theory than in practice, though, because some funds invest in an eclectic mix of stocks. Don't get bogged down with the names of funds — funds sometimes have misleading names and don't necessarily do what their names imply. The investment strategies of the fund and the fund's typical investments are what matter. The following characteristics are what you need to pay attention to:

- **Company size:** The first dimension on which a stock fund's stock selection differs is based on the size of the company — small, medium, and large companies — in which the fund invests. The total market value *(capitalization)* of a company's outstanding stock defines the categories of stocks that the fund invests in. A company's capitalization is simply the going price of its shares multiplied by the number of shares. (The term *capitalization* is often shortened to "cap," so you may hear financial folks tossing around terms like *large cap* and *small cap*.) The dollar amounts used to define the categories are arbitrary, and as stock prices increase over time, investment market analysts have moved up their cutoffs:

  - Canadian small-company stocks, for example, are usually defined as stocks of companies that possess total market capitalization of less than $500 million. (In the United States, small-cap companies have market values of less than $2 billion.)

  - Medium-capitalization Canadian stocks have market values between $500 million and $1 billion. (The market value of U.S. mid-capitalization companies is between $2 billion and $10 billion.)

  - Large-capitalization Canadian stocks are those of companies with market values greater than $1 billion. (In the United States, large-capitalization stocks have a market value greater than $10 billion.)

  - Why care about the size of the companies that a fund holds? Historically, smaller companies pay lower dividends but appreciate more. They have more volatile share prices but tend to produce slightly higher total returns. Larger companies' stocks tend to pay greater dividends and on average are less volatile and produce slightly lower total returns than small-company stocks. Medium-size companies' stocks, as you may suspect, fall between the two.

- **Growth versus value:** Stock fund managers and their funds are further categorized by whether they invest in growth or value stocks.

  - *Growth stocks* have high prices in relation to the company's assets, profits, and potential profits. Growth companies typically experience rapidly expanding revenues and profits. These companies tend to reinvest most of their earnings in the company to fuel future expansion; thus, these stocks pay low dividends. For example, Research in Motion (RIM) pays no dividends and reinvests most of its profits in its business.

- *Value stocks* are priced cheaply in relation to the company's assets, profits, and potential profits. Value stocks tend to pay higher dividends than growth stocks and historically have actually produced higher total returns than growth stocks.

- Mutual fund companies sometimes use other terms to describe other types of stock funds. *Aggressive growth funds* tend to invest in the most growth-oriented companies and may undertake riskier investment practices, such as frequent trading. *Growth and income funds* tend to invest in stocks that pay higher-than-average dividends, thus offering the investor the potential for growth and income. *Income funds* tend to invest more in higher-yielding stocks. Bonds usually make up the other portion of income funds.

✓ **Company location:** Stocks and the companies that issue them are also divvied up based on the location of their main operations and headquarters. Funds that specialize in Canadian stocks are, not surprisingly, called *Canadian stock funds.* Funds that can invest anywhere in the world, including Canada, are called *global funds,* and those that can invest in any country except for Canada are referred to as *international funds.*

By putting together two or three of these major classifications, you can start to comprehend all those silly and lengthy names that mutual funds give their stock funds. You can have funds that focus on large-company value stocks or small-company growth stocks. You can add in U.S., international, and world-wide funds to further subdivide these categories into more fund types. As a result, you can have international stock funds that focus on small-company stocks or growth stocks.

You can purchase several stock funds, each focusing on a different type of stock, to diversify into different types of stocks. Two potential advantages result from doing so:

✓ First, not all your money rides in one stock fund and with one fund manager.

✓ Second, each of the different fund managers can look at and track particular stock investment possibilities.

Using the selection criteria we outline in the section "The Keys to Successful Fund Investing," earlier in this chapter, the following sections describe the best stock funds that are worthy of your consideration. The funds differ primarily in terms of the types of stocks they invest in. Keep in mind as you read through these funds that they also differ in their tax-friendliness (see Chapter 3). If you invest inside a retirement plan, you don't need to worry about tax-friendliness.

Canadian stock funds

Of all the different types of funds offered, Canadian stock funds are the largest category. Stock funds differ mainly in terms of the size of the companies that they invest in and in whether the funds focus on growth or value companies. Some funds do all these things, and some may even invest a bit overseas.

The only way to know for sure where a fund currently invests (or where the fund may invest in the future) is to ask. To start your information search, you can call the mutual fund company that you're interested in or visit its Web site. You can also read the fund's annual report. Don't waste your time looking for this information in the fund's prospectus because it doesn't give you anything beyond general parameters that guide the range of investments. The prospectus doesn't tell you what the fund currently invests in or has invested in.

For mutual funds that you hold outside of retirement plans, you have to pay income tax on distributed dividends and capital gains. As we discuss in Chapter 3, long-term capital gains and stock dividends are taxed at lower rates than ordinary income and other investment income.

Here's our short list of Canadian stock funds:

- ✔ Altamira Precision Canadian Index (index fund)
- ✔ Bissett Canadian Equity
- ✔ Chou RRSP
- ✔ GBC Canadian Growth
- ✔ iShares Canadian Composite Index (ETF)
- ✔ Mawer New Canada (small caps)
- ✔ Phillips, Hager & North Community Values Canadian Equity
- ✔ RBC O'Shaughnessy Canadian Equity
- ✔ Resolute Performance (small caps)
- ✔ Saxon Stock
- ✔ TD Canadian Index - e (index fund only available online)

Canadian dividend funds

Dividend funds invest in preferred shares that pay fixed dividends, as well as in common shares of large blue-chip companies that pay high yields, such as the big banks. The goal of these funds is to maximize the amount of dividend income.

Changes to the tax system in 2005 reduced the tax rate on *eligible dividends,* which, broadly speaking, are dividends paid out by publicly traded companies. This change meant that in most provinces, and for people in most tax brackets, dividends have the lowest tax rate, lower even than capital gains. (Beginning in 2010, the tax rates on dividends will be raised modestly.)

For the 2008 tax year, the marginal tax rate on dividends for those in the lowest tax bracket (approximately $9,600 to $37,885) was actually negative. This means you not only don't pay any tax on your dividend income, but that income earns you a tax credit that can be used to reduce your overall tax bill. For those earning between $37,886 and $75,769, dividend tax rates ranged from −1.4 percent in British Columbia to around 15 percent in Quebec and Newfoundland. For people in the $75,770 to $123,184 bracket, the approximate marginal tax rate on dividends ranged from 12 percent to 26 percent, depending on the province. Finally, those earning more than $123,184 faced a tax rate of anywhere from 16 percent to almost 30 percent on dividends.

If you're looking for a steady flow of income on your investments with a low tax rate, consider these dividend funds:

- Bissett Dividend Income
- Claymore S&P/TSX CDN Preferred Share ETF
- iShares CDN Dividend Index (ETF)
- RBC Canadian Dividend
- Phillips, Hager & North Dividend Income
- TD Dividend Growth U.S. stock funds

The United States accounts for almost half of the world's stock market capitalization, so it makes sense to allocate a portion of your portfolio to American investments. Although investors were richly rewarded for holding U.S. stocks in the late 1990s, don't forget that it was one of the biggest and best bull markets in history. Don't expect that kind of return, and remember that other markets — including Canada's — will likely outpace the U.S. market from time to time.

Here's our short list of U.S. stock funds:

- Chou Associates
- iShares Canadian S&P 500 index (ETF)
- McLean Budden American Equity
- RBC O'Shaughnessy U.S. Value (and U.S. Growth)
- TD U.S. Index (index fund)
- TD U.S. Mid-Cap Growth

International stock funds

For diversification and growth potential, you should include stock funds that invest overseas as part of your portfolio. Normally, you can tell that you're looking at a fund that focuses its investments overseas if its name contains words such as *international* (usually foreign only) or *global* (foreign and Canadian)

As a general rule, avoid foreign funds that invest in just one country, regardless of whether that country is Australia, Zimbabwe, or anywhere in between. As with investing in a sector fund that specializes in a particular industry (see the following section), this lack of diversification defeats the whole purpose of investing in funds. Funds that focus on specific regions, such as Southeast Asia, are better but still generally problematic because of poor diversification and higher expenses than other, more-diversified international funds.

If you want to invest in more geographically limiting international funds, take a look at funds that invest in broader regions, such as investing just in Europe, Asia, and the volatile but higher-growth-potential emerging markets in Southeast Asia and Latin America.

In addition to the risks normally inherent with stock fund investing, changes in the value of foreign currencies relative to the Canadian dollar cause price changes in the international securities. A decline in the value of the Canadian dollar helps the value of foreign stock funds (and conversely, a rising dollar versus other currencies can reduce the value of foreign stocks). Some foreign stock funds hedge against currency changes. Although this hedging helps reduce volatility a bit, it does cost money.

Here are our picks for diversified global and international funds that may meet your needs:

- ✔ Altamira Precision International Currency Neutral (index fund)
- ✔ AGF International Stock Class
- ✔ Mackenzie Cundill Recovery (small and mid-caps)
- ✔ Mackenzie Cundill Value
- ✔ Mawer World
- ✔ RBC International Index Currency Neutral (index fund)
- ✔ Saxon World Growth (small and mid-caps)
- ✔ Templeton Growth
- ✔ TD Managed Index Maximum Portfolio (index fund)
- ✔ TD International Index-e (index fund only available online)

Sector funds

Sector funds invest in securities in specific industries. In most cases, you should avoid sector funds for a number of reasons, including the following:

- ✓ **Lack of diversification:** Investing in stocks of a single industry defeats a major purpose of investing in mutual funds — you give up the benefits of diversification. Also, even if you're lucky enough to jump into a sector fund just before it becomes "hot," you can't assume that the fund will pick the right securities within that sector.

- ✓ **High fees:** They tend to carry much higher fees than other mutual funds.

- ✓ **Taxable distributions:** Many sector funds have high rates of trading or turnover of their investment holdings. Investors who use these funds outside of retirement plans have to pay the taxman for the likely greater taxable distributions that this trading produces.

The only types of specialty funds that may make sense for a small portion (10 percent or less) of your entire investment portfolio are funds that invest in real estate or precious metals. These funds can help diversify your portfolio because they can perform better during times of higher inflation — which often depresses bond and stock prices. (However, you can comfortably skip these funds because diversified stock funds tend to hold some of the same stocks as these specialty funds.) Here are some details about these two specialty fund types:

- ✓ Real estate funds: Real estate investment trusts (REITs) are stocks of companies that invest in real estate. REITs typically invest in properties such as apartment buildings, shopping centers, and other rental properties. REITs allow you to invest in real estate without the hassle of being a landlord. Just as it's a hassle to evaluate REIT stocks, you can always invest in a mutual fund of REITs.

  REITs usually pay healthy levels of dividends, which for most people are the most tax-friendly way to receive earnings on investments. Some good funds to choose from are CIBC Canadian Real Estate, Dynamic Focus Plus Real Estate, and Sentry Select REIT. You can also invest in a REIT ETF, the iShares Canadian REIT Sector index.

- ✓ Precious metals: If you expect high inflation, consider a gold fund. But know that these funds swing wildly in value and aren't for the faint of heart; over the long term, such funds provide lousy returns — on about par with increases in the cost of living. Good gold funds to choose from are AGF Precious Metals Fund, CIBC Precious Metals Fund, RBC Precious Metals Fund, and Sprott Gold and Precious Minerals Fund.

Don't buy bullion itself; storage costs and the concerns over whether you're dealing with a reputable company make buying gold bars a pain. Also avoid futures and options, which are gambles on short-term price movements (see Chapter 1 for more information).

The Best Bond Funds

Bond funds can make you money in the same three ways that a stock fund can — through dividends, capital gains distributions, and appreciation. However, most of the time, the bulk of your return in a bond fund comes from dividends.

Although an overwhelming number of bond fund choices exists (thousands, in fact), not that many remain after you eliminate high-cost funds (those with loads and high ongoing fees), low-performance funds (which are often the high-cost funds), and funds managed by fund companies and fund managers with minimal experience investing in bonds. Here are the aspects to consider when choosing bond funds:

- **Length to maturity:** Bond fund objectives and names usually fit one of three maturity categories — short-, intermediate-, and long-term. You can earn a higher yield from investing in a bond fund that holds longer-term bonds, but as we explain in Chapter 7, such bond prices are more sensitive to changes in interest rates.

- **Quality:** Generally speaking, the lower a bond issuer's credit rating, the riskier the bond. As with the risk associated with longer maturities, a fund that holds lower-quality bonds should provide higher returns for the increased risk you take. A higher yield is the bond market's way of compensating you for taking greater risk. Funds holding higher-quality bonds provide lower returns but more security.

- **Loads and fees:** After you settle on the type of bonds that you want, a bond fund's costs — its sales commissions and annual operating fees — are a huge consideration. Stick with no-load funds that maintain lower annual operating expenses.

- **Tax implications:** Pay attention to the taxability of the dividends that bonds pay. If you're investing in bonds inside of retirement accounts, you want taxable bonds. If you invest in bonds outside of retirement accounts, the choice between taxable versus tax-free depends on your tax bracket (see Chapter 3).

Invest in bond funds only if you have sufficient money in an emergency reserve. If you invest money for longer-term purposes, particularly retirement, you need to come up with an overall plan for allocating your money among a variety of different funds, including bond funds. (See the section "Allocating for the long term," earlier in this chapter.)

Avoiding yield-related missteps

When selecting bond funds to invest in, investors are often led astray as to how much they can expect to make. The first mistake is to look at recent performance and assume that you'll get that return in the future. Investing in bond funds based on recent performance is tempting right after a period where interest rates have declined (1990s and early 2000s), because declines in interest rates pump up bond prices and, therefore, bond fund total returns. Remember that an equal but opposite force waits to counteract pumped-up bond returns — bond prices fall when interest rates rise.

Don't get us wrong: Past performance is an important issue to consider. In order for performance numbers to be meaningful and useful, you must compare bond funds that are comparable (such as intermediate-term funds that invest exclusively in high-grade corporate bonds).

Bond mutual funds calculate their yield after subtracting their operating expenses. When you contact a mutual fund company seeking a fund's current yield, make sure that you understand what time period the yield covers. Fund companies are supposed to give you the *SEC yield,* which is a standard yield calculation developed by the Securities and Exchange Commission that allows for fairer comparisons among bond funds. The SEC yield reflects the bond fund's yield to maturity. The SEC yield is the best yield to use when you compare funds because it captures the effective rate of interest that an investor can receive in the future.

Unfortunately, if you select bond funds based on advertised yield, you're almost guaranteed to purchase the wrong bond funds. Bond funds and the mutual fund companies that sell them can play more than a few games to fatten a fund's yield. Such sleights of hand make a fund's marketing and advertising departments happy because higher yields make it easier for salespeople and funds to hawk their bond funds. But remember that yield-enhancing shenanigans can leave you poorer. Here's what you need to watch out for:

- ✔ **Lower quality:** In comparing one short-term bond fund to another, you may discover that one pays 0.5 percent more and decide that it looks better. However, it turns out that the higher-yielding fund invests 20 percent of its money in junk (non-investment grade) bonds, whereas the other fund fully invests in high-quality bonds.

- ✔ **Longer maturities:** Bond funds can usually increase their yield just by increasing their maturity a bit. If one long-term bond fund invests in bonds that mature in an average of 17 years, and another fund has an average maturity of 12 years, comparing the two is a classic case of comparing apples and oranges.

✔ **Giving your money back without you knowing it:** Some funds return a portion of your principal in the form of dividends. This move artificially pumps up a fund's yield but depresses its total return. When you compare bond funds, make sure that you compare their total return over time (in addition to making sure that the funds have comparable portfolios of bonds).

✔ **Waiving of expenses:** Some bond funds, particularly newer ones, waive a portion or even all their operating expenses to temporarily inflate the fund's yield. Yes, you can invest in a fund that has a sale on its operating fees, but you'd also buy yourself the bother of monitoring things to determine when the sale is over. Bond funds that engage in this practice often end sales quietly when the bond market is performing well. Don't forget that if you sell a bond fund (held outside of a retirement plan) that has appreciated in value, you owe taxes on your profits.

Treading carefully with actively managed bond funds

Some bond funds are aggressively managed. Managers of these funds possess a fair degree of latitude to purchase and trade bonds that they think will perform best in the future. For example, if a fund manager thinks interest rates will rise, she usually buys shorter-term bonds and keeps more of a fund's assets in cash. The fund manager may invest more in lower-credit-quality bonds if she thinks that the economy is improving and that more companies will prosper and improve their credit standing.

Aggressively managed funds are a gamble. If interest rates fall instead of rise, the fund manager who moved into shorter-term bonds and cash suffers worse performance. If interest rates fall because the economy sinks into recession, the lower-credit-quality bonds will likely suffer from a higher default rate and depress the fund's performance even further.

Some people think the "experts" have no trouble predicting which way interest rates or the economy is heading. The truth is that economic predictions are always difficult, and the experts are often wrong. Few bond fund managers have been able to beat a buy-and-hold approach.

Trying to beat the market can lead to getting beaten! In recent years, increasing numbers of bond funds have fallen on their faces after risky investing strategies backfired. Interestingly, bond funds that charge sales commissions (loads) and higher ongoing operating fees are the ones that are more likely to blow up, perhaps because managers of these funds are under more pressure to pump up returns to make up for higher operating fees.

It's fine to invest some of your bond fund money in funds that try to hold the best position for changes in the economy and interest rates, but remember that if these fund managers are wrong, you can lose more money. Over the long term, you'll probably do best with efficiently managed funds that stick with an investment objective and don't try to time and predict the bond market. Index funds that invest in a relatively fixed basket of bonds so as to track a market index of bond prices are a good example of this passive approach.

Short-term bond funds

Of all bond funds, short-term bond funds are the least sensitive to interest rate fluctuations. The stability of short-term bond funds makes them appropriate investments for money that you seek a better rate of return on than a money market fund can produce for you. But with short-term bond funds, you also have to tolerate the risk of losing a percent or two in principal value if interest rates rise.

Short-term bonds work well for money that you earmark for use in a few years, such as the purchase of a home or a car, or for money that you plan to withdraw from your retirement account in the near future.

A few good short-term bond choices include the following:

- ✔ CIBC Canadian Short-Term Bond Index (index fund)
- ✔ Fidelity Canadian Short Term Bond
- ✔ iShares Canadian Short-Term Bond Index (ETF)
- ✔ Phillips, Hager & North Short-Term Bond and Mortgage
- ✔ TD Short Term Bond

Long-term bond funds

Long-term bond funds are more volatile than short-term bond funds. If interest rates on long-term bonds increase substantially, you can easily see the principal value of your investment decline 10 percent or more. (See the discussion in Chapter 7 of how interest rate changes impact bond prices.)

Long-term bond funds are generally used for retirement investing in one of two situations:

- ✔ Investors don't expect to tap their investment money for a decade or more.
- ✔ Investors want to maximize current dividend income and are willing to tolerate volatility.

Don't use these funds to invest money that you plan to use within the next five years, because a bond market drop can leave your portfolio short of your monetary goal.

We recommend looking at the following long-term bond funds:

- ✔ Beutel Goodman Income
- ✔ iShares Canadian Bond Index (ETF of corporate and government bonds)
- ✔ iShares Canadian Government Bonds Index (ETF of government bonds)
- ✔ McLean Budden Fixed Income
- ✔ Phillips, Hager & North Bond
- ✔ TD Canadian Bond index – e (index fund only available online)

The Best Hybrid Funds

Hybrid funds invest in a mixture of different types of securities. Most commonly, they invest in both bonds and stocks. These funds are usually less risky and less volatile than funds that invest exclusively in stocks; in an economic downturn, bonds usually hold value better than stocks.

Hybrid funds make it easier for investors who are skittish about investing in stocks to hold stocks because they reduce the volatility that normally comes with pure stock funds. Because of their extensive diversification, hybrid funds are excellent choices for an investor who doesn't have much money to start with.

Hybrid funds come in two forms:

- ✔ **Balanced funds** generally try to maintain a fairly constant percentage of investment in stocks and bonds.
- ✔ **Asset allocation funds,** by contrast, normally adjust the mix of different investments according to the portfolio manager's expectations. Some asset allocation funds, however, tend to keep more of a fixed mix of stocks and bonds, whereas some balanced funds shift the mix around quite frequently. (Although the concept of a manager being in the right place at the right time and beating the market averages sounds good in theory, most funds that shift assets fail to outperform a buy-and-hold approach.)

Here's our recommended short list of great balanced-type mutual funds:

- ✔ Bissett Canadian Balanced
- ✔ CIBC Monthly Income
- ✔ Concordia Strategic Balanced
- ✔ Mawer Canadian Balanced RSP
- ✔ McLean Budden Balanced Growth
- ✔ RBC Monthly Income
- ✔ Saxon Balanced
- ✔ Standard Life Monthly Income
- ✔ TD Monthly Income

The Best Money Market Funds

As we explain in Chapter 7, money market funds are a safe, higher-yielding alternative to bank accounts. Money market funds can invest only in the highest credit-rated securities, and their investments must have an average maturity of less than 180 days. The short-term nature of these securities effectively eliminates the risk of money market funds being sensitive to changes in interest rates.

The securities that money market funds use are extremely safe. General-purpose money market funds invest in Treasury bills, guaranteed investment certificates, and short-term corporate debt that the largest and most credit-worthy companies issue.

When shopping for a money market fund, consider these factors:

- ✔ **Expenses:** Within a given category of money market funds (general and Treasury bill), money market fund managers invest in the same basic securities. The market for these securities is pretty darn efficient, so "superstar" money market fund managers may eke out an extra 0.1 percent per year in yield, but not much more.

Select a money market fund that does a good job controlling its expenses. The operating expenses that the fund deducts before payment of dividends are the biggest determinant of yield. All other things being equal (which they usually are with different money market funds), lower operating expenses translate into higher yields for you.

You have no need or reason to tolerate annual operating expenses of greater than 1 percent. Some top-quality funds charge 0.75 percent or less annually. Remember, lower expenses don't mean that a fund company cuts corners or provides poor service. Lower expenses are possible in most cases because a fund company is successful in attracting a lot of money to invest.

✔ **Tax consequences:** With money market funds, all your return comes from interest. What you actually get to keep of these returns (on non-retirement plan investments) is what is left over after the federal and provincial governments take their cut of your earnings. Where possible, hold money market funds inside a tax-deferred retirement plan or Tax-Free Savings Account.

✔ **Location of other funds:** Consider what other investing you plan to do at the fund company where you establish a money market fund. Suppose that you decide to make mutual fund investments in stocks and bonds at TD Canada Trust. Then keeping a money market fund at a different firm that offers a slightly higher yield may not be worth the time and administrative hassle, especially if you don't plan on keeping much cash in your money market fund.

✔ Most mutual fund companies don't have many local branch offices. Generally, this fact helps fund companies keep their expenses low so they can pay you greater money market fund yields. You may open and maintain your mutual fund account via the fund's toll-free phone lines, the mail, or the company's Web site. You don't really get much benefit, except psychological, if you select a fund company with an office in your area. But we don't want to diminish the importance of your emotional comfort level.

Using the criteria that we just discussed, we recommend in this section the best money market funds — those that offer competitive yields, access to other excellent mutual funds, and other commonly needed money market services.

General money market funds

Here are the best money market funds to consider:

✔ Franklin Templeton Money Market

✔ McLean Budden Money Market

✔ Phillips, Hager, & North Canadian Money Market

How to contact fund providers

Here are the phone numbers and Web sites you can use to contact the mutual fund companies we discuss in this chapter:

AGF Management: 800-268-8583; www.agf.com

Altamira Investment Services: 888-270-3941; www.altamira.com

iShares / Barclays Global Investors: 866-474-2737; ca.ishares.com

Beutel Goodman & Company: 800-461-4551; www.beutel-can.com

Bissett Funds: 800-387-0830; www.franklintempleton.ca

Chou Associates Management: 888-357-5070; www.choufunds.com

CI Mutual Funds: 800-792-9355; www.ci.com

CIBC Funds: 800-465-2422; www.cibc.com/ca/mutual-funds

Claymore Investments: 866-417-4640; www.claymoreinvestments.ca

Empire Life (Concordia Strategic): 800-561-1268; www.empire.ca

Fidelity Investments Canada: 800-263-4077; www.fidelity.ca

Franklin Templeton Investments: 800-387-0830; www.franklintempleton.ca

GBC Asset Management: 800-668-7383; www.gbc.ca

Invesco Trimark: 800-874-6275; www.invescotrimark.com

Mackenzie Financial: 800-387-0614; www.mackenziefinancial.com

Manulife Funds: 888-588-7999; www.manulife.ca

Mawer Investment Management: 800-889-6248; www.mawer.com

McLean Budden Funds: 800-884-0436; www.mcleanbudden.com

Phillips, Hager & North Investment Management: 800-661-6141; www.phn.com

RBC Funds: 800-769-2511; www.rbcfunds.com

Resolute Funds: www.resolutefunds.com

Saxon Mutual Funds: 888-287-2966; www.saxonfunds.com

TD Funds: 866-567-8888; www.tdassetmanagement.com

Canadian Treasury bill money market funds

Consider Canadian Treasury bill money market funds if you prefer a money market fund that invests solely or primarily in T-bills, which maintain the safety of government backing.

We recommend these funds that invest primarily in Canadian Treasury bills:

- ✔ Altamira T-Bill
- ✔ CIBC T-Bill
- ✔ Franklin Templeton Treasury Bill
- ✔ RBC Canadian T-Bill
- ✔ TD Canadian T-Bill

Chapter 9

Choosing an Investment Dealer

*Y*ou can invest in most securities — such as the stocks and bonds that we discuss in Chapters 4 through 7 — on your own, without using an investment adviser, if you buy mutual funds direct from fund providers. But someday, you may need investment services. Investment advisers execute your trades to buy or sell stocks, bonds, and other securities.

Consider setting up an investment account for one or more of the following reasons:

✔ If you hold or invest in individual stocks and bonds

✔ If you seek to invest in and hold mutual funds from a variety of fund companies through a single account

✔ If you want to invest in newer exchange-traded funds (see Chapter 8)

In this chapter, we explain the ins and outs of discount brokers to help you find the right broker for your investment needs.

Getting Your Money's Worth: Discount Brokers

When you hear the word *discount,* you probably think of adjectives like *cheap, inferior quality,* and such. However, when it comes to the investment industry, the discount brokers who place your trades at substantial discounts can offer you even better value and service than full-service investment dealers. The following list offers some of the reasons why discount brokers give you more bang for your buck:

- ✔ Discount brokers can place your trades at a substantially lower price because they have much lower overhead.

- ✔ Discount brokers tend not to rent the posh downtown office space, complete with mahogany-panelled conference rooms, in order to impress customers.

- ✔ Discounters don't waste tons of money employing economists and research analysts to produce forecasts and predictive reports.

In addition to lower commissions, another major benefit of using discount brokers is that they generally work on salary. Working on salary removes a significant conflict of interest that continues to get commission-paid investment advisers and dealers into trouble. Although many of these dealers today claim to offer financial planning, the reality is that commission-paid advisers aren't any different from other salespeople, whether the product is cars, copy machines, or computers. People who sell on commission to make a living aren't inherently evil, but given the financial incentives they have, you might not receive holistic, in-your-best-interest investing counsel from them.

Ignoring the salespeople's arguments

One of the many sales tactics of high-commission investment dealers is to try to disparage discounters by saying things such as "You'll receive poor service from discounters." Our own experience, as well as that of others, suggests that in many cases, discounters actually offer *better* service.

Many of the larger discounters, such as those run by the big banks, have convenient branch offices that offer help, including assistance with filling out paperwork and access to independent research reports. And as we discuss in Chapter 8, you can buy *no-load* (commission-free) mutual funds that are run by management teams that make investment decisions for you. Such funds can be bought from mutual fund companies as well as through many discount brokerage firms.

High-commission dealers used to argue that discount brokerage customers received worse trade prices when they bought and sold. This assertion is a bogus argument because all brokerage firms use a computer-based trading system for smaller retail trades. Trades are processed in seconds. High-commission investment dealers also say that discounters are only "for people who know exactly what they're doing and don't need any help." This statement is also false.

Birth of the discount broker

Prior to 1975, all securities brokerage firms charged the same fee, known as a *commission,* to trade stocks and bonds. In the United States, the Securities and Exchange Commission (SEC), the federal government agency responsible for overseeing investment firms and their services, regulated commissions.

Beginning May 1, 1975 — known in the brokerage business as "May Day" — brokerage firms were free to compete with one another on price, like companies in almost all other industries. Most of the firms in existence at that time, such as Prudential, Merrill Lynch, E. F. Hutton, and Smith Barney, largely continued

with business as usual, charging relatively high commissions. Canadians finally got the benefits of deregulated commissions in 1983, when the Toronto and Montreal stock exchanges deregulated the retail brokerage industry here.

Deregulation led to the birth of a new type of brokerage firm, the discount broker. Discount brokerage firms charge substantially lower commissions — typically 50 to 75 percent lower — than the other firms. Today, discount brokers, which include many online brokers, abound and continue to capture the lion's share of new business.

Selecting a discount broker

Which discount broker is best for you depends on your needs and wants. In addition to fees, consider how important having a local branch office is to you. If you seek to invest in mutual funds, the discount brokerage firms that we list later in this section offer access to good funds. In addition, these firms offer money market funds into which you can deposit money awaiting investment or proceeds from a sale.

Here are our top picks for discount brokers:

- ✔ **BMO InvestorLine** (888-776-6886; www.bmoinvestorline.com): Bank of Montreal's discount brokerage offers an easy-to-use Web site that's been thoughtfully put together. The site has numerous useful tools, including good asset allocation and financial planning features. InvestorLine is also known for good customer service, and investors can access a load of useful research. The downside to InvestorLine is its transaction costs. Especially for investors with smaller accounts, commissions are higher than those of many other discount brokers.

- ✔ **Qtrade Investor** (877-787-2330; www.qtrade.ca): Qtrade not only offers low commissions but also keeps improving its offerings, including an expanded stock research section. Qtrade also offers online GIC purchases. Qtrade has strong customer service, and you can easily get a real person on the phone should you need assistance.

✔ **Questrade** (888-783-7866; www.questrade.com): This privately held firm has some of the lowest fees available. Recently, the brokerage offered a commission option of just $4.95 for stock trades. Questrade also is rare in allowing investors to hold U.S. dollars inside their RRSPs, which saves you charges for exchanging currencies.

✔ **TD Waterhouse** (800-465-5463; www.tdwaterhouse.ca): TD Waterhouse has a solid range of competitive services. You can choose from TD's solid in-house funds as well as from a wide selection of other funds. TD Waterhouse also offers several "e-funds" that boast bargain-basement-level management expenses — the *MER* or *management expense ratio* — if you buy them online.

All the preceding firms offer mutual funds from many fund companies in addition to their family of funds (if they have a family of funds). In other words, you may purchase non-TD mutual funds through TD's brokerage department. Other discounters with good service and competitive rates are certainly available, including those of the other big banks not mentioned here, so shop around if you desire. Note, however, that you may have to pay a transaction fee to buy funds from firms that don't offer their own family of funds.

Examining your online trading motives

If trading online attracts you, first examine why you're motivated to do so. Tracking prices daily (or, even worse, hourly) and frequently checking your account balances leads to addictive trading. Even a low fee of $5 or $10 per trade doesn't really save you any money if you trade a lot and rack up significant total commissions. And, even if you do well, you'll pay more in capital gains taxes. Don't forget that as with trading through a full-service investment dealer, you also lose the *spread* (difference between the bid and ask prices when you trade stocks and bonds), in addition to the explicit commission rates that online brokers charge.

Frankly, trading online is also an unfortunately easy way for people to act impulsively and emotionally when making important investment decisions. If you're prone to such actions, or you find yourself tracking and trading investments too closely, use the Internet to check account information and gather factual information, and stay away from this form of trading.

Know that most of the best investment firms allow you to trade via touch-tone phone. In most cases, touch-tone phone trading is discounted when you compare it to trading through a live broker, although it's admittedly less glamorous than trading through a Web site.

Some brokers also offer account information and trading capabilities via personal digital assistants, which, of course, add to your costs. Digital assistants can also promote addictive investment behaviours.

Investment Web sites also push the surging interest in online trading with the pitch that you can beat the market averages and professionals at their own game if you do your own research and trade online. Beating the market and professionals is highly unlikely. However, you can save some money trading online, but probably not as much as the hype has you believe.

Considering other costs

Discount brokerage customers often shop for low costs. However, simply talking with enough people who have traded online and reviewing online message boards where customers speak their minds clearly show that shopping merely for low-cost trading prices often causes the investor to overlook other important issues.

✔ Some discounters charge fees for real-time stock quotes (as opposed to quotes that may be 15 to 20 minutes old and are free). Some brokers whack you $20 here and $50 there for services such as wiring money or simply closing your account. Also beware of "inactivity fees" that some brokers levy on accounts that have infrequent trading. So before you sign up with any broker, make sure that you examine its entire fee schedule.

✔ When you buy or sell an investment, you may have cash sitting around in your brokerage account. Not surprisingly, the online brokers pitching their cheap online trading rates in numbers 8 centimeters (3 inches) high don't reveal their money market rates in such large type (if at all). Some don't pay interest on the first $1,000 or so of your cash balance, and even then, some companies pay half a percent to a full percent less than their best competitors. In the worst cases, some online brokers have paid up to 3 percent less. Under those terms, you'd earn up to $150 less in interest per year if you averaged a $5,000 cash balance during the year.

Examining service quality

Common complaints among customers of online brokers include slow responses to e-mail queries, long dead time as you wait to speak with a live person to answer questions or resolve problems, delays in opening accounts and receiving literature, unclear statements, incorrect processing of trading requests, and slow Web response during periods of heavy traffic. With a number of firms that we called, we experienced phone waits of up to ten minutes and were transferred several times to retrieve answers to simple questions, such as whether the firm carried a specific family of mutual funds.

When you shop for an online broker, check your prospects thoroughly. Call for literature and see how long reaching a live human being takes. Ask some questions and see how knowledgeable and helpful the representatives are. For non-retirement plans, if the quality of the firm's year-end account statements concern you, ask prospective brokerages to send you a sample. Try sending some questions to the broker's Web site and see how accurate and timely the response is. If you're a mutual fund investor, check out the quality of the funds that the company offers — don't allow the sheer number of funds that the company offers impress you. Also, inquire about the interest rates that the company pays on cash balances, as well as the rates that the company charges on margin loans, if you want such borrowing services.

Consider checking online message boards to see what current and past customers of the firm say about the firms that you're considering. Most online brokers that have been around for more than six months lay claim to a number-one rating with some survey or ranking of online brokers. Place little value on such claims.

Transact business only with firms that offer sufficient account insurance (enough to protect your assets) through the Canadian Investor Protection Fund (CIPF). The severe stock market downturn in the early 2000s led to the first of what is likely to be many major shakeouts, and you need to protect yourself.

Considering Full-Service Investment Dealers

Although the use of discount brokers is now widespread, a great number of Canadians still work with full-service investment dealers, whom they continue to regard as the traditional "stockbrokers." That is, in return for access to his or her company's research, advice on structuring your portfolio, and other services, you compensate your adviser through commissions when you buy and sell. These commissions have declined somewhat with the advent of discount brokerages, but transactions through a full-service investment dealer will still cost you a lot compared with what you'd pay a discount broker. Many Canadians maintain both a discount brokerage account and an account with a full-service investment dealer.

Why you should keep your securities in an investment dealer or discount brokerage account

When most investors purchase stocks or bonds today, they don't receive the actual paper certificate demonstrating ownership. Investment dealer and discount brokerage accounts often hold the certificate for your stocks and bonds on your behalf. Holding your securities through an account is beneficial because there is an extra fee to issue certificates.

Sometimes people hold stock and bond certificates themselves — this practice was more common among your parents' and grandparents' generations. The reason: During the Great Depression, many investment dealers failed and took people's assets down with their sinking ships. Since then, various reforms have greatly strengthened the safety of money and the securities that you hold in an investment account.

Just as the CDIC insurance system backs up money in bank accounts, the CIPF (Canadian Investor Protection Fund) provides insurance to customers of investment dealers and discount brokerage firms that are members of the fund. The base level of insurance is $1,000,000 per account held with each financial institution. However, many firms purchase additional protection — some as high as $100 million total!

Investment firms don't often fail these days, but unlike during the Depression, the CIPF protects you if they do. However, the CIPF coverage doesn't protect you against a falling stock market. If you invest your money in stocks, bonds, or whatever that plunge in value, that's your own problem!

Besides not having to worry about losing your securities if a dealer fails, another good reason to hold securities with an investment dealer or discount broker is so you don't lose them — literally! Surprising numbers of people — the exact number is unknown — have lost their stock and bond certificates. Those who realize their loss can contact the issuing firms to replace them, but doing so takes a good deal of time. However, just like future goals and plans, some certificates are simply lost, and owners never realize their loss. This financial fiasco sometimes happens when people die and their heirs don't know where to look for the certificates or the securities that their loved ones held.

Another reason to hold your securities in an account is that doing so cuts down on processing all those dividend cheques. For example, if you own a dozen stocks that each pays you a quarterly dividend, you must receive, endorse, and otherwise deal with 48 separate cheques. Some people enjoy this practice — they say that doing so is part of the "fun" of owning securities. Our advice: Stick all your securities in one brokerage account that holds your paid dividends. These accounts offer you the ability to move these payments into a reasonably good-yielding money market fund. Most of the better investment dealers and discount brokers even allow you to reinvest stock dividends in the purchase of more shares of that stock at no charge.

Given the higher costs, why do people stick with full-service investment dealers? They may feel they benefit from the research they receive. They may look to a full-service investment dealer for advice on larger financial planning issues. Or maybe it's just what their parents did, and setting up an account with Dad's — or Mom's — dealer was a rite of passage. Some people simply like to be able to say "My investment dealer says . . ." just like they enjoy being able to talk about their lawyer, their accountant, and so on.

Full-service investment dealers have one major strike against them: The more you buy and sell, the more money they make, plain and simple. That's not to say there aren't good, competent, trustworthy full-service dealers out there — there are. But if you're going to deal with one, you need to take a few basic steps in order to get your money's worth.

Your first step should be to educate yourself before you go any further with your full-service investment dealer — or before you open an account with one. Knowing what products and approach will best suit your circumstances will go a long way toward helping ensure your interests come first. Next, have a frank discussion about the commissions you'll pay. Most dealers know that discount brokerages are a big competitive force, and are usually willing to reduce their commissions to keep your business. For instance, you could propose that when an investment comes from your own research and home-work, you pay the commission that you'd otherwise pay a discount broker. In this way you can keep your investments in one place and keep costs down while still drawing on your dealer's knowledge and advice.

Another strike against full-service investment dealers is that they often won't recommend no-load funds because they won't make a commission. Consider proposing a flat fee — say, 1 percent — to your dealer to buy into these funds. In many cases, that will be close to what you may end up paying with some discounters, once you count in the many buried fees that often exist.

The biggest benefit of using a full-service investment dealer — and one not to be underestimated — is that he can serve as a sober second opinion. Too many individual investors fail to even match the market indexes because they're too quick to sell when prices fall and too slow to buy when prices rise. If a full-service investment dealer saves you from selling at discount prices when the market corrects, she may more than earn her keep.

Part III
Getting Rich with Real Estate

The 5th Wave   By Rich Tennant

©RICHTENNANT

"Of course I could never afford a shoe this size if I weren't collecting rents from a tennis shoe across town and two ski boots in Whistler."

In this part . . .

Owning a home and investing in real estate are time-proven methods for building wealth. However, if you're not careful, you can easily fall prey to a number of pitfalls. In this part, you discover the right and wrong ways to purchase real estate and how to build your real estate empire. Even if you don't want to be a real estate tycoon, you also see how simply owning your own home can help build your net worth and accomplish future financial goals.

Chapter 10

Investing in a Home

For most people, buying a home in which to live is their first, best, and only real estate investment. Homes may require a lot of financial feeding, but over the course of your life, owning a home (instead of renting) can make and save you money. Although the pile of mortgage debt seems daunting in the years just after your purchase, someday your home may be among your biggest assets. (And, yes, real estate is still a good investment despite its recent declines in the late 2000s in many areas. Like stocks, real estate does well over the long term but doesn't go continuously higher. Smart investors take advantage of down periods as times to buy at lower prices just like they do when their favourite retail stores are having a sale.)

Even though your home consumes a lot of dough (mortgage payments, property taxes, insurance, maintenance, and so on) while you own it, it can help you accomplish important financial goals, such as

✔ **Retiring:** By the time you hit your 50s and 60s, the size of your monthly mortgage payment, relative to your income and assets, should start to look small or non-existent. Relatively low housing costs can help you afford to retire or cut back from full-time work. Some people are choosing to sell their homes and buy less-costly ones or to rent the homes out and use some or all of the cash to live on in retirement. Other homeowners enhance their retirement income by taking out a reverse mortgage to tap the *equity* (market value of the home minus the outstanding mortgage debt) that they've built up in their properties.

✔ **Pursuing your small-business dreams:** Running your own business can be a source of great satisfaction. Financial barriers, however, prevent many people from pulling the plug on a regular job and taking the entrepreneurial plunge. You may be able to borrow against the equity that you've built up in your home to get the cash you need to start your own business. Depending on what type of business you have in mind, you may even be able to run your enterprise from your home. (We discuss small-business issues in more detail in Part IV.)

✔ **Financing university:** Although it may seem like only yesterday that your kids were born, soon enough they're ready for an expensive four-year undertaking: university. Borrowing against the equity in your home is a viable way to help pay for your kids' educational costs.

Perhaps you won't use your home's equity for retirement, a small business, educational expenses, or other important financial goals. But even if you decide to pass your home on to your children, charity, or a long-lost relative, it's still a valuable asset and a worthwhile investment. This chapter explains how to make the most of it.

The Buying Decision

We believe that most people should buy and own a home. But homeowner-ship isn't for everybody and certainly not at all times in your adult life.

The decision about if and when to buy a home can be complex. Money matters, but so do personal and emotional issues. Buying a home is a big deal — you're settling down. Can you really see yourself coming home to this same place day after day, year after year? Of course, you can always move, but now you've got a financial obligation to deal with.

Weighing the pros and cons of ownership

To hear some people — particularly enthusiastic salespeople in the real estate business — everybody should own a home. You may hear them say things like the following:

✔ Buy a home for the tax break.

✔ Renting is like throwing your money away.

As we discuss later in this chapter, it's true that the profit you make when you sell the home in which you've been living — your *primary residence* — is tax-free. However, many people end up living in their home for many, many years — perhaps for the rest of their lives — while others use all the profits from one home along with extra savings in order to buy a larger property as their family grows. Tax-free profits are great, but they often don't get redirected to your retirement or other investment account. Don't buy a home just because of the tax break.

As for renting, it isn't necessarily "throwing your money away." In fact, renting can have a number of benefits:

✔ **In some communities, with a given type of property, renting is less costly than buying.** Happy and successful renters we've seen include people who pay low rent, perhaps because they've made housing sacrifices. If you can sock away 10 percent or more of your earnings while renting, you're probably well on your way to accomplishing your future financial goals.

✔ **You can save money and hopefully invest in other financial assets.** Stocks, bonds, and mutual funds (see Part II) are quite accessible and useful in retirement. Most homeowners, by contrast, have a substantial portion of their wealth tied up in their homes. (Accessibility is a double-edged sword because it may tempt you as a cash-rich renter to blow the money in the short term.)

✔ **Renting has potential emotional and psychological rewards.** First is the not-so-inconsequential fact that you have more flexibility to pack up and move on. You may have a lease to fulfill, but you can renegotiate it if you need to move on. As a homeowner, you have a major monthly payment to take care of — to some people, this responsibility feels like a financial ball and chain. After all, you have no guarantee that you can sell your home in a timely fashion or at the price you desire if you want to move.

Although renting has its benefits, renting has at least one big drawback: exposure to inflation. As the cost of living increases, your landlord can keep increasing your rent (unless you live in a rent-controlled unit). If you're a homeowner, however, the big monthly expense of the mortgage payment doesn't increase during the existing term of your mortgage, assuming that it is a fixed-rate mortgage. (Your property taxes, homeowners insurance, and maintenance expenses are exposed to inflation, but these expenses are usually much smaller in comparison to your monthly mortgage payment or rent.)

Here's a quick example to show you how inflation can work against you as a long-term renter. Suppose that you're comparing the costs of owning a home that costs $300,000 to renting a similar property for $1,200 a month. (If you're in a high-cost urban area and these numbers seem low, please bear with us and focus on the numbers and accompanying insights, which you can apply to higher-cost areas.) Buying at $300,000 sounds a lot more expensive than renting, doesn't it? But this isn't a fair apples-to-apples comparison. You must compare the monthly cost of owning to the monthly cost of renting. Figure 10-1 does just that over 25 years.

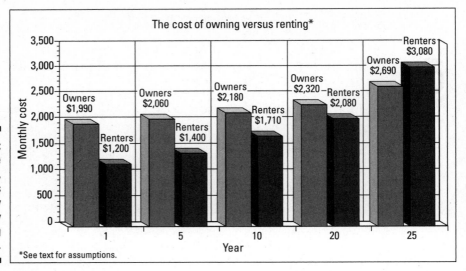

Figure 10-1:
Because
of inflation,
renting is
generally
more costly
in the long
run.

As you can see in Figure 10-1, although it costs more in the early years to own, owning should be less expensive in the long run. Renting is higher in the long term because all of your rental expenses increase with inflation. ***Note:*** We haven't factored in the potential change in the value of your home over time. Over long periods of time, home prices tend to appreciate, which makes owning even more attractive.

The example in Figure 10-1 assumes that if you buy, you make a 25 percent down payment, and that your mortgage is at 7.5 percent. We also assume that the cost of your insurance, property taxes, and maintenance starts at $450 a month, and those costs increase by 4 percent each year. If you rent, the assumption is the rate of inflation of your monthly rental cost is also 4 percent per year. Note that if inflation is lower, renting doesn't necessarily become cheaper in the long term. In the absence of inflation, your rent should escalate less, but your homeownership expenses (property taxes, maintenance, and insurance), which are subject to inflation, should increase less too. And with low inflation, you can probably renew your mortgage at a lower interest rate, which reduces your monthly mortgage payments. With low or no inflation, owning can still cost less, but the savings versus renting aren't as dramatic as when inflation is greater.

Recouping transaction costs

Financially speaking, we advise that you wait to buy a home until you can see yourself staying put for a minimum of three years. Ideally, we'd like you to think that you have a solid chance of staying with the home for five or more years. Why? Buying and selling a home cost big bucks, and you generally need at least five years to recoup your transaction costs. Some of the expenses you'll face include

- **Inspection fees:** You shouldn't buy a property without thoroughly checking it out, so you'll incur inspection expenses. Good inspectors can help you identify problems with the plumbing, heating, and electrical systems. They also check out the foundation, roof, and so on and let you know whether termites are living in the house.

- **Appraisal fee:** Your lender may require you to get your home appraised so that it can have an independent assessment of the home's value. An appraisal typically costs from $150 to $300 or more.

- **Survey fee:** Unless the sellers have recently had a survey done of the property, you'll need to have a new one prepared. Done by a registered land surveyor, a survey is simply a drawing of your property that lets you and your lender ensure that the buildings you're buying are indeed on your property, that your neighbours' homes aren't on your land, and that any buildings meet zoning regulations. An up-to-date survey is generally needed before you can legally be awarded title. A survey will typically cost around $400 to $500.

- **Legal fees:** Although you can prepare an offer to purchase yourself and tend to the closing costs, using a lawyer to at least search the title is usually advisable. A title search is carried out to determine that the vendor actually owns the home and has the right to sell it to you, and that the property doesn't have any claims against it. You can save some money by using a paralegal, but it's generally best to use a lawyer. In British Columbia and Quebec, lawyers are the only folks legally allowed to complete the purchase. Using a lawyer also gives you valuable insurance. If the lawyer certifies that the seller has the right to sell you the property and that it doesn't have any claims against it — known as *free and marketable title* — and this later proves to be wrong, you can pursue a claim against the lawyer.

- **Title insurance:** When you buy a home, you and your lender need to protect yourselves against the chance — albeit small — that the property seller doesn't actually legally own the home that you're buying. That's where title insurance comes in — it protects you financially from unscrupulous sellers.

Knowing when to buy

If you're considering buying a home, you may be concerned whether home prices are poised to rise or fall. No one wants to purchase a home that then plummets in value. And who wouldn't like to buy just before prices go on an upward trajectory?

It's not easy to predict what's going to happen with real estate prices in a particular city, province, or country over the next one, two, or three or more years. (Just think about how quickly the subprime mortgage crisis hit in 2008. A year earlier you would have been hard-pressed to find more than the odd voice in the wilderness warning that house prices were set to drop in a number of regions.) Ultimately, the economic health and vitality of an area drive the demand and prices for homes in that area. An increase in jobs, particularly ones that pay well, increases the demand for housing. And when demand goes up, so do prices.

If you first buy a home when you're in your 20s, 30s, or even your 40s, you may end up as a homeowner for several decades. Over such a long time, you may experience lots of ups and downs, but

probably more ups than downs, so we wouldn't be too concerned about trying to predict what's going to happen to the real estate market in the near term. We know some long-term renters who avoided buying homes decades ago because they thought that prices were expensive. Consequently, they missed out on tremendous appreciation in real estate values.

That said, you may be, at particular times in your life, ambivalent about buying a home. Perhaps you're not sure that you'll stay put for more than three to five years. Therefore, part of your home-buying decision may hinge on whether current home prices in your local area offer you a good value. The level of real estate prices as compared to rent, the state of the job market, and the number of home listings for sale are useful indicators of the housing market's health. Trying to time your purchase has more importance if you think that you may move in less than five years. In that case, avoid buying in a high market. If you expect to move so soon, renting generally makes more sense because of the high costs of buying and selling real estate.

- ✔ **Moving costs:** You can transport all your furniture, clothing, and other personal belongings yourself, but your time is worth something, and your moving skills are likely limited. Besides, do you want to end up in a hospital emergency room after you're pinned at the bottom of a staircase by a runaway couch?

- ✔ **Real estate agents' commissions:** A commission of 5 to 7 percent of the purchase price of most homes is paid to the real estate salespeople and the companies they work for.

On top of all these transaction costs of buying and then selling a home, you'll also face maintenance expenses — for example, fixing leaky pipes and painting. To cover all the transaction and maintenance costs of homeownership, the value of your home needs to appreciate about 15 percent over the years that you own it just for you to be as well off financially as if you had continued renting. Fifteen percent! If you need or want to move elsewhere in a few years, counting on that kind of appreciation in those few years is risky. If you happen to buy just before a sharp rise in housing prices, you may get this much appreciation in a short time. But you can't count on this upswing — you're more likely to lose money on such a short-term deal.

Some people invest in real estate even when they don't expect to live in the home for long and may consider turning their home into a rental if they move within a few years. Doing so can work well financially in the long haul, but don't underestimate the responsibilities that come with rental property, which we discuss in Chapter 11.

Deciding How Much to Spend

Buying a home is a long-term financial commitment. You'll probably choose to repay the money you borrow to purchase your home (your *mortgage*) over 25 years. This is called the *amortization*. Over the years, your home will also need maintenance. So before you decide to buy, take stock of your overall financial health.

If you have good credit and a reliable source of employment, lenders will eagerly offer to loan you money. They'll tell you how much you may borrow from them — the maximum that you're qualified to borrow. But that doesn't mean that you *should* borrow the maximum.

If you buy a home without considering your other monthly expenditures and long-term goals, you may end up with a home that dictates much of your future spending. Have you considered, for example, how much you need to save monthly to reach your retirement goals? How about the amount that you want to spend on recreation and entertainment?

If you want to continue your current lifestyle, you have to be honest with yourself about how much you can really afford to spend as a homeowner. First-time homebuyers in particular run into financial trouble when they don't understand their current spending. Buying a home can be a wise decision, but it can also be a huge burden. And there are all sorts of nifty things to buy for a home. Some people prop up their spending habits with credit cards — a dangerous practice.

Don't let your home control your financial future. Before you buy a property or agree to a particular mortgage, be sure that you can afford to do so — be especially careful not to ignore your retirement planning (if you hope to someday retire). Start by reading Chapter 3. After reading the following sections, you can also check out Chapter 12, where we cover mortgages and financing options in greater detail.

Looking through lenders' eyes

All mortgage lenders want to gauge your ability to repay the money that you borrow, so you have to pass a few tests. Mortgage lenders calculate the maximum amount that you can borrow to buy a piece of real estate.

For a home in which you will reside, lenders total your monthly housing expenses. They define your housing costs as:

Mortgage payment   +   Property taxes   +   Condominium maintenance fees
(and sometimes heating)   (for condominium buyers)

Most lenders don't want any more than 30 to 32 percent of your monthly gross (pre-tax) income going toward your housing expense. The maximum amount you'll be able to borrow will typically be where the corresponding monthly payments come to just under a third of your pre-tax income. (Lenders don't usually consider the maintenance and upkeep expenses that come with owning a home.) This is known as the *gross debt service ratio*.

If you're self-employed, determining what a lender will allow you to borrow is much less formulaic. Lenders will typically want to see your financial statements and income tax returns for the last few years. Just how much you'll be able to borrow is often worked out on an individual basis. Lending ratios vary slightly from lender to lender.

Although lenders may not care where you spend money outside your home, they do care about your other debt. A lot of other debt, such as credit cards or auto loans, diminishes the funds that are available to pay your housing expenses. Lenders know that having other debt increases the possibility that you may fall behind or actually default on your mortgage payments.

If you have consumer debt that requires monthly payments, lenders calculate another ratio to determine the maximum that you can borrow. Lenders add the amount that you need to pay down your other consumer debt to your monthly housing expense.

Consumer debt is bad news even without considering that it hurts your qualification for a mortgage. Consumer debt is costly and encourages you to live beyond your means. Get rid of it — curtail your spending and adjust to living within your means. If you can't live within your means as a renter, doing so is going to be even harder as a homeowner.

Homeownership tax savings

Any profit you make when you sell your home is generally tax-free. In addition to a house, this includes condos and townhouses, as well as a share in a co-operative housing corporation.

To qualify, the property you're selling has to be what's called your *principal residence* — you or your spouse or child must have "ordinarily inhabited" the property. This means you can't claim the exemption on empty land or a building that you rent out and have never lived in. You don't have to live there the majority of the year to call a property your "principal residence."

Your principal residence doesn't have to be a "house" in the traditional sense. You are, however, limited to designating a single property as your principal residence in any given year. If you have a home and a cottage, for example, you could choose to designate the home as your principal residence for some years and the cottage for others.

When you sell a property, just how much of your gain will be tax-free is determined by a formula that looks at how many years you owned it, how many years it was your principal residence, and the overall increase in value. If you move out of your home, but rather than sell you choose to rent it out, you can generally still call it your "principal" residence — and claim the tax-break — for up to four years. You need to file a special election along with your tax return for the year in which you begin renting out your home. You can't, however, claim another property as your residence during that time, even if it is one in which you are living full-time.

Determining your down payment

Another factor to consider when you decide how much you should borrow is that most lenders require you to purchase *mortgage insurance* if your down payment is less than 20 percent of your home's purchase price. Mortgage insurance protects the lender from getting stuck with a property that may be worth less than the mortgage you owe, in the event that you default on your loan. On a moderate-size loan, mortgage insurance can add hundreds of dollars per year to your payments.

If you have to take mortgage insurance to buy a home with less than 20 percent down, keep an eye on your home's value and your loan balance. Over time, the value of your property should appreciate and your loan balance should decrease as you make monthly payments. After your mortgage represents 80 percent or less of the market value of the home, you can get rid of the mortgage insurance (doing so entails contacting your lender and usually requires you to pay for an appraisal).

What if you have so much money that you can afford to make *more* than a 20 percent down payment? How much should you put down then? (This problem doesn't usually arise — most buyers, especially first-time buyers, struggle to get a 20 percent down payment together.) The answer depends on what else you can or want to do with the money. If you're considering other investment opportunities, determine whether you can expect to earn a higher rate of return on those other investments versus the interest rate that you'll pay on the mortgage. During the past century, stock market and real estate investors have enjoyed average annual returns of around 8 to 10 percent per year. So if you borrow mortgage money at around 6 to 7 percent, in the long term you should come out a couple of percent ahead if you use the money you would have put toward a larger down payment to invest in such growth investments. You aren't guaranteed, of course, that your investments will earn 8 to 10 percent yearly. (Remember that past returns don't guarantee the future.) And don't forget that all investments come with risk. The advantage of putting more money down for a home and borrowing less is that it's essentially a risk-free investment (as long as you have adequate insurance on your property).

If you prefer to put down just 20 percent and invest more money elsewhere, that's fine. Just don't keep the extra money (beyond an emergency reserve) under the mattress, in a savings account, or in bonds that pay less interest than your mortgage costs you in interest. Invest in stocks, real estate, or a small business. Otherwise, you don't have a chance at earning a higher return than the cost of your mortgage, and you're therefore better off paying down your mortgage.

Selecting Your Property Type

If you're ready to buy a home, you must make some decisions about what and where to buy. If you grew up in the suburbs, your image of a home may include the traditional single-family home with a lawn, a couple of kids, and the family pets. But single-family homes, of course, aren't the only or even the main types of residential housing in many areas, especially in some higher-cost, urban neighbourhoods. Other common types of higher-density housing include the following:

✔ **Condominiums:** These are generally apartment-style units that are stacked on top of and adjacent to one another. Many condo buildings were originally apartments that were converted — through the sale of ownership of separate units — into condos. When you purchase a condominium, you purchase a specific unit as well as a share of the common areas (for example, the pool, grass and other plantings, entry and hallways, laundry room, and so on).

✔ **Townhouses:** *Townhouse* is just a fancy way of saying attached or row home. Think of a townhouse as a cross between a condominium and a single-family house. Townhouses are condo-like because they're attached (generally sharing walls and a roof) and are homelike because they're often two-storey buildings that come with a small yard.

✔ **Cooperatives:** *Cooperatives* (usually called co-ops) resemble apartment and condominium buildings. When you buy a share in a cooperative, you own a share of the entire building, including some living space. Unlike in a condo, you generally need to get approval from the cooperative association if you want to remodel or rent your unit to a tenant. In some co-ops, you must even gain approval from the association for the sale of your unit to a proposed buyer. Co-ops are generally much harder to obtain loans for and to sell, so we don't recommend that you buy one unless you get a good deal and can easily obtain a loan.

All types of shared housing (the types of housing in the preceding list) offer two potential advantages:

✔ First, this type of housing generally gives you more living space for your dollars. This value makes sense because with a single-family home, a good chunk of the property's cost is for the land that the home sits on. Land is good for decks, recreation, and children who want to roll around on the grass (or in the snow), but you don't live "in" it the way you do with your home. Shared housing maximizes living space for the housing dollars that you spend.

✔ Another benefit of shared housing is that, in many situations, you're not personally responsible for general maintenance. Instead, the homeowners' association (which you pay into) takes care of it. If you don't have the time, energy, or desire to keep up a property, shared housing can make sense. Shared housing units may also give you access to recreation facilities, such as a pool, tennis courts, and exercise equipment.

So why doesn't everyone purchase shared housing? Well, as investments, single-family houses generally perform better in the long run. In a good real estate market, single-family houses tend to outperform other housing types. Shared housing is easier to build (and to overbuild) — and the greater supply tends to keep its prices from rising as much. Single-family houses tend to attract more potential buyers — most people, when they can afford it, prefer a stand-alone home, especially for the increased privacy.

If you can afford a smaller single-family house instead of a larger shared-housing unit, buy the single-family house. Shared housing makes more sense for people who don't want to deal with building maintenance and who value the security of living in a larger building with other people. Also know that shared-housing prices tend to hold up better in developed urban environments. If possible, avoid shared housing units in suburban areas where the availability of developable land makes building many more units possible, thus increasing the supply of housing and slowing growth in values.

If shared housing interests you, make sure that you have the property thoroughly inspected. Also, examine the trend in maintenance fees over time to ensure that these costs are under control. (See Chapter 11 for more specifics on how to check out property.)

Finding the Right Property and Location

Some people know where they want to live, so they look at just a handful of properties and then buy. Most people take much more time — finding the right house in a desired area at a fair price can take a lot of time. Buying a home can also entail much compromise when you buy with other family members (particularly spouses).

Be realistic about how long it may take you to get up to speed about different areas and to find a home that meets your various desires and concerns. If you're a normal person with a full-time job and you're confined to occasional weekends and evenings to look for a house, three to six months is a short time period to settle on an area and actually find and successfully negotiate on a property. Six months to a year isn't unusual or slow. Remember that you're talking about an enormous purchase that you'll come home to daily.

Real estate agents can be a big barrier to taking your time with this monumental decision. Some agents are pushy and want to make a sale, get their commission, and move on to the next client. As a buyer, don't work with such agents — they can make you miserable, unhappy, and broke. If necessary, begin your search without an agent to avoid this outside pressure. See Chapter 12 for additional information on working with an agent.

Keep an open mind

Before you start your search, you may have an idea about the type of property and location that interests you or that you think you can afford. You may think, for example, that you can afford only a condominium in the neighbourhood that you want. But if you take the time to check out other communities, you may find another area that meets most of your needs and has affordable single-family homes. You'd never know that, though, if you narrowed your search too quickly.

Even if you've lived in an area for a while and think that you know it well, look at different types of properties in a variety of locations before you start to narrow your search. Be open-minded and make sure that you know which of your many criteria for a home you *really* care about. You'll likely have to be flexible with some of your preferences.

After you focus on a particular area or neighbourhood, make sure that you see the full range of properties available. If you want to spend $250,000 on a home, look at properties that are more expensive. Unless an area is experiencing a boom, real estate usually sells for less than its listing price, and you may feel comfortable spending a little bit more after you see what you can purchase if you stretch your budget a little bit. Also, if you work with an agent, make sure that you don't overlook homes that are for sale by their owners (that is, properties not listed with real estate agents). Otherwise, you may miss out on some good prospects.

Research, research, research

Thinking that you can know what an area is like from anecdotes or from a small number of personal experiences is a mistake. You may have read or heard that someone was mugged in a particular area. That doesn't make that area dangerous — or more dangerous than others. *Get the facts.* Anecdotes and people's perceptions often aren't accurate reflections of the facts. Check out the following key items:

- ✔ **Amenities:** Hopefully, you don't spend all your time at work, slaving away to make your monthly mortgage payment. We hope that you have time to use parks, sports and recreation facilities, and so on. You can drive around the neighbourhood you're interested in to get a sense of these attractions. Most real estate agents just love to show off their favorite neighbourhoods. Cities and towns can also mail you information booklets that detail what they have to offer and where you can find it.

- ✔ **Schools:** If you have kids, you care about this issue a lot. Unfortunately, many people make snap judgments about school quality without doing their homework. Visit the schools and don't blindly rely on test scores. Talk to parents and teachers and discover what goes on at the schools.

If you don't have (or want!) school-age children, you may be tempted to say, "What the heck do I care about the quality of the schools?" You need to care about the schools because even if you don't have kids, the quality of the local schools and whether they're improving or faltering has a direct bearing on the value of your property. Consider these issues even if they're not important to you, because they can affect the resale value of your property.

- ✔ **Property taxes:** What will your property taxes be? Property tax rates vary from community to community. Check with the town's assessment office or with a good real estate agent.

- ✔ **Crime:** Call the local police department or visit your public library to get the facts on crime. Cities and towns keep all sorts of crime statistics for neighbourhoods — use them!

- ✔ **Future development:** Check with the planning department in towns that you're considering living in to find out what types of new development and major renovations are in the works. Planning people may also be aware of problems in particular areas.

- ✔ **Catastrophic risks:** Are the neighbourhoods that you're considering buying a home in susceptible to major risks, such as floods, tornadoes, mudslides, fires, or earthquakes? Although homeowner's insurance can protect you financially, consider how you may deal with such catastrophes emotionally — insurance eases only the financial pain of a home loss. All areas have some risk, and a home in the safest of areas can burn to the ground. Although you can't eliminate all risks, you can at least educate yourself about the potential catastrophic risks in various areas.

If you're new to an area or don't have a handle on an area's risks, try a number of different sources. Knowledgeable and honest real estate agents may help, but you can also dig for primary information. Contact Environment Canada as well as the Public Safety and Emergency Preparedness Canada office (www. ocipep.gc.ca) to find out about potential flooding and earthquake risks in the area you're considering. Insurance companies and agencies can also tell you what they know about risks in particular areas.

Understand market value

Over many months, you'll perhaps look at dozens of properties for sale. Use these viewings as an opportunity to find out what places are worth. The listing price isn't what a house is worth — it may be, but odds are it's not. Property that is priced to sell usually does just that — it sells. Properties left on the market are often overpriced. The listing price on such properties may reflect what an otherwise greedy or uninformed seller and his agent hope that some fool will pay.

Of the properties that you see, keep track of the prices that they end up selling for. (Good agents can help you obtain this information.) Properties usually sell for less than the listed price. Keeping track of selling prices gives you a good handle on what properties are really worth and a better sense of what you can afford.

Pound the pavement

After you set your sights on that special home, thoroughly check out the surroundings — you should know what you're getting yourself into.

Go back to the neighbourhood in which the property is located at different times of the day and on different days of the week. Knock on a few doors and meet your potential neighbours. Ask questions. Talk to property owners as well as renters. Because they don't have a financial stake in the area, renters are often more forthcoming with negative information about an area.

After you decide where and what to buy, you're ready to try to put a deal together. We cover issues common to both home and investment property purchases — such as mortgages, negotiations, inspections, and so on — in Chapter 12.

Chapter 11

Investing in Real Estate

*I*f you've already bought your own home (and even if you haven't), using real estate as an investment may interest you. Over the decades and generations, real estate investing, like the stock market and small-business investments, has generated tremendous wealth for participants. (Please see Chapter 2 for more on the rate of return from good real estate investments.)

Real estate is like other types of ownership investments, such as stocks, where you have an ownership stake in an asset. Although you have the potential for significant profits, don't forget that you also accept greater risk. Real estate isn't a gravy train or a simple way to get wealthy. Like stocks, real estate goes through good and bad performance periods. Most people who make money investing in real estate do so because they invest and hold property over many years. The vast majority of people who don't make money in real estate don't because they make easily avoidable mistakes. In this chapter, we discuss how to make the best real estate investments and avoid the rest.

Outlining Real Estate Investment Attractions

As we discuss in Chapter 1, many types of people build their wealth by investing in real estate. Some people focus exclusively on property investments, but many others build their wealth through the companies they started or through other avenues and then diversify into real estate investments. What do these wealthy folks know, and why do they choose to invest in real estate? In the following sections, we cover some of real estate's attractions.

Real estate, like all investments, has its pros and cons. Investing in real estate is time intensive and carries investment and other risks. Invest in real estate because you enjoy the challenge and because you want to diversify your port-folio (an advantage of real estate is that its value doesn't move in lockstep with other investments, such as stocks or small-business investments that you hold). Don't take this route because you seek a get-rich-quick outlet.

Limited land

The supply of buildable, desirable land on planet Earth is limited. And because people are prone to reproduce, demand for land and housing con-tinues to grow. Land and what you can do with it are what make real estate valuable. Cities and islands such as Hawaii, Hong Kong, Vancouver, San Francisco, Toronto, Los Angeles, and New York City have the highest housing costs around because land is limited in these places.

Leverage

Real estate is different from most other investments in that you can borrow 80 to 90 percent (or more) of the value of the property to buy it. Thus, you can use your small down payment of 10 to 20 percent of the purchase price to buy, own, and control a much larger investment; this concept is called *leverage*. Of course, you hope that the value of your real estate goes up — if it does, you make money on your original dollars invested, as well as on the money that you borrowed.

Here's a quick example to illustrate. Suppose that you purchase a rental property for $150,000 and make a $30,000 down payment. Over the next three years, imagine that the property appreciates to $180,000. Thus, you have a profit (on paper at least) of $30,000 on an investment of just $30,000. In other words, you've made a 100 percent return on your investment. (Note that in this scenario, we ignore whether your expenses from the property exceed the rental income that you collect.)

Leverage is good for you if property prices appreciate, but leverage can also work against you. If your $150,000 property decreases in value to $120,000, even though it's dropped only 20 percent in value, you actually lose (on paper) 100 percent of your original $30,000 investment. If you have an out-standing mortgage of $120,000 on this property and you need to sell, you actually must pay money into the sale to cover selling costs, in addition to losing your entire original investment. Ouch!

Appreciation and income

Another reason that real estate is a popular investment is that you can make money from it in two major ways:

✔ First, you hope and expect that over the years, your real estate investments will appreciate in value. The appreciation of your properties compounds, tax-deferred, during your years of ownership. You don't pay tax on this profit until you sell your property.

If you sell a property for more than you paid for it — particularly if you have been renting it out for several years — your profits will generally be deemed to be capital gains. That's a heck of a deal when you consider that capital gains are taxed at half the rate of ordinary income.

✔ In addition to making money from your properties' increase in value, you can also make money from the ongoing business that you run — renting the property. You rent out investment property to make a profit based on the property's rental income that (hopefully) exceeds your expenses (mortgage, property taxes, insurance, maintenance, and so on). Unless you make a large down payment, your monthly operating profit will usually be small or non-existent in the early years of rental property ownership. Over time, your operating profit, which is subject to ordinary income tax, should rise as you increase your rental prices faster than your expenses. During soft periods in the local economy, however, rents may rise more slowly than your expenses (or rents may even fall).

Ability to "add value"

You as a small investor can't add value to stocks by "fixing them up," but you may have some good ideas about how to improve a property and make it more valuable. Perhaps you can fix up a property or develop it further and raise the rental income and resale value accordingly. Through legwork, persistence, and good negotiating skills, you can purchase a property below its fair market value.

Relative to investing in the stock market, tenacious and savvy real estate investors can more easily buy property below its fair market value. You can do the same in the stock market, but the scores of professional, full-time money managers who analyze stocks make finding bargains more difficult.

Ego gratification

Face it, investing in real estate appeals to some investors because land and buildings are tangible. Although few admit it, some real estate investors get an ego rush from a tangible display of their wealth. You can drive past investment real estate and show it off to others. In an article in *The New York Times* titled "What My Ego Wants, My Ego Gets," Donald Trump publicly admitted what most everyone else knew long ago: He holds his real estate investments partly for his ego. Trump confessed of his purchase of the famed Plaza Hotel in the Big Apple, "I realized it was 100 percent true — ego did play a large role in the Plaza purchase and is, in fact, a significant factor in all of my deals."

Real estate investing isn't as wonderful as they say

If you've read some of the many real estate investment books that have been published over the years, you may need to slightly deprogram yourself. Too often, authors attempt to make real estate investments sound like the one and only sure way to become a multimillionaire with little effort. Consider the following statements made by real estate book authors. Our rebuttals to their claims follow:

"Rather than yielding only a small interest payment or dividend, real estate in prime locations can appreciate 20 percent a year or more."

Bank accounts, bonds, and stocks pay interest or dividends that typically amount to 2 to 6 percent per year (the total return on stocks averages about 8 to 10 percent per year). However, bank accounts and bonds aren't comparable investments to stocks or real estate — they're far more conservative and liquid and therefore don't offer the potential for double-digit returns. Stock market investing is comparable to investing in real estate, but you shouldn't go into real estate investments *expecting* annual returns of 20 percent or more. Those who purchased good Toronto or Vancouver real estate in the 1950s and held onto it for the next three decades earned handsome returns as the population of this area boomed. Finding areas like these — and knowing how long to hold on to investments in these areas — is easier said than done. With real estate investments, over the long haul you can expect to earn 8 to 12 percent per year, but not 20 percent or more.

"A good piece of property can't do anything but go up!"

Any city, town, or community has good pieces of real estate. But that doesn't mean that communities can't and won't have slow or depressed years. Real estate in some parts of the prairies, for example, has appreciated quite slowly — at or just above the rate of inflation — for periods as long as a generation or more.

"Real estate is the best way of preserving and enhancing wealth. . . . [it] stands head and shoulders above any other form of investment."

Investing in stocks or in a small business is every bit as profitable as investing in real estate. In fact, more great fortunes have been built in small business than in any other form of investment. Over the long term, stock market investors have enjoyed (with far less hassle) average annual rates of return comparable to real estate investors' returns.

Longer-term focus

One problem with investing in the securities markets, such as the stock market, is that prices are constantly changing. Television news programs, Web sites, BlackBerrys, and other communication devices dutifully report the latest price quotes. From our observations and discussions with individual investors, we've seen how the constant reports on changes in the financial markets cause some investors to lose sight of the long term and the big picture. In the worst cases, large short-term drops like we saw in late 2008 lead investors to panic and sell at what end up being bargain prices. Or headlines about big increases pull investors in lemming-like fashion into an overheated and peaking market. Because all you need to do is click your computer mouse or dial a toll-free phone number to place your sell or buy order, some stock market investors fall prey to irrational snap judgments.

Like the stock market, the real estate market is constantly changing. However, to a real estate investor, short-term, day-to-day, and week-to-week changes are invisible. Publications don't report the value of your real estate holdings daily, weekly, or even monthly, and that's a good thing because it encourages a longer-term focus. If prices do decline over the months and years, you're much less likely to sell in a panic with real estate. Preparing a property for sale and eventually getting it sold take a good deal of time, and this barrier to quickly selling helps keep your vision in focus.

Figuring Out Who Should Avoid Real Estate Investing

Real estate investing isn't for everyone; not even close. Most people do better financially when they invest their ownership holdings in a diversified portfolio of stocks, such as through stock mutual funds. Shy away from real estate investments that involve managing property if you fall into either of the following categories:

- ✔ **You're time starved and anxious.** Buying and owning investment property and being a landlord take a lot of time. If you fail to do your homework before purchasing real estate, you can end up overpaying — or buying a heap of trouble. As for managing a property, you can hire a property manager to help with screening and finding good tenants and trouble-shooting problems with the building, but this step costs money and still requires some time involvement. Also, remember that most tenants don't care for a property the same way property owners do. If every little scratch or carpet stain sends your blood pressure skyward, avoid distressing yourself as a landlord.

✔ **You're not interested in real estate.** Some people simply don't feel comfortable and informed when it comes to investing in real estate. If you've had experience and success with stock market investing, that's a good reason to stick with it and avoid real estate. Over long periods of time, both stocks and real estate provide comparable returns.

Examining Simple, Profitable Real Estate Investments

Investing in rental real estate that you're responsible for can be a lot of work. With rental properties, you have all the headaches of maintaining a property, including finding and dealing with tenants, without the benefits of living in and enjoying the property.

Unless you're extraordinarily interested in and motivated to own investment real estate, start with and perhaps limit your real estate investing to a couple of much simpler yet still profitable methods that we discuss in this section.

A place to call home

During your adult life, you need a roof over your head. However, you may be able to sponge off your folks or some other relative for a number of years. If you're content with this arrangement, you can minimize your housing costs and save more for a down payment and possibly toward other goals. Go for it, if your relatives will!

But what if neither you nor your relatives are up for the challenge? For the long term, because you need a place to live, why not own real estate instead of renting it? Real estate is the only investment that you can live in or rent to produce income. You can't live in a stock, bond, or mutual fund! Unless you expect to move within the next few years, buying a place probably makes good long-term financial sense. In the long term, owning usually costs less than renting and allows you to build equity in an asset. Read Chapter 10 to find out more about profiting from homeownership.

Real estate investment trusts

Real estate investment trusts (REITs) are entities that generally invest in different types of property, such as shopping centres, apartments, and other rental buildings. For a fee, REIT managers identify and negotiate the purchase of properties that they believe are good investments and manage these properties, including all tenant relations. Thus, REITs are a good way to invest in real estate for people who don't want the hassles and headaches that come with directly owning and managing rental property.

Surprisingly, most books that focus on real estate investing neglect REITs. Why? We've come to the conclusion that they do so for three major reasons:

- ✔ First, if you invest in real estate through REITs, you don't need to read a long, complicated book on real estate investment.

- ✔ Second, real estate agents write many of these books. Not surprisingly, the real estate investment strategies touted in these books include and advocate the use of such agents. You can buy REITs without real estate agents.

- ✔ Finally, a certain snobbishness prevails among people who consider themselves to be "serious" real estate investors. One real estate writer/investor went so far as to say that REITs aren't "real" real estate investments.

Please. No, you can't drive your friends by a REIT and show it off. But those who put their egos aside when making real estate investments are happy that they considered REITs and have enjoyed double-digit annual gains over the decades.

Converting your home into a rental

If you move into another home, turning your current home into a rental property may make sense. After all, it saves you the time and cost of finding a separate rental property.

Unfortunately, many people make the mistake of holding on to their current home for the wrong reasons when they buy another. This situation often happens when homeowners must sell their home in a depressed market (such as existed in many areas in the late 2000s). Nobody likes to lose money and sell their home for less than they paid for it. Thus, some owners hold on to their homes until prices recover.

If you plan to move and want to keep your current home as a long-term investment property, you can. But turning your home into a short-term rental is usually a bad move for a couple of reasons:

- ✔ First, you may not want the responsibilities of a landlord, yet you force yourself into the landlord business when you convert your home into a rental.

- ✔ Second, if the home eventually does rebound in value, you owe tax on the profit if your property is a rental when you sell it and don't buy another rental property.

You can research and purchase shares in individual REITs, which trade as securities on the major stock exchanges. An even better approach is to buy a mutual fund that invests in a diversified mixture of REITs (see Chapter 8).

In addition to providing you with a diversified, low-hassle real estate investment, REITs offer an additional advantage that traditional rental real estate doesn't: You can easily invest in REITs with money inside a tax-deferred account (for example, an RRSP). As with traditional real estate investments, you can even buy REITs and mutual fund REITs with borrowed money.

Evaluating Direct Property Investments

Every year several publications put out lists of the wealthiest people. (They generally leave out mobsters and drug kingpins — the money must be made through seemingly legitimate and legal channels.) Numerous people get on these lists primarily because of their real estate investments. For others, real estate was an important secondary factor that contributed to their wealth.

Consider Marcel Adams. Born in Romania, Mr. Adams was forced into a labour camp during the Second World War, escaped his native country, and landed in Canada in the 1950s. After working as a hide tanner and trader in Quebec City, he got into real estate and began building strip malls and shopping centres. After he'd built up his cash flow and minimized his debts, he moved into the lending business with Les Placements Jeton Bleu Inc. (Blue Chip Investments). The company specialized in lending money at high rates to high-risk commercial real estate ventures. In the early 1990s, real estate prices plummeted, dozens of owners defaulted on their over-leveraged properties, and Mr. Adams's company took them back. The company expanded to own many buildings and malls, including some of Quebec's most well-known shopping centres. At one point, Mr. Adams's worth was estimated to be over $900 million.

If you think you're cut out to be a landlord and are ready for the responsibility of buying, owning, and managing rental real estate, you have lots of direct real estate investment options from which to choose.

Before you begin this potentially treacherous journey, we strongly recommend that you read Chapter 10. Many concepts you need to know to be a successful real estate investor are similar to those you need to know when you buy a home. The rest of this chapter focuses on issues that are unique to real estate investing.

Ideally, you should plan to make real estate investments that you hold until, and perhaps through, your retirement years, although some investors prefer to buy properties, improve them, and then move on. But what should you buy? The following is our take on various real estate investments.

Residential housing

Your best bet for real estate investing is to purchase residential property. People always need a place to live. Residential housing is easier to understand, purchase, and manage than most other types of property, such as office and retail property. If you're a homeowner, you already have experience locating, purchasing, and maintaining residential property.

The most common residential housing options are single-family houses, condominiums, and townhouses. You can also purchase multiunit buildings. In addition to the considerations that we address in Chapter 10, from an investment and rental perspective, consider the following issues when you decide what type of property to buy:

- **Tenants:** Single-family homes with just one tenant (could be a family, a couple, or a single person) are simpler to deal with than multiunit apartment buildings that require the management and maintenance of multiple renters and units.

- **Maintenance:** From the property owner's perspective, condominiums are generally the lowest-maintenance properties because most condominium associations deal with issues such as roofing, gardening, and so on for the entire building. Note that as the owner, you're still responsible for maintenance that is needed inside your unit, such as servicing appliances, interior painting, and so on. Beware, though, that some condo complexes don't allow rentals.

  With a single-family home or apartment building, you're responsible for all the maintenance. Of course, you can hire someone to do the work, but you still have to find the contractors and coordinate and oversee the work.

- **Appreciation potential:** Look for property where simple cosmetic and other fixes may allow you to increase rents. Such improvements can increase the market value of the property. Although condos may be easier on the unit owner to maintain, they tend to appreciate less than homes or apartment buildings, unless the condos are located in a desirable urban area. One way to add value to some larger properties is to "condo-ize" them. In some areas, if zoning allows, you can convert a single-family home or multiunit apartment building into condominiums. Keep in mind, however, that this metamorphosis requires significant research, both on the zoning front as well as with estimating remodelling and construction costs.

- **Cash flow:** As we discuss in the "Examining and estimating cash flow" section later in the chapter, your rental property brings in rental income that you hope covers and exceeds your expenses. The difference between the rental income you collect and the expenses you pay out is known as your *cash flow*.

Unless you can afford a large down payment (25 percent or more), the early years of rental property ownership may financially challenge you. Making a profit in the early years from the monthly cash flow with a single-family home is hard because such properties usually sell at a premium price relative to the rent that they can command. Remember, you pay extra for the land, which you can't rent. Also, the downside to having just one tenant is that when you have a vacancy, you have no rental income.

Apartment buildings, particularly those with more units, can generally produce a small positive cash flow, even in the early years of rental ownership. With all properties, as time goes on, generating a positive cash flow gets easier as you pay down your mortgage debt and hopefully increase your rents.

Unless you really want to minimize maintenance responsibilities, avoid condominium investments. Single-family home investments are generally more straightforward for most people. Just make sure that you run the numbers (we show you how in the "Examining and estimating cash flow" section, later in this chapter) on your rental income and expenses to see whether you can afford the negative cash flow that often occurs in the early years of ownership. Apartment building investments are best left to sophisticated investors who like a challenge and can manage more complex properties. As we discuss in Chapter 12, do thorough inspections before you buy any rental property.

Land

If tenants are a hassle and maintaining a building is a never-ending pain, why not invest in land? Buy land in an area that will soon experience a building boom, hold on to it until prices soar, and then cash in. Such an investment idea sounds good in theory. In practice, however, making the big bucks through land investments isn't easy. Although land doesn't require upkeep and tenants, it does require financial feeding.

Investing in land is a cash drain, and because it costs money to purchase land, you also have a mortgage payment to make. Mortgage lenders charge higher interest rates on loans to purchase land because they see it as a more speculative investment. You don't get depreciation tax write-offs because land isn't depreciable. You also have property tax payments to meet, as well as other expenses. However, with land investments, you don't receive income from the property to offset these expenses.

If you decide that you someday want to develop the property, that will also cost you a hefty chunk of money. Obtaining a loan for development is challenging and more expensive (because it's riskier for the lender) than obtaining a loan for a developed property.

Identifying many years in advance which communities will experience rapid population and job growth isn't easy. Land in those areas that people believe will be the next hot spot already sells at a premium price. If property growth doesn't meet expectations, appreciation will be low or non-existent.

If you decide to invest in land, be sure that you

- ✔ **Can afford it:** Tally up the annual carrying costs to see what your cash drain may be. What are the financial consequences of this cash outflow? For example, will you be able to fund your tax-advantaged retirement plans? If you can't, count the lost tax benefits as another cost of owning land.

- ✔ **Understand what further improvements the land needs:** Running utility lines, building roads, landscaping, and so on all cost money. If you plan to develop and build on the land that you purchase, research what these things may cost. Make sure that you don't make these estimates with your rose-tinted sunglasses on — improvements almost always cost more than you expect.

- ✔ **Know its zoning status:** The value of land depends heavily on what you can develop on it. Never purchase land without thoroughly understanding its zoning status and what you can and can't build on it. Also research the disposition of the planning department and nearby communities. Areas that are anti-growth and anti-development are less likely to be good places for you to invest in land, especially if you need permission to do the type of project that you have in mind. Beware that zoning can change for the worse — sometimes a zoning alteration can reduce what you can develop on a property and, consequently, the property's value.

- ✔ **Become familiar with the local economic and housing situations:** In the best of all worlds, you want to buy land in an area that is home to rapidly expanding companies and that has a shortage of housing and developable land. We discuss how to research these issues in the upcoming section "Deciding Where and What to Buy."

Commercial real estate

Ever thought about owning and renting out a small office building or strip mall? If you're really motivated and willing to roll up your sleeves, you may want to consider commercial real estate investments. Generally, you're better off not investing in such real estate because it's much more complicated than investing in residential real estate. It's also riskier from an investment and tenant-turnover perspective. When tenants move out, new tenants sometimes require extensive and costly improvements, which you'll likely need to provide to compete with other building owners.

If you're a knowledgeable real estate investor and you like a challenge, there are two good reasons to invest in commercial real estate:

- ✔ Your analysis of the local market suggests that it's a good time to buy.
- ✔ You can use some of the space to run your own small business.

Just as owning your home is generally more cost-effective than renting over the years, so it is with commercial real estate if — and this is a big if — you buy at a reasonably good time and hold the property for many years.

So how do you evaluate the state of your local commercial real estate market? Examine the supply-and-demand statistics over recent years. How much space is available for rent, and how has that changed over time? What is the vacancy rate, and how has that changed in recent years? Also investigate the rental rates, usually quoted as a price per square foot. See the next section, "Deciding Where and What to Buy," to find out how to gather this kind of information.

One way to tell that purchasing a commercial property in an area is a bad idea is if the supply of available space has increased faster than demand, leading to falling rental rates and higher vacancies. A slowing local economy and a higher unemployment rate also spell trouble for commercial real estate prices. Each market is different, so make sure you check out the details of your area. In the next section, we explain where you can find such information.

Deciding Where and What to Buy

If you're going to invest in real estate, you can do tons of research to decide where and what to buy. Keep in mind, though, that as in other aspects of life, you can spend the rest of your life looking for the perfect real estate investment, never find it, never invest, and miss out on lots of opportunities, profit, and even fun. In the following sections, we explain what to look for in a community and area that you seek to invest in.

We're not suggesting that you need to conduct a nationwide search for the best areas. In fact, investing in real estate closer to home is best because you're probably more familiar with the local area and you should have an easier time researching and managing local property.

Considering economic issues

People need a place to live, but an area doesn't generally attract homebuyers if no jobs exist. Ideally, look to invest in real estate in communities that maintain diverse job bases. If the local economy relies heavily on jobs in a small number of industries, that dependence increases the risk of your real estate investments. Statistics Canada tracks this data — you'll find their number in the blue pages of your local telephone book, or visit www.statcan.gc.ca. A good local library should also have this data.

Also, consider which industries are more heavily represented in the local economy. If most of the jobs come from slow-growing or shrinking employment sectors, real estate prices are unlikely to rise quickly in the years ahead. On the other hand, areas with a greater preponderance of high-growth industries stand a greater chance of faster price appreciation.

Also, check out the unemployment situation and examine how the jobless rate has changed in recent years. Good signs to look for are declining unemployment and increasing job growth. Statistics Canada also tracks this information.

Evaluating the real estate market

The price of real estate, like the price of anything else, is driven by supply and demand. The smaller the supply and the greater the demand, the higher prices climb. Some real estate investors find out this fact the hard way. One such investor (John Reed, who also writes about real estate) lost all the money he had made in 15 years of apartment investing as a result of owning apartments in Texas when overbuilding occurred in the mid-1980s.

Ouch! Imagine investing for 15 years and then losing it all! Credit was loose in some areas during the 1980s, which led to a building boom. But in many parts of Texas, as in some other parts of North America, a ton of buildable land existed. This abundance of land and available credit inevitably led to over-building. When the supply of anything expands at a much faster rate than demand, prices usually fall.

Upward pressure on real estate prices tends to be greatest in areas with little buildable land. This characteristic was one of the things that attracted Eric to real estate in the San Francisco Bay Area decades ago. If you look at a map of this area, you can see that the city of San Francisco and the communities to the south are on a peninsula. Ocean, bay inlets, and mountains bound the rest of the Bay Area. More than 80 percent of the land in the greater Bay Area isn't available for development because state and federal government parks, preserves, and other areas protect the land from development or the land is impossible to develop. Of the land available for development, nearly all of it in San Francisco and the vast majority of it in nearby counties had been developed.

In the long term, the lack of buildable land in an area can be a problem. Real estate prices that are too high may cause employers and employees to relocate to less expensive areas. If you want to invest in real estate in an area with little buildable land and sky-high prices, run the numbers to see whether the deal makes economic sense. (We explain how to do this later in this chapter.)

In addition to buildable land, consider these other important real estate market indicators to get a sense of the health, or lack thereof, of a particular market:

- **Building permits:** The trend in the number of building permits tells you how the supply of real estate properties may soon change. A long and sustained rise in permits over several years can indicate that the supply of new property may dampen future price appreciation.

- **Vacancy rates:** If few rentals are vacant, that means more competition and demand for existing units, which bodes well for future real estate price appreciation. Conversely, high vacancy rates indicate an excess supply of real estate, which may put downward pressure on rental rates as many landlords compete to attract tenants.

- **Listings of property for sale and number of sales:** Just as the construction of many new buildings is bad for future real estate price appreciation, increasing numbers of property listings are also an indication of potential future trouble. As property prices reach high levels, some investors decide that they can make more money cashing in and investing elsewhere. When the market is flooded with listings, prospective buyers can be choosier, exerting downward pressure on prices. At high prices (relative to the cost of renting), more prospective buyers elect to rent, and the number of sales relative to listings drops.

  A sign of a healthy real estate market is a decreasing and relatively low level of property listings, indicating that the demand from buyers meets or exceeds the supply of property for sale from sellers. When the cost of buying is relatively low compared with the cost of renting, more renters can afford and choose to purchase, thus increasing the number of sales.

- **Rents:** The trend in rental rates that renters are willing and able to pay over the years gives a good indication as to the demand for housing. When the demand for housing keeps up with the supply of housing and the local economy continues to grow, rents generally increase. This increase is a positive sign for continued real estate price appreciation. Beware of buying rental property subject to rent control — the property's expenses may rise faster than you can raise the rents.

Examining property valuation and financial projections

How do you know what a property is really worth? Some say it's worth what a ready, willing, and financially able buyer is willing to pay. But some buyers pay more than what a property is truly worth. And sometimes buyers who are patient, do their homework, and bargain hard are able to buy property for less than its fair market value.

Crunching some numbers to figure what revenue and expenses a rental property may bring is one of the most important exercises you can go through when you determine a property's worth and decide whether you should buy it. In the sections that follow, we walk you through these important calculations.

Examining and estimating cash flow

Cash flow is the difference between the money that a property brings in and what goes out for its expenses. If you pay so much for a property that its expenses (including the mortgage payment and property taxes) consistently exceed its income, you have a money drain on your hands. Maybe you have the financial reserves to withstand the temporary drain for the first few years, but you need to know upfront what you're getting yourself into.

One of the biggest mistakes that novice rental property investors make is in failing to realize all the costs associated with investment property. In the worst cases, some investors end up in personal bankruptcy from the drain of *negative cash flow* (expenses exceeding income). In other cases, we've seen negative cash flow hamper people's ability to accomplish important financial goals.

The second biggest mistake rental property investors make is in believing the financial statements that sellers and their real estate agents prepare. Just as an employer views a resume, you should always view such financial statements as advertisements rather than sources of objective information. In some cases, sellers and agents lie. In most cases, these statements contain lots of projections and best-case scenarios.

For property that you're considering purchasing, ask for a copy of the Canada Revenue Agency Form T776 (Statement of Real Estate Rentals) from the property seller's federal income tax return. When most people complete their tax returns, they try to minimize their revenue and maximize their expenses — the opposite of what they and their agents normally do on the statements they sometimes compile to hype the property sale. Confidentiality and privacy aren't issues when you ask for Form T776 because you're asking only for this one schedule and not the person's entire income tax return. (If the seller owns more than one rental property for which financial data is compiled, he can simply black out this other information if he doesn't want you to see it.)

Refuting the wisdom of buying in the "best" areas

Some people, particularly those in the real estate business, say, "Buy real estate in the best school districts" or "Buy the least expensive home in the best neighbourhood." Conventional wisdom is often wrong, and these examples prove that.

Remember that as a real estate investor, you hope to profit from someday selling your properties, many years in the future, for a much higher price than you purchased them. If you buy into the "best," there may not be as much room for growth.

Take school districts, for example. Conventional wisdom says that you should look at the test scores of different districts and buy real estate in the best (that is, highest-scoring) districts. But odds are that real estate in those areas is probably already priced at a premium level. If things deteriorate, such an area may experience more decline than an area where property buyers haven't bid prices up into the stratosphere.

The biggest appreciation often comes from those areas and properties that benefit the most from improvement. Identifying these in advance isn't easy, but look for communities where the trend in recent years has been positive. Even some "average" areas perform better in terms of property value appreciation than today's "best" areas.

You should prepare financial statements based on facts and a realistic assessment of a property (see Figures 11-1, 11-2, and 11-3). There's a time and a place for unbridled optimism and positive thinking, such as when you're lost in a major snowstorm. If you think pessimistically, you may not make it out alive! But deciding whether to buy a rental property is not a life-or-death situation. Take your time and do it with your eyes and ears open and with a healthy degree of skepticism.

The monthly rental property financial statement that you prepare in Figures 11-1 through 11-3 is for the present. Over time, you hope and expect that your rental income will increase faster than the property's expenses, thus increasing the cash flow. If you want, you can use this financial statement for future years' projections as well.

Valuing property

Examining and estimating a property's cash flow is an important first step to figuring a property's value. But on its own, a building's cash flow doesn't provide enough information for you to intelligently decide whether to buy a particular real estate investment. Just because a property has a positive cash flow doesn't mean that you should buy it. Real estate generally sells for less and may have better cash flow in areas that investors expect to earn lower rates of appreciation.

In the stock market, you have more clues about a specific security's worth. Most companies' stocks trade on a daily basis, so you at least have a recent sales price to start with. Of course, just because a stock recently traded at $20 per share doesn't mean that it's worth $20 per share. Investors may be overly optimistic or pessimistic.

Just as you should evaluate a stock versus other comparable stocks, so too should you compare the asking price of a property with other comparable real estate. But what if all real estate is overvalued? Such a comparison doesn't necessarily reveal the state of inflated prices. In addition to comparing a real estate investment property to comparable properties, you need to also perform some local area evaluations of whether prices from a historic perspective appear too high, too low, or just right. To answer this last question, see Chapter 10.

	Per Month
Rents: Ask for copies of current lease agreements and also check comparable unit rental rates in the local market. Ask if the owner made any *concessions* (such as a month or two of free rent), which may make rental rates appear inflated. Make your offer contingent on the accuracy of the rental rates.	$_____
Garage rentals: Some properties come with parking spaces that the tenants rent. As with unit rental income, make sure that you know what the spaces really rent for.	+$_____
Laundry income: Dirty laundry isn't just on the evening news — it can make you wealthier! Don't underestimate or neglect to include the cost of laundry machine maintenance when you figure the expenses of your rental building.	+$_____
Other income: Other potential income streams for residential properties can include late charges, vending, Internet services, storage, concierge services, and so on. For commercial properties, common area maintenance charges (CAM) and telecommunications income, among others sources, are possible.	+$_____
Vacancy allowance: Keeping any rental occupied all the time is difficult, and finding a good tenant who is looking for the type of unit(s) that you have to offer may take some time. You can do occasional maintenance and refurbishing work in between tenants. Allow for a vacancy rate of 5 to 10 percent (multiply 5 to 10 percent by the rent figured in the first line).	–$_____
TOTAL INCOME	=$_____

Figure 11-1: Monthly rental property financial statement (Page 1 of 3).

(continued)

	Per Month
Mortgage: Enter your expected mortgage payment.	$_____
Property taxes: Ask a real estate person, mortgage lender, or your local assessor's office what your annual property tax bill would be for a rental property of comparable value to the one that you're considering buying. Divide this annual amount by 12 to arrive at your monthly property tax bill.	+$_____
Utilities: Get copies of utility bills from the current owner. Get bills over the previous 12-month period — a few months won't cut it because utility usage may vary greatly during different times of the year. (In a multiunit building, it's a plus for each unit to have a separate utility meter so that you can bill each tenant for what he/she uses.)	+$_____
Insurance: Ask for a copy of the current insurance coverage and billing statement from the current owner. If you're considering buying a building in an area that has floods, earthquakes, and so on, make sure that the cost of the policy includes these coverages. Although you can insure against most catastrophes, we would avoid buying property in a flood-prone area. Flood insurance does not cover lost rental income.	+$_____
Water: Again, ask the current owner for statements that document water costs over the past 12 months.	+$_____
Garbage: Get the bills for the last 12 months from the owner.	+$_____
Repairs/maintenance/cleaning: You can ask the current owner what to expect and check the tax return, but even doing this may provide an inaccurate answer. Some building owners defer maintenance. (A good property inspector can help to ferret out problem areas before you commit to buy a property.) Estimate that you'll spend at least 1 to 2 percent of the purchase price per year on maintenance, repairs, and cleaning. Remember to divide your annual estimate by 12!	+$_____
Rental advertising/management expenses: Finding good tenants takes time and promotion. If you list your rental through rental brokers, they normally take one month's rent as their cut. Owners of larger buildings sometimes have an on-site manager to show vacant units and deal with maintenance and repairs. Put the monthly pay for that person on this line or the preceding line. If you provide a below-market rental rate for an on-site manager, make sure that you factor this into the rental income section.	+$_____
Extermination/pest control: Once a year or every few years, you likely need to take care of pest control. Spraying and/or inspections generally start at $200 for small buildings.	+$_____
Legal, accounting, and other professional services: Especially with larger rental properties, you'll likely need to consult with lawyers and tax advisers from time to time.	+$_____
TOTAL EXPENSES	=$_____

Figure 11-2:
Monthly rental property financial statement (Page 2 of 3).

	Per Month
Total Income (from Page 1)	$_____
Total Expenses (from Page 2)	−$_____
CASH FLOW (Pretax Profit or Loss)	=$_____
Depreciation: The tax law allows you to claim a yearly tax deduction for depreciation, but remember that you can't depreciate land. Break down the purchase of your rental property between the building and land. You can make this allocation based on the assessed value for the land and the building or on a real estate appraisal. Residential property is depreciated at 4 or 5 percent per year of the remaining undepreciated value, depending on the type of building and when it was purchased. (You're generally limited to half that rate in the year you make your purchase.) For example, say you buy a residential rental property for $300,000 and $200,000 of that is allocated to the building, which can be depreciated at 4 percent. In the first year, you can take $4,000 as a depreciation tax deduction ($200,000 × ½ of 0.02%). The next year you can claim 4 percent of the remaining undepreciated value of $196,000 or $7,840, as your depreciation expense.	−$_____
NET INCOME	=$_____

Figure 11-3: Monthly rental property financial statement (Page 3 of 3).

Important note: Although depreciation is a deduction that helps you reduce your profit for tax purposes, it doesn't actually cost you money. Your cash flow from a rental property is the revenue minus your out-of-pocket expenses.

Here are the pros and cons of the different approaches you can use to value property:

- ✔ **Appraisers:** The biggest advantage of hiring an appraiser is that she values property for a living. An appraisal also gives you some hard numbers to use for negotiating with a seller. Hire a full-time appraiser who has experience valuing the type of property that you're considering. Ask for examples of a dozen similar properties in the area that she has appraised in the past three months.

  The drawback of appraisers is that they cost money. A small home may cost several hundred dollars to appraise, and a larger multiunit building may cost $1,000 or more. The danger is that you can spend money on an appraisal for a building that you don't end up buying.

- ✔ **Real estate agents:** If you work with a good real estate agent (we discuss how to find one in Chapter 12), ask him to draw up a list of comparable properties and help you estimate the value of the property you're considering buying. The advantage of having your agent help with this analysis is that you don't pay extra for this service.

The drawback of asking an agent what to pay for a property is that his commission depends on your buying a property and on the amount that you pay for that property. The more you're willing to pay for a property, the more likely the deal flies, and the more the agent makes on commission.

✔ **Do-it-yourself:** If you're comfortable with numbers and analysis, you can try to estimate the value of a property yourself. The hard part is identifying comparable properties. It's usually impossible to find identical properties, so you need to find similar properties and then make adjustments to their selling price so you can do an apples-to-apples comparison.

Among the factors that should influence your analysis of comparable properties are the date the properties sold; the quality of their locations; lot size; building age and condition; the number of units; the number of rooms, bedrooms, and bathrooms; and whether they have garages, fireplaces, and yards. A real estate agent can provide this information, or you can track it down for properties that you've seen or that you know have recently sold.

For example, if a similar property sold six months ago for $250,000 but prices overall have decreased 3 percent in the last six months, subtract 3 percent from the sales price. Ultimately, you have to attach a value or price to each difference between comparable properties and the one that you're considering buying. Through a series of adjustments, you can then compare the value of your target property to others that have recently sold.

These approaches aren't mutually exclusive — you probably want to at least review the numbers and analysis that an appraiser or real estate agent puts together.

Finding the information you need

When you evaluate properties, you need to put on your detective hat. If you're creative and inquisitive, you soon realize that this isn't a hard game to play. You can collect useful information about a property and the area in which it's located in many ways.

The first place to begin your inquiries is with the real estate agent who listed the property for sale. One thing that most agents love to do is talk and schmooze. Try to understand why the seller is selling. This knowledge helps you negotiate an offer that's appealing to the seller.

As for specifics on the property's financial situation, as we explain in the earlier section "Examining and estimating cash flow," ask the sellers for specific independent documents, including Form T776 from their tax return. Hire inspectors to investigate the property's physical condition (we advise you on hiring inspectors in Chapter 12).

Local government organizations can be treasure troves of information about their communities. You can also see the other recommended sources in Chapter 10, as well as some other sources that we suggest earlier in this chapter.

Digging for a Good Deal

Everyone likes to get a deal or feel like they bought something at a relatively low price. How else can you explain the North American retail practice of sales? merchandise is first overpriced, and what doesn't sell quickly enough is then marked down to create the illusion that you're getting a bargain! Some real estate sellers and agents do the same thing. They list property for sale at an inflated price and then mark it down after they realize that no one will pay their asking price. "$30,000 price reduction!" the new listing screams. Of course, this reduction isn't a deal.

Purchasing a piece of real estate at a discount is possible. Without doing a lick of work, you can make money simply by purchasing a property at a discount — one of the ultimate thrills of capitalism!

Scores of books claim to have the real estate investment strategy that can beat the system. Often these promoters claim that you can become a multimillionaire through investing in distressed properties. A common strategy is to purchase property that a seller has defaulted on or is about to default on. Or how about buying a property in someone's estate through probate court? Maybe you'd like to try your hand at investing in a property that has been condemned or has toxic-waste contamination!

It's possible to get a good buy and purchase a problem property at a discount larger than the cost of fixing the property. However, these opportunities are hard to find, and sellers of such properties are often unwilling to sell at a discount that's big enough to leave you much room for profit. If you don't know how to thoroughly and correctly evaluate the property's problems, you can end up overpaying.

In some cases, the strategies these real estate gurus advocate involve taking advantage of people's lack of knowledge. If you can find a seller in dire financial straits and desperate for cash, you may get a bargain buy on the home. (You may struggle with the moral issues of buying property cheaply this way.)

Other methods of finding discounted property take lots of time and digging. Some involve cold-calling property owners to see whether they're interested in selling. This method is a little bit like trying to fill a job opening by interviewing people you run into on a street corner. Although you may eventually find a good candidate this way, if you factor in the value of your time, the deal seems like less of a bargain.

Without making things complicated or too risky, you can use some of the following time-tested and proven ways to buy real estate at a discount to its fair market value:

✔ **Find a motivated seller:** Be patient and look at lots of properties, and sooner or later you'll come across one that someone needs to sell (and these aren't necessarily the ones advertised as having a motivated seller). Perhaps the seller has bought another property and needs the money to close on the recent purchase. Having access to sufficient financing can help secure such deals.

✔ **Buy unwanted properties with fixable flaws:** The easiest problems to correct are cosmetic. Some sellers and their agents are lazy and don't even bother to clean a property. One single-family home that Eric bought had probably three years' worth of cobwebs and dust accumulated. It seemed like a dungeon at night because half the light bulbs were burned out.

Painting; tearing up old, ugly carpeting; refinishing hardwood floors; and putting new plantings in a yard are relatively easy jobs. They make the property worth more and make renters willing to pay higher rent. Of course, these tasks take money and time, and many buyers aren't interested in dealing with problems. If you have an eye for improving property and are willing to invest the time that coordinating the fix-up work requires, go for it! Just make sure that you hire someone to conduct a thorough property inspection before you buy. (See Chapter 12 for more details.)

Be sure to factor in the loss of rental income if you can't rent a portion of the property during the fix-up period. Some investors have gone belly up from the double cash drain of fix-up expenses and lost rents.

✔ **Buy when the real estate market is depressed:** When the economy takes a few knocks and investors rush for the exits (like the downturn in the late 2000s), it's time to go shopping! Buy real estate when prices and investor interest are down. During times of depressed markets, obtaining properties that produce a positive cash flow (even in the early years) is easier. In Chapter 10, we explain how to spot a depressed market.

✔ **Check for zoning opportunities:** Sometimes, you can make more productive use of a property. For example, you can legally convert some multiunit apartment buildings into condominiums. Some single-family residences may include a rental unit if local zoning allows for it. A good real estate agent, contractor, and the local planning office in the town or city where you're looking at the property can help you identify properties that you can convert. If you're not a proponent of development, then you probably won't like this strategy.

If you buy good real estate and hold it for the long term, you can earn a healthy return from your investment. Over the long haul, having bought a property at a discount becomes an insignificant issue. You make money from your real estate investments as the market appreciates and as a result of your ability to manage your property well. So don't obsess over buying property at a discount, and don't wait for the perfect deal, because it won't come along.

Recognizing Inferior Real Estate "Investments"

Some supposedly "simple" ways to invest in real estate rarely make sense because they're near-certain money losers. In this section, we discuss real estate investments that you should generally (but not always) avoid.

Second/vacation homes

Some folks dream of having a weekend cottage or condo — a place you can retreat to when crowded urban or suburban living conditions get on your nerves. When it's not in use, you may rent out your vacation home and earn some income to help defray part of the maintenance expenses.

If you can realistically afford the additional costs of a second, or vacation, home, we're not going to tell you how to spend your extra cash. Investment real estate is property that you rent out 90 percent or more of the time. Most second-home owners we know rent their property out very little — 10 percent or less of the time. As a result, second homes are usually money drains. Even if you do rent your second home most of the time, high tenant turnover decreases your net rental income.

Now, we have seen some people make a decent return with second homes that were infrequently rented. Usually, these homes are held over many years and located in areas that have become increasingly popular.

Part of the allure of a second home is the supposed tax benefits. Even when you qualify for some or all of them, tax benefits only partially reduce the cost of owning a property. We've seen more than a few cases in which the second home is such a cash drain that it prevents its owners from making tax-deductible contributions to retirement savings plans.

If you don't rent out a second home property most of the time, ask yourself whether you can afford such a luxury. Can you accomplish your other financial goals — saving for retirement, paying for the home in which you live, and so on — with this added expense? Keeping a second home is more of a consumption than an investment decision.

Time-shares

Time-shares are near-certain money losers. With a time-share, you buy a week or two of ownership or usage of a particular unit, usually a condominium, in a resort location. If you pay $8,000 for a week of "ownership," you pay the equivalent of more than $400,000 a year for the whole unit ($8,000/week × 52 weeks). However, a comparable unit nearby may sell for only $150,000. The extra markup pays the salespeople's commissions, administrative expenses, and profits for the time-share development company. (This little analysis also ignores the not-so-inconsequential ongoing time-share maintenance fees, which can easily run $200 per year or more.) People usually get hoodwinked into buying a time-share when they're enjoying a vacation someplace. Vacationers are easy prey for salespeople who, often using high-pressure sales tactics, want to sell them a souvenir of the trip. The cheese in the mousetrap is an offer of something free (for example, a free night's stay in a unit) for going through the sales presentation. As one regretful buyer told Tony, "I went in for a free pina colada and came out with a condo!"

If you can't live without a time-share, consider buying a used one. Many previous buyers, who almost always have lost much of their original investment, try to dump their time-shares. This fact tells you something about time-shares. You may be able to buy a time-share from an existing owner at a fair price, but why commit yourself to taking a vacation in the same location and building at the same time each year? Many time-shares let you trade your weeks; however, doing so is usually a hassle, and you're limited by what time slots you can trade for, which are typically dates that other people don't want.

Limited partnerships

In Chapter 2, we give you good reasons to avoid limited partnerships. High sales commissions and ongoing management fees burden limited partnerships sold through investment dealers and financial planners who work on commission. Quality real estate investment trusts (REITs), which we discuss earlier in this chapter, are infinitely better alternatives. REITs, unlike limited partnerships, are also completely liquid.

Scams

Wanting to make a lot of money in a hurry is very North American. Real estate investors with lofty expectations for high returns become bait for various hucksters who promise these investors great riches. It's bad enough when the deck is stacked against you. Even worse is to put your money into scams.

First Pension, for example, was a U.S. outfit, run by loan broker William Cooper, that bilked investors out of more than $100 million. First Pension was sold as a limited partnership that invested in mortgages. Using a Ponzi-type (pyramid) scheme, Cooper used the money from new investors to pay dividends to earlier investors. Time-shares, a truly terrible investment that we discuss earlier in this chapter, have also been subject to bankruptcy and fraud problems.

Hundreds of thousands of viewers fall prey annually to infomercial hucksters. Among the more infamous real estate infomercial promoters is Tom Vu. At his seminars, according to *The Los Angeles Times,* he says, "Well, if you make no money with me, you a loser." Vu, who came to the United States from Vietnam in the mid-1970s, claims to have made a fortune investing in real estate by using a fairly simple system. He says that he searches for property owners who are in debt up to their eyeballs and offers to buy their properties with no money down. By finding desperate sellers, he says, you can buy real estate at a big discount from its fair market value.

Vu actually makes his money from running high-priced seminars to teach you basic real estate techniques that you can read in a book that costs about $20. Vu, however, charges up to $15,000 for a five-day seminar! As if overpaying this much isn't enough, Vu's former "students," who filed a number of lawsuits that included a class action suit, say that his methods don't work and that he reneged on his promises to go into partnership on properties they identified. A number of states investigated Vu's practices, have barred further Vu seminars in their states, and are seeking compensation for victims. Unfortunately, Vu appears to have moved much of his money overseas. Other real estate seminar hucksters such as Robert Allen and Ed Buckley saw their seminar enterprises end up in bankruptcy, sunk by the claims of their unhappy students.

Other scams also abound. Stephen Murphy was a real estate investor who claimed to make a fortune buying foreclosed commercial real estate and wrote and self-published a book to share his techniques with the public. Murphy's organization contacted the people who bought his book and pitched them into collaborating with him on property purchases that supposedly would return upwards of 100 percent or more per year. However, Murphy had other ideas, and he siphoned off nearly two-thirds of the money for himself and for promotion of his books! He even hoodwinked Donald Trump into writing praise for his book and work: "I really admire Steve Murphy. . . . Steve commands some very wise, intelligent . . . and unique purchasing strategies." No kidding!

If an investment "opportunity" sounds too good to be true, it is. If you want to invest in real estate, avoid the hucksters and invest directly in properties that you can control or invest through reputable REITs (or REIT mutual funds), which we discuss earlier in this chapter.

Chapter 12

Real Estate Financing and Deal Making

*I*n this chapter, we discuss issues such as understanding and selecting mortgages, working with real estate agents, negotiating, and other important details that help you put a real estate deal together. We also provide some words of wisdom about taxes and selling your property that may come in handy down the road. (In Chapter 10, we cover what you need to know to purchase a home, and in Chapter 11, we review the fundamentals of investing in real estate.)

Financing Your Real Estate Investments

Unless you're affluent or buying a low-cost property, you likely need to borrow some money, via a mortgage, to finance your property acquisition. Without financing, your dream to invest in real estate will remain just that — a dream. So first, you've got to maximize your chances of getting approved for a loan, which, unfortunately, got a lot tougher in the late 2000s because of the soft real estate market in many parts of the country. Shopping wisely for a good mortgage can save you thousands, perhaps even tens of thousands, of dollars in extra interest and fees. Don't get saddled with a loan that you may not be able to afford someday and that could push you into foreclosure or bankruptcy.

Getting your loan approved

Even if you have perfect or near-perfect credit, you may encounter financing problems with some properties. And of course, not all real estate buyers have a perfect credit history, tons of available cash, and no debt. With the soft real estate market of the late 2000s, lenders tightened credit standards to avoid making loans to people likely to default. If you're one of those borrowers who ends up jumping through more hoops than other borrowers do to get a loan, don't give up hope. Few borrowers are perfect from a lender's perspective, and many problems are fixable.

The best defence against loan rejection is avoiding it in the first place. To head off potential rejection before you apply for the loan, you can sometimes disclose to your lender anything that may cause a problem. For example, if you already know that your credit report indicates some late payments from when you were out of the country for several weeks five years ago, write a letter that explains this situation.

Solving down payment problems

Most people, especially when they make their first real estate purchase, are strapped for cash. In order to qualify for the most attractive financing, lenders typically require that your down payment be at least 20 percent of the property's purchase price. The best investment property loans sometimes require 20 to 30 percent down for the best terms. In addition, you need reserve money to pay for other closing costs, such as title insurance and loan fees.

If you don't have 20-plus percent of the purchase price available, don't despair — you can still own real estate with the following strategies.

Checking out high-ratio mortgages

You may be able to put down as little as 5 percent of the purchase price and still get a mortgage. However, if you put down less than 20 percent of the value of the property, you're required by law (under the National Housing Act) to purchase mortgage insurance for your loan.

The insurance protects your lender in the event that you can't make your payments and you default on a high-ratio mortgage. The premium you'll pay is calculated on the full value of your mortgage — not just the amount beyond 80 percent of the property's value that you can borrow under a regular mortgage.

As a result of the subprime loan crisis, in 2008 the government brought in a rule requiring that any new insured mortgages must have an *amortization* — the number of years you take to pay back your home loan — of no more than 35 years. The new rules, which came into effect in late 2008, also required those taking out a new insured mortgage to meet certain credit requirements. In addition, zero-money-down mortgages were banned, with a new requirement that to get a new mortgage, borrowers must have at least a 5 percent down payment.

Mortgage insurance is available from the federal government's Canada Mortgage and Housing Corporation (CMHC). You can also purchase mortgage insurance from Genworth Financial Capital, which evolved out of GE Mortgage Insurance Canada. A third choice is newcomer AIG United Guaranty.

The rate you'll pay is determined by the size of your down payment compared with the value of the property. In the late 2000s, for example, insurers were charging about 1.75 percent if you were borrowing from 80 to 85 percent of the purchase price. For updated rates, visit the CMHC Web site at cmhc-schl.gc.ca/en. Rates for Genworth can be found at www.genworth.ca, and for AIG at www.aigug.ca.

You can choose either to pay the premium as a lump sum or to have it added to your mortgage amount. Adding it to your mortgage means you'll pay the premium several times over due to the extra interest you'll incur. Usually you'll also have to pay an application fee that can be as high as a few hundred dollars.

Considering the Home Buyers' Plan

Under the federal government's Home Buyers' Plan, you can borrow up to $25,000 from your RRSP to buy (or build) a home. Your spouse can also borrow an additional $25,000 from his or her RRSP, meaning you can take out a combined maximum of $50,000 if you're jointly purchasing a property.

The program is open to you only if you haven't owned a home and lived in it for the last five years. You're also ineligible if your spouse, and this includes those living in common-law, has owned a home in which you've lived over the same period.

Any money you borrow under the plan is treated as an interest-free loan you're making to yourself. The money doesn't have to be included in your income for that year, and you don't have to pay any tax on the withdrawal.

You have to start repaying the money you borrowed in the second year after you borrowed it. You must repay the full amount over 15 years, and are required to repay at least $1/15$ each year. If you miss a payment or part of a payment, that amount is included in your taxable income for that year, and you'll have to pay tax on it at your full marginal tax rate (the rate you pay on the highest, or last, dollars of income in any year).

Although it seems like a good deal, the Home Buyers' Plan has some significant costs:

- ✔ If making RRSP contributions is already a challenge, you may find it tough to make your repayments.

- ✔ You don't get a tax deduction for the repayments, because you're simply replacing money the government let you borrow interest-free — and tax-free — from your plan. If the tax savings from your RRSP contributions are an important factor in your finances, you need to consider the impact on your cash flow of having to replace that money as well as having to come up with the money to repay your loan.

- ✔ The plan can do damage to the long-term growth of your RRSP. When you withdraw money, you lose all its potential tax-free compounding until it's repaid to your plan. In addition, if you feel you'll be able to get together only the required repayments, you will also lose out on the tax savings and compound growth of the new RRSP contributions you could have used that money for.

The younger you are, the more costly this lost growth becomes. While your home's appreciation will likely offset the loss, it won't boost your retirement income unless you sell your property and move to a less expensive home, or take out a *reverse mortgage*. (A reverse mortgage allows you to trade some or all of the equity in your home for a series of payments to yourself. The money you receive, along with interest charges, is eventually paid back using the proceeds from the sale of your home, usually after you and your spouse die.)

Before you tap your retirement savings, get hold of a financial planning calculator (these are included with most personal finance planning software, and are also available at many Web sites) and calculate how much using the Home Buyers' Plan will decrease the future value of your RRSP. We address retirement planning issues in more detail in Chapter 3.

Investigating other options

Borrowing from your RRSP or taking out a high-ratio home loan aren't the only ways to deal with a lack of money for a down payment. Here are some other options to consider:

- ✔ **Postpone your purchase:** If you don't want the cost and strain of extra fees and bad mortgage terms, you can also postpone your purchase. Go on a financial austerity program and boost your savings rate.

- ✔ **Consider lower-priced properties:** Smaller properties and ones that need some work can help keep down the purchase price and the required down payment.

- ✔ **Find a partner:** Make sure that you write up a legal contract to specify what happens if a partner wants out. Family members sometimes make good partners. Your parents, grandparents, and maybe even your siblings may have some extra cash they'd like to lend, invest, or even give to you as a gift!

- ✔ **Look into seller financing:** Some property owners or developers may finance your purchase with as little as 5 to 10 percent down. However, you can't be as picky about such seller-financed properties because a limited supply is available and many that are available need work or haven't yet sold for other reasons.

Improving your credit rating

Late payments, missed payments, or debts that you never bothered to pay can tarnish your credit rating and squelch a lender's desire to offer you a mortgage. If you're turned down for a loan because of your less-than-stellar credit history, request (at no charge to you) a copy of your credit report from the lender that turned down your loan.

But if you think that your credit history may be a problem, the first thing to do is get the facts. Thanks to consumer legislation, you have the right to obtain a credit report for free from both of the main credit bureaus in Canada. To get a copy of your credit rating, contact either of the following credit bureaus:

- ✔ **Equifax:** www.equifax.ca; 1-800-465-7166
- ✔ **TransUnion:** www.tuc.ca; 1-800-663-9980

In order to obtain your report you'll need to provide the companies with signed photocopies of two pieces of ID, as well as your name, address, and social insurance number.

If you visit the Web sites of either credit bureau, you'll find it all but impossible to see that the companies will send you a free report in the mail. At both sites, it looks as if your only option is to pay a fee for an online report. In addition, both companies pitch a number of unnecessary credit services.

Explain any credit report problems to your lender. If the lender is unsympathetic, try calling other lenders. Tell them your credit problems up front and see whether you can find a lender willing to offer you a loan. Mortgage brokers may also be able to help you shop for lenders in these cases. (We discuss working with mortgage brokers later in this chapter.)

Sometimes you may feel that you're not in control when you apply for a loan. In reality, you can fix a number of credit problems yourself, and you reap great rewards (access to better loan terms, including lower interest rates) for doing so. And you can often explain those that you can't fix. Remember that some lenders are more lenient and flexible than others. Just because one mortgage lender rejects your loan application doesn't mean that all the others will as well.

If any erroneous information is listed on your credit report, get on the phone to the credit bureaus and start squawking. If specific creditors are the culprits, call them too. Keep notes from your conversations and make sure that you put your case in writing and have your comments added to your credit report. If the customer service representatives you talk with are no help, send a letter to the president of each company. Let the head honcho know that his or her organization caused you problems in obtaining credit. For more information on examining and disputing items on your credit report and managing credit in general, check out the Financial Consumer Agency of Canada Web site at www.fcac-acfc.gc.ca.

Another common credit problem is having too much consumer debt when you apply for a mortgage. The more credit card, auto loan, and other consumer debt you rack up, the less mortgage you qualify for. If you're turned down for the mortgage, take it as a well-meaning nudge to get rid of this high-cost debt. Hang on to the dream of buying real estate and use it as motivation to keep paying off your debts a priority.

To find out more about how credit scores work and techniques to improve yours, please see the latest edition of our book *Personal Finance For Canadians For Dummies* (Wiley).

Dealing with low appraisals

Even if you have sufficient income, a clean credit report, and an adequate down payment, the lender may turn down your loan if the appraisal of the property you want to buy comes in lower than the amount you agreed to pay for the property.

Assuming you still like the property, renegotiate a lower price with the seller by using the low appraisal to strengthen your case. With a low appraisal on a property that you already own and are refinancing, you obviously need to follow a different path. If you have the cash available, you can simply put more money down to get the loan balance to a level for which you qualify. If you don't have the cash, you may need to try another lender or forgo the refinance until you save more money or until the property value rises. (We discuss refinancing in more detail later in this chapter.)

In rare cases, lenders sometimes lowball (intentionally undervalue) an appraisal on refinances to sabotage a loan. A lender may do so, for example, if your current mortgage is under better terms (from their point of view). If you suspect that the lender is sabotaging your appraisal, ask for a copy of your appraisal, to which you are entitled. If you have comparable sale prices of homes from your area that support your case, go back to the lender and see what he or she has to say.

Handling insufficient income

If you're self-employed or you've changed jobs, your current income may not resemble your past income or, more importantly, your income may not be what a mortgage lender likes to see in respect to the amount that you want to borrow. A simple (but often impossible) way around this problem is to make a larger down payment. For example, if you put down 30 percent or more, you may be able to get a stated-income or no-documentation loan. Another option is to get mortgage insurance, which is offered by the Canada Mortgage and Housing Corporation (CMHC), as well as private insurers such as Genworth Financial (www.genworth.ca) and AIG United Guaranty (www.aigug.ca). Because of the real estate market downturn and the rise in foreclosures in the late 2000s, fewer lenders are willing to make these sorts of loans, but they aren't extinct just yet.

If you can't make a large down payment, another option is to get a co-signer for the loan — your relatives may be willing. As long as they aren't overextended themselves, they may be able to help you qualify for a larger loan than you can get on your own. As with partnerships, put your agreement in writing so that no misunderstandings occur.

Understanding the differences between short-term and long-term mortgages

Most mortgage lenders offer you the option of taking out a home loan for anywhere from six months to five years. You can even take a mortgage for seven or even ten years, but these are less common.

The period of time you arrange to borrow money for your home is called the *term*. When your term is up, your loan agreement comes to an end, or *matures*. The term of your mortgage is completely separate from the *amortization* you choose — the number of years over which you spread out the repayment of your principal and the interest charges. Most mortgages are amortized over 25 years.

When your mortgage's term is up, you have the choice of renewing with your existing lender or taking your mortgage elsewhere. Each time your mortgage matures, you're also free to choose whatever term you wish for your new loan.

You can stick with the same term, or choose a longer or shorter term. In general, the shorter the term, the lower the interest rate you'll pay. For instance, your lender might offer you an interest rate of 6 percent on a six-month term, 6.75 percent on a three-year term, and 7.5 percent on a five-year term.

Choosing a longer term of four or five years means you don't have to concern yourself about what happens to interest rates for a while, at least as they affect your home loan. Your payments are set and guaranteed for the entire period. That makes longer-range budgeting easier, as it removes uncertainty from that part of your required expenses, which for many people is a frequent source of stress. The drawback is that, as we note earlier, you'll pay a higher interest rate. Think of it as an insurance premium.

A short-term mortgage that lasts, say, only six months or one year puts you at the whim of interest rate fluctuations much more frequently. If rates trend upward, each time your mortgage renews you'll be hit by higher payments. Conversely, if rates are falling, you'll be able to enjoy lower payments much sooner than those who lock into longer terms.

Choosing between a short-term and long-term mortgage

Whether to go for a short- or long-term loan is an important decision in the real estate buying process. You need to weigh the pros and cons of each and decide what's best for your situation *before* you go out to purchase real estate or refinance.

In the real world, most people ignore this sensible advice. The excitement of purchasing a home or other piece of real estate tends to cloud judgment. In our experience, few buyers look at their entire financial picture before they make a major real estate decision.

Unfortunately, too many people let their interest rate crystal ball dictate whether they should take a short- or long-term mortgage. For example, those who think interest rates can only go up find long-term mortgages attractive.

You can't predict the future course of interest rates. Even the professional financial market soothsayers and investors can't accurately predict where rates are heading. If you could foretell this information, you could make a fortune investing in bonds and interest-rate futures and options. So cast aside your crystal ball, consider the following statistics, and then ask yourself the vital question that follows to help you decide whether a short-term or long-term mortgage will work best for you.

Assessing the cost

When many people are trying to decide between a short- and long-term mortgage, they focus on how much they can save over the next little while, and then factor in their sense of whether interest rates will rise in the future.

Much more important, though, is to get a sense of each option's total cost over the full life of your loan. Several studies have assessed how homeowners would have fared if they either continually renewed a short-term mortgage or stuck with five-year terms. Going back to 1980 when short-term mortgages were first made available, the studies found that 85 to over 90 percent of the time, the least expensive choice was to continually roll over a short-term mortgage. One study found that for a $200,000 mortgage, the average cost of five-year terms versus a series of one-year terms was an extra $2,000 of interest a year.

Continually renewing a five-year term costs more because short-term rates are almost always lower than long-term rates. In order for a series of short-term mortgages to cost more than a five-year term, interest rates over that time must rise enough so that the one-year rate increases beyond the five-year rate, and stays there for a good percentage of that time.

Of course, that's just the numbers side of your decision. You also need to consider how comfortable you are with the extra uncertainty that choosing short-term mortgages brings.

Determining how comfortable you are with taking risk

How much of a gamble can you take with the size of your monthly mortgage payment? For example, if your job and income are unstable and you need to borrow an amount that stretches your monthly budget, you can't afford much risk. If you're in this situation, you may want to stick with a long-term mortgage. You may also sleep better with a long-term mortgage if you're buying your first home and have little savings to fall back on should interest rates rise in a year or two and hit you with much higher monthly payments.

If you're in a position to take the financial risks associated with mortgage payments that may change every six months or year, you have a better chance of saving money with a shorter-term mortgage. Your interest rate starts lower and stays lower when the overall level of interest rates stays unchanged. Even if rates go up, there's a good possibility they will come back down over the life of your loan. Sticking with your short-term mortgage for better and for worse will likely help you come out ahead in the long run.

A short-term mortgage makes more sense if you borrow less than you're qualified for. Or perhaps you can save a sizable chunk — more than 10 percent — of your monthly income. If your income significantly exceeds your spending patterns, you may feel less anxiety about fluctuating interest rates. If you do choose a short term, you may feel more financially secure if you have a hefty financial cushion (at least six months' to as much as a year's worth of expenses reserved) that you can access if rates go up.

Don't take a short-term mortgage because the lower interest rate allows you to afford the property you want to buy (unless you're absolutely certain your income will rise to meet possible future payment increases). Try setting your sights on a property you can afford to buy with a longer-term mortgage.

Understanding the differences between open and closed mortgages

Another decision you'll have to make when setting up your mortgage is whether you want to be able to pay some or all of it off or to be able to refinance. Although this is possible with most mortgages, you may have to pay so much in penalties that it's not worthwhile if you have a closed mortgage. In contrast, there are typically no restrictions or penalties in paying off an open mortgage. Here are other key distinctions between these two types of mortgages:

- ✔ **Closed mortgage:** With this mortgage type, you agree to the specific conditions and interest rate on your loan for the entire term of your loan. If interest rates drop significantly in the meantime, you may be prevented from *refinancing* — ending your agreement and working out a new loan. If you're permitted to refinance, you'll likely have to pay a financial penalty that compensates the lender for the extra interest given up by allowing you to renegotiate your agreement. In most cases, this penalty will eliminate any gain from negotiating a new mortgage at the prevailing lower interest rates.

- ✔ **Open mortgage:** This mortgage type gives you the right to pay off some or all of the loan whenever you wish without incurring any penalties. This can be useful if interest rates are falling rapidly and you want to take advantage of them. An open mortgage is also a good idea if you know you'll be coming into a significant sum that will allow you to pay off your mortgage, or if you'll be selling your home in the near future. Because of this extra flexibility, open mortgages have higher interest rates than closed mortgages.

Choosing an open, closed, or convertible mortgage

If you know you'll be paying off your mortgage or selling your property in the near future, an open mortgage makes sense because of the flexibility to end your loan whenever you want without penalty.

In most other cases, paying higher interest rates for an open mortgage usually doesn't put you ahead. If you're going to be coming into a large sum of money, you could simply choose a short term and pay down your principal when the term is up. Even if you choose a longer term, most lenders allow you to pay off a reasonable chunk of your loan — typically 10 percent — once a year. If you're considering an open mortgage because interest rates appear to be heading steadily downward, you can simply select a short term — say six months or a year — so that you can soon renew at (hopefully) a lower interest rate and with lower monthly payments.

If you're like most people, you want to pay as little as you can but also want some protection against a sudden and large jump in rates. In that case, a good choice is a *convertible mortgage*. Convertible mortgages vary slightly from lender to lender, but the basic concept is the same. You agree to a short-term closed mortgage — either six months or one year, usually at or close to the same interest rate as a closed mortgage for the same term. However, at any point during the term, you can convert your loan to a different term. For instance, if you choose a six-month term and rates start rising rapidly, you can simply lock in a five-year rate at the prevailing level to protect yourself against rates being much higher by the time your existing term ends.

The attraction of a convertible mortgage is that it allows you to avoid paying the premium for longer-term fixed rates. At the same time, you're protected against rapidly rising rates because you can lock in for a longer term at any time, instead of either having to wait until your current term expires or paying a hefty penalty to refinance early. If rates are the same or lower when your current mortgage matures, you can just sign up for another six-month or one-year convertible mortgage.

Check the fine print. For instance, if you choose to convert to a different term, your lender may restrict you to a five-year term. The major drawback to a convertible mortgage is that if you do decide to convert while the mortgage is in existence, you can't change lenders, which eliminates much of your ability to bargain for a better rate. Unless you work out a rate discount ahead of time, when you convert you'll have to pay the going or posted rate for the new term you select. This means your rate will likely be anywhere from a quarter to three-quarters or more of a percent higher than you could otherwise negotiate.

Understanding other mortgage fees

In addition to the ongoing interest rate, lenders tack on all sorts of other upfront charges in processing your loan. Get an itemization of these other fees and charges in writing from all lenders that you're seriously considering (we explain how to find the best lenders for your needs in the next section). You need to know the total of all lender fees so you can accurately compare different lenders' loans and determine how much closing on your loan will cost you. Other mortgage fees can pile up in a hurry. Here are the common ones you may see:

- **Application and processing fees:** Most lenders charge a few hundred dollars to work with you to complete your paperwork and funnel it through their loan evaluation process. Should your loan be rejected, or if it's approved and you decide not to take it, the lender needs to cover its costs. Some lenders return this fee to you upon closing with their loan.

- **Credit report charge:** Most lenders charge you for the cost of obtaining your credit report, which tells the lender whether you've repaid other loans on time. Your credit report should cost about $50.

- **Appraisal fee:** The property for which you borrow money needs to be valued. If you default on your mortgage, a lender doesn't want to get stuck with a property that's worth less than you owe. The cost for an appraisal typically ranges from several hundred dollars for most residential properties to as much as $1,000 or more for larger investment properties.

To minimize your chances of throwing money away on a loan that you may not qualify for, ask the lender whether there is any reason your loan request may be denied. Be sure to disclose any problems on your credit report or any problems with the property that you're aware of. Lenders may not take the time to ask about these sorts of things in their haste to get you to complete their loan applications.

Finding the best lenders

You can easily save thousands of dollars in interest charges and other fees if you shop around for a mortgage deal. It doesn't matter whether you do so on your own or hire someone to help you, but you should shop because much money is at stake!

Shopping yourself

Many mortgage lenders compete for your business. Although having a large number of lenders to choose from is good for keeping interest rates lower, it also makes shopping a chore.

Real estate agents can refer you to lenders with whom they've done business. Those lenders don't necessarily offer the most competitive rates — the agent simply may have done business with them in the past or received client referrals from them.

Look in the real estate section of a large, local weekend newspaper for charts of selected area lender interest rates. Just as with Internet sites that advertise lender rates, these tables are by no means comprehensive or reflective of the best rates available. In fact, many of these rates are sent to newspapers for free by firms that distribute mortgage information to mortgage brokers. Use them as a starting point and call the lenders that list the best rates.

Shopping through a mortgage broker

A competent mortgage broker can be a big help in getting you a good loan and closing the deal, especially if you're too busy or disinterested to dig for a good deal on a mortgage. A good mortgage broker also keeps abreast of the many different mortgages in the marketplace. He or she can shop among lots of lenders to get you the best deal available. The following list presents some additional advantages to working with a mortgage broker:

- An organized and detail-oriented mortgage broker can help you through the process of completing all those tedious documents that lenders require.
- Mortgage brokers can help polish your loan package so the information you present is favourable yet truthful.
- The best brokers can also help educate you about various loan options and the pros and cons of available features.

Be careful when you choose a mortgage broker, because some brokers are lazy and don't shop the market for the best current rates. Even worse, some brokers may direct their business to specific lenders so they can take a bigger cut or commission.

A mortgage broker typically gets paid a percentage, usually 0.5 to 1 percent, of the loan amount. This commission is completely negotiable, especially on larger loans that are more lucrative.

You need to ask what the commission is on loans that a broker pitches. Some brokers may be indignant that you ask — that's their problem. You have every right to ask — it's your money.

Even if you plan to shop on your own, talking to a mortgage broker may be worthwhile. At the very least, you can compare what you find with what brokers say they can get for you. Again, be careful. Some brokers tell you what you want to hear — that is, that they can beat your best find — and then can't deliver when the time comes.

When to consider a home equity loan

Home equity loans, also known as second mortgages, allow you to borrow against the equity in your home in addition to the mortgage that you already have (a first mortgage).

A home equity loan may benefit you if you need more money for just a few years or if your first mortgage is at such a low interest rate that refinancing it to get more cash would be too costly. Otherwise, we advise you to avoid home equity loans.

If you need a larger mortgage, why not refinance the first one and wrap it all together? Home equity loans often have higher interest rates than comparable first mortgages. That's because they're riskier from a lender's perspective because the first mortgage lender gets first claim against your property if you file bankruptcy or you default on the mortgage.

One attraction of a home equity loan is that when you use your home as the security for a line of credit, the interest rate is usually the lowest available for consumer loans. You can borrow only the amount you need at the time you need it, and you can repay any or all of your borrowings at any time. These features mean you pay interest only on money you actually need, and you can cut your interest charges as soon as you have money available to pay down your loan.

If your loan broker quotes you a really good deal, make sure that you ask who the lender is. (Most brokers refuse to reveal this information until you pay the necessary fee to cover the appraisal and credit report.) You can check with the actual lender to verify the interest rate that the broker quotes you and make sure that you're eligible for the loan.

Working with Real Estate Agents

When you purchase real estate, if you're like most people, you enlist the services of a real estate agent. A good agent can help screen property so you don't spend all of your free time looking at potential properties, negotiating a deal, helping coordinate inspections, and managing other preclosing items.

Recognizing agent conflicts of interest

All real estate agents, good, mediocre, and awful, are subject to a conflict of interest because of the way they're compensated — on commission. We must say that we respect real estate agents for calling themselves what they are. Real estate agents don't hide behind an obscure job title, such as "shelter consultant." (Many financial "planners," "advisers," or "consultants," for example, actually work on commission and sell investments and life insurance and, therefore, are really stockbrokers and insurance brokers, not planners or advisers.)

Real estate agents aren't in the business of providing objective financial counsel. Just as car dealers make their living selling cars, real estate agents make their living bringing together real estate buyers and sellers. Never forget this fact as a buyer.

The pursuit of a larger commission may encourage an agent to get you to do things that aren't in your best interests, such as the following:

- **Buy, and buy sooner rather than later:** If you don't buy, your agent doesn't get paid for all the hours she spends working with you. The worst agents fib and use tricks to motivate you to buy. They may say that other offers are coming in on a property that interests you, or they may show you a bunch of dumps and then one good listing to motivate you to buy the one good listing.

- **Spend more than you should:** Because real estate agents get a percentage of the sales price of a property, they have a built-in incentive to encourage you to spend more on a property than what fits comfortably with your other financial objectives and goals. An agent doesn't have to consider or care about your other financial needs.

- **Purchase their company's listings:** Agents also may have a built-in incentive (higher commission) to sell their own listings.

- **Buy in their territory:** Real estate agents typically work a specific territory. As a result, they usually can't objectively tell you the pros and cons of the surrounding regions.

- **Use people who scratch their backs:** Some agents refer you to brokers, lenders, inspectors, and title insurance companies that have referred customers to them. Some agents also solicit and receive referral fees (or bribes) from mortgage lenders, inspectors, and contractors to whom they refer business.

Finding a good agent

A mediocre, incompetent, or greedy agent can be a real danger to your finances. Whether you're hiring an agent to work with you as a buyer or seller, you want someone who is competent and with whom you can get along. Working with an agent costs a good deal of money, so make sure you get your money's worth.

Interview several agents and check references. Ask agents for the names and phone numbers of at least three clients with whom they've worked in the past six months in the geographical area in which you're looking. By narrowing the period during which they worked with references to six months, you maximize the chances of speaking with clients other than the agent's all-time-favourite clients.

As you speak with an agent's references, look for these traits in any agent that you're considering working with, whether as a buyer or seller:

- **Full-time employment:** Some agents work in real estate as a second or even third job. Information in this field changes constantly — keeping track of it is hard enough on a full-time basis. It's hard to imagine a good agent being able to stay on top of the market while moonlighting elsewhere.

- **Experience:** Hiring someone with experience doesn't necessarily mean looking for an agent who's been an agent for decades. Many of the best agents come into the field from other occupations, such as business and teaching. Agents can acquire some sales, marketing, negotiation, and communication skills in other fields, but experience in real estate does count.

- **Honesty and integrity:** You need to trust your agent with a lot of information. If the agent doesn't level with you about what a neighbourhood or particular property is really like, you suffer the consequences.

- **Interpersonal skills:** An agent must get along not only with you but also with a whole host of other people who are involved in a typical real estate deal: other agents, property sellers, inspectors, mortgage lenders, and so on. An agent needs to know how to put your interests first without upsetting others.

- **Negotiation skills:** Putting a real estate deal together involves negotiation. Is your agent going to exhaust all avenues to get you the best deal possible? Most people don't like the sometimes aggravating process of negotiation, so they hire someone else to do it for them. Be sure to ask the agent's former client references how the agent negotiated for them.

- **High quality standards:** Sloppy work can lead to big legal or logistical problems down the road. If an agent neglects to recommend an inspection, for example, you may get stuck with undiscovered problems after the deal is done.

Agents who pitch themselves as buyers' brokers claim that they work for your interests. Agents who represent you as a buyer's broker still get paid only when you buy. And agents still get paid a commission that's a percentage of the purchase price, so they still have an incentive to sell you a piece of real estate that's more expensive because their commission increases.

Buying without a real estate agent

You can purchase property without an agent if you're willing to do some additional legwork. You need to do the things that a good real estate agent does, such as searching for properties, scheduling appointments to see them, determining fair market value, negotiating the deal, and coordinating inspections.

If you don't work with an agent, have a lawyer review the various contracts, unless you're a legal expert. Having someone else not vested in the transaction look out for your interests helps your situation. Real estate agents generally aren't legal experts, so getting legal advice from a lawyer is generally better. One possible drawback to working without an agent is performing the negotiations yourself. Negotiating can be problematic if you lack these skills or get too caught up emotionally in the situation.

Some agents market themselves as *top producers,* which means that they sell a relatively larger volume of real estate. This title doesn't count for much for you, the buyer. In fact, you may use this information as a potential red flag for an agent who focuses on completing as many deals as possible. Such an agent may not be able to give you the time and help that you need to get the house you want.

When you buy a home, you need an agent who is patient and who allows you the necessary time to educate yourself and helps you make the decision that's best for you. The last thing you need or want is an agent who tries to push you into making a deal.

You also need an agent who is knowledgeable about the local market and community. If you want to buy a home in an area where you don't currently live, an informed agent can have a big impact on your decision.

Finding an agent with financing knowledge is a plus for buyers, especially first-time buyers or those with credit problems. Such an agent may be able to refer you to lenders that can handle your type of situation, which can save you a lot of legwork.

Closing the Deal

After you locate a property that you want to buy, and you understand your financing options, the real fun begins. Now you have to put the deal together. The following sections discuss key things to keep in mind.

Negotiating 101

When you work with an agent, the agent usually carries the burden of the negotiation process. But even if you delegate responsibility for negotiating to your agent, you still should have a strategy in mind. Otherwise, you may overpay for real estate.

Find out about the property and the owner before you make your offer. How long has the property been on the market? What are its flaws? Why is the owner selling? The more you understand about the property you want to buy and the seller's motivations, the better your ability is to draft an offer that meets everyone's needs. Some listing agents love to talk and will tell you the life history of the seller. Either you or your agent may be able to get them to reveal helpful information about the seller.

Also, bring facts to the bargaining table. Get comparable sales data to support your price. Too often, homebuyers and their agents pick a number out of the air when they make an offer. If you were the seller, would you be persuaded to lower your asking price? Pointing to recent and comparable home sales to justify your offer price strengthens your case.

Remember that price is only one of several negotiable items. Sometimes sellers fixate on selling their homes for a certain amount. Perhaps they want to get at least what they paid for it themselves several years ago. You may get a seller to pay for certain repairs or improvements or to offer you an attractive loan without all the extra fees that a bank charges. Also, be aware that the time for closing on the purchase is a bargaining point. Some sellers may need cash soon and may concede other terms if you can close quickly. Likewise, the real estate agent's commission is negotiable.

Finally, try to leave your emotions out of any property purchase. This is easier said than done and hardest to do when you purchase a home in which you'll live. Try, as best you can, not to fall in love with a property. Keep searching for other properties even when you make an offer because you may be negotiating with an unmotivated seller.

Inspecting the property

Unless you've built homes and other properties and performed contracting work yourself, you probably have no idea what you're getting yourself into when it comes to furnaces and termites.

Spend the money and time to hire inspectors and other experts to evaluate the major systems and potential problem areas of the home. Because you can't be certain of the seller's commitment, we recommend that you do the inspections *after* you've successfully negotiated and signed a sales contract. Although you won't have the feedback from the inspections to help with this round of negotiating, you can always go back to the seller with the new information. Make your purchase offer contingent on a satisfactory inspection.

Hire people to help you inspect the following features of the property. (With multiunit rental property, be sure to read Chapter 11 for other specifics that you need to check out, such as parking.)

- Overall condition of the property (for example, is the paint peeling, are the floors level, are appliances present and working well, and so on?)
- Electrical, heating and air conditioning, and plumbing systems
- Foundation
- Roof
- Pest control, dry rot, and mould
- Seismic/slide/flood risk

Inspection fees often pay for themselves. If you uncover problems that you weren't aware of when you negotiated the original purchase price, the inspection reports give you the information you need to go back and ask the property seller to fix the problems or reduce the property's purchase price.

Never accept a seller's inspection report as your only source of information. When a seller hires an inspector, he or she may hire someone who isn't as diligent and critical of the property. Review the seller's inspection reports if available, but get your own as well. Also, beware of inspectors who are popular with real estate agents. They may be popular because they help agents close deals by not bothering to document all the property's problems.

As with other professionals whose services you retain, interview a few different inspection companies. Ask which systems they inspect and how detailed a report they can prepare for you. Consider asking the company that you're thinking of hiring for customer references. Ask for names and phone numbers of three people who used the company's services within the past six months. Also, request from each inspection company a sample of one of its reports.

The day before you close on the purchase, take a brief walk-through of the property to make sure that everything is still in the condition it was before and that all the fixtures, appliances, curtains, and other items the contract lists are still there. Sometimes, sellers ignore or don't recall these things, and consequently, they don't leave what they agreed to in the sales contract.

Shopping for title insurance

Some mortgage lenders require *title insurance* to protect against someone else claiming legal title to your property. This can happen, for example, when a husband and wife split up, and the one who remains in the home decides to sell and take off with the money. If the title lists both spouses as owners, the spouse who sells the property (possibly by forging the other's signature) has no legal right to do so. The other spouse can come back and reclaim rights to the home even after it has been sold. In this event, both you and the lender can get stuck holding the bag. (If you're in the enviable position of paying cash for a property, buying title insurance is still wise, even though a mortgage lender won't prod you to do so. You need to protect your investment.)

Title insurance fees may vary from company to company. Don't simply use the company that your real estate agent or mortgage lender suggests — shop around. When you call around for title insurance fee quotes, make sure that you understand all the fees. Many companies tack on all sorts of charges for things such as courier fees and express mail. If you find a company with lower prices and want to use it, consider asking for an itemization in writing so you don't receive any unpleasant surprises.

An insurance company's ability to pay claims is always important. Provincial and federal insurance departments monitor and regulate title insurance companies. Title insurers rarely fail, and regulators generally do a good job shutting down financially unstable ones. Check with your province's department if you're concerned. You can also ask the title insurer for copies of its ratings from insurance-rating agencies.

Selling Real Estate

You should buy and hold real estate for the long term. If you do your homework, buy in a good area, and work hard to find a fairly priced or underpriced property, why sell it quickly and incur all the selling costs, time, and hassle to locate and negotiate another property to purchase?

Some real estate investors like to buy properties in need of improvement, fix them up, and then sell them and move on to another. Unless you're a contractor or experienced real estate investor and have a real eye for this type of work, don't expect to make a windfall or even to earn back more than the cost of the improvements. The process of buying, fixing, and flipping can be profitable, but it's not as easy as the home-improvement television shows and some books would have you believe. In fact, it's more likely that you'll erode your profit through the myriad costs of frequent buying and selling. The vast majority of your profits should come from the long-term appreciation of the overall real estate market in the communities that you own property in.

Use the reasons that you bought in an area as a guide if you think you want to sell. Use the criteria that we discuss in Chapter 11 as a guideline. For example, if the schools in the community are deteriorating and the planning department is allowing development that will hurt the value of your property and the rents you can charge, you may have cause to sell. Unless you see significant problems like these in the future, holding good properties over many years is a great way to build your wealth and minimize transaction costs.

Negotiating real estate agents' contracts

Most people use an agent to sell real estate. As we discuss in "Finding a good agent," earlier in this chapter, selling and buying a home demand agents with different strengths. When you sell a property, you want an agent who can get the job done efficiently and for as high a sales price as possible.

As a seller, you should seek agents who have marketing and sales expertise and who are willing to put in the time and money necessary to sell your house. Don't be impressed by an agent just because she works for a large company. What matters more is what the agent can do to market your property.

When you list a property for sale, the contract you sign with the listing agent includes specification of the commission you pay the agent if he succeeds in selling your property. In most areas of the country, agents usually ask for a 6 percent commission for single-family homes. In an area that maintains lower-cost housing, agents may ask for 7 percent. For small multifamily properties and commercial properties, commissions are often in the 3 to 5 percent range. (Rates are notably higher in Quebec, where the standard rate is 8 percent.)

Regardless of the commission an agent says is "typical," "standard," or "what my manager requires," always remember that you can negotiate commissions. Because the commission is a percentage, you have much greater ability to get a lower commission on a higher-priced property. If an agent makes 6 percent selling both a $200,000 and a $100,000 property, the agent makes twice as much on the $200,000 property. Yet selling the higher-priced property doesn't usually take twice as much work.

If you live in an area with higher-priced properties, you may be able to negotiate a 5 percent commission. For expensive properties, a 4 percent commission is reasonable. You may find, however, that your ability to negotiate a lower commission is greatest when an offer is on the table. Because of the cooperation of agents who work together through the multiple listing service

(MLS), if you list your real estate for sale at a lower commission than most other properties, some agents won't show it to prospective buyers. For this reason, you're better off having your listing agent cut his take instead of cutting the commission that you pay to a real estate agent who brings a buyer for your property to you.

In terms of the length of the listing agreement, three months is reasonable. If you give an agent too long to list your property (6 to 12 months), the agent may simply toss your listing into the multiple listing database and not expend much effort to get your property sold. Practically speaking, you can fire your agent whenever you want, regardless of the length of the listing agreement, but a shorter listing may motivate your agent more.

Selling without a real estate agent

The reason for selling real estate without an agent is usually to save the commission that an agent deducts from your property's sale price. If you have the time, energy, and marketing experience, you can sell sans agent and possibly save some money.

The major problem with attempting to sell real estate on your own is that you can't list it in the MLS, which, in most areas, only real estate agents can access. If your property isn't listed in the MLS, many potential buyers never know that your home is for sale. Agents who work with buyers don't generally look for or show their clients properties that are for sale by owner or listed with discount brokers.

Several companies have tried to find a middle ground, offering home sellers low commissions or flat fees, while giving them access to MLS. These include erealty.ca (www.erealty.ca), which operates in British Columbia, and two Ontario companies, Home@ease Realty Inc. (www.homeatease.ca) and Flatfee Realty Inc. (www.flatfeerealty.ca).

Besides saving you time, a good agent can help ensure that you're not sued for failing to disclose known defects of your property. If you decide to sell on your own, have access to a legal adviser who can review the contracts. Take the time to educate yourself about the many facets of selling property for top dollar.

Part IV
Savouring Small Business

The 5th Wave   By Rich Tennant

"Here's my business plan for the Jazz Store. I think we should just fake the budget, improvise the marketing, and make up the long-range goals as we go along."

In this part . . .

Although the businesses may be small, the potential for earning profits and finding a fulfilling career isn't. Here, we explain such things as how to develop a business plan, identify marketable products or services, find customers, and wallop the competition! If starting your own shop seems either too overwhelming or too uninspiring, you also find out how to buy an existing business.

Chapter 13

Assessing Your Appetite for Small Business

In This Chapter

▶ Knowing what it takes to be a successful entrepreneur

▶ Exploring alternatives to starting your own company

▶ Looking at small-business investment options

▶ Mapping out your small-business plans

Many people dream about running their own companies, and for good reason. If you start your own business, you can pursue something that you're passionate about, *and* you have more control over how you do things. Plus, successful business owners can reap major economic bounties.

But tales of entrepreneurs becoming multimillionaires focus attention on the financial rewards without revealing the business and personal challenges and costs associated with being in charge. Consider what your company has to do well to survive and succeed in the competitive business world:

✔ Develop products and services that customers will purchase

✔ Price your offerings properly and promote them

✔ Deal with the competition

✔ Manage the accounting

✔ Interpret lease contracts and evaluate office space

✔ Keep current with changes in your field

✔ Hire, train, and retain good employees

Business owners also face personal and emotional challenges, which rarely get airtime among all the glory of the rags-to-riches tales of multimillionaire entrepreneurs. Major health problems, divorces, fights, and lawsuits among family members who are in business together, the loss of friends, and even suicides have been attributed to the passions of business owners who are consumed with winning or who become overwhelmed by their failures.

Had enough already? We're not trying to *scare* you, but we do want you to be *realistic* about starting your own business. Maybe you do have the right stuff to run your own company, but most people don't.

Testing Your Entrepreneurial IQ

The keys to success and enjoyment as an entrepreneur vary as much as the businesses do. But if you can answer yes to most of the following questions, you probably have the qualities and perspective needed to succeed as a small-business owner.

Don't be deterred by the questions that you can't answer in the affirmative. A perfect entrepreneur doesn't exist. Part of succeeding in business is knowing what you can't do, as well as what you can do, and finding creative ways (or people) to help you.

1. **Are you a self-starter? Do you like challenges? Are you persistent? Are you willing to do research to solve problems?**

   Running your own business isn't glamorous most of the time, especially in the early years. You have many details to mind and things to do. Success in business is the result of doing lots of little things well. If you're accustomed to working for large organizations where much of the day is spent attending meetings and keeping up on office politics and gossip, with little accountability, you probably won't enjoy or succeed at running your own business.

2. **Do you value independence and self-control?**

   Particularly in the early days of your business, you need to enjoy working on your own. When you leave a company environment and work on your own, you give up a lot of socializing. Of course, if you work in an unpleasant environment or with people you don't really enjoy socializing with, venturing out on your own may be a plus.

   If you're a people person, many businesses offer lots of contact. But you must recognize the difference between socializing with co-workers and networking with business contacts and customers.

3. **Can you develop a commitment to an idea, product, or principle?**

   Most entrepreneurs work about 50 hours per week, 50 or so weeks a year — that's about 2,500 hours per year. If the product, service, or cause that you're pursuing doesn't excite you and you can't motivate others to work hard for you, you're going to have a long year!

One of the worst reasons to start your own business is for the pursuit of great financial riches. Don't get us wrong — if you're good at what you do and you know how to market your services or products, you may make more money working for yourself. But for most people, money isn't enough of a motivation, and many people make the same or less money on their own than they did working for a company.

4. **Are you willing to make financial sacrifices and live a reduced life-style before and during your early entrepreneurial years?**

"Live like a student, before and during the start-up of your small business" was the advice that Eric's best business school professor, James Collins, gave him before he started his business. With most businesses, you expend money during the start-up years and likely have a reduced income compared to the income you received while working for a company. You also have to buy your own benefits.

To make your entrepreneurial dream a reality, you need to live within your means both before and after you start your business. But if running your own business really makes you happy, sacrificing expensive vacations, overpriced luxury cars, the latest designer clothing, and $4 lattes at the corner cafe shouldn't be too painful.

5. **Do you recognize that when you run your own business, you must still report to bosses?**

Besides the allure of huge profits, the other reason some people mistakenly go into business for themselves is that they're tired of working for other people. Obnoxious, evil bosses can make anyone want to become an entrepreneur.

When you run your own business, you may have customers and other bosses who are miserable to deal with. Fortunately, even the worst customers usually can't make your life anywhere near as miserable as the worst bosses. (If you have enough customers, you can simply decide not to do business with such misfits.)

6. **Can you withstand rejection, naysayers, and negative feedback?**

"I thought every no that I got when trying to raise my funding brought me one step closer to a yes," says Alex Popov, an entrepreneur. Unless you come from an entrepreneurial family, don't expect your parents to endorse your "risky, crazy" behaviour. Even other entrepreneurs can ridicule your good ideas. Some people (especially parents) simply think that working for a giant company makes you safer and more secure (which, of course, is a myth, because corporations can lay you off in a snap). It's also easier for them to say to their friends and neighbours that you're a big manager at a well-known corporation (such as Cadillac Fairview, Nortel, or WorldCom) than to explain that you're working on some kooky business idea out of a spare bedroom. (How secure do you think those former employees of Nortel and WorldCom feel now about having lost their jobs at their former large company?)

7. **Are you able to identify your shortcomings and hire or align yourself with people and organizations that complement your skills and expertise?**

   To be a successful entrepreneur, you need to be a bit of a jack-of-all-trades: marketer, accountant, customer service representative, administrative assistant, and so on. Unless you get lots of investor capital, which is rare for a true start-up, you can't afford to hire help in the early months, or perhaps even years, of your business.

   Partnering with others or buying certain services or products rather than trying to do everything yourself may make sense for you. And over time, if your business grows and succeeds, you should be able to afford to hire more help. If you can be honest with yourself and surround and partner yourself with people whose skills and expertise complement yours, you can build a winning team!

8. **Do you deal well with ambiguity? Do you believe in yourself?**

   When you're on your own, determining when and if you're on the right track is difficult. Some days, things don't go well — and such days are much harder to take flying solo. Therefore, being confident, optimistic, and able to work around obstacles are necessary skills.

9. **Do you understand why you started the business or organization and how you personally define "success"?**

   Many business entrepreneurs define success by such measures as sales revenue, profits, number of branch offices and employees, and so on. These are fine measures, but other organizations, particularly non-profits, have other measures. For example, the Sierra Club of Canada seeks to "develop a diverse, well-trained grassroots network working to protect the integrity of our global ecosystems."

   To accomplish such goals as affecting public policy and public opinion about issues such as the environment and health, money is necessary, but such a cause-focused organization has a "bottom line" very different from a for-profit organization.

10. **Can you accept lack of success in the early years of building your business?**

    A few rare businesses are instant hits, but most businesses take time to build momentum — it may take years, perhaps even decades. Some successful corporate people suffer from anxiety when they go out on their own and encounter the inevitable struggles and lack of tangible success as they build their companies.

Myths of being an entrepreneur

Many myths persist about what it takes to be an entrepreneur, partly because those who aren't entrepreneurs tend to hang out with others who aren't. The mass media's popularization of "successful" entrepreneurs such as Bill Gates, Donald Trump, and Oprah Winfrey leads to numerous misperceptions and misconceptions, including these often-cited nuggets:

✔ **You have to be well-connected or know "important" people.** We think that being a decent human being is far more important. Enough rude, inconsiderate, and self-centred people are in the business world (and, yes, some of them do succeed in spite of their character flaws), and if you're not that way, you'll be able to meet people who can help you in one way or another. But remember that looking in the mirror shows you your best and most trusted resource.

✔ **You need to have an MBA or some other fancy degree.** Many successful entrepreneurs — Bill Gates and Steve Jobs, for example — don't even have university degrees, for goodness' sake. Perusing _Forbes_ magazine's lists of the most financially successful small companies shows that about 15 percent of the CEOs didn't earn a university degree and about half don't have advanced degrees! These statistics are even more amazing when you consider that a relatively large number of entrepreneurs with humble backgrounds leave or are forced out of the successful enterprises they started.

We're not saying that a good education isn't worthwhile in general and that it can't help you succeed in your own business. But a formal education isn't _necessary_.

✔ **You need to be a genius.** Intelligence is admittedly a difficult thing to measure, but the majority of entrepreneurs have IQs under 120, and a surprising percentage have IQs under the average of 100 — more entrepreneurs, in fact, have IQs under 100 than have IQs greater than 130!

✔ **You must be a gregarious, big-egoed extrovert.** Although some studies show that more entrepreneurs are extroverted, many entrepreneurs are not.

✔ **You have to be willing to take a _huge_ risk.** Some people focus on the potential for failure. Consider the worst-case scenario — if your venture doesn't work out, you can always go back to a job similar to the one you left behind. Also, recognize that risk is a matter of perception, and as with investments, people completely overlook some risks. What about the risk to your happiness and career if you stay in a boring, claw-your-way-up-the-corporate-ladder kind of job? You always risk a layoff when you work for a company. An even greater risk is that you'll wake up in your 50s or 60s and think that it's too late to do something on your own and wish you had tried sooner.

Considering Alternative Routes

Sometimes, entrepreneurial advocates imply that running your own business or starting your own non-profit is the greatest thing in the world and that all people would be happy owning their own business if they just set their mind to it. The reality is that some people won't be blissful as entrepreneurs. If you didn't score highly on our ten-question entrepreneur assessment in the preceding section, don't despair. You can probably be happier and more successful doing something other than starting your own business.

Some people are better off working for someone else. Consider the following options.

Being an entrepreneur inside a company

A happy medium is available for people who want the challenge of running their own show without giving up the comforts and security that come with a company environment — for example, you can manage an entrepreneurial venture at a company. That's what John Kilcullen, president and chief executive officer of IDG Books Worldwide (former publisher of the *For Dummies* books), did when he helped launch the book publishing division of IDG in 1990. (IDG Books was subsequently bought by John Wiley & Sons, Inc., in 2001.)

Kilcullen had publishing industry experience and wanted to take on the responsibility of growing a successful publishing company. But he also knew that being a player in the book publishing industry takes a lot of money and resources. Because he was a member of the founding team of the new IDG Books division, Kilcullen had the best of both worlds.

Kilcullen always had a passion to start his own business but found that most traditional publishers weren't interested in giving autonomy and money to a division and letting it run with the ball. "I wanted the ability to build a business on my own instincts . . . the appeal of IDG was that it was decentralized. IDG was willing to invest and provide the freedom to spend as we saw fit."

If you're able to secure an entrepreneurial position inside a larger company, in addition to significant managerial and operational responsibility, you can also negotiate your share of the financial success you help create. The parent company's senior management wants you to have the incentive that comes from sharing in the financial success of your endeavours. Bonuses, stock options, and the like are often tied to a division's performance.

Investing in your career

Some people are happy or content as employees. Companies need and want lots of good employees, so you can find a job if you have skills, a work ethic, and the ability to get along with others.

You can improve your income-earning ability and invest in your career in a variety of different ways:

✔ **Work:** Be willing to work extra hours and take on more responsibility, but do so within reason. Those who take extra initiative and then deliver really stand out in a company where many people working on a salary have a time-clock, 9-to-5 mentality. But be careful that the extra effort doesn't contribute to workaholism, a dangerous addiction that causes too many people to neglect important personal relationships and their own health. Don't bite off more than you can chew — otherwise, your supervisors won't have faith that they can count on you to deliver. Find ways to work smarter, not just longer, hours.

✔ **Read:** One of the reasons that you don't need a PhD, master's degree, or even an undergraduate university degree to succeed in business is that you can find out a lot on your own. You can gain insight by doing, but you can also gain expertise by reading a lot. A good bookstore has no entrance requirements, such as an elevated high school grade point average — you only have to walk through the doors. A good book isn't free, but it costs a heck of lot less than taking more university or graduate courses!

✔ **Study:** If you haven't completed your university or graduate degree and the industry you're in values those who have, consider investing the time and money to finish your education. Speak with others who have taken that path and see what they have to say.

Exploring Small-Business Investment Options

Only your imagination limits the ways that you can make money with small businesses. Choosing the option that best meets your needs isn't unlike choosing other investments, such as in real estate (see Part III) or in the investment industry (see Part II). Following are the major ways you can invest in small business and what is and isn't attractive about each option.

Starting your own business

Of all your small-business options, starting your own business involves the greatest amount of work. Although you can perform this work on a part-time basis in the beginning, most people end up working in their business full time.

For most of our working years, we've both run our own businesses, and overall, we both really like it. In our experience with small-business owners, we've seen many people of varied backgrounds, interests, and skills achieve success and happiness running their own businesses.

Don't start a business for tax write-offs

"Start a small business for fun, profit, and huge tax deductions," a financial advice book declares, adding that "the tax benefits alone are worth starting a small business." A seminar company offers a course titled "How to Have Zero Taxes Deducted from Your Pay Cheque." This tax seminar tells you how to solve your tax problems: "If you have a sideline business, or would like to start one, you're eligible to have little or no taxes taken from your pay."

All this sounds too good to be true — and of course it is. Not only are the strategies sure to lead to Canada Revenue Agency (CRA) audit purgatory, but such books and seminars may also seduce you to pony up $100 or more for audiotapes or notebooks of "inside information."

Unfortunately, many self-proclaimed self-help gurus state that you can slash your taxes simply by finding a product or service that you can sell on the side of your regular employment. The problem, they argue, is that as a regular wage earner who receives a paycheque from an employer, you can't write off many of your other (personal) expenses. Open a sideline business, they say, and you can deduct your personal expenses as business expenses.

The pitch is enticing, but the reality is something quite different. You have to spend money to get tax deductions, and the spending must be for legitimate purposes of your business in its efforts to generate income. If you think that taking tax deductions for your hobby is worth the risk because you won't get caught unless you're audited, the odds are stacked against you. The CRA audits an extraordinarily large portion of small businesses that show regular losses.

The bottom line is that you need to operate a real business for the purpose of generating income and profits, not tax deductions. It used to be that the CRA placed a lot of importance on whether an undertaking had "a reasonable expectation of profit." The problem is that the test was done after the fact. It wasn't uncommon for people to be turned down when they tried to claim their losses as legitimate deductions, since in hindsight it's a lot easier to see why a failed business didn't have a fighting chance in the first place.

More importantly, the rule set a much higher standard for entrepreneurs than it did for larger companies that regularly deduct the cost of misguided blunders, ill-advised takeovers, and pie-in-the-sky planning. What's more, many of today's successful businesses would never have got off the ground if the entrepreneurs behind them had listened to all the reasons they were "bound to fail" offered up by naysayers. Sometimes, too, businesses launched on a foolhardy premise manage to survive and often thrive thanks to good luck and fortuitous timing.

The good news for entrepreneurs is that in 2002, the Supreme Court greatly reduced the importance of the "reasonable expectation of profit" test, making it just one of many factors that the tax department considers when assessing the commercial viability of an enterprise. At the same time, the Court emphasized that a taxpayer's business smarts — or complete commercial naïveté — are not to be considered when assessing whether expenses qualify as business losses.

If you have rung up losses for three years or more, and want to continue to claim your future losses, you may still have to convince the CRA that you're seriously trying to make a profit and run a legitimate business. The bottom line is that you need to operate a real business for the purpose of generating income and profits, not tax deductions. And remember that deducting any expenses that aren't directly applicable to your business is illegal.

Most people perceive starting their own business as the riskiest of all small-business investment options. But if you get into a business that uses your skills and expertise, the risk isn't nearly as great as you may think. Suppose that you teach and make $35,000 per year and you want to set up your own tutoring service, making a comparable amount of money. If you find through your research that others who perform these services charge $40 per hour, you need to actually tutor about 20 or so hours per week, assuming that you work 50 weeks per year. Because you can run this business from your home (which can possibly generate small tax breaks) without purchasing new equipment, your expenses should be minimal.

Instead of leaving your job cold turkey and trying to build your business from scratch, you can start moonlighting as a tutor. Over a couple of years, if you can build the tutoring up to ten hours per week, you're halfway to your goal. If you leave your job and focus all your energies on your tutoring business, getting to 20 hours per week of billable work shouldn't be a problem. Still think starting a business is risky?

Many businesses can be started with little money by leveraging your existing skills and expertise. If you have the time to devote to building "sweat equity," you can build a valuable company and job. As long as you check out the competition and offer a valued product or service at a reasonable cost, the principal risk with your business is that you won't do a good job marketing what you have to offer. If you can market your skills, you should succeed. See Chapter 14 for more details on starting and running your own business.

Buying an existing business

If you don't have a specific idea for a business that you want to start, but you have business management skills and an ability to improve existing businesses, consider buying an established business. Although you don't have to go through the riskier start-up period if you take this route, you'll likely need more capital to buy a going enterprise.

You also need to be able to deal with potentially sticky personnel and management issues. The history of the organization and the way things work predates your ownership of the business. If you don't like making hard decisions, firing people who don't fit with your plans, and coercing people into changing the way they did things before you arrived on the scene, buying an existing business likely isn't for you. Also realize that some of the good employees may be loyal to the old owner and his or her style of running the business, so they may split when you arrive.

Some people perceive that buying an existing business is safer than starting a new one, but buying someone else's business can actually be riskier. You'll have to shell out far more money up front, in the form of a down payment, to buy a business. If you don't have the ability to run the business and it does poorly, you may lose much more financially. Another risk is that the business may be for sale for a reason — perhaps it's not very profitable, it's in decline, or it's generally a pain in the posterior to operate.

Good businesses that are for sale don't come cheaply. If the business is a success, the current owner has removed the start-up risk from the business, so the price of the business should include a premium to reflect this lack of risk. If you have the capital to buy an established business and you have the skills to run it, consider going this route. Chapter 15 discusses how to buy a good business.

Investing in someone else's business

If you like the idea of profiting from successful small businesses but don't want the day-to-day headaches of being responsible for managing the enterprise, you may want to invest in someone else's small business. Although this route may seem easier, fewer people are actually cut out to be investors in other people's businesses.

Investing for the right reasons

Consider investing in someone else's business if you meet the following criteria:

- You have sufficient assets so that what you invest in small privately held companies is a small portion (20 percent or less) of your total financial assets.

- You can afford to lose what you invest. Unlike investing in a diversified stock mutual fund (see Chapter 8), you may lose all of your investment when you invest in a small, privately held company.

- You're astute at evaluating financial statements and business strategies. Investing in a small, privately held company has much in common with investing in a publicly traded firm. The difference is that private firms aren't required to produce comprehensive, audited financial statements that adhere to certain accounting principles the way that public companies are. Thus, you have a greater risk of not receiving sufficient or accurate information when you evaluate a small private firm.

Putting money into your own business (or someone else's) can be a high-risk — but potentially high-return — investment. The best options are those that you understand well. If you hear about a great business idea or company from someone you know and trust, do your research and make your best judgment. That company or idea may well be a terrific investment.

Before you invest, ask to see a copy of the business plan and compare it with the business plan model that we suggest later in this chapter. Thoroughly check out the people running the business. Talk to others who don't have a stake in the investment and benefit from their comments and concerns. But don't forget that many a wise person has rained on the parade of what turned out to be a terrific business idea.

Avoiding investing mistakes

Although some people are extra careful when they invest other people's money, know that many small-business owners seek investors' money for the wrong reasons. Some business owners are impatient and perhaps don't understand the feasibility of making do with a small amount of capital (a process called *bootstrapping,* which we discuss in Chapter 14).

Other businesses need money because they're in financial trouble. Consider the small furniture retailer that conducted a stock offering to raise money. On the surface, everything seemed fine, and the company made it onto the *Inc.* 500 list of fast-growing small companies. But it turns out that the company wanted to issue stock because it expanded too quickly and didn't sell enough merchandise to cover its high overhead. The company ended up in bankruptcy.

Another problem with small businesses that seek investors is that many small-business owners may take more risk and do less upfront planning and homework with other people's money. Many well-intentioned people fail at their businesses. Take the MBA from a top business school — we'll call him Jacob — who convinced an investor to put up about $300,000 to purchase a small manufacturing company. Jacob put a small amount of his own money into the business and immediately blew about $100,000 on a fancy computer scheduling and order-entry system.

Likewise, Jacob wasn't interested much in sales (a job that the previous owner managed), so he hired a sales manager. The sales manager he hired was a disaster — many of the front-line salespeople fled to competitors, taking key customers with them. By the time Jacob came to his senses, it was too late — the disaster had unfolded. He tried to cut costs, but doing so hurt the quality and timeliness of the company's products. The business dissolved, and the investor lost everything.

Drawing Up Your Business Plan

If you're motivated to start your own business, the next step is to figure out what you want to do and how you're going to do it; in other words, you need a *business plan.* You need a general plan that helps you define what you think you want to do and the tasks you need to perform to accomplish your goal. The business plan — which is essential for your own planning, obtaining loans, and showing to potential investors — should be a working document or blueprint for the early days, months, and years of your business.

You don't need a perfectly detailed plan that spells out all the minutiae. Making such an involved plan is a waste of your time because things change and evolve.

The amount of detail your plan needs depends on your goals and the specifics of your business. A simple, more short-term focused plan (ten pages or so) is fine if you don't aspire to build an empire. However, if your goal is to grow, hire employees, and open multiple locations, then your plan needs to be longer (20 to 50 pages) to cover longer-term issues. If you want outside investor money, a longer business plan is a necessity.

As you put together your plan and evaluate your opportunities, open your ears and eyes. Expect to do research and to speak with other entrepreneurs and people in the industry. Most people will spend time talking with you as long as they realize that you don't want to compete with them. And for more details on crafting a business plan, check out *Business Plans For Canadians For Dummies,* by Paul Tiffany, Steven D. Peterson, and Nada Wagner (Wiley).

Identifying your business concept

What do you want your business to do? What product or service do you want to offer? Maybe your business goal is to perform tax-preparation services for small-business owners. Or perhaps you want to start a consulting firm, open a restaurant that sells healthy fast food, run a gardening service, or manufacture toys.

Your concept doesn't have to be unique to survive in the business world — witness the legions of self-employed consultants, plumbers, tax preparers, and restaurant owners. The existence of many other people who already do what you want to do validates the potential for your small-business ideas. We know many wage slaves who say they would love to run their own business if they could only come up with "the idea." Most of these people still dream about their small-business plans as they draw their Canada Pension Plan cheques. Being committed to the idea of running your own business is more important than developing the next great product or service. In the beginning, the business opportunities you pursue can be quite general to your field of expertise or interest. What you eventually do over time will evolve.

We're not saying that an innovative idea lacks merit. A creative idea gives you the chance to hit a big home run, and the first person to successfully develop a new idea can achieve big success.

Wet blankets throughout history

"This 'telephone' has too many shortcomings to be seriously considered as a means of communication. The device is inherently of no value to us." — Western Union internal memo in response to Alexander Graham Bell's telephone, 1876.

"The concept is interesting and well formed, but in order to earn better than a C, the idea must be feasible." — A Yale University management professor in response to Fred Smith's paper proposing reliable overnight delivery service. Smith went on to found Federal Express Corporation.

"We don't tell you how to coach, so don't tell us how to make shoes." — A large sporting shoe manufacturer to Bill Bowerman, inventor of the waffle shoe and cofounder of NIKE, Inc.

"So we went to Atari and said, 'Hey, we've got this amazing thing, even built with some of your parts, and what do you think about funding us? Or we'll give it to you. We just want to do it. Pay our salary, we'll come work for you.' And they said, 'No.' So then we went to Hewlett-Packard, and they said, 'Hey, we don't need you. You haven't got through college yet.'" — Steve Jobs, speaking about attempts to get Atari and Hewlett-Packard interested in his and Steve Wozniak's personal computer. Jobs and Wozniak founded Apple Computer.

"'You should franchise them,' I told them. 'I'll be your guinea pig.' Well, they just went straight up in the air! They couldn't see the philosophy.... When they turned us down, that left Bud and me to swim on our own." — Sam Walton, describing his efforts to get the Ben Franklin chain interested in his discount retailing concept in 1962. Walton went on to found Wal-Mart.

"We don't like their sound, and guitar music is on the way out." — Decca Recording Company in rejecting The Beatles, 1962.

In 1884, John Henry Patterson was ridiculed by his business friends for paying $6,500 for the rights to the cash register — a product with "limited" or no potential. Patterson went on to found National Cash Register (NCR) Corporation.

"What's all this computer nonsense you're trying to bring into medicine? I've got no confidence at all in computers and I want nothing whatsoever to do with them." — A medical professor in England to Dr. John Alfred Powell, about the CT scanner.

"That is good sport. But for the military, the airplane is useless." — Ferdinand Foch, Commander in Chief, Allied Forces on the Western Front, World War I.

"The television will never achieve popularity; it takes place in a semidarkened room and demands continuous attention." — Harvard Professor Chester L. Dawes, 1940.

These quotations are reprinted with permission from *Beyond Entrepreneurship, Turning Your Business into an Enduring Great Company,* James C. Collins and William C. Lazier, Prentice Hall.

Even if you aspire to build the next billion-dollar company, you can put a twist on older concepts. Suppose that you're a veterinarian, but you don't want a traditional office where people must bring their cats and dogs for treatment. You believe that because many people are starved for free time, they want a vet who makes house calls. Thus, you open your Vet on Wheels business.

You may also want to franchise the business and open locations around the country. However, you can also succeed by doing what thousands of other vets are now doing and have done over the years with a traditional office.

Outlining your objectives

The reasons for starting and running your own small business are as varied as the entrepreneurs behind their companies. Before you start your firm, it's useful to think about what you're seeking to achieve. Your objectives need not be cast in concrete and will surely change over time. If you like, you can write a short and motivating mission statement.

When you ask an MBA, especially one from a big-name school, to think about objectives, he or she usually says something like, "My goal is to run a $20 million company in seven years." Financial objectives are fine, but don't make your objectives strictly financial unless money is the only reason that you want to run your own business.

Introductory economics courses teach students that the objective of every for-profit firm is to maximize profits. As with many things taught in economics courses, this theory has one problem — it doesn't hold up in reality. Most small-business owners we know don't manage their businesses maniacally in the pursuit of maximum profits. The following list gives you some other possible objectives to consider:

- **Working with people you like and respect:** Some customers may buy your products and services, and some employees and suppliers may offer you their services for a good price, but what if you can't stand working with them? If you have sufficient business or just have your own standards, you can choose whom you do business with.

- **Educating others:** Maybe part of your business goal is to educate the public about something that you're an expert in. We know that when we started our businesses, we both saw educating people about personal finance and investing as a core part of our companies' purpose.

- **Improving an industry/setting a higher standard:** Perhaps part of your goal in starting your business is to show how your industry can better serve its customers. Having an ideal and putting it into practice can be very rewarding and a terrific motivator that helps you get through tough stretches.

Of course, you can't accomplish these objectives without profits, and doing these things isn't inconsistent with generating greater profits. But if your objectives are more than financial or your financial objectives aren't your number-one concern, don't worry — that's usually a good sign. Remember the expression "Do what you love, the money will follow."

Analyzing the marketplace

The single most important area to understand is the marketplace in which your business competes. To be successful, your business must not only produce a good product or service, but it must also reach customers and convince them to buy your product at a price at which you can make a profit. You should discern what the competition has to offer, as well as its strengths and vulnerabilities. In most industries, you also need to understand government regulations that affect the type of business you're considering.

Meeting customer needs

If the market analysis is the most important part of the business plan, then understanding your potential customers is the most important part of your market analysis. If you don't understand your desired customers and their needs, don't expect to have a successful business.

If you're in a business that sells to consumers, consider your customers' gender, age, income, geographic location, marital status, number of children, education, living situation (rent or own), and the reasons they want your product or service. Who are your prospective customers? Where do they live, and what do they care about? If you sell to businesses, you need to understand similar issues. What types of businesses may buy your product or services? Why?

The best way to get to know your potential customers is to get out and talk to them. While more time-consuming, live interviews allow you to go with the flow of the conversation, improvise questions, and probe more interesting areas. Although you can e-mail or mail paper-based surveys to many people with a minimal investment of your time, the response rate is usually quite low, and the answers are usually not very illuminating. To encourage better response, offer a product or service sample or some other promotional item to those who help you with your research. Doing so attracts people who are interested in your product or service, which helps you define your target customers.

Also, try to get a sense of what customers do pay and will pay for the products or services that you offer. Analyzing the competition's offerings helps, too. Some products or services also require follow-up or additional servicing. Understand what customers need and what they'll pay for your services.

If you want to raise money from investors, include some estimates of the size of the market for your product or services. Of course, such numbers are ballpark estimates, but sizing the market for your product helps you estimate profitability, the share of the market needed to be profitable, and so on.

Besting the competition

Always examine the products, services, benefits, and prices that competitors offer. Otherwise, you go on blind faith that what you offer stacks up well versus the alternatives in the industry.

You first need to decide whether you have a realistic chance of winning the consumer choice battle. We think you'll agree that going into the same discount warehouse retailing business and competing head-to-head with Real Canadian Superstore, Costco, or Rona is crazy.

Examine your competitors' weaknesses so you can exploit them. Rather than trying to beat them on their terms, maybe you've identified a need for a neighbourhood pet supply store that offers a more specialized range of pet supplies than the big-selling brands of dog and cat food that warehouse stores sell. Providing knowledgeable customer sales representatives to answer customer questions and make product suggestions can also give you a competitive edge. These advantages may allow you to surpass the warehouse stores on three counts: convenience of location for people in your neighbourhood, breadth of product offerings, and customer assistance.

Don't make the mistake of thinking that even if you have a completely innovative product or service that no other business currently offers, you don't have competitors. All businesses have competitors. In the event that you've developed something truly unique that has little competition, your success will surely breed competition as imitators follow or attempt to leapfrog your lead.

Complying with regulations

Most businesses are subject to some sort of regulation. If you want to start a retail business, for example, few communities permit you to run it out of your home. If you lease or purchase a private location, the zoning laws in that location may restrict you. Therefore, you need to check what you can and can't sell at that location. Check with the zoning department of your city or town — don't simply believe a real estate agent or property owner who says, "No problem!" That person's goal, after all, is to sell the property.

If you were going to start a veterinary practice, you would quickly discover that special zoning is required to use a piece of real estate for a vet's office. Convincing a local zoning board to allow a new location to get such special zoning is quite difficult, if not impossible, in some areas.

Many businesses face other local, provincial, and even federal regulatory issues, including ordinances, laws, and the need for specific licences and filings. For example, if you were opening a restaurant, you'd have to heed ordinances and laws that regulate everything from signage to operating hours to your ability to serve alcohol. And you'd be subject to an amazing array of health codes, building codes, and fire codes, to name a few.

If you enter an industry that you're relatively new to, ask questions and open your ears to find out more about where you should locate and how you should design your business. Speak to people who are currently in the field and your local chamber of commerce to see what, if any, licences or filings you must complete. Read books on the subject and check the newsstand and local library for trade magazines that may deal with your questions. Libraries have books and online services that can help you locate specific articles on topics that interest you.

Delivering your service or product

Every business has a product or service to sell. How are you going to provide this product or service? Suppose you want to start a business that delivers groceries and runs errands for busy people or older and disabled people who can't easily perform daily tasks for themselves. Delineate the steps that you'll take to provide the service. When potential customers call you to inquire about your business, what kinds of information do you want to record about their situation? Create a pricing sheet and other marketing literature (discussed in the next section) that you can mail curious potential customers. After someone calls and says, "I want to hire you," you need to collect more details. Try drawing up an information sheet that prompts you for the information that you need (for example, address, promised delivery time, desired items, and so on).

You need to map out a system that you can work with before you dive into running your business. Your system may evolve over time — you can be guaranteed of that — but a tentative game plan has great value.

If you want to manufacture a product, you definitely need to scope out the process you're going to use. Otherwise, you have no idea how much time the manufacturing process may take or what the process may cost.

As your business grows and you hire employees to provide services or create your products, the more you codify what you do, the better your employees can replicate your good work.

Marketing your service or product

After you get more in-depth information about your company's services or products, you need to find more specific information about the following:

✔ **How much will you charge for your services and products?** Look at what competing products and services cost. Estimating your costs helps you figure out what you need to charge to cover your costs and make a reasonable profit.

✔ **How will you position your product and services versus the competition?** Remember the local pet supply store example that we mention in the earlier section "Besting the competition"? It positions itself as a convenient store equipped with a broad selection and knowledgeable customer assistance. Books similarly position themselves in the book marketplace. We hope, in your mind, that our financial books are down-to-earth, practical, answer-oriented, and educational.

✔ **Where will you sell your product or service?** Business consultants label this decision the *distribution channel* question. For example, if you're going to go into the hula-hoop manufacturing business, you may consider selling via mail order and the Internet, through toy stores, or through discount warehouse stores. Selling through each of these different distribution channels requires unique marketing and advertising programs. If you market a product or service to companies, you need to find out who the key decision makers are at the company and what will persuade them to buy your product or service.

Having a great product or service isn't enough if you keep it a secret — you gotta get the word out. It's doubtful that you have the budget or want to reach the same region that television and radio advertising reach.

Start marketing your product to people you know. Develop a punchy, informative one-page letter that announces your company's inception and the products or services it offers, and mail it to your contacts. Include an envelope with a reply form that allows recipients to provide the addresses of others who may be interested in what you have to offer. Send these folks a mailing as well, mentioning who passed their names along to you.

Finding and retaining customers is vital to any business that wants to grow and be profitable. One simple, inexpensive way to stay in touch with customers you've dealt with or others who have made inquiries and expressed interest in your company's offerings is via a mailing list. Once a quarter, once a year, or whatever makes sense for your business, send out a simple, professional-looking postcard or newsletter announcing new information about your business and what customer needs you can fulfill. Such mailings also allow you to remind people that you're still in business and that you provide a wonderful product or service. Computer software gives you a fast, efficient way to keep a customer mailing list up to date and to print mailing labels.

E-mailing this information has the attraction of no out-of-pocket expenses. However, due to the deluge of junk e-mail most people get, your e-mail is likely to be deleted without being opened. At least a snail-mailed postcard will get the attention of prospective customers, even if only for a brief period.

Organizing and staffing your business

Many small businesses are one-person operations. So much the better for you — you have none of the headaches of hiring, payroll, and so on. You only have to worry about you — and that may be a handful in itself!

But if you would rather manage the work being done instead of doing all the work yourself, and if you hope to grow your business, you'll eventually want to hire people. (We explain the best way to fill your personnel needs in Chapter 14.) Give some thought now to the skills and functional areas of expertise that future hires need. If you want to raise money, the employment section of your business plan is essential to show your investors that you're planning long-term.

Maybe you'll want an administrative assistant, researcher, marketing person, or sales representative. What about a training specialist, finance person, or real estate person if your company expands? Consider the background that you want in those you hire, and look at the types of people that similar companies select and hire.

You should also consider what legal form of organization — for example, a sole proprietorship, partnership, incorporated company, and so on — your business will adopt. We address this topic in Chapter 14.

Projecting finances

An idea often becomes a bad idea or a business failure if you neglect to consider, or are unrealistic about, the financial side of the business you want to start. If you're a creative or people-person type who hates numbers, the financial side may be the part of the business plan that you most want to avoid. Don't! Doing so can cost you tens of thousands of dollars in avoidable mistakes. Ignoring the financial side can even lead to the bankruptcy of a business founded with a good idea.

Before you launch your business, you should do enough research so you can come up with some decent estimates to address these financial issues.

Financial projections are mandatory, and knowledgeable investors will scrutinize them if you seek outside money. You also need to think through how and when investors can cash out.

Start-up and development costs

Spending money to get your business from the idea stage to an operating enterprise is inevitable. Before the revenue begins to flow in, you'll incur expenditures as you develop and market your products and services. Therefore, you need to understand what you must spend money on and the approximate timing of the needed purchases.

If you were going to build a house, you would develop a list of all the required costs. How much are the land, construction, carpeting, landscaping, and so on going to cost? You can try to develop all these cost estimates yourself, or you can speak with local builders and have them help you. Likewise, with your business, you can hire a business consultant who knows something about your type of business. However, we think you're best served by doing the homework yourself — you discover a lot more, and it's cheaper.

If you're going to work in an office setting, at home or in another space, you need furniture (such as a desk, chair, filing cabinets, and so on), a computer, printer, and other office supplies. Don't forget to factor in the costs of any licences or government registrations you may need.

If you run a retailing operation, you need to also estimate your cost for establishing an initial inventory of goods. Remember, selling your inventory takes time, especially when you first start up. And because it's a new business, suppliers won't give you months on end to pay for your initial inventory. Be realistic — otherwise, the money that you tie up in inventory can send you to financial ruin.

Income statement

Preparing an estimated *income statement* that summarizes your expected revenue and expenses is a challenging and important part of your business plan. (We explain the elements of an income statement in Chapter 6.) Preparing an income statement is difficult because of all the estimates and assumptions that go into it. As you prepare your estimated income statement, you may discover that making a decent profit is tougher than you thought. This section of your business plan helps you make pricing decisions.

Consider the Vet on Wheels business idea that we discuss in the "Identifying your business concept" section, earlier in this chapter. What range of veterinary services can you provide if you make house calls? You can't perform all the services that you can in a larger office setting. What equipment do you need to perform the services? How much should you charge for the services? You need to estimate all these things to develop a worthwhile income statement. You should be able to answer these questions from the insights and information you pulled together regarding what customers want and what your competitors are offering.

With service businesses in which you or your employees sell your time, be realistic about how many hours you can bill. You may end up being able to bill only a third to half of your time, given the other management activities you need to perform.

Because building a customer base takes several years, try to prepare estimated income statements for the first three years. In the earlier years, you have more start-up costs. In later years, you reap more profits as your customer rolls expand. Having income statements for several years is also essential if you're seeking investor money.

Balance sheet

An income statement measures the profitability of a business over a span of time, such as a year, but it tells you nothing of a business's resources and obligations. That's what a *balance sheet* does. Just as your personal balance sheet itemizes your personal assets (for example, investments) and liabilities (debts you owe), a business balance sheet details a company's assets and liabilities.

If you operate a cash business — you provide a service and are paid for that service, and you don't hold any inventory, for example — a balance sheet has limited use. An exception is if you're trying to get a bank loan for your service business.

A detailed balance sheet isn't as important as tracking your available cash, which will be under pressure in the early years of a business because expenses can continue to exceed revenue for quite some time.

A complete balance sheet is useful for a business that owns significant equipment, furniture, inventory, and so on. The asset side of the balance sheet provides insight into the financial staying power of the company. For example, how much cash does your business have on hand to meet expected short-term bills? Conversely, the liability side of the ledger indicates the obligations, bills, and debts the company has coming due in the short and long term.

See Chapter 6 for more information on all the elements of a balance sheet.

Writing an executive summary

An *executive summary* is a 2- to 3-page summary of your entire business plan that you can share with interested investors who may not want to first wade through a 40- to 50-page plan. The executive summary whets the prospective investor's appetite by touching on the highlights of your entire plan. Although you should put this summary at the beginning of your plan document, we list this element last because you're not going to be able to write an intelligent summary of your plan until you flesh out the body of your business plan.

Chapter 14

Starting and Running a Small Business

. . . .

. . . .

After you research and evaluate the needs of your business, at some point you need to decide whether to actually start your business. In reference to his business plan, Alex Popov, founder of Smart Alec's, a healthy fast-food restaurant, says, "Something just clicked one day, and I said to myself, 'Yes, this is a business that is viable and appropriate now.'"

Most entrepreneurs experience this sudden realization, including us — we've experienced it with every business that we've ever started. If you really want to, you can conduct and analyze market research and crunch numbers until the cows come home. Even if you're a linear, logical, analytic, quantitative kind of person, you need to make a gut-level decision in the final analysis: Do you want to jump in the water and start swimming, or do you want to stay on the sidelines and remain a spectator? In our opinion, watching isn't nearly as fun as doing. If you feel ready but have some trepidation, you're normal — just go for it!

Starting Up: Your Preflight Checklist

When you decide to take off into the world of small-business ownership, you also need to ponder and make some decisions about a number of important issues. Just like a pilot before launching an airplane into flight, you need to make sure that all systems are in order and ready to do the job. If your fuel tanks aren't adequately filled, your engines clean and in working order, and your wing flaps in the proper position, you may never get your business off the ground.

Preparing to leave your job

The top reasons that wannabe entrepreneurs remain wannabe entrepreneurs are the psychological and financial aspects. Financial and emotional issues cause many aspiring entrepreneurs to remain their employers' indentured servants and cause those who do break free to soon return to their bondage. You may never discover that you have the talent to run your own business, and perhaps have a good idea to boot, unless you prepare yourself financially and psychologically to leave your job.

The money side of this self-exploration is easier to deal with than your mind, so we'll start with that. Dealing with a net reduction in the income you bring home from work — at least in the early years of your business — is a foregone conclusion for the vast majority of small-business opportunities that you may pursue. Accept this fact and plan accordingly.

Do all you can to reduce your expenses to a level that fits the entrepreneurial life you want to lead. You must examine your monthly spending patterns now to make your budget lean, mean, and entrepreneurially friendly. Determine what you spend each month on your rent (or mortgage), groceries, eating out, telephone calls, insurance, and so on. Unless you're one of those organized computer geeks — someone who keeps all this data detailed in a software package — you need to whip out your chequebook register, ATM receipts, credit card statements, and anything else that documents your spending habits. Don't forget to estimate your cash purchases that don't leave a trail, like when you eat lunch out or spend $35 on gas.

Don't tell us that everything you spend your money on is a necessity and that you can't cut anywhere. Question your expenditures! If you don't, continuing to work as an employee will be a necessity, and you'll never be able to pursue your entrepreneurial dream.

Beyond the bare essentials of food, shelter, health care, and clothing, most of what you spend money on is *discretionary* — that is, you spend money on things you don't need, like luxuries. Even the amount that you spend on the necessities, such as food and shelter, is probably only part necessity and may include a fair amount of luxury and waste. If you need a helping hand and an analyst's eye in preparing and developing strategies for reducing your spending, pick up a copy of the latest edition of our book *Personal Finance For Canadians For Dummies* (published by Wiley).

If reducing your spending is the most important financial move you can make before and during the period that you start your business, the second-best thing you can do is to figure how you'll manage the income side of your personal finances. The following list gives you some proven strategies to ensure that you earn enough income to live on:

- ✓ **Transition gradually.** One way to pursue your entrepreneurial dreams (and not starve while doing so) is to continue working part time in a regular job while you work part time at your own business. If you have a job that allows you to work part time, seize the opportunity. Some employers may even allow you to maintain your benefits.

  In addition to ensuring a steady source of income, splitting your time allows you to adjust to a new way of making a living. Some people have a hard time adjusting to their new lifestyle if they quit their jobs cold turkey and plunge headfirst into full-time entrepreneurship.

  Another option is to completely leave your job but line up a chunk of work that provides a decent income for at least some of your weekly work hours. Consulting for your old employer is a time-tested first "entrepreneurial" option with low risk.

- ✓ **Get/stay married.** Actually, as long as you're attached to someone who maintains a regular job and you manage your spending so you can live on that person's income alone, you're golden! Just make sure that you talk things through with the love of your life to minimize misunderstandings and resentments. Maybe someday you can return the favour!

Valuing and replacing your benefits

One money dilemma you may encounter deals with the benefits that your employer provides. For many people, walking away from these benefits is both financially and emotionally challenging. Benefits are valuable, but you may be surprised by how efficiently you can replicate them in your own business.

Extended health care benefits

Some prospective entrepreneurs fret over finding new extended health care benefits. Unless you have a significant existing medical problem (known as a pre-existing condition), getting this coverage as an individual isn't difficult.

The first option to explore is whether your existing coverage through your employer's group plan can be converted into individual coverage.

Don't just buy continuing coverage because it's available. Before you do, explore other health plans on your own. You may find you can purchase similar benefits at a lower cost. Also, get proposals for individual coverage from major health plans in your area. Investigate the cost and value of coverage from Blue Cross, Liberty Health, Ingle Health, and other major health plan offerers in your area. Look into joining your local chamber of commerce or board of trade, which often offer insurance plans to their members. Take a high deductible, if available, to keep costs down.

Long-term disability insurance

For most people, their greatest asset is their ability to earn money. If you suffer a disability and can't work, how would you manage financially? Long-term disability insurance protects your income in the event of a disability.

Before you leave your job, secure an individual long-term disability policy. After you leave your job and are no longer earning steady income, you won't qualify for a policy. Most insurers want to see at least six months of self-employment income before they'll write you a policy. If you become disabled during this time, you're uninsured and out of luck — that's a big risk to take!

Check with any professional associations that you belong to or could join to see whether they offer long-term disability plans. As with many employer-based programs, association plans are sometimes less expensive because of the group's purchasing power.

Life insurance

If you have dependents who count on your income, you need life insurance. And unlike with disability insurance, in the vast majority of cases, you can purchase a life insurance policy at a lower cost than you can purchase additional coverage through your employer.

Retirement plans

If your employer offers a retirement savings program, such as a pension plan or a deferred profit sharing plan, don't despair about not having these when you head out on your own. For starters, what you've already earned and accumulated while employed is yours as long as you've been in the plan the required amount of time to own the benefits, known as *vesting*. And when you're self-employed you can continue — or start — putting money into an RRSP. As long as you earn an income from your enterprise, you'll be able to take advantage of RRSPs, which allow you to sock away a hefty chunk of your earnings on a tax-deductible basis.

Other benefits

Yes, employers offer other benefits that you may value. For example, you *seem* to get paid holidays and vacations. In reality, though, your employer simply spreads your salary over all 52 weeks of a year, thus paying you for actually working the other 47 weeks or so out of the year. You can do the same by building the cost of this paid time off into your product and service pricing.

Another "benefit" of being an employee is that your employer pays half of your Canada Pension Plan or Quebec Pension Plan contributions. When you're self-employed, you have to pay the full amount yourself. However, you get to claim half that amount — the "employer's contribution" — as a deduction from your taxable income. You also get a 15.5 percent federal tax credit for the other half — the "employee's share" — which also generally gets you an accompanying provincial tax credit. As with vacations and holidays, you can build the cost of this tax into your product and service pricing. Just think: Your employer could pay you a higher salary if it wasn't paying CPP on your behalf.

Some employers offer other insurance plans, such as dental or vision care plans. Ultimately, these plans cover small out-of-pocket expenditures that aren't worth insuring. Don't waste your money purchasing such policies when you're self-employed. If you want this sort of coverage, look for a plan that includes it as part of a wider range of health coverage. Whether you're self-employed or incorporated, the premiums for health and dental insurance are generally deductible from your business income.

Financing Your Business

When you create your business plan (which we explain how to do in Chapter 13), you should estimate your start-up and development costs. You can start many worthwhile small businesses with little capital. The following sections explain methods for financing your business.

No matter what type of business you have in mind and how much money you think you need to make it succeed, be patient. Start small enough that you don't need outside capital (unless you're in an unusual situation where your window of opportunity is now, but it will close if you don't get funding soon). Starting your business without outside capital instills the discipline required for building a business piece by piece over time. The longer you can wait to get a loan or an equity investment, the better the terms are for you and your business because the risk is lower for the lender or investor.

Bootstrapping

Making do with a small amount of capital, and spending it as you can afford to, is known as *bootstrapping*. Bootstrapping is just a fancy way of saying that a business lives within its means. This forces a business to be more resourceful and less wasteful. Bootstrapping is also a great training mechanism for producing cost-effective products and services. It offers you the advantage of getting into business in the first place with little capital.

Millions of successful small companies were bootstrapped at one time or another. Like small redwood saplings that grow into towering trees, small companies that had to bootstrap in the past can eventually grow into multi-million-dollar and even multi-billion-dollar companies. For example, Magna International, one of the world's largest suppliers to the auto industry, started off as a one-man tool and die shop opened by founder Frank Stronach. Then there's the Jim Pattison Group, Canada's third largest privately held company, which employs some 27,000 people. Entrepreneur Jim Pattison began by borrowing the money to buy a car dealership by using his home and life insurance policy as collateral. Microsoft, Motorola, Sony, and Disney were all bootstrapped, too.

Whether you want to maintain a small shop that employs just yourself, hire a few employees, or dream about building the next Canadian Tire, Research in Motion, or Tim Hortons, you need capital. However, misconceptions abound about how much money a company needs to achieve its goals and sources of funding.

"There's an illusion that most companies need tons of money to get established and grow," says James Collins, former lecturer at the Stanford Graduate School of Business and coauthor of the best-sellers *Built to Last* and *Good to Great: Why Some Companies Make the Leap . . . and Others Don't.* "The Silicon Valley success stories of companies that raise gobs of venture capital and grow 4,000 percent are very rare. They are statistically insignificant but catch all sorts of attention," he adds.

Studies show that the vast majority of small businesses obtain their initial capital from personal savings and family and friends rather than outside sources, such as banks and venture capital firms. A Harvard Business School study of the *Inc.* 500 (500 large, fast-growing private U.S. companies) found that more than 80 percent of the successful companies were started with funds from the founder's personal savings. The median start-up capital was a modest $10,000, and these are successful, fast-growing companies! Slower-growing companies tend to require even less capital.

With the initial infusion of capital, many small businesses can propel themselves for years after they develop a service or product that brings in more cash flow. For example, Jim Gentes, the founder of Giro, the bike helmet manufacturer, raised $35,000 from personal savings and loans from family and friends to make and distribute his first product and then used the cash flow for future products.

Eventually, a successful, growing company may want outside financing to expand faster. Raising money from investors or lenders is much easier after you demonstrate that you know what you're doing and that a market exists for your product or service.

As we explain in the section "Preparing to leave your job," earlier in this chapter, aspiring entrepreneurs must examine their personal finances for opportunities to reduce their own spending. If you want to start a company, the best time for you to examine your finances is many years before you want to hit the entrepreneurial path. As with other financial goals, advance preparation can go a long way toward helping start a business. The best funding source and easiest investor to please is you.

Alan Tripp, founder and CEO of Score Learning, a chain of storefront interactive learning centres, planned for seven years before he took the entrepreneurial plunge. He funded his first retail centre fully from personal savings. He and his wife lived frugally to save the necessary money. Tripp's first centre proved the success of his business concept: retail learning centres where kids can use computers to improve their reading, math, and science skills. With a business plan crafted over time and hard numbers to demonstrate the financial viability of his operation, Tripp then successfully raised funds from investors to open many more centres. (Kaplan Inc. ultimately bought out his company.)

Some small-business founders put the cart before the horse and don't plan and save for starting their business the way Tripp did. And in many cases, small-business owners want capital but don't have a clear plan or need for it.

Borrowing from banks

If you're starting a new business or have been in business for just a few years, borrowing, particularly from banks, may be difficult. Borrowing money is easier when you don't really need to do so. No one knows this fact better than small-business owners do.

Small-business owners who successfully obtain bank loans do their home-work. To borrow money from a bank, you generally need a business plan, three years of financial statements and tax returns for the business and its owner, as well as projections for the business. Hunt around for banks that are committed to and understand the small-business marketplace.

Canada Small Business Financing Program

The Canada Small Business Financing (CSBF) Program guarantees some small-business loans provided by banks, credit unions, and many trust, loan, and insurance companies. Because many small businesses lack collateral and pose a higher loan risk, banks would not otherwise make many of these loans. In addition to guaranteeing loans for existing businesses, the CSBF backs loans to start-ups. The loans, which can go as high as $250,000, can be used to finance the purchase of assets, leasehold improvements, computer acquisitions, and so on, and are available to sole proprietorships, partner-ships, and incorporated companies.

If you choose a floating-rate loan, the interest rate can't be more than 3 per-cent above the lender's *prime lending rate*, the rate they charge their lowest-risk corporate borrowers. You can also choose a fixed-rate loan: In this case, the interest rate can't be greater than 3 percent over the lender's residential mortgage rate for a similar term.

For more information, call the Small Business Loans Administration branch of Industry Canada at 613-954-5540. You can also find them online at strategis.ic.gc.ca.

Business Development Bank of Canada

Another good potential source of funds is the Business Development Bank of Canada (BDC). For start-ups or companies in their first 12 months of ringing up sales, the BDC offers working capital you can use to boost an existing line of credit. You may also be able to get financing for buying equipment and for marketing and other start-up costs. Financing is also available for buying a franchise.

BDC is worth looking into because it offers a number of financing options that can be very valuable to newer businesses. For instance, you may be able to spread out repayment of your loan over a number of years. You may also be able to fit your repayments to your projected cash flow, including a schedule that suits the seasonality of your business, or payments that grow as your business grows.

For businesses already on their way, the BDC offers working capital loans as well as loans for expanding your existing premises or constructing new facili-ties. It also provides financing for a range of other undertakings, including product and market research, sales planning, feasibility studies, and developing marketing and distribution plans.

The BDC is also a good place to turn for counselling and consulting services. It offers programs to assist small businesses on a number of fronts, including developing a business plan, strategic planning, human resources, finance, and assessing opportunities for growing your business.

To get more information on BDC's services and how to contact a local office, call 1-888-463-6232. BDC also has an informative Web site at www.bdc.ca.

Other sources of bank financing

Other potential sources of financing include the following:

- ✔ **Credit unions:** These institutions can be another source of financial help, and small businesses are generally a key target market for credit unions. Credit unions also are generally more willing to make personal loans to individuals.

- ✔ **Credit cards:** If you've got the itch to get your business going but can't wait to save the necessary money and lack other ways to borrow, the plastic in your wallet may be your ticket to operation. You can acquire some credit cards at interest rates of 10 percent or less. Because credit cards are unsecured loans, if your business fails and you can't pay back your debt, your home equity and assets in retirement accounts aren't at risk.

Borrowing from yourself

You can use your RRSP as another potential source of capital. However, any money you take out of your plan will be taxed as income at your full *marginal tax rate* (the rate you pay on your highest, or last, dollar of income in the year). If you do withdraw money from your RRSP, your plan administrator has to retain some of the money to help pay the tax on the withdrawal. This is known as a *withholding tax*. The tax is 10 percent on withdrawals up to $5,000, 20 percent on withdrawals of between $5,001 and $15,000, and 30 percent on amounts over $15,000. Quebec charges a withholding tax of 16 percent, regardless of the amount, in addition to the federal withholding tax.

If you use your RRSP savings for your business, you'll increase your cash flow if you take out several smaller chunks rather than one large amount. For instance, if you need to take $9,000 out of your RRSP, instead of taking it out as one lump sum, make two withdrawals, one for $5,000 and one for $4,000.

The withholding tax will often not be enough to cover the total tax bill on your withdrawal. That means the following spring you may need to find extra money in order to pay the outstanding tax on your withdrawal. Far more importantly, taking money out of your plan can be an expensive way to fund your business. For example, say you borrow $20,000 from your RRSP. If you left that money in your plan and it compounded annually by 10 percent, it would grow to almost $135,000 in 20 years' time.

You can also borrow against the equity in your home or other real estate to ease your access to capital, because it acts as security on your loan and allows you to get a lower interest rate.

Borrowing from family and friends

Because they know you and hopefully like and trust you, your family and friends may seem like a good source of investment money for your small business. They also have the added advantage of offering you better terms than a banker, wealthy investor, or venture capitalist.

Before you solicit and accept money from those you love, consider the pitfalls:

✔ First, defaulting on a loan made by a large, anonymous lender if your business hits the skids is one thing, but defaulting on a loan from your dear relatives can make future Thanksgiving meals mighty uncomfortable!

✔ Second, most entrepreneurs receive surprisingly little encouragement from people they're close to. Most parents, for example, think you've severed some of your cerebral synapses if you announce your intention to quit your job with the lofty job title, decent pay, and benefits. The lack of emotional support can discourage you far more than the lack of financial support.

From entrepreneurs we've observed, we've found that family investments in a small business work best under the following conditions:

✔ You prepare and sign a letter of agreement that spells out the terms of the investment or loan, as if you're doing business with a banker or some other investor you know for business purposes only. We also recommend clearly disclosing the risk of losing one's entire investment. As time goes on, people have selective recall. Putting things in writing reminds everyone what was agreed to.

✔ You're quite certain that you can repay the loan.

✔ You can start your business with an equity investment. With an equity investment, a person is willing and able to lose all the money invested but hopes to hit a home run while helping you with your dream.

Courting investors and selling equity

Beyond family members and friends, private individuals with sufficient money — also known as wealthy individuals — are your next best source of capital if you want an equity investor (and not a loan from a lender). Before you approach wealthy people, you must have a good business plan, which we explain how to prepare in Chapter 13. A worthwhile *angel investor* (a wealthy individual who invests in small companies) should have a track record of success with somewhat similar businesses that she's funded and should bring other things to the table besides money, such as strategic advice, helpful business contacts, and so on.

Although you want such people to care about your business, it's best if their investment in your business is no more than 5 to 10 percent of their total investment portfolio. No one wants to lose money, but doing so is less painful if you diversify well. A $10,000 investment from a millionaire is 1 percent of his portfolio.

Finding people who may be interested in investing isn't difficult, but you need to be persistent and creative. Consider these approaches:

- Consulting tax advisers and lawyers you know may have contacts
- Networking with successful entrepreneurs in similar fields
- Considering customers or suppliers of your business who like your business and believe in its potential

Finding your way to wealthy individuals who don't know you may prove fruitful as well. Alex Popov, whom we introduce at the beginning of this chapter, sent hundreds of letters to people who lived in upscale neighbourhoods. The letter, a one-page summary of Alex's investment opportunity, got an astounding 5 percent response for interest in receiving a business plan. Ultimately through this search method, Popov found one wealthy investor who funded his entire deal.

Determining how much of the business you're selling for the amount invested isn't easy. Basically, the equity percentage should hinge upon what the whole business is worth (see Chapter 15 for details on how to value a business). If your whole business is worth $500,000 and you're seeking $100,000 from investors, that $100,000 should buy 20 percent of the business.

New businesses are the hardest to value — yet another reason you're best off trying to raise money *after* you demonstrate some success. The farther along you are, the lower the risk to an investor and the lower the cost to you (in terms of how much equity you must give up) to raise money.

Deciding Whether to Incorporate

Most businesses operate as sole proprietorships. The term *sole proprietorship* doesn't mean that only one person owns the business, but rather that for legal and tax purposes, your business is not a corporation. If you run a sole proprietorship, you report your business income and costs on your tax return on the Statement of Business Activities (Form T2124). Certain professionals such as doctors, lawyers, and engineers, are required to use the Professional Income and Expenses form (T2032). You attach these to your personal income tax return, the T1 General.

Incorporating, which establishes a distinct legal entity under which you do business, takes time and costs money. Therefore, incorporation must offer some benefits.

Because corporations are legal entities distinct from their owners, they offer features that a proprietorship or partnership doesn't. For example, corporations can have shareholders who own a piece or percentage of the company. These shares can be sold or transferred to other owners, subject to any restrictions in the shareholder's agreement. Corporations also offer *continuity of life,* which simply means that they can continue to exist despite an owner's death or the owner's transfer of her stock in the company.

Don't waste your money incorporating if you simply want to maintain a corporate-sounding name. If you operate as a sole proprietor, you can choose to operate under a different business name ("doing business as," or d.b.a.) without the cost and hassles of incorporating.

Obtaining liability protection

A major reason to consider incorporation is liability protection. Incorporation effectively separates your business from your personal finances, thereby better protecting your personal assets from lawsuits that may arise from your business.

Before you incorporate, ask yourself (and perhaps others in your line of business or advisers — legal, tax, and so on — who work with businesses like yours) what can or may cause someone to sue you. Then see whether you can purchase insurance to protect against these potential liabilities. Insurance is superior to incorporation because it pays claims, and people can still sue you, even if you're incorporated. If you incorporate and someone successfully sues you, your company must cough up the money for the claim, and doing so may sink your business. (You may also have to offer personal guarantees for obtaining financing for an incorporated business, which also exposes you legally.) Only insurance can cover such financially destructive claims.

People can also sue you if, for example, they slip and suffer an injury while on your property. To cover these types of claims, you can purchase a property or premises liability policy from an insurer.

Accountants, doctors, and a number of other professionals can buy liability insurance, and in fact, are sometimes required to do so by regulators or professional bodies. A good place to start searching for liability insurance is through the associations for your profession. Even if you're not a current member, check out the associations anyway — you may be able to access the insurance without membership, or you can join the association long enough to sign up. (Associations also sometimes offer competitive rates on disability insurance.)

Paying corporate taxes

A big difference between operating as a sole proprietor and as a corporation is that the government taxes a corporation's profits differently from those realized in a sole proprietorship. Which is better for your business depends on your situation.

Suppose that your business performs well and makes lots of money. If your business isn't incorporated, the government taxes all profits from your business on your personal tax return in the year that your company earns those profits. If you intend to use these profits to reinvest in your business and expand, incorporating can potentially save you some tax dollars.

Resist the short-term temptation to incorporate just so you can have money left in the corporation taxed at a lower rate. If you want to pay yourself the profits in the future, you can end up paying more taxes. Why? Because you first pay taxes at the corporate tax rate in the year that your company earns the money, and then you pay taxes again on your personal income tax return when the corporation pays you.

Another reason not to incorporate, especially in the early months of a business, is that you can't immediately claim the losses for an incorporated business on your personal tax return. Because most businesses produce little revenue in their early years and have all sorts of start-up expenditures, losses are common.

The general federal corporate tax rate is 22 percent. In addition, corporations pay provincial tax of around 12 percent. If your enterprise qualifies as a *Canadian-controlled private corporation,* the federal tax rate is just 13 percent on the first $400,000 of active business income. Income over this level is taxed at the general 22 percent federal corporate tax rate. In order to qualify, the corporation has to be resident in Canada, and not controlled by any combination of non-residents or public corporations.

The provinces also have reduced small-business tax rates for the first $400,000 or $500,000 (depending on the province) of small-business income. As a result, a corporation with profits that qualify as "small-business income" will be taxed at anywhere from about 14 to 21 percent. The tax rate on profits above the threshold amount ranges from around 32 percent to 38 percent, depending on the province.

Making the decision

If you're totally confused about whether to incorporate because your business is undergoing major financial changes, it's worth getting competent professional help. The hard part is knowing where to turn, because finding one adviser who can put together all the pieces of the puzzle (financial, legal, and taxes) is challenging. Also be aware that you may get wrong or biased advice.

Although many lawyers and tax advisers don't understand the business side of business, try to find one who does, or you may also need a business adviser. Lawyers who specialize in advising small businesses can help explain the legal issues. Tax advisers who perform a lot of work with business owners can help explain the tax considerations.

If you've weighed the factors and you still can't decide, our advice is to keep your business simple — don't incorporate. Why? Because doing the paperwork for incorporating costs time and money, and corporations have additional reporting requirements. In addition, should you decide being incorporated is not beneficial, unincorporating also takes time and money. Start off your business as a sole proprietorship and then take it from there. Wait until the benefits of incorporating your business clearly outweigh the costs and drawbacks.

Finding and Keeping Customers

When you write your business plan (see Chapter 13), you need to think about your business's customers. Just as the sun is the centre of our solar system, everything in your business revolves around your customers. If you take care of your customers, they'll take care of you and your business for many years.

The first thing we recommend doing is putting together a mailing list of people you know who may be interested in what you're offering. Draft and mail an upbeat, one-page letter that provides an overview of what your business offers. As you have news — successes to report, new products and services, and so on — do another mailing. Short letters get read more than something that looks like another glossy advertising newsletter. Most people are busy and don't care about your business enough to read something lengthy.

In addition to mailings, other successful ways to get the word out and attract customers are limited only to your imagination and resourcefulness. Consider the following ideas:

- ✔ If your business idea is indeed innovative or somehow different, or if you have grand expansion plans, add some local media people to your mailing list and send them the one-page updates on your business, too. Everybody from newspaper, radio, and television business reporters to Web site writers and bloggers are always looking for story ideas. Just remember to make your press releases informational and not an advertisement.

- ✔ If your business seeks customers in a specific geographic area, blanket that area by mailing your one-page letter or delivering it door to door. You can include a coupon that offers your products or services at a reduced cost (perhaps at your cost) to get people to try them. Make sure that people know that this is a special opening-for-business bargain.

After you attract customers, treat them as you would like to be treated by a business. If customers like your products and services, they not only come back to buy more when the need arises, but they also tell others. Satisfied customers are every business's best cost-effective marketers.

We never cease to be amazed by how many businesses have mediocre, poor, or downright awful customer service. One reason for poor service is that as a business grows, its employees are on the customer service front lines. If you don't hire good people and give them the proper incentives to service customers, many of them won't do it. For most employees on a salary, the day-to-day servicing of customers may be just an annoyance for them.

One way to make your staff care about customer service is to base part of their pay on the satisfaction of the customers they work with. Tie bonuses and increases at review time to this issue. You can easily measure customer satisfaction with a simple survey form.

Treating the customer right starts the moment the selling process begins. Honesty is an often-underused business tool. More than a few salespeople mislead and lie in order to close a sale. Many customers discover after their purchase that they've been deceived, and they get angry. These unethical businesses not only likely lose future business from customers but also surely — and justifiably — lose referrals.

If your business doesn't perform well for a customer, apologize and bend over backward to make the customer happy. Offer a discount on the problem purchase or, if possible, a refund on product purchases. Also, make sure that you have a clear return-and-refund policy. Bend that policy if doing so helps you satisfy an unhappy customer or rids you of a difficult customer.

Setting Up Shop

No matter what type of business you have in mind, you need space to work from, whether it's a spare room in your home, shared office space, or a small factory. You also need to outfit that space with tools of your trade. This section explains how to tackle these tasks.

Finding business space and negotiating a lease

You may be in the market for office or retail space unless you can run your business from your home. Finding good space and buying or leasing it takes tons of time if you do it right.

In the early months and years of your business, buying an office or a retail building generally doesn't make sense. The down payment consumes important capital, and you may end up spending lots of time and money on a real estate transaction for a location that may not interest you in the long term. Buying this type of real estate rarely makes sense unless you plan to stay put for five or more years.

Leasing a space for your business is far more practical. Renting office space is simpler than renting retail space because a building owner worries less about your business and its financial health. Your business needs more credibility to rent retail because your retail business affects the nature of the strip mall or shopping centre where you lease. Owners of such properties don't want quick failures or someone who does a poor job of running his business.

Because renting retail space is harder, if you and your business don't have a track record with renting space, getting references is useful. If you seek well-located retail space, you must compete with national chains like Tim Hortons, so you'd better have an A+ credit rating and track record. Consider subletting — circulate flyers to businesses that may have some extra space in the area where you want to locate your business. Also prepare financial statements that show your creditworthiness (personally and in business).

Agents list most spaces for lease. Working with an agent can be useful, but the same conflicts exist as with residential agents (see Chapter 12). You should also examine spaces for lease without an agent, where you deal with the landlord directly. Such landlords may give you a better deal, and they don't worry about recouping an agent's commission.

The biggest headaches with leasing space are understanding and negotiating the lease contract. Odds are that the lessor presents you with a standard, preprinted lease contract that she says is fair and is the same lease that everyone else signs. Don't sign it! This contract is the lessor's first offer — have an expert review it and help you modify it. Find yourself a lawyer who regularly deals with such contracts.

Office leases are usually simpler than retail leases. About the most complicated issue you face with office leases is that they can be *full service,* which includes janitorial benefits. Retail leases, however, are almost always *triple-net,* which means that you as the tenant pay for maintenance (for example, resurfacing the parking lot, cleaning, and gardening), utilities, and property taxes. You're correct to worry about a triple-net retail lease because you can't control many of these expenses. For example, if the property is sold, property taxes can jump. Here are provisions to keep in mind when dealing with a triple-net lease:

- Compare your site's costs to other sites to evaluate the deal that the lessor offers you.

- Your lease contract needs to include a cap for the triple-net costs at a specified limit per square foot.

- Try to make sure that the lease contract doesn't make you responsible for removal costs for any toxic waste you may discover during your occupation. Also exclude increased property taxes that the sale of the property may cause.

- If feasible, get your landlord to pay for remodelling — it's cheaper for the landlord to do it and entails fewer hassles for you.

- With retail leases, get an option for renewal — this is critical in retail, where location is important. The option should specify the cost — for example, something like 5 percent below market, as determined by arbitration.

- Get an option that the lease can be transferred to a new owner if you sell the business.

If you really think that you want to purchase (not lease) because you can see yourself staying in the same place for at least five years, read Chapter 11.

Should you work from home?

You may be able to run a relatively simple small business from your home. If you have the choice of running your business out of your home versus securing outside office space, consider the following issues:

✔ **Cost control:** As we discuss earlier in this chapter, bootstrapping your business can make a lot of financial and business sense. If you have space in your home that you can use, then you've found yourself a rent-free business space. (If you're considering buying a larger home to have more space, then you can't really say that your home office is rent-free.)

✔ **Business issues:** What are the needs of your business and customers? If you don't require fancy office space to impress others or to meet with clients, work at home. If you operate a retail business that requires lots of customers coming to you, getting outside space is probably the best (and legally correct) choice. Check with the governing authorities of your town or city to find out what local regulations exist for home-based businesses.

✔ **Discipline:** At home, do you have the discipline to work the number of hours that you need and want, or will the kitchen goodies tempt you to make half a dozen snack trips? Can you refrain from turning on the television every hour for late-breaking news? The sometimes amorphous challenge of figuring out how to grow the business may cause you to focus your energies elsewhere.

✔ **Family matters:** Last but not least, your home life should factor into where you decide to work. One advantage to working at home when you're a parent is that you can be a more involved parent. If nothing else, you can spend the one to two hours per day that many people spend commuting with your kids! Just make sure that you try to set aside work hours, during which time your office is off limits.

Ask other family members how they feel about your working at home. Be specific about what you plan to do, where, when, and how. Will clients come over? What time of day and where in the home will you meet with them? You may not think that your home office is an imposition, but your spouse may. Home business problems come between many couples. If you're single and living alone, of course, home life is less of an issue.

Equipping your business space

You can easily go overboard spending money when leasing or buying office space and outfitting that space. The most common reason that small-business owners spend more than they should is to attempt to project a professional, upscale image. You can have an office or retail location that works for you and your customers without spending a fortune if you observe some simple rules:

✔ **Buy — don't lease or finance — equipment.** Unless you're running a manufacturing outfit where the cost of buying equipment is prohibitive, try to avoid borrowing and leasing. If you can't buy office furniture, computers, cash registers, and so on with cash, then you probably can't afford them! Buying such things on credit or leasing them — leasing is invariably the most expensive way to go — encourages you to spend beyond your means.

Consider buying used equipment, especially furniture, which takes longer to become obsolete. The more popular a piece of equipment, the more beneficial it is for you to purchase rather than lease: If many other businesses would be willing to buy the equipment, you'll have an easier time unloading it if you ever want to sell it. Leasing may make more sense with oddball-type equipment that is more of a hassle and costly for you to unload after a short usage period.

✔ **Don't get carried away with technological and marketing gadgets.** Many small-business owners we speak with spend all sorts of money on items such as laptops, smart phones, and continual roving Internet capability because they feel the need to be "competitive" and "current." Don't forget the virtues of picking up the phone or meeting in person — these forms of communication are much more personal ways of doing business.

Voice mail is one device that many small-business owners find worth spending money on. Voice mail sounds more professional than an answering machine and can handle simultaneous calls with ease. Best of all, voice mail can save you money on administrative help.

Bootstrap-equipping your office makes sense within certain limits (see "Bootstrapping," earlier in this chapter). If customers come to you, of course, you don't want a shabby-looking store or office. However, that doesn't mean that you have to purchase the Rolls Royce equivalent of everything that you need for your office.

Accounting for the Money

One of the less glamorous aspects of running your own business is dealing with accounting. Unlike when you work for an employer, you must track your business's income, expenses, and taxes (for you _and_ your employees). Although you may be able to afford to hire others to help with these dreary tasks, you must know the inner workings of your business to keep control of your business, to stay out of trouble with the tax authorities, and to minimize your taxes. The following sections show you how to handle the accounting aspect of your business.

Tax record keeping and payments

With revenue hopefully flowing into your business and expenses surely heading out, you must keep records to help satisfy your tax obligations and to keep a handle on the financial status and success of your business. You can't accurately complete the necessary tax forms for your business if you don't properly track your income and expenses. And should the Canada Revenue Agency (CRA) audit you — the probability of being audited as a small-business owner is about four times higher than when you're an employee at a company — you'll need to prove some or even all of your expenses and income.

In order to keep your sanity, and keep the CRA at bay, make sure that you do the following:

✔ **Pay your taxes each quarter and on time.** When you're self-employed, you're responsible for the accurate and timely filing of all taxes that you owe on your income on a quarterly basis. You must pay taxes by the 15th of March, June, September, and December (unless the 15th falls on the weekend, in which case the payment is due the Monday that follows the 15th). To pay correctly, call the Canada Revenue Agency — you'll find the number for your local office in the blue pages of your telephone book — and ask for Form T2WS3 (Calculating Quarterly Instalment Payments). This form includes an easy-to-use estimated tax worksheet to help you calculate your quarterly tax payments. Mark the due dates for your quarterly taxes on your calendar so you don't forget!

If you have employees, you need to withhold taxes from each paycheque they receive. You must use the money that you deduct from their paycheques to make timely payments to the Canada Revenue Agency. In addition to income tax, you need to withhold and send in Canada Pension Plan (or Quebec Pension Plan) and Employment Insurance premiums. Pay these premiums immediately and *never* use the money to fund your business needs.

Use a payroll service to ensure that your payments are made on time and correctly to all the different places that these tax filings need to go.

✔ **Keep your business accounts separate from your personal accounts.** The CRA knows that small-business owners, as a group, cheat more on their tax returns than do company employees. One way that dishonest entrepreneurs cheat is hiding business income and inflating business expenses. Thus, the CRA looks skeptically at business owners who use and commingle funds in personal chequing and credit card accounts for business transactions.

Although you may find opening and maintaining separate business accounts bothersome, do so. And remember to pay for only legitimate business expenses through your business account. You'll be thankful come tax preparation time to have separate records. Having separate records can also make the CRA easier to deal with if and when you're audited.

✔ **Keep good records of your business income and expenses.** You can use file folders, software, or a shoebox to collect your business income and expense records, but just do it! When you need to file your annual return, you want to be able to find the documentation that allows you to figure your business income and expenses. For most people, the file folder system works best. If your business is small, one folder for income and one for your expenses will do. Computer software can help you with this drudgery as well. Because you must go through the hassle of entering the data, software is more useful with larger small businesses and in those businesses that process lots of cheques or expenses.

Charging expenses on a credit card or writing a cheque can make the documentation for most businesses easier. These methods of payment leave a paper trail that simplifies the task of tallying up your expenses come tax time, and they make the CRA auditor less grumpy in the event that he audits you. (Just make sure that you don't overspend, as many people do with credit cards!)

How to (legally) pay lower taxes

Every small business must spend money, and spending money in your business holds the allure of lowering your tax bill. But don't spend money on your business just for the sake of generating tax deductions. Spend your money to make the most of the tax breaks that you can legally take. The following are some examples of legal tax breaks:

✔ **Appreciate depreciation.** If you buy a computer, printer, furniture, or other equipment — called *capital assets* — you can't simply deduct the price as a business expense. Instead, you have to spread the cost over a number of years. Each year, you're allowed a deduction for the decrease in the value — the wear and tear — of the equipment (for example, computers, desks, chairs — even that funky espresso machine) you use in your business. The income tax system refers to this as *capital cost allowance,* or *CCA.*

Normally, equipment for your business is *depreciated* over a number of years. With depreciation, you claim a yearly tax deduction for a portion of the total purchase price of the equipment. Different types of equipment are grouped into different CCA classes, which have different allowable rates of depreciation. For instance, computer hardware can be depreciated at 30 percent annually, while furniture can be depreciated at 20 percent annually. Each year, your maximum deduction is equal to the allowable depreciation, or *CCA rate,* times the remaining undepreciated value of the assets. In addition, in the year you purchase an asset, you can claim a deduction of only one-half of the regular CCA.

For example, say you buy a new desk and chair for $4,000. Furniture can be depreciated at 20 percent, so you'd normally get a deduction for $800. However, in the first year, you can claim only half that, or $400. The next year you can claim a deduction worth 20 percent of the remaining undepreciated value of $3,600 ($4,000 – $400), worth $720.

You're not required to claim the maximum allowable CCA each year. The undepreciated amount simply gets carried ahead to the next year. This can be a profitable strategy. Consider that in the early years of most businesses, profits are low. When your business is in a low tax bracket, the value of your deductions is low. If your business grows, you may come out ahead if you don't claim some or all of the allowable deduction for some of your early-year big-ticket purchases, instead postponing claiming the expenses until your income — and therefore your marginal tax rate — is higher.

✔ **Make the most of your auto deductions.** If you use your car for business, you can claim a deduction for a portion of the expenses, usually based on the kilometers you drive for business compared with the overall kilometres you put on your vehicle. You can also claim a deduction for the depreciation (capital cost allowance), again using the same percentage. However, the CRA puts a ceiling on the purchase cost you can use when doing your calculations. The maximum price you can use for calculating your CCA is $26,000 for cars bought in 1998 or 1999, $27,000 for cars bought in 2000, and $30,000 for cars bought in 2001 through 2009.

If you lease a vehicle, the deduction you can claim is also limited, depending on the year you entered into the lease. For 1998–1999, the maximum monthly deductible lease amount is $650, for 2000 the maximum is $700, and for 2001–2009 it's $800. Your actual allowable deduction may be less than this amount, because the CRA also uses a complex formula to come up with another ceiling. If you borrow money to purchase a vehicle, the maximum interest expense allowed is $300 a month.

✔ **Deduct travel, meal, and entertainment expenses.** You can deduct these expenses as long as they're for a bona fide business purpose. You need to be aware of certain restrictions, however. For instance, say you live in Winnipeg and fly to Honolulu for a week for a convention. You spend three days at a seminar for business purposes, and then the other four days snorkelling and getting skin cancer on Waikiki Beach. You can deduct the expenses for only the three days of your trip that you devoted to business. In most cases, however, you can deduct the full cost of getting there and back. Note that you're allowed to deduct only the cost of a maximum of two conventions a year. Furthermore, the convention has to be held in a location that's part of the normal area of the sponsoring organization.

You can only deduct 50 percent of meal and entertainment expenses, so don't spend frivolously on business trips and think you can deduct everything. Even if you're out of town at a convention, you can deduct only 50 percent of the cost of any meals.

The Canada Revenue Agency doesn't allow business deductions for club dues, such as for health, business, airport, or social clubs; or for entertainment such as executive boxes at sports stadiums. If you entertain others for business purposes at a club, you can deduct the cost subject to the limitations noted above.

Keeping a Life and Perspective

David Packard, co-founder of Hewlett-Packard, said, "You are likely to die not of starvation for opportunities, but of indigestion of opportunities."

Most small businesses succeed in keeping their owners more than busy — in some cases, too busy. If you provide needed products or services at a fair price, customers will beat a path to your door. Your business will grow and be busier than what you can personally handle. You may need to start hiring people. We know small-business owners who work themselves into a frenzy and put in 70 or more hours a week.

If you enjoy your work so much so that it's not really work and you end up putting in long hours because you enjoy it, terrific! But success in your company can cause you to put less energy into other important aspects of your life that perhaps don't come as easily.

Although careers and business successes are important, don't place these successes higher than fourth on your overall priority list. You can't replace your health, family, and friends — but you can replace a job or a business.

Chapter 15

Purchasing a Small Business

. . . .

. . . .

*E*ach year, hundreds of thousands of small businesses change hands. This chapter is for those of you who want to run or invest in an existing small business but don't want to start the business yourself. And of course, this chapter can show you how to make good money and have fun along the way!

Examining the Advantages of Buying

We don't want to scare you off if you want to start a business. However, buying someone else's business works better for some people than others. The following list reflects the main advantages of buying a business:

✔ **You avoid start-up hassles and headaches.** Starting a business from scratch requires dealing with many issues. In the early years, beyond formulating a business plan, you must also deal with a variety of issues, such as developing a marketing plan, finding customers, locating space, hiring employees, and incorporating. If you buy a good existing business, you buy into an ongoing enterprise with customers, assets, and hopefully profits (although you still need to fix any problems the business may have).

Think about the learning curve for the type of business you're considering purchasing. Buying an existing business makes more sense if the business is complicated. For example, purchasing a business that manufactures musical instruments makes more sense than purchasing a plumbing business that requires plumbing know-how and a few tools to start up. Unless you've built musical instruments before and understand the intricacies of the production process, starting such a business from scratch is quite risky and perhaps foolhardy. (However, purchasing an existing plumbing business may still make sense if, for example, you don't want to build a stable of customers from scratch.)

✔ **You reduce risk.** Although investing in something with a solid track record is still far from a sure thing, your risk may be significantly lower than the risk involved in a start-up. After a business has an operating history and offers a product or service with a demonstrated market, some of the risk in the company is removed. Looking at historic financial statements also helps you make more accurate financial forecasts than you could make with a start-up venture.

✔ **You enhance your ability to attract investor or lender money.** You should have less difficulty raising money from investors and lenders for your existing business than with a start-up. Attracting most investors to something that's more than an idea is easier. And for the amount that they invest, investors demand a smaller piece of an existing business than they would with an investment in an idea.

✔ **You want to enter a business where buying an existing business is your only ticket in.** You can enter some businesses — such as bottlers or car dealerships — only through your purchase of a business that already exists.

✔ **You can find businesses where you can add value.** Some entrepreneurs who start businesses don't see the potential for growth or don't want to grow their business — they may be burned out, content with their current profit, or simply ready to retire. Finding businesses where the potential exists to improve operating efficiency and to expand into new markets isn't too hard. Relative to investing in stocks or real estate (see Parts II and III), finding small companies that are undervalued relative to the potential that they can offer is easier for a business-minded person.

Just because you think you see potential to improve a business, don't pay a high price based on your high expectations. You can be wrong — you may be looking at the business through rose-coloured glasses. Even if you're correct about the potential, don't pay the current owner for the hard work and ingenuity you'll bring to the business if you purchase it. Offer a fair price based on the value of the business *now* — we explain how to figure this value in the section "Evaluating a Small Business," later in this chapter.

Understanding the Drawbacks of Buying

Just as everyone doesn't enjoy running or cooking, some people don't enjoy the negatives that come with buying an existing business. If the following issues don't turn you off, purchasing an existing business may be right for you:

✔ **You buy the baggage.** When you buy an existing business, the bad comes with the good, and all businesses include their share of the bad. The business may employ problem employees, for example, or it may have a less-than-stellar reputation in the marketplace. Even if the employees are good, they and the company culture may not mesh with where you want to take the company in the future.

Do you have the ability to motivate people to change — or to fire them if they don't? Do you have the patience to work at improving the company's products and reputation? You need these types of skills and traits to run and add value to a company. Some people enjoy and thrive on such challenges, and others find such pressures hard to swallow. Think back on your other work experiences for information about what challenges you've tackled and how you felt about them.

✔ **You need to do a lot of inspection.** If you think that buying a company is easier than starting one, think again. You must know what you're buying *before* you buy. So you need to do a thorough inspection, perform due diligence, kick the tires, or whatever you want to call it. For example, you need to rip apart financial statements to ascertain whether the company is really as profitable as it appears and to determine its financial health.

After you close the deal and the cheques and/or money are transferred, you can't change your mind. Unless a seller commits fraud or lies (which is difficult and costly for a buyer to prove legally), it's "buyer beware" about the quality of the business you're buying. In "Evaluating a Small Business," later in this chapter, we cover the homework you need to do before you buy.

✔ **You need more capital.** Existing businesses have value, which is why you generally need more money to buy a business than to start one. If you're short of cash, starting a company is generally a lower-cost path.

✔ **Lower risk means lower returns.** If you purchase a good business and run it well, you can make decent money. In some cases, you can make a lot of money. But you generally have less upside and potential for hitting it really big than with a business you start. Those who have built the greatest wealth from small businesses are generally those who have started them rather than those who bought existing ones.

✔ **You don't get the satisfaction of creating a business.** Whether for their ego or their psyche, entrepreneurs who build their own businesses get a different experience than those who buy someone else's enterprise. You can make your mark on a business you buy, but doing so takes a number of years. Even then, the business is never completely your own creation.

Prerequisites to Buying a Business

Not everyone is cut out to succeed when buying an existing business. Even if you have sufficient funds for the purchase, you may be blind to a whole host of problems and pitfalls and can end up losing your entire investment.

Conversely, some people with little money for buying a business succeed wildly. You can purchase a good small business with little or, in rare cases, no money down. So what, then, are the traits common to people who successfully buy and operate an existing small business?

Business experience

First, you should have business experience and background. If you were an economics or business major in university and you took accounting and other quantitatively oriented courses, you're off to a good start.

 Even better than academic learning is work experience in the type of business that you want to buy. If you want to run a restaurant, go work in one. Consider the experience as paid on-the-job training for running your own restaurant.

If you've worked as a consultant on business management issues with a variety of industries, you also have a good background. However, the danger in having done only consulting is that you're usually not on the front lines, where most of the serious operational business issues arise.

Should none of the previous examples apply to you, we won't say that you're doomed to fail if you buy a business, but we will say that the odds are against you.

 If you don't have business experience, you'll likely do far better in your first business venture after some remedial work. Get some hands-on experience, which is more valuable than any degree or credential you can earn through course work. There's no substitute for the real-life experiences of marketing to and interacting with customers, grappling with financial statements, dealing with competitive threats, and doing the business of business. However, we don't endorse skipping academic course work. You may, in fact, be required to get a credential to be able to do the work you want to do. If you don't need a specific credential, taking selected courses and reading good business books (we recommend some in Chapter 18) can boost your knowledge.

Financial resources

To purchase a business, as with real estate, you need to make a down payment on the purchase price. In most cases, you must put down 25 to 30 percent. Bankers and business sellers who make loans to business buyers normally require such down payments to protect their loan. Small-business buyers who make sizable down payments are less likely to walk away from a loan obligation if the business gets into financial trouble.

If you lack sufficient capital for a down payment, try asking family or friends to invest. You can also set your sights on a less expensive business or seek business owners willing to accept a smaller down payment. If you can find a business for sale whose owner wants less than 20 percent down, you may be on to something good. Be careful, though, because an owner who accepts such a small down payment may have a difficult time selling because of problems inherent in the business or because the business is overpriced.

Sometimes you can purchase existing small businesses with a loan from the selling owner. Also, check for loans with banks or credit unions in your area that specialize in small-business loans. (See Chapter 14 for other financing ideas.)

Focusing Your Search for a Business to Buy

Unless you're extraordinarily lucky, finding a good business to buy takes a great deal of time. If you spend time outside of your work hours, finding a quality business right for you to buy can easily take a year or two. Even if you can afford to look full time, finding and closing on a business can still take you many months.

Above all else, it pays to be persistent, patient, and willing to spend time on things that don't lead immediately to results. You must be willing to sort through some rubbish. If you require immediate gratification in terms of completing a deal, you can make yourself miserable in your search or rush into a bad deal.

You're going to end up spinning your wheels (and likely end up with the wrong type of business for yourself) unless you set some boundaries for your business search. You don't need to be rigid or to precisely define every detail of the business you want to purchase, but you do need to set some parameters so you can start laying the groundwork to purchase.

Each person has unique shopping criteria. The following list exemplifies some useful ones to narrow your search:

- **Size/purchase price:** The money you have available to invest in a business determines the size of business that you can afford. As a rough rule, figure that you can afford to pay a purchase price of about three times the amount of cash you have earmarked for the business. For example, if you have $50,000 in the till, you should look at buying a business for about $150,000. Because many business sellers overprice their businesses, you can probably look at businesses listed at a price above $150,000, perhaps as high as $200,000.

- **Location:** If you're already rooted and don't want to move or deal with a long commute, the business's location further narrows the field. Although you may be willing to look at a broader territory, maybe even nationally if you're willing to relocate, evaluating businesses long-distance is difficult and costly. Unless you want a highly specialized type of company, try to keep your business search local.

- **Industry:** Industry-specific expertise you want to use in the business you buy can help whittle the pool of businesses down further. If you don't have industry-specific expertise, we highly recommend that you focus on some specific niches in industries that interest you or that you know something about. Focusing on an industry helps you conduct a more thorough search and find higher-quality companies. The industry knowledge you accumulate in your search process can pay big dividends during your years of ownership in the business.

If you have a hard time brainstorming about specific industries, use this trick to jump-start your creativity — take a walk through the Yellow Pages! Many business types known to exist in your area are listed alphabetically. You also may want to buy a business in a sector that is experiencing fast growth so that you, too, can ride the wave. Check out *Profit* magazine's annual list of Canada's 100 fastest-growing companies. In addition, the magazine compiles a list of 50 of the country's fastest-growing start-ups, ranked by their two-year growth rate. Also, look at *Inc.* magazine's annual *Inc.* 5,000 list of the fastest-growing private companies in the United States.

- **Opportunity to add value:** Some buyers want to purchase a business with untapped opportunities or problems that need fixing. As with real estate, however, many people are happier leaving the fixer-uppers to the contractors. Some businesses without major problems can offer significant untapped potential.

After you define your shopping criteria, you're ready to go to the market-place of businesses for sale. We recommend that you type up your criteria on a single page so you can hand it to others who may put you in touch with businesses for sale. The following sections give you the best techniques for identifying solid businesses that meet your needs.

Perusing publications

If you're focused on specific industry sectors, you may be surprised to learn that all sorts of specialty newsletters and magazines are out there. Just think of the fun you can have reading publications such as *Canadian Plastics, Alternative Energy Retailer, Welding Canada, Specialty Foods Merchandising, Coal Mining Newsletter,* or *Gas Turbine World!* Specialty publications not only get you into the thick of an industry, they also advertise businesses for sale or business brokers who work in the industry.

Conducting literature searches of general interest business publications can help you identify articles on your industry of interest. The *Reader's Guide to Periodicals* and online computer searches can help you find the articles. Web sites worth examining include Industry Canada's (www.gc.ca), the federal government's site for entrepreneurs (www.canadabusiness.ca), as well as *Profit* magazine's Web site (www.canadianbusiness.com).

A useful U.S. reference publication that you can find in public libraries with decent business sections is a two-volume set titled *Small Business Sourcebook* (Gale). Organized alphabetically by industry, this reference contains listings of publications, trade associations, and other information sources.

Networking with advisers

Speak with accountants, lawyers, bankers, and business consultants who specialize in working with small businesses. These advisers are sometimes the first to hear of a small-business owner's desire to sell. Advisers may also suggest good businesses that aren't for sale but whose owners may consider selling (see the next section).

Knocking on some doors

Some business owners who haven't listed their businesses for sale may be thinking about selling, so if you approach enough businesses that interest you, you may find some of these not-yet-on-the-market businesses with owners interested in selling. You can increase the possibility of finding your desired business, and you may get a good deal on such a business because you can negotiate with the seller from the beneficial position of not having to compete with other potential buyers.

Instead of calling on the phone or literally knocking on the business's door, start your communications by mail. Sending a concise letter of introduction explaining what kind of business you're looking for and what a wonderful person you are demonstrates that you're investing some time in this endeavour. Follow up with a call a week or so after you send the letter.

Working with business brokers

Numerous small businesses for sale list their enterprises through business brokers. Just as a real estate agent makes a living selling real estate, a business broker makes a living selling businesses.

Business brokers generally sell smaller small businesses — those with less than $1 million in annual sales. These businesses tend to be family-owned or sole proprietorships, such as restaurants, dry cleaners, other retailers, and service firms. About half of such small businesses are sold through brokers. Most business brokerage firms sell different types of businesses. Some firms, however, specialize in one industry or a few industries.

One advantage of working with brokers to buy a business is that a broker can expose you to other businesses you may not have considered (a doughnut shop, for example, instead of a restaurant). Brokers can also share their knowledge with you — like the fact that you need to get up at 4 a.m. to make doughnuts. Still want to buy a doughnut shop?

The pitfalls of working with brokers are numerous:

- **Commission:** Brokers aren't your business advisers; they're salespeople. That fact doesn't make them corrupt or dishonest, but it does mean that their interests aren't aligned with yours. Their goal is to do a deal and do the deal soon. And the more you pay for your business, the more they make. Business brokers typically get paid 10 to 12 percent of the sales price of the business. Technically, the seller pays this fee, but as with real estate deals done through brokers, the buyer actually pays. Remember, if a broker isn't involved, the seller can sell for a lower price and still clear more money, and the buyer is better off, too.

- **Undesirable businesses:** Problem businesses are everywhere, but a fair number end up with brokers when the owners encounter trouble selling on their own.

- **Packaging:** This problem relates to the preceding two. Brokers help not-so-hot businesses look better than they really are. Doing so may involve lying, but more typically, it involves stretching the truth, omitting negatives, and hyping potential. (Owners who sell their business themselves may do these things as well.)

You (and your advisers) need to perform the due diligence on a business that you may buy. Never, ever trust or use the selling package that a broker prepares for a business as your sole source of information. *Remember:* Brokers, as well as sellers, have been known to stretch the truth, lie, and commit fraud.

- **Access to limited inventory:** Unlike a real estate agent (who can access all homes listed with brokers for sale in an area through a shared listing service), a business broker can generally tell you only about his office's listings. (Confidentiality is an issue because a shared listing service increases the number of people who can find out that a business is for sale and the particulars of the sale. This may cause some customers to find another company to do business with and may lead some key employees to leave as well.)

If you want to work with a business broker, use more than one. Working with a larger business brokerage firm or one that specializes in listing the type of business you're looking for can maximize the number of possible prospects you see.

- **Few licensing requirements:** The business brokerage field isn't tightly regulated. The majority of regions have no requirements — anyone can hang out a shingle and work as a business broker. Some regions allow those with investment dealer licences to operate as business brokers, whereas others require real estate licenses.

You can find business brokers in the Yellow Pages under "Business Brokers." Ads for businesses for sale may lead you to a broker as well. You can also ask tax, legal, and business consultants for names of good brokers they may know. If you find a broker you think you'd like to work with, check references from other buyers who have worked with the broker. Be sure that the broker works full time and has solid experience. Some business brokers dabble in it part time and make a living in other ways.

Ask the broker you're interested in for the names of several buyers of similar businesses whom they've worked with over the past six months. By narrowing the field to only your particular business interest, the broker can't just refer you to the three best deals of his career. Also, check whether anyone has filed complaints against the brokerage with the local Better Business Bureau (although the BBB favours member companies more and is less likely to entertain and retain complaints against members) and provincial regulatory departments (consumer and commercial relations, attorney general, and so on) that oversee business brokers.

Considering a Franchise or Multilevel Marketing Company

Among the types of businesses that you may buy are franchises and multi-level marketing companies. Both of these types of businesses offer more of a prepackaged and defined system for running a business. Although both types may be worth your exploration, significant pitfalls can trip you up, especially with multilevel marketing companies.

Finding a franchise

Purchasing a good franchise can be your ticket into the world of small-business ownership. Some companies expand their locations through selling replicas, or *franchises,* of their business. When you purchase a franchise, you buy the local rights for a specified geographic territory to sell the company's products or services under the company's name and to use the company's system of operation. In addition to an upfront franchisee fee, franchisers also typically charge an ongoing royalty.

Franchising makes up a huge part of the business world. Companies that franchise — such as McDonald's, Canadian Tire, Pizza Hut, H&R Block, Grand & Toy, Midas Muffler, Second Cup, Century 21 Real Estate, Holiday Inn, Avis, Subway, and Foot Locker — account for more than US$1 trillion in sales globally each year.

Franchise advantages

When you purchase a new franchise, you don't already have customers — just like starting a business, you must find them, although the parent company should have a track record and multiple locations with customers. (You can also purchase existing franchises from owners who want to sell.)

So why would you want to pay a good chunk of money to buy a business without customers?

✔ **Proven business:** A company that has been in business for a number of years and has successful franchisees proves the demand for the company's products and services and shows that the company's system for providing those products and services works. The company has worked out the bugs and hopefully solved common problems. As a franchise owner, you benefit from and share in the experience that the parent company has gained over the years.

✔ **Name-brand recognition:** Some consumers recognize the company name of a larger and successful franchise company and may be more inclined to purchase its products and services. Some consumers feel more comfortable getting a muffler job done at franchiser Midas Muffler rather than hunting around and calling Discount Muffler World or Manny's Muffler Bazaar from a yellow pages listing. The comfort that comes from dealing with Midas may stem from the influence of advertisements, recommendations of friends, or your own familiarity with Midas's services, perhaps in another part of the country. Most free-standing small businesses for sale in a community lack name-brand recognition.

✔ **Centralized purchasing power:** You would hope and expect that Midas, as a corporation made up of hundreds of locations, buys mufflers at a low price — volume purchasing generally leads to bigger discounts. In addition to possibly saving franchisees money on supplies, the parent company can also take the hassle out of figuring out where and how to purchase supplies. Again, most unattached small businesses that you could buy won't offer this advantage, although quality business associations can provide some of these benefits.

Franchise pitfalls

As with purchasing other small businesses, pitfalls abound in buying a franchise. Franchises aren't for everyone. Here are some common problems that may cause you to reconsider buying a franchise:

✔ **You're not the franchise type.** When you buy a franchise, you buy into an established system. People who like structure and following established rules and systems adapt more easily to the franchise life. But if you're the creative sort who likes to experiment and change things, you may be an unhappy franchisee. Unlike starting your own business, where you can get into the game without investing lots of your time and money, buying a franchise that you end up not enjoying can make for an expensive learning experience.

✔ **You may be locked in to buying overpriced supplies.** Centralized, bulk purchasing through the corporate headquarters supposedly saves franchisees time and money on supplies and other expenditures. Some franchisers, however, take advantage of franchisees through large mark-ups on proprietary items that franchisees must buy from the franchisers.

✔ **The franchise is unproven.** If the company's concept hasn't stood the test of time, don't make yourself a guinea pig. Some franchisers show more interest in simply selling franchises to collect the upfront franchise money. Reputable franchisers want to help their franchisees succeed so they can collect an ongoing royalty from the franchisees' sales.

Work-from-home "opportunities"

"We made $18,269.56 in just 2½ weeks! Remarkable, home-based business! We do over 90 percent of the work for you! Free info: 800-555-8975."

"You can be earning $4,000 to $10,000 each month in less than 30 days! We'll even help you hire agents to do the work for you . . . FREE!"

You can find lots of ad copy like this, especially in magazines that small-business owners and wannabe small-business owners read. In most cases, these ads come from grossly overhyped multilevel marketing companies. In other ads, no legitimate company exists; instead, a person (or two or three) simply tries to sell you some "information" that explains the business opportunity. This information may cost several hundred dollars or more. Such packages end up being worthless marketing propaganda and rarely provide useful information that you couldn't find at a far lower cost or no cost at all.

Never buy into anything promoted in these sorts of ads that companies (or people) pitch to you through the mail or over the phone.

✔ **The franchise is a pyramid scheme.** Unscrupulous, short-term-focused business owners sometimes attempt to franchise their businesses and sell as many franchises as they can as quickly as possible. Some push their franchisees to sell franchises. The business soon focuses on selling franchises rather than operating a business that sells a product or service well. In rare cases, franchisers engage in fraud and sell next to nothing, except the hopes of getting rich quick.

Evaluating a franchise

Make sure that you do plenty of homework before you agree to buy a franchise. You may be tempted to cut corners in reviewing a franchise from a long-established company. Don't. You may not be right for the specific franchise, or perhaps the "successful" company has mostly been good at keeping problems under wraps.

In "Evaluating a Small Business," later in this chapter, we explain the homework you should complete prior to buying an existing business. Read that section, especially if you want to purchase an existing franchise from another franchisee.

Considering a multilevel marketing company

A twist, and in most cases a bad one, on the franchising idea is *multilevel marketing (MLM) companies*. Sometimes known as network companies, MLMs can be thought of as a poor person's franchise. We know dozens of people who have been sorely disappointed with the money and time they've spent on MLMs.

In companies that use multilevel marketing, representatives who work as independent contractors solicit customers as well as recruit new representatives, known in the industry as your *downline*. For those weary of traditional jobs, the appeal of multilevel marketing is obvious. You can work at home, part time if you want. You have no employees. You don't need any experience. Yet you're told you can still make big bucks ($10,000, $25,000, $50,000, or more per month). If your parents raised you right, however, you should be skeptical of deals like these.

A big problem to watch out for is the business equivalent of the pyramid scheme — businesses that exist to sign up other people. Beware MLM companies that advocate that you "Sell directly to those that you have direct influence over. The system works great because you don't need to resell month after month. It's an opportunity for anybody — it's up to them how much work they want to put into it."

Any MLM examination should start with the company's product or service. How does its product or service stack up to the competition on price and quality? Contact the Better Business Bureau in the city where the MLM company is headquartered to see what kinds of complaints are on file.

The bottom line on any network marketing "opportunity" is to remember that it's a job. No company is going to pay you a lot of money for little work. As with any other small-business venture, if you hope to earn a decent income, multilevel marketing opportunities require at least three to five years of low income to build up your business. Most people who pay to buy into networks make little money, and many quit and move on.

Also, think twice before you sign up relatives, friends, and co-workers — often the first people whom network marketers encourage you to sell to. A danger in doing business with those people whom you have influence over is that you put your reputation and integrity on the line. You could be putting your friendships and family relations on the line as well.

Quality multilevel marketing companies are the exception

A number of network companies have achieved success over the years. Amway, Herbalife, and Mary Kay have stood the test of time and achieved significant size. Amway founders Richard De Vos and Jay Van Andel achieved multibillionaire status.

Not all multilevel companies are created equal, and few are worth a look. However, Mary Kay, which sells primarily makeup and skin care products, is an example of a successful network company with a 30-plus year history. Mary Kay has hundreds of thousands of sales representatives and does business worldwide. Although not shy about the decent money that its more successful salespeople make, Mary Kay doesn't hype the income potential. According to the company, the top 50 percent of local Canadian sales directors earn anywhere from under $20,000 to over $100,000 per year, but this income comes after many years of hard work. Mary Kay rewards top sellers with gifts, such as the famous pink Cadillac.

The ingredients for Mary Kay's success include competitive pricing, personal attention, and social interaction, which many stores don't or can't offer their customers. "We make shopping and life fun . . . we make people look and feel good," says Mary Gentry, one of Mary Kay's sales directors.

Mary Kay encourages prospective Mary Kay reps to try the products first and then host a group before they sign up and fork over the $150 to purchase a showcase of items to sell. To maximize sales, the company encourages Mary Kay representatives to keep a ready inventory because customers tend to buy more when products are immediately available. If reps want out of the business, they can sell their inventory back to the company at 90 cents on the dollar originally paid, a good sign that the company stands behind its product.

Do your homework and remember that due diligence requires digging for facts and talking to people who don't have a bias or reason to sell to you. Do the same homework that we recommend for franchises in the "Evaluating a Small Business" section, later in this chapter. Be skeptical of multilevel marketing systems, unless the company has a long track record and many people who are happy. Assume that an MLM company isn't worth pursuing until your extensive due diligence proves otherwise.

Quality multilevel marketing companies make sense for people who really believe in and want to sell a particular product or service and don't want to or can't tie up a lot of money buying a franchise or other business. Just remember to check out the MLM company, and realize that you won't get rich in a hurry, or probably ever.

Evaluating a Small Business

If you put in many hours, you may eventually come across a business that interests and intrigues you so much that you consider purchasing it. As with purchasing a piece of real estate, major hurdles stand between you and ownership of the business. You need to inspect what you want to buy, negotiate a deal, and finalize a contract — done correctly, these processes take a lot of time.

Doing due diligence

The Canadian legal system presumes a person is innocent until a court finds that person is guilty beyond a reasonable doubt. When you purchase a business, however, you must assume that the selling business owner is guilty of making the business appear better than what it is (and possibly lying) until you prove otherwise.

We don't want to sound cynical, but a business owner can use more than a few tricks to make a business look more profitable, financially healthier, and more desirable than it really is. You can't decide how much inspection or due diligence to conduct on a business based on your gut-level feeling.

Because you can't guess what hidden surprises exist in a business, you must dig for them. Until you prove to yourself beyond a reasonable doubt that these surprises don't exist, don't go through with a business purchase.

When you find a business that you think you want to purchase, you absolutely, positively must do your homework before you buy. However, just as with purchasing a home, you don't want to expend buckets of money and time on detailed inspections until you can reach an agreement with the seller. What if you deal with a seller who is unrealistic about what the business is worth? You need to perform the most serious, time-consuming, and costly due diligence after you have an accepted offer to purchase a business. Make such inspections a contingency in your purchase contract.

Ultimately, if you're going to buy a business, you need to follow a plan similar to, but likely shorter than, the business plan we present in Chapter 13. Addressing such issues in a plan goes a long way toward helping you perform your due diligence.

Following are some additional questions you need to answer about a business you're contemplating purchasing. (Address as many of the questions as possible before you make your offer.)

Questioning profits

Don't blindly take the profit from the bottom line of a business's financial statement as the gospel. As part of your due diligence, ask a tax adviser to perform an audit after you negotiate a deal.

Even if the financial statements of a business are accurate, you (and your tax adviser) must still look for subtle problems that can make the profits of the business appear better than they truly are. The issues that we tell you to look for in Chapter 6, when you analyze the financial statements of public companies that issue stock, also apply to evaluating the financial statements of small companies.

If necessary, factor out one-time events from the profit analysis. For example, if the business last year received an unusually large order that is unlikely to be repeated and hasn't been the norm in the past, subtract this amount from the profitability analysis. Also, examine the owner's salary to see if it's low for the field. Owners can reduce their draw to a minimum or pay family members less than fair market salaries to pump up the profitability of their company in the years before they sell.

Also examine whether the rent or mortgage expense may change when you buy the business. Consider what will happen to profits when you factor in your expected rent or mortgage costs.

✔ **Why is the owner selling?** Ask the owner or the owner's advisers why the owner wants to sell and why now. The answers may shed insight on the owner's motivations and need to sell. Some owners want to bail when they see things getting worse.

✔ **What is the value of the assets you want to buy?** This value includes not only equipment but also "soft" assets, such as the firm's name and reputation with customers and suppliers, customer lists, patents, and so on. Interview key employees, customers, suppliers, advisers, and competitors. Ask key customers and key employees whether they would still be loyal to the business if you took it over.

✔ **What do the financial statements reveal?** Search for the same things that you would look for in a company whose stock you're considering purchasing. (See Chapter 6 for how to read financial statements and what to look for.) Don't take the financial statements at face value simply because they're audited. The accountant who did the audit may be incompetent or chummy with the seller.

One way to check for shenanigans is to ask the seller for a copy of the business's tax returns. Owners are more likely to try to minimize reported revenue and maximize expenses on their tax return to keep from paying more tax. After you have an accepted purchase offer, ask a tax adviser experienced in such matters to do an audit (see the "Questioning profits" sidebar in this chapter for more information).

✔ **If the company leases its space, what does the lease contract say?** A soon-to-expire lease at a low rate can ruin a business's profit margins. With a retail business, the ability to maintain a good location is also vital. Check *comparables* — that is, what other similar locations lease for — to see whether the current lease rate is fair, and talk to the building owner to discover his plans for the building. Ask for and review (with the help of a legal adviser) the current owner's lease contract.

✔ **What liabilities, including those that may be hidden "off" the balance sheet, are you buying with a business?** Limit liabilities, such as environmental contaminations, through a contract. Conduct legal searches for liens, litigation, and tax problems.

✔ **What does a background check turn up on the owners and key employees?** Do they have good business experience, or do they have criminal records and a trail of unpaid debts?

Determining a business's value

After you find what you think is a good business and do your homework, you're ready to make an offer. Negotiating takes time and patience. Unless you're legally savvy, find a lawyer who focuses her practice on small-business dealings. Have a lawyer review and work with your contract. Also consider obtaining input from a qualified tax adviser.

Good advisers can help you inspect what you're buying and look for red flags in the company's financial statements. Advisers can also help structure the purchase to protect what you're buying and to gain maximum tax benefits. If you work with a business broker, use a lawyer and accountant as well.

The price a business is listed for is often in excess — sometimes grossly so — of the business's true worth. Look at what similar businesses have sold for as a starting point for valuing a business you want to buy. Smart homebuyers or real estate investors look at comparable properties when they're ready to make an offer.

When you look at sales of comparable businesses, figure the multiple of earnings these businesses sold for. In Chapter 5, we discuss how the price/earnings ratio works for evaluating the value of larger, publicly traded companies. Because they're less well established and riskier from an investment standpoint, small, privately held businesses sell for a lower multiple of earnings than comparable, but larger, companies.

Some advisers and business brokers advocate using a multiple of revenue to determine the value of a business. Revenue is a poor proxy for profitability: Two businesses in the same field can have identical revenue yet quite different profitability because of how well they're run, the pricing of their products and services, and the types of customers they attract.

In addition to looking at the sales price of other businesses relative to earnings, you can also consider the value of a company's assets. The so-called *book value* of a company's assets is what the assets are worth per the company's balance sheet. Check these figures to ensure that their asset values are correct. Another, more conservative way to value such assets is to consider the liquidation/replacement cost.

Part V
Investing
Resources

That's the Harrisons. Never have I seen an investment portfolio start so strong and go south so quickly.

In this part . . .

Everywhere you turn these days, you're bombarded with investing tidbits, sound bites, trivia, advice, and opinions. In this important part, we help you to evaluate the reliability of a given source. Whether you're reading a magazine, newspaper article, or a book, perusing an Internet site, using software, watching television, or listening to the radio, you need to know how to evaluate what's worth considering and what to ignore.

Chapter 16

Selecting Investing Resources

. . . .

In This Chapter

▶ Overcoming information and advice overload

▶ Evaluating investing resources

. . . .

*I*n the past, finding financial information was much simpler, largely because the available resources were limited. You could subscribe to publications such as *Kiplinger's Personal Finance* magazine for general money issues and a local big-city newspaper for daily stock prices. The hard-core investor had *The Globe and Mail* with its "Report on Business," the *National Post* with its "Financial Post" section, or *The Wall Street Journal* delivered daily.

Times have changed, though. Today's investor faces information overload. Radio, television, magazines, newspapers, books, the Internet, family, friends, neighbours, and cabdrivers — everywhere you turn, someone is offering investing opinions, tips, and advice. You can't pick up a newspaper or magazine or turn on the television or radio without bumping into articles, stories, segments, and entire programs devoted to investment issues.

Chosen wisely, the best investing resources can further your investment knowledge and enable you to make better decisions. Because investment information and advice is so widespread, and constantly growing, knowing how to sift through it is just as important as finding out what the best resources are today. Throughout the rest of the book, we name the best investment resources that we're familiar with, but in this chapter, we explain how you can separate the good from the mediocre and awful.

Dealing with Information Overload

Early in the year 2000, one of Eric's clients, Roseanne, called him in a near panic. "Eric, I'm not satisfied with my investments. Why are so many of my friends doubling and tripling their money in technology stocks, and my mutual funds are going nowhere? Everywhere I turn, people are talking about these high-growth companies. I want my piece of the pie, too!" Eric explained to her that many of her diversified mutual funds held some technology stocks as well as stocks in many other industries. He also reminded her that because she was nearing 50 years of age, she had a healthy helping of bonds in her portfolio as well.

She urged Eric to put her money in some technology stocks and technology-focused funds, but he stood his ground. He further encouraged her to read this book wherein we highlighted technology stocks as a bubble waiting to burst (see Chapter 5). We're glad to say that Roseanne followed Eric's advice, and now, years later, she is, too. During the severe stock market decline in the early 2000s, technology stocks got clobbered, but other market segments (such as bonds and value-oriented stocks) actually increased in value. (Even by the late 2000s, tech stocks were nowhere near attaining their prior levels — the NASDAQ index has been trading at half or less than the highs it reached in 2000.)

A major reason that so many people were talking about making money with technology stocks was that so many media outlets (radio, television, Web sites, and so on) were talking about these investments and other personal money management issues around the clock. Why is everybody in the media and publishing world putting out investing information? Has money become that much more complicated over the years? Are there simply more media and publishing executives who want to help us?

The following list explains some of the reasons that investing has become such a hot topic:

- ✔ **Communications options are expanding.** Over the past generation, the number of television channels has mushroomed as a result of cable television. Flip through your cable channels at any hour of the day, and you see infomercials that promise to make you a real estate tycoon or stock market day trader in your spare time. The explosion of the Internet has introduced a whole new medium. Now, at a relatively low cost, anybody can publish a Web page.

   The accessibility of these communications media allows just about anyone with an animated personality and a few bucks to appear to be an expert. These newer communications options are primarily structured around selling advertising rather than offering quality content.

- ✔ **Economic change breeds uncertainty.** Global competition and technological advances are causing most industries to undergo dramatic changes in much shorter periods of time. Although jobs are relatively plentiful for many with particular training and skills, fear of job loss and financial instability runs high. Economic change and widespread cynicism about the ability of the Canada Pension Plan or the Quebec Pension Plan to provide a reasonable retirement income to baby boomers has also caused many to seek investment guidance.

✔ **Investment choices and responsibilities are increasing.** More employees are forced to take responsibility for saving money for their retirement and deciding how to invest that money. In the past, more employers offered pension plans. In these plans, the employer set aside money on behalf of employees and retained a pension manager who decided how to invest it. All the employees had to do was learn the level of benefits that they had earned and when they could begin drawing a monthly cheque.

With today's retirement plans, such as RRSPs and companies' money-purchase pension plans, employees need to educate themselves about how much money they need to save and how to invest it. In addition to mastering retirement planning and investment allocation, individuals face a dizzying number of financial products, such as the tens of thousands of mutual funds that are on the market.

✔ **Our society is too money focused.** The pages of tabloid papers and magazines are filled with highly paid movie and sports celebrities and wealthy corporate executives. Other warning signs abound for a society that too often cares more about money than people and human relationships. Some people view hiring someone else to raise their children as a luxury of wealth. Others spend tens of thousands of dollars on fancy, financed cars that require years of work to pay off. People don't spend enough time with our children and then are puzzled why the teen suicide rate has tripled in the past two generations.

Read the next section to find out how you can filter out the best information and advice and skip the rest.

Separating Financial Fact from Fiction

Just because more sources offer investing advice doesn't mean that you should read, listen to, or watch much of it. In this section, we offer prescriptions for how to intelligently choose among all the available financial information sources.

Understanding how advertising corrupts

The first rule for maximizing your chances of finding the best investing information and advice is to recognize that there are no free lunches. Too many people get sucked into supposedly free resources.

The Internet is packed with scores of "free" investing sites. Turn on your television or radio and you come across mountains of "free" stuff. Of course, someone is paying for all this "free" content, and it's all there for some reason. Most of the free Internet sites are run by investment companies or someone else with something to sell. What these sites give away is nothing but subtle and not-so-subtle advertising for whatever products and services they sell. Advertising also foots the bill in the vast majority of cases involving free investment advice on TV and radio.

As we discuss in Chapter 18, many investing and personal finance books aren't free from subtly veiled advertising aims, either. Some authors choose to write books that are the equivalent of an infomercial for something else — such as high-priced seminars — that the "author" really wants to sell. Such writers aren't interested in educating and helping you as much as they are seeking to sell you something. So, for example, an author might write about how complicated the investing markets are and some indicators he follows to time investments. However, at the end of such a book, the author might say that investing is too complicated to do on your own and that you really need a personal investment manager — which, to no great surprise, the author happens to be.

Whether in print or on the Internet, television, or radio — and whether it's overt or subtle — advertising often compromises the quality of the investment advice it accompanies.

We won't say that you can't find some useful investment resources in media with lots of advertising. You can find some good investing programs on radio and television and some helpful investing sites on the Internet. However, these resources are the exception to the rule that where there's a lot of advertising, there's little valuable information and advice. Likewise, just because magazines and newspapers have quite a bit of advertising doesn't mean that some of their columnists and articles aren't worthy of your time.

In the following sections, we outline the problems that advertising can cause within all the media outlets.

Influencing content

Many organizations, such as newspaper and magazine publishers and radio and television stations that accept ads, say that their ad departments are separate from their editorial departments. The truth, however, is that in most of these organizations, advertisers wield influence over the content. At a minimum, the editorial environment must be perceived as conducive to the sale of the advertiser's product.

The stock market cable television channels, for example, carry many ads from brokers catering to investors who pick and trade their own stocks. Furthermore, such stations carry ads from firms that purport to teach you how to make big bucks day trading (see Chapter 5). Not surprisingly, such stations offer many "news" segments on their shows that cater to stock traders and condone and endorse foolish strategies, such as day trading, instead of condemning them. Instead of asking themselves what's in the best interests of their viewers, listeners, and readers, executives at too many media and publishing firms ask what will attract attention and advertisers.

Corrupting content

In most organizations, advertisers can have a direct and adulterating influence on editorial content. Specifically, some media organizations and publishers simply won't say anything negative about a major advertiser or will highlight and praise investment companies that are big advertisers.

More than a few media outlets have attempted to edit out critical comments that we've made about companies with lousy products that turned out to be their advertisers. Some editors simply say that they don't want to bite the hand that feeds them. Others are less candid about why they remove such criticism. The bottom line is still the same: Advertisers' influence squashes freedom of speech and, more importantly, prevents readers, viewers, and listeners from getting the truth and best advice. (By the way, we don't write for organizations that edit our work in such a fashion.)

Producing low-quality content

Because of the previously mentioned reasons and an overall lack of concern for the value of information and advice, some investing resources cut corners on the quality of their content. Because consumers often pay nothing or next to nothing for many investment resources, the media have an incentive to sell advertising space and not to hire high-quality writers who can offer sound advice to readers.

Recognizing quality resources

With the tremendous increase in the coverage of investing and other personal money issues, more and more journalists are writing about increasingly technical issues — often in areas in which they have no expertise.

(This is true in traditional print publications as well as in the so-called blogosphere online.) Some of these writers provide good information and advice. Unfortunately, some dish out bad advice. In fields such as medicine or the law, you wouldn't be so willing to take advice from non-experts. Why should you care any less about your money?

How can you know what's good and whom you can trust? Although we can suggest resources that we hold in high regard (and do so throughout this book, especially in Chapters 17, 18, and 19), we recognize that you may encounter many different investment resources and you need to understand *how* to tell the best from the rest. The answer to the question, dear reader, rests in educating thyself. The more knowledgeable you are about both sound and flawed investment strategies, the better able you are to tell good from not-so-good or even truly awful investment resources.

The best thing to do when you encounter a financial magazine, newspaper, Web site, or other resource for the first time is to investigate it. The following sections suggest some investigative work you should do before you take anyone's investment advice.

Following the money

All things being equal, you have a greater chance of finding quality content when subscription fees account for the bulk of a company's revenue, and advertising accounts for little or none of the revenue. This generalization, of course, is just that — a generalization. Some publications that derive a reasonable portion of their revenues from advertising have some good columns and content. Conversely, some relatively ad-free sources aren't very good.

Figuring out their philosophy and agenda

Readers of our books can clearly understand our philosophies about investing. We advocate buying and holding, not trading and gambling. We explain how to build wealth through proven vehicles, including stocks, real estate, and small-business ownership. Our guiding beliefs are clearly detailed on the Cheat Sheet in the front of this book.

Unfortunately, many publications and programs don't make it as easy for you to see or hear their operating beliefs. You may have to do some homework. For example, with a radio program, you probably have to listen to at least portions of several shows to get a sense of the host's investment philosophies. Warning signs include publications and programs that make investing sound overly complicated and that imply or say you won't succeed or do as well if you don't hire a financial adviser or follow your investments like a hawk.

Considering whether the information is constructive

Just about everywhere you turn these days — radio, television, and the Internet — you can get up-to-the-minute updates on financial markets around the globe. Although most investors have a natural curiosity about how their investments are doing, from our experience, the constant barrage of updates causes a loss of focus on the big picture. In many cases, publishing and media companies report what we call the "noise" rather than the news of the day. Some companies are far worse about doing so than others.

Over the next week, take a close look at how you spend your time keeping up with financial news and other information. Do the programs and publications that you most heavily use really help you better understand and map out sound investment strategies, or do they end up confusing, overwhelming, and paralyzing you with bits and pieces of contradictory and often hyped noise? We're not saying that you should tune these resources out completely, but we are saying that you should devote less time to the noise of the day and more time to self-education. How can you do that? Read a few good books (a topic that we discuss in detail in Chapter 18).

Considering their qualifications

Examine the backgrounds, including professional work experience and education credentials, of a resource's writers, hosts, and/or anchors. If such information isn't given or easily found, that's usually a red flag. People with something to hide, or a lack of something significantly redeeming to say about themselves, usually don't promote their backgrounds.

Of course, just because someone seems to have a relatively impressive background doesn't mean that she has your best interests in mind or has honestly presented her qualifications. For example, *Forbes* journalist William P. Barrett was skeptical of financial author Suze Orman's biographical and business claims. He investigated and presented a sobering review of Orman's stated credentials and qualifications in *Forbes* magazine — revealing that they were largely exaggerated. A writer for the *San Francisco Chronicle* later substantiated this fact.

So what's the lesson to be learned from this story? You can't accept stated credentials and qualifications at face value, for the simple reason that some people don't tell the truth. You can increase your chances of being tipped off to hucksters by being skeptical. In fact, Barrett started his investigation of Orman because of the sheer outrageousness of the number of new clients that Orman claimed to be getting each year.

Chapter 17

Perusing Periodicals, Radio, and Television

. . . .

In This Chapter

▶ Sifting through financial magazines and newspapers

▶ Surveying radio and television programs

▶ Steering clear of most investment newsletters

. . . .

*A*ll the news that's fit to print or broadcast — in newspapers, magazines, and newsletters, and on radio and television programs — inundates us with investing information and advice. In this chapter, we explain what to look for — and what to look out for — when you tune in to these media sources in the hopes of investing better.

In Print: Magazines and Newspapers

Visit a newsstand and you find many investing publications as well as general interest publications with investing columns. We've written investing articles for various magazines and newspapers. Some of the experiences have been enjoyable, others okay, and a few miserable. The best publications and editors we've written for take seriously their responsibility to provide quality information and advice to their readers.

Taking the scribes to task

In this section, we discuss the problems with magazine and newspaper investment articles.

Highlighting hype and horror

Whenever the stock market suffers a sharp decline, many in the media bring out the gloom and doom. Front-page headlines such as "The Beginning of the End" torment investors about holding on to their stocks. An avalanche of such articles, like that seen in late 2002 and early 2003, often coincides with a bottoming stock market. When the stock and real estate markets slid in the late 2000s, scores of "the sky is falling" pieces similarly populated the pages. At the end of 2008, a cursory glance at the headlines might have made you think investing in the stock market was truly a thing of the past.

Another particularly popular subject for such reporting is the cost of a university education. (See, you can write a sentence about the cost of education without including the word *skyrocketing*.) Scores of articles horrify parents with estimates of the expected costs associated with sending Junior to campus. The typical advice: Start saving and investing early so you don't have to tell Junior that you can't afford to send him to university.

The sky-high-cost-of-post-secondary-education stories typify another failing of the horror stories. The *horror* is the story, and the accompanying advice can be shortsighted. Completely overlooked and ignored are the tax and financial aid consequences of the recommended investment strategies. For example, if parents don't take advantage of tax-deductible retirement plans and instead save outside them, they pay more in taxes. Sound investing decisions require a holistic approach that acknowledges that people have limited money and must make these sorts of trade-offs.

Offering poor advice

To sell their publications, magazines and newspapers sometimes entice readers with promises of high returns. This can easily lead to crummy advice.

Consider the gaffe made by a *Money* magazine piece titled "Where to Get Safe, High Yields." The title itself should have been a red flag: It's impossible to find a *safe* high yield. To get high yields, you must be willing to accept more risk. In the *Money* article, three of the recommended investments were limited partnerships (LPs) sold through commission-based advisers. These products' high commissions and ongoing fees doomed even the luckiest of investors to mediocre or dismal investment returns.

The *Money* article even asserted that investors could earn annual returns as high as 18 percent on some LPs. Students of the financial markets know that the best ownership investments, such as stocks and real estate, return no more than 10 to 12 percent per year over the long haul. To expect more is to hold unrealistic expectations.

Quoting experts who are not

Historically, one way that journalists have attempted to overcome technical gaps in their knowledge is to interview and quote financial experts. Although this may add to the accuracy and quality of a story, journalists who aren't experts themselves have difficulty telling qualified experts from hacks. (See Chapter 16 for a discussion of examining the qualifications of writers who offer up financial guidance.)

One glaring example of this phenomenon that continues to amaze us is how many newspaper and magazine financial writers quote unproven advice from investment newsletter writers. As we discuss in the section "Investment Newsletters," later in this chapter, the predictive advice of many newsletter writers is often wrong and causes investors to earn lower returns and missed investment gains due to frequent trading than if they simply bought and held. Journalists who simply parrot this type of information and provide an endorsement that unqualified sources are "experts" do readers an immense disservice.

In some ways, what's worse than quoting unqualified experts is when financial writers start to believe they themselves can predict the future with only a cursory investigation or explanation. Consider the *Globe and Mail* columnist who advised in April 2000 — just a few weeks into the eventual collapse of the high tech sector — that "the correct way to think of Cisco, Nortel et al. is as tech blue chips, not much different than banks, merchandisers and manufacturers. These are essential stocks that investors and money managers will flock to for the foreseeable future."

Even in October 2000, the same columnist said Nortel was still a "great company" and commented that "Nortel could go lower, or it could rebound quickly. Long term, it's hard to imagine a company with brighter business prospects, but that's just one opinion."

One opinion, indeed! Nortel's shares, of course, would go on to fall to as low as $0.67, and in early 2009, the company filed for bankruptcy.

Focusing on noise and minutiae

Daily financial press writers also contribute to today's shortsighted investment environment and encourage readers to adopt similarly misguided outlooks. It's common for daily newspaper charts to show the stock market's movements at five-minute intervals throughout the previous day. This focus on the noise of the day causes nervous investors to make panicked, emotionally based decisions, such as deciding to sell *after* major stock market falls.

Of course, the daily print media aren't the only ones chronicling the minutiae. As we discuss elsewhere, other media, including television, radio, and the Internet, cause many investors to lose sight of the long term and the big picture.

The short length of newspaper and magazine articles can easily lead writers to oversimplify complex issues and offer flawed advice. For example, some pieces on mutual funds focus on a fund's returns and investment philosophies, devoting little, if any, space to the risks or tax consequences of investing in recommended funds.

Making the most of periodicals

So what should you do if you want to find out more about investing but don't want to be overloaded with information? Educate yourself and be selective. If you're considering subscribing to financial publications, go to the library first and review some old issues. Were the information and advice useful and error free? The more you know, the easier it is to separate the wheat from the chaff.

Shy away from publications that purport to be able to predict the future — few people can, and those who can are usually busy managing money. Unfortunately, as the financial markets got more volatile in the late 1990s and early 2000s, and then again in the late 2000s, we witnessed more and more publications promoting columnists and headlines that attempted to prognosticate the future.

Read bylines and biographies and get to know writers' strengths and weaknesses. Ditto for the entire publication. Any writer or publisher can make mistakes. Some make many more than others — follow their advice at your own peril. Start by evaluating advice in the areas that you know the most about. For example, if you're interested in investing in RIM or Intel and are reasonably familiar with the computer industry, find out what the publications say about technology investments.

And remember that you're not going to outfox the financial markets, because they're reasonably efficient (see Chapter 4). Spend your time seeking information and advice that help you flesh out your goals and develop a plan rather than trolling for the next hot stock tip or worrying about short-term trends.

Radio and Television Programs

As you move from the world of magazines and newspapers to radio and television, the entertainment component usually increases. In this section, we highlight some common problems with radio and television programs and offer some recommendations for the better programs.

Looking at problems with radio and television programs

We've been guests on hundreds of radio and television programs. Just as Dorothy discovered in *The Wizard of Oz,* seeing how things work behind the scenes tends to deglamorize these mediums. Here are the main problems we've discovered from our years observing radio and television.

You often get what you pay for

Some of the worst financial advice is brought to you, not surprisingly, for "free." Because listeners don't pay for money and investing shows on radio or television, advertising often drives who and what gets on the air, as we discuss in Chapter 16. But we've found that some of the worst offenders are local radio advice programs.

Some of these shows are "hosted" by a person who is nothing more than a financial salesperson. That person's first, and sometimes only, motivation for wanting to do the show is to pick up clients. Many local radio investing programs are hosted by a local investment dealer (who usually calls himself a financial consultant or planner). A dealer who reels in just one big fish a month — a person with, say, $300,000 to invest — can generate commissions totalling $15,000 by selling investments with a 5 percent commission.

But radio suffers from more than dealers trolling for new clients, as evidenced by the case of Sonny Bloch, a New York radio personality who was indicted for fraud. The Securities and Exchange Commission in the United States found that Bloch was receiving kickbacks from investment brokers for endorsing some pretty crummy investment products on his nationally syndicated radio show. The SEC also filed a complaint against Bloch for defrauding investors of millions of dollars to supposedly purchase some radio stations. Instead, according to the SEC, Bloch and his wife used hundreds of thousands of dollars to purchase a condominium. Partners in a precious metals firm (DeAngelis Brothers Collectibles) that Bloch regularly endorsed on the air were arrested for theft and ended up in bankruptcy.

We know from personal experience what too many radio stations look for in the way of hosts for financial programs. The host's integrity, knowledge, and lack of conflict of interest don't matter. Willingness to work for next to nothing helps: One radio station program director said she liked the broker who was hosting a financial talk show because the broker was willing to work for so little compensation from the radio station. Never mind the fact that the broker rarely gave useful advice and was obviously trolling for new clients. That didn't matter to the program director, who said, "We're in the entertainment business."

Information and hype overload

At 9:30 a.m. EST, the Toronto and New York stock exchanges open, and transactions start streaming across the bottom of television screens tuned to financial cable stations. Changes in the major market indexes — the TSX Composite, Dow Jones Industrial Average, the S&P 500, and the NASDAQ index — also flash on the screen. In fact, these indexes are updated almost every five *seconds* on the screen. Far more exciting than a political race or sporting event, this event never ends and offers constant change and excitement. Even after the markets close, reporting of still-open overseas markets continues. The performance of futures of stock market indexes then appears on-screen.

All of this reporting and data don't make us better investors. Although the conventionally accepted notion is that this information overload levels the playing field for the individual investor, we know too many investors who make emotionally based decisions prodded by all this noise, prognostication, opinion, and hearsay.

Poor method of guest selection

Some journalists, often in an effort to overcome their own lack of knowledge, like to interview "experts." A classic example of this problem is the media exposure that author Charles Givens used to receive. Givens became a darling of the media and the public following unprecedented, consecutive three-day appearances on NBC's *Today* show. Givens regularly held court on the talk show circuit with the likes of Larry King and Oprah Winfrey.

The Givens case highlights some of the media's inability to distinguish between good and bad experts. It's relatively easy for the financially sophisticated to see the dangerous, oversimplified, and biased advice that Givens offers in his books. In his first best-seller, *Wealth Without Risk,* Givens recommended investing in limited partnerships and provided a phone number and address of a firm, Delta Capital Corp. in Florida, where readers could buy the partnerships. Those who bought these products ended up paying hefty sales commissions and owning investments worth half or less of their original value. Besides the problematic partnerships he recommended, court proceedings against Givens in a number of states uncovered that he owned a major share of Delta Capital.

Other investing advice from Givens that gives pause: In his chapters on investing, he said that the average yearly return you'll earn investing in mutual funds will be 25 percent or 30 percent. The reality: An investor would be fortunate to earn half of these inflated returns.

So how did Givens get on all these programs? He had a shrewd publicist, and the show producers either didn't read his books and/or were themselves financially illiterate. Talk shows and many reporters often don't take the time to check out people like Givens. Most of the time, the books are never read. Producers, who themselves usually don't know much about investing, often decide to put someone on the air on the basis of a press kit or a call from a publicist.

Slim pickings in Canada

Unfortunately, Canada lacks solid and dependable radio and television programming about investing. The recession in the late 2000s took what were already slim pickings and reduced the field to next to nothing. As advertisers slashed spending, television networks scaled back programming even further. Unfortunately, unless investment shows bring in large audiences and ad dollars, it's unlikely we'll see any change in the near future. Simply put, we don't have a large enough population for a sufficient critical mass to support good programming on investing or small business.

One of the dangers of business and investing programs is that the entertainment component can overshadow common sense. The best example of this in Canada is *Dragon's Den,* adapted from a Japanese series by the CBC (as well as the BBC in the United Kingdom). On the program, small-business owners and would-be entrepreneurs have a few minutes to make a pitch for funding to five wealthy businesspeople, the so-called dragons. Although the program can be entertaining, its premise involves the dragons' making a decision to invest in a matter of minutes, with scant details. If you're considering investing in a small business, you shouldn't make an offer without spending many hours if not days turning the proposal inside out. At the same time, it's never wise to agree to a partnership of this kind without getting to know the background and personality of the people involved.

Just as the economy was collapsing in the late 2000s, CBC Newsworld launched a new program called *Fortune Hunters.* The program's host, Diane Buckner, was a host for *Venture,* a worthwhile program on the trials and triumphs of small-business owners. (Sadly, after more than two decades, the show was cancelled in 2007.) In contrast, *Fortune Hunters* focuses on "hot trends" and the entrepreneurs who are trying to find ways to turn them into profitable businesses. *Fortune Hunters* offers insights into how to think critically about an idea for a business, in part due to the comments of the program's experts on concepts from Canada and around the world.

Investment Newsletters

Particularly in the newsletter business, prognosticators fill your mailbox with promotional material making outrageous claims about their returns. Private money managers, not subject to the same scrutiny and auditing requirements as mutual funds, can do the same.

Be especially wary of any newsletters making claims of high returns. Stephen Leeb's *Personal Finance* newsletter, for example, claims that he has developed a brilliant proprietary model, which he calls the "Master Key Indicator." His model supposedly has predicted the last 28 upturns in the market in a row without a single miss. The odds of doing this, according to Leeb, are more than 268 million to 1! The ad goes on to claim that Leeb's "Master Key" market-timing system could have turned a $10,000 investment over 12 years into $39.1 million, a return of 390,000 percent!

Turns out that this outrageous claim was based on *backtesting,* looking back over historic returns and creating "what if" scenarios. In other words, Leeb didn't turn anyone's $10,000 into $39 million. Much too late after that ad appeared, the SEC finally charged Leeb with false advertising. Leeb settled out of court for a mere $60,000 fine (far less than he cost investors).

According to the *Hulbert Financial Digest,* the worst investment newsletters have underperformed the market averages by dozens of percentage points; some would even have caused you to lose money during a decade when the financial markets performed extraordinarily well. U.S. newsletter purveyor Joe Granville, for example, has long been known for making outrageous and extreme stock market predictions and is often quoted in financial publications. He claims to have the number-one-rated newsletter — omitting to mention that it was number one for one year only (in 1989). Over the subsequent decade — one of the best decades ever for the stock market (with U.S. stocks more than quadrupling in value) — followers of Granville's advice *lost* 99 percent of their investments!

Be highly suspicious of past investment performance claims made by investment newsletters. Don't believe a track record unless a reputable accounting firm with experience doing such audits has audited it. In order for you to make sound investing choices, you don't need predictions and soothsayers. If you choose to follow these and you're lucky, little harm will be done. But more often than not, you can lose lots of money by following their predictions. Stay far away from publications that purport to be able to tell what's going to happen next. No one has a crystal ball.

The best investment publications can assist you with research and ideas. For individual stock selection, please see our recommended resources in Chapter 6.

If you're looking for ongoing advice and commentary, select newsletters that have a conservative, long-term, and anti–crystal ball philosophy. The best newsletters will admit outright that they cannot — and will not — try to predict just which stock or fund will serve up the next investing home run. Instead, they see their role as reinforcing sound investing fundamentals, providing useful background and analysis, and informing readers of significant changes or news in the areas they cover. One example of a Canadian newsletter that focuses on stocks in this manner is *The Investment Reporter,* published weekly by MPL Communications. Another choice is *The Successful Investor,* which is published monthly. Visit www.thesuccessfulinvestor.com for more information.

The *Canadian Mutual Fund Adviser,* also from MPL, provides good long-term advice on mutual funds coupled with a decidedly realistic and grounded view of the markets in general.

Chapter 18

Selecting the Best Investment Books

Over the years, we've read hundreds of investing and financial books. We hope you haven't subjected yourself to this task!

Although most books have something to offer, too many investing books are burdened with biased, wrongheaded advice and misinformation. As a non-expert, you may have a hard time sifting through the heap for the tidbits of treasure. The bad stuff can pollute your otherwise intelligent thinking and cause you to make investing mistakes that millions before you have made.

We hope we're not the first people to tell you not to believe everything you read. Publishing is no different from any other business — companies are in it to make money. As with other industries, the short-sighted desire to reap quick profits causes some companies to publish content that seems attractive in the short term but is toxic to readers in the long term. In this chapter, we help you sift through the confusion to find books worth reading.

Beware of Infomercial Books

The worst books tend to confuse more than they convey. Why would an author want to do that? Well, some authors have an incentive to make things complicated and mysterious. Their agenda may be to sell you a high-priced newsletter or persuade you to turn your money over to them to manage.

Here's what one book "author" said: "Royalties, schmoyalties . . . I write books to hook people into my monthly newsletter. I can make $185 per year off of a $195 newsletter sale. You can't do that with a book." You sure can't. However, this salesman isn't satisfied to just turn out books that are short on information and advice but long on pitches to keep up with the latest market developments through his newsletter. When you subscribe to his newsletter, you're told that the financial markets are so complicated and change so rapidly that the newsletter is really no substitute for using his money-management service!

The worst books steer you toward purchasing a crummy investment product that the author has a vested interest in selling you. Unfortunately, most publishers don't do their homework to check out prospective authors. They don't care what the author is up to, or whether the author is really an expert on the topic, as long as she's willing and able to write and promote a saleable book. Authors who run around the country conducting seminars and making publicity appearances are a plus to the publisher.

As a cautionary tale, consider a fellow called Wade Cook. In his books and seminar promotional materials, Wade Cook claimed to be able to teach people how to earn monthly returns of 20 percent or more (that's right — not yearly but *monthly!*) by using his stock market investing strategies.

Cook's self-published best-selling books were short on specifics and were largely infomercials for his high-priced seminars. Cook's get-rich-quick investment seminars — which cost a whopping $4,695 — had been so successful at attracting attendees that Cook's company, Profit Financial Corporation, went public and generated more than $100 million in revenues annually! Cook wasn't shy about promising people they could get rich quick without much effort. Here's a passage from his book *Stock Market Miracles:*

> *I want millions of dollars and I don't want to have to work a 9 to 5 job to get them. Boy, that's a conundrum. It's almost impossible to work a typical American job, with average income and accumulate millions. Yes, in 40 to 50 years maybe, but who wants to wait that long? That's the rub — accomplishing the task of having millions without having to work for millions.*
>
> *You see my method is simple. I want to use a small amount of money — risk capital if you will — to generate cash flow which will exponentially generate more income.*

Cook promised his followers several hundred percent annualized returns by teaching them how to successfully gamble (not invest) in the stock market. Cook's "techniques" included trading in and out of stocks and options on stocks after short holding periods of weeks, days, or even hours.

Cook's trading strategies were loosely based upon *technical analysis* — that is, examining a stock's price movements and volume history through charting. (See Chapter 6 for more details on the foolishness of technical analysis.) Cook's investment seminar, which was offered in cities throughout the country, was marketed to folks like this: "If you aren't getting 20 percent per month, or 300 percent annualized returns on your investments, you need to be there."

Steven Thomas, a truck driver, went to a seminar with his wife so both of them could follow and implement Cook's strategies. In addition to spending $4,695 on the seminar, they also spent another $2,000 on audiotapes and videotapes. Six months later, Steven spent $1,500 on a paging system from Cook's company. The results: Thomas eventually lost $36,000 on investments made following Cook's strategies, which he borrowed against his home's equity. "I saw this as an opportunity to quit my job and just invest in the stock market," says Thomas. "This has had a terrible impact on my family, and I'm super-depressed."

Of course, if Cook had indeed earned the 300 percent annual returns his seminars claimed to be able to teach the masses how to achieve, he would have, in about a decade, become the world's wealthiest individual if he had invested just $1 million of the income he supposedly earned in real estate. Look out, Bill Gates and Warren Buffett! Any investor starting with just $10,000 would vault to the top of the list of the world's wealthiest people in about 15 years if Cook's teachings really worked!

So how did Cook get his start in the investing world? Here's what his Web site said:

> He was a taxicab driver in the '70s. Borrowing $500 from his father, Wade Cook started buying real estate. His innovative ideas and gutsy follow-through enabled him to turn that $500 into several million. But that's nothing compared with what he's doing on Wall Street. Starting with $1,300, using his "Rolling Rock" and "Range Rider" methods, he's showing students how to create millions.

> Why is Wade so smart? He says he's "street smart." What he discovered driving a cab changed his life forever. While his fellow cabbies were out looking for the big runs, Wade was taking every little run he could find — $4 here, $5 here. You see it costs $2 just to get into a cab (something called a meter drop) even if you only go two blocks. At the end of a month, Wade made three times what every other taxicab driver made. Now, Wade applies his "meter drop" technique to his stock market investment business — making a ton of money on a lot of little deals.

Although Cook's investment return expectations were completely unrealistic, he got away with claiming hyped and undocumented returns for many years because he didn't manage money for others. In the United States, seminar promoters and newsletter writers face no SEC scrutiny of their inflated performance claims or what they do in their seminars as long as no securities laws are violated. The SEC refers to such organizations as *nonregulated entities*.

Of course, Cook wasn't the first person to profit in this fashion. Numerous other seminar promoters and authors (some are discussed later in this chapter) have made big bucks as well, including the Beardstown investment club, which couldn't document its supposedly market-beating returns of 23-plus percent per year (see the next section for details). In addition to puffed-up expected stock market returns, there's more to Cook's past than simply driving a taxi. According to *Smart Money* magazine, Cook's dubious business practices had him in trouble throughout the '80s. At the end of his real estate seminars, which touted that average people could become millionaires by buying property with little money down, Cook began peddling stock in his own business ventures.

By 1990, state securities regulators in six states — Missouri, Utah, Minnesota, Illinois, Oregon, and Arizona — issued Cook cease-and-desist orders for selling securities without a license, selling unregistered securities, and omitting material facts — like the fact that he had declared bankruptcy in 1987. In fact, Arizona charged that Cook had duped $390,841 out of 150 investors by selling unregistered securities, funnelling $48,000 of that money into a Scottsdale home purchase and federal income tax payments. The state ordered him to pay back the money and slapped him with a $150,000 penalty.

Cook answered by filing bankruptcy (again). Cook then moved back to his home state of Washington, where he didn't lie low for long. His new company, Profit Financial Corporation, became wildly successful by selling his Wall Street Workshop seminars and publishing his two stock-picking books. The attorneys general of several states sought millions of dollars in consumer refunds and sued the company. The states alleged the company lied about its investment track record. (Now that's a big surprise — this company claimed you would make 300 percent per year in stocks!) Cook's company settled the blizzard of state and Federal Trade Commission (FTC) lawsuits against his firm by agreeing to accurately disclose its trading record in future promotions and to give refunds to customers who were misled by past inflated return claims.

Although Profit Financial Corporation was a public company, SEC documents indicated that it wasn't exactly shareholder friendly. Cook set up a rather clever business structure whereby the public company (of which he is the majority owner) was required to pay him for the right to print his words and teach his methods. This enabled Cook to funnel much of the revenue stream directly into his pockets before it ever got to the shareholders. According to SEC filings, Cook's total corporate compensation in one year exceeded $8 million! According to a report by Bloomberg News, Cook's firm lost a whopping 89 percent of its own money trading in 2000. As Deb Bortner, director of the Washington State Securities Division and president of the North American Securities Administrators Association, observed, "Either Wade is unable to follow his own system, which he claims is simple to follow, or the system doesn't work."

And if there weren't enough unsavoury aspects to Cook's financial dealings, Cook was sentenced in 2007 to more than seven years in federal prison for tax evasion, filing false tax returns, and obstructing a tax investigation, and was ordered to pay nearly $4 million in additional taxes.

The moral of the story: Be highly skeptical and suspicious of investing books that direct you to high-priced seminars and other expensive products and services from the author. The best investing books, which we recommend later in this chapter, seek to instruct and educate.

Ignore Unaudited Performance Claims

Book authors avoid careful scrutiny of claims of especially high returns. But if a performance claim hasn't been independently audited, don't believe it.

Remember also that the stock market, over the long term, provides annualized returns of about 10 percent. View skeptically any prognosticator or author claiming substantially higher returns that sound too good to be true.

Some book publishers are happy to look the other way or even to solicit and encourage great boasts that they use in the packaging to sell books. Consider these two examples: *The Beardstown Ladies' Common-Sense Investment Guide: How We Beat the Stock Market — and How You Can, Too* and *The Whiz Kid of Wall Street's Investment Guide* by Matt Seto.

The Beardstown investment club claimed a whopping 23.4 percent annual return since the club's inception in 1983. In the book, the authors advocated forming an investment club, pooling your money, and using a simple stock selection method to beat the pants off the market and the suspendered managers of mutual funds. The bulk of this book walked readers through how this investment club evaluated and selected individual stocks.

As for Seto's book, it boasted, "Matt Seto manages a portfolio that consistently outperforms 99 percent of all mutual fund managers . . . and returns an annual average of 34 percent." In his book, this 17-year-old investing genius told readers to forget bonds, real estate, and mutual funds and grow rich by investing entirely in individual stocks.

Each of these books made performance claims that were prominently displayed and marketed. The returns of the Beardstown club and Seto, versus the market averages, would have placed them shoulder to shoulder with the legendary Peter Lynch, of the now famous Fidelity Magellan fund, and Warren Buffett, an investor whom Peter Lynch described as "the Greatest Investor of them all." Problem is, neither book contained information on how these investment gurus calculated their returns, nor were the authors able to substantiate their claimed returns when asked to.

When Eric first wrote about the Beardstown book for _The San Francisco Examiner,_ he offered to work with an accounting firm to calculate the club's returns if the club supplied the necessary information. Eric asked the same of Seto when he read his book. Neither of these authors could supply the documentation to prove their claims, and they backpedalled when pressed.

Initially, the Beardstown club said it would send the information, but months passed, and it never arrived. The club's media spokesperson then told Eric that the club has "chosen not to make our return an issue. . . . we're not out to be bragging." This statement was surprising, given the claims prominently plastered all over the book.

A later piece in _Chicago_ magazine proved that although the Beardstown investment club claimed 23 percent per year returns versus 14 percent for the market, the club actually tremendously underperformed the market and earned only 9 percent per year. The publisher of the Beardstown book, Buena Vista Publishing (which was doing business as Hyperion and Seth Godin Productions), was ultimately sued. The book publisher settled the lawsuit in 2002. Under the terms of the settlement, buyers of the Beardstown investment club's books, audiotapes, or videotapes received certificates that could be redeemed for other books published by Hyperion.

Do you think the Beardstown ladies would have gotten their book deal (and landed on best-seller lists) if the facts had been known? Seto, likewise, couldn't prove his claim of an astounding 34 percent return.

Investing and Business Books Worth Reading

Exceptional investing books — ones that are readable, educational, and insightful — are rare. Some of the better investment and business books are technical in nature and are written by career investment folks, so don't be surprised if they require more than one read. Make the investment of time; it'll pay big dividends (and capital gains!). Following are our picks for books that are worth the trouble of tracking down and reading.

A Random Walk Down Wall Street

Now in its ninth edition, *A Random Walk Down Wall Street* (Norton), by Burton Malkiel, is a classic that was first published in 1973. Malkiel is an entertaining and intelligent writer. Drawing from examples from this century and others, Malkiel teaches how *speculative bubbles* (frenzied buying) and fear and greed, as well as economic and corporate fundamentals, can move the financial markets.

One fundamental premise of his book is that the financial markets can't be predicted, especially in the short term. Common sense confirms this premise: If someone could figure out a system to forecast the markets and make a fortune, then that person wouldn't waste time writing a book, publishing a newsletter, and so on. Malkiel, in fact, is one of the pioneers and proponents of *index mutual funds,* which simply invest in a relatively fixed basket of securities in order to track the overall market performance rather than to attempt to beat it. (See Chapter 8 to find out about index funds and how to use them.)

Needless to say, many Bay Street types aren't enamoured of this book. As Malkiel says, the very term *random walk* is considered an "obscenity." But Malkiel presents a mountain of compelling arguments and data to support his case that most Wall Street firms and their investment research aren't worthy of an investor's hard-earned money. Malkiel explains how to look at some common-sense indicators, such as whether the stock and bond markets are fairly valued and your own personal goals and desire to take risk, to develop a thoughtful and successful investment plan. Instead of trying to predict the future, Malkiel explains how the level of risk an investor accepts with investments will ultimately determine future returns.

Money Logic

Should you invest in this stock or that mutual fund? If you choose mutual funds, should it be fund X or fund Y? And does paying the extra management fees on segregated funds that guarantee you your principal back after a set number of years make financial sense? *Money Logic: Financial Strategies for the Smart Investor* (Stoddart), written by Moshe A. Milevsky with Michael Posner, tackles these and other common investment quandaries with thoughtful discussion.

Although the book is out of print, it's worthwhile tracking down a copy or borrowing one from your local library. Milevsky, who teaches risk management at York University, uses historical data and mathematical logic to offer practical advice on what information to focus on in order to make sound choices. Among the common concerns he addresses are how to assess the value that managers bring to funds, whether the guarantee of getting your principal back after a certain number of years is worth the extra management expense fees charged by segregated funds, and why and how much international diversification is a good idea.

Stocks for the Long Run

Finance professor Jeremy J. Siegel loves investing data, especially examining it over long time periods. In *Stocks for the Long Run: The Definitive Guide to Financial Market Returns and Long-Term Investment Strategies,* 4th Edition (McGraw-Hill), Siegel presents an analysis of U.S. stock and bond returns since 1802! The book is packed with charts and graphs, some of which you won't readily comprehend unless you're the analytic, graphical sort. Even so, Siegel provides comprehensive discussion of the worldwide financial markets as well as how the economic environment affects stocks. The book focuses on stock market investing, although it also discusses bonds if for no other reason than to compare their returns and risk to stocks.

Canadian Small Business Kit For Dummies

Many small businesses fail because of a lack of upfront planning. Sure, we may have a bias towards the books with a bright yellow cover. That said, *Canadian Small Business Kit For Dummies* (Wiley) can help you to think your idea through, and lay a strong foundation to raise your odds of succeeding. The authors explain the differences between being a sole proprietorship and incorporating, and point to possible benefits and problems. The included CD-ROM contains many common business forms.

Built to Last and Good to Great

Some people may think that *Built to Last: Successful Habits of Visionary Companies* (HarperCollins) is just for the small number of people who want to build a large company. However, the book, written by management consultant James Collins and Stanford Business School Professor Jerry Porras, is an excellent book for all entrepreneurs and people who work in leadership positions in companies, as well as people interested in investing in individual stocks. Rarely does a great book make it to the business best-seller lists, but *Built to Last* did.

The book presents the findings from an extensive six years' worth of research into what's behind the success of companies such as 3M, Boeing, Ford, Hewlett-Packard, Motorola, Sony, and Wal-Mart, all of which have achieved great success in their respective industries over many years. The average company in the Collins and Porras study was founded in 1897. In all, the authors tracked 18 extraordinary companies (referred to as the gold-medal winners in their respective industries) and compared the traits of these companies with those of similarly long-lived but less successful peer companies (in the same industries).

Collins and Porras's findings not only yield insight into how to build or identify a great business in which to invest but also destroy some commonly held myths. For example, some people feel that a great idea is behind every great company. This concept is wrong, and in fact, according to the authors' research, companies founded on the basis of a great idea can lead to focusing on the idea rather than laying the groundwork for building a great company. Sony's founder, for example, wrote a nine-page philosophical prospectus setting the stage for this great company, yet he had few product ideas in his firm's early days. Early products, such as a rice cooker, failed miserably.

Great, visionary companies are rigid and unyielding when it comes to respecting their core ideologies and principles. On the other hand, such companies tinker and experiment to stimulate positive change and innovation. And despite their often-stunning financial success, great companies usually have an aspiration higher than or equal to maximizing profits: fulfilling a purpose and being driven by values. This book is packed with insights, information, and examples, so don't expect to absorb all of its contents in one reading.

Collins subsequently wrote another outstanding book, *Good to Great: Why Some Companies Make the Leap . . . And Others Don't* (HarperCollins), which he calls the prequel to *Built to Last*. In *Good to Great*, Collins presents the engaging and insightful results of another long-term study of numerous companies that over time moved from being average companies to outstanding companies. As with *Built to Last*, this newer book can assist readers not only with managing their own small businesses but also with selecting companies to invest in.

Chapter 19

Investigating Internet and Software Resources

In This Chapter

▶ Choosing investing software

▶ Recognizing Internet pitfalls and opportunities

▶ Finding the best investing Web sites

*T*housands of investing software packages and Web sites claim to enable you to more easily make profitable investments. As with most other advertising claims, the reality of using your computer for investing and other tasks falls short of the promises and the hype.

In this chapter, we show you ways that your computer may help you with your investing challenges and chores. Throughout this discussion, however, please remember several important caveats:

✔ Some highly successful investors don't use their computers (or they use them infrequently) to deal with their investments.

✔ You may subject yourself to information overload and spend a fair amount of money without seeing many benefits if you don't choose wisely.

✔ Don't believe everything you read, especially in the online world, where filters and editors are often absent. (Of course, as we discuss elsewhere in this book, filters and editors don't guarantee that you'll find quality investment advice and information when you read financial publications.)

Evaluating Investment Software

Good investment software should be user-friendly and provide quality information for making sound decisions. Software that helps you make personal investment decisions also needs to provide, if applicable, well-founded advice.

Which software is best for you depends on what you're trying to accomplish, as well as your level of investment knowledge and computer savvy. Software can help you with a variety of investment tasks, from tracking your investments to researching, planning, and placing trades through your computer (a topic that we discuss in Chapter 9). The following sections help you find the best software for your needs.

Investment-tracking software

Software that can help you with investment tracking falls into one of two main groups:

- ✔ Personal finance software that also includes investment-tracking capabilities
- ✔ Software that focuses exclusively on investment tracking

The broader personal finance packages such as *Quicken* and *Microsoft Money* are more user-friendly and are probably more familiar if you already use these packages' other features (such as a bill-paying feature).

In the following sections, we outline what we see as the advantages and disadvantages of using tracking software based on your needs and offer a few alternative approaches to tracking your investments.

The benefits

Investment-tracking software offers a number of positive features that may appeal to you:

- ✔ **Organization:** One of the best benefits of these packages is that using them can help you get organized. If you enter your investments into the program, the software can help you make sure that you don't lose track of your holdings. Of course, if your home burns to the ground and you don't have a backup copy of your files or software off-site, you have to start your documentation from scratch.

✔ **At-a-glance access:** In addition to organizing all of your investment information in one place, investment software allows you to track original purchase price, current market values, and rates of return on your investments. If you have accounts at numerous investment firms, using software can reduce some of the complications involved in tracking your investing kingdom.

✔ **Overall return data:** People usually know their GIC and bond yields, but ask most people investing in individual stocks and bonds what the total return was on their entire portfolio, and at best, you'll get a guess. It's the rare person who can quote you total returns or tell you whether her returns are on pace to reach her future financial goals. If someone does know her investments' returns, she probably doesn't know whether that return is good, bad, or otherwise. Feel good having made 22 percent on your portfolio of stocks last year? Maybe you wouldn't if an index of comparable stocks was up 35 percent over the same period.

Investment-tracking software can be more useful for stock traders. In our experience, stock traders, the people who would most benefit from using these programs, often don't track their overall returns. If they did, they could calculate the benefit (or lack thereof) of all their trading.

The drawbacks

Many software makers produce programs that claim to solve investment-tracking quandaries. (Numerous financial Web sites offer tracking tools as well.) However, investment-tracking software isn't a painless panacea for investors who want to track their investments and returns.

Many people buy these programs thinking that the programs will, after a small investment of time, simplify their investment lives. Our review of many investment-tracking packages suggests that you should be prepared to make a substantial time commitment to find out how to use them and should know that other, less high-tech alternatives may be more efficient and enlightening. Also know that a good portion of program users tire of entering all the required data and then feel guilty for falling behind.

If you want to see what your investment returns have been over the years, be aware that entering historic data from your account statements (if you can find them) is a time-consuming process, regardless of which package you use. To calculate your returns, you generally need to enter what's known as the adjusted cost base of each new investment that you make as well as all your reinvestments of dividends, interest, and capital gains distributions (such as those made on mutual funds). Ugh!

The alternatives

If you're not into data entry, here are some alternative routes to consider:

- **Organization:** Keeping a current copy of each of your investment statements in a binder or file folder can accomplish the same result of organizing all of your holdings.

- **At-a-glance access:** Investment software can track all the facts and figures for all of your investments — purchase price, market value, rates of return, and so on. But you can accomplish the same things by consolidating your investments at one investment company. (See our discussion of discount brokers in Chapter 9.)

- **Overall return data:** You can easily estimate the return of your overall portfolio by using an old-fashioned paper and pencil. Simply weight the return of each investment by the portion of your portfolio that's invested in it. For example, with a simple portfolio equally divided between two investments that returned 10 percent and 20 percent, respectively, your overall portfolio return would be 15 percent ($10 \times 0.50 + 20 \times 0.50 = 15$). If you're not adding to or taking money from a portfolio, you can simply compare the portfolio's value at year end to the prior year end.

People who make investments at various times throughout the year and want to know what their actual returns were during the year can use software to get answers. Unless you're a frequent trader and are trying to measure the success of your trading, knowing the exact returns based on the precise dates that you fed money into investments has limited value. This fact is especially true if you're a regular, dollar-cost-averaging investor (see Chapter 3). Also know that increasing numbers of investment companies are providing personal return data via their Web site and/or on account statements.

And if you're a buy-and-hold mutual fund investor, a path that we find great value in, tracking software gives you limited benefits because of the time that entering your data requires. Mutual funds and many other published resources tell you what a fund's total return was for the past year, so you don't need to enter every dividend and capital gain distribution.

Investment research software

Investment research software packages usually separate investment beginners (and others who don't want to spend a lot of their time managing their money) from those who enjoy wallowing in data and conducting primary research. If you already have a plan in mind and just want to get on with investing, then go for it! But even if you don't want to conduct more specific research, some of the packages that we discuss in this section can also help you conduct online investment transactions and track an investment's performance.

Understanding how software calculates returns

Most software programs calculate returns in one of two ways. First, the programs can calculate your effective or "internal" rate of return (IRR) by comparing the original amounts you invested to the current market value. Of those programs that we've tested that calculate IRR — and some don't — the results were accurate. After you calculate your returns, knowing how they compare with relevant market averages would be nice. Unfortunately, not all programs allow you to compare your performance to various market indexes.

The tax or cost-basis method is the second way software may calculate your returns. All the packages that we've reviewed calculate your adjusted cost base for accounting purposes. Your adjusted cost base is your original investment plus reinvested dividends and capital gains, for which you have already paid taxes in a non-retirement account. To get an accurate adjusted cost base, you need to key in all of your investments, including reinvested distributions. Time-starved investors can take solace in the fact that most investment companies, particularly larger mutual fund providers, provide adjusted cost base information for you upon request or when you sell an investment.

Some packages provide only this adjusted cost base information and don't report actual returns. Adjusted cost base reports make your returns look less generous because reinvested distributions increase your original investment and seemingly reduce your returns. We know from experience that investors often look at adjusted cost base reports and assume that the reports tell them what their investment returns are. This happens partly because of the adjusted cost base reports' misleading names, such as "investment performance" or "investment analysis."

The difference between the rate of return using the adjusted cost base and IRR methods is generally substantial. For the data used in our research, the adjusted cost base method software calculated a 2.7 percent annual return, and the IRR method software calculated a 13 percent annual return. The actual portfolio's total return was 13 percent, but an investor using a software package that calculates only adjusted cost base is led to believe that her profit was just 2.7 percent (which is correct for tax purposes only for a non-retirement plan).

Is all this calculation method mumbo jumbo too technical for your taste? Because they already have the data on your accounts, more investment firms can and hopefully someday will be able to send you your account's performance numbers. To date, surprisingly few investment firms provide personal investment returns.

You may have the problems of sifting through too much data and differentiating the best from the mediocre and the downright awful. And unless cost is no object, you need to make sure that you don't spend too much of your loot simply accessing the information.

Before you plunge into the data jungle and try to become the next Peter Cundill or Warren Buffett and pick individual stocks, be honest about your reasons for wanting to research. Some investors fool themselves into believing that their research will help them beat the markets. Few investors, even so-called professionals, ever do. Witness the fact that over long time periods (ten-plus years), mutual funds that invest in a market index, such as the Toronto Stock Exchange Composite, outperform about three-quarters of their actively managed peers thanks to the index fund's lower operating expenses (see Chapter 8).

Researching individual securities

If you like to invest in individual securities, the Canadian Shareowners Association Stock Selection Guide software (about $200) helps you research individual companies. You can enter the data yourself or purchase it in electronic form from the association. The association has information on over 6,000 Canadian and U.S. companies.

The data, available on CD or online, costs about $230 annually for unlimited downloads. You can also choose to have the data mailed out to you on disc every two months for slightly more. You can order the software and data by calling the Canadian Shareowners Association at 800-268-6881, or by visiting its Web site at www.shareowner.com. We discuss the association in more detail in Chapter 6. Another good option is the *Value Line Investment Analyzer,* which helps you research individual stocks using the data that the Value Line Investment Survey provides (as we discuss in Chapter 6). This software package lets you sift through Value Line's data efficiently. You can also use it to track your stock portfolio.

A two-month introductory offer for Value Line's software costs US$75 (US$95 for the "Plus Edition," which also tracks small- and medium-company stocks), and an annual subscription costs US$598 for monthly updates (US$995 for the more comprehensive version). The software is available from Value Line at 800-654-0508 or by visiting its Web site at www.valueline.com.

Morningstar, which is better known for its mutual fund information, has followed in Value Line's footsteps in providing lots of data on individual stocks. Morningstar's *Principia for Stocks* has data and features equivalent to what Value Line's Plus Edition offers. This program is intended for those with in-depth knowledge of how to analyze stocks and is most definitely not for beginners. An annual subscription to *Principia for Stocks* with monthly updates costs US$675. You can reach Morningstar at 800-735-0700 or visit its Web site at www.morningstar.ca. Morningstar offers a number of ways to tap in to the more basic stock data it collects through its Web site, which we discuss in the next section.

Researching ETFs and mutual funds

For ETFs and mutual funds, ShareOwner, Morningstar, and Value Line all publish a number of software packages. These packages are geared toward more sophisticated investors who understand mutual funds and how to select them. For more on how to pick winning funds, see Chapter 8.

Investigating Internet Resources

As people interested in managing their money surf the Internet, thousands of Web sites have sprung up to meet the demand. Although the low barriers to entry in the online world make it easy for scammers and incompetents to flog their wares and flawed advice, this medium can offer some helpful resources if you know where to look and how to discern the good from the not-so-good.

The U.S. Securities and Exchange Commission shutters numerous online scams, such as the one that bilked investors out of more than $3.5 million by promising to double investors' money in four months in a fictitious security they called "prime bank."

Although you may be smart enough to avoid offers that promise pie in the sky, you're far more likely to fall for unsound financial advice, which is in abundance online. You can find plenty of self-serving advertorial content and bad advice online, so you should be wary and cautious. The next section offers tips for evaluating Internet resources.

Evaluating online resources

Fraud and bad financial advice existed long before the Internet ever came around. The SEC describes online scams as "new medium, same message." The tips in the following sections can help you find the nuggets of helpful online advice and avoid the land mines.

Checking out agendas

Get an idea of who's behind a site before you trust its information. When navigating the Internet for investment purposes, remember that financial service companies that want to sell you something erect the vast majority of sites. Thus, the "free" entrance fee to these sites is driven by companies wanting you to buy what they're selling.

Some sites go to extraordinary lengths — including providing lots of information and advice and attempting to conceal the identity of the company that runs the site — to disguise their agendas. Therefore, don't turn to the Web for advice or opinions, which usually aren't objective. Approach online financial calculators with skepticism. Most are simplistic and biased.

Many Web sites have icons that you can click to see some background on the site's sponsor and to find out whether the site solicits potential advertisers. With a simple click, you can quickly see that a site purporting to be a reference service of the best small-company stocks in which to invest may be nothing more than an online Yellow Pages of companies that paid the site an advertising fee. Look for sites that exercise quality control in what they post and use sensible screening criteria for outside information or companies they list.

Just because every Tom, Dick, and Jane can easily and at relatively low cost set up an Internet site doesn't mean that their Web sites and advice are worthy of your time. Not surprisingly, the financial companies with reputations for integrity offline are the ones that offer some of the best integrity online. For example, as we discuss later in this chapter, the leading and most investor-friendly investment companies often have the best education-oriented Web sites.

Soliciting grassroots customer feedback

The Internet can be a useful place to do consumer research. The more enlightening message board conversations that we've encountered start with someone asking what others thought about particular financial service firms, such as investment dealers. If you're investigating a certain financial service, the Internet can be an efficient way to get feedback from other people who have experience dealing with that firm.

To find a dozen people offline who have done business with a given firm, you'd probably have to speak with hundreds of people. Online, finding customers is a snap. Those who feel wronged by a particular firm are more than willing to share their gripes through sites such as www.PlanetFeedback.com. As in the offline world, though, don't believe everything you hear, and watch out for employees of a given firm who post flattering comments about their firms and dis the competition.

Verifying advice and information offline

Enhance the value of the online information you gather by verifying it elsewhere. You can do some fact checking both online and offline. For example, if you're contemplating the purchase of some stock based on financial data you read on an investing site, first check out those numbers at the library or at one of the Web sites we recommend later in this chapter.

Lots of Internet investment advice (and most of the scams) focus on smaller companies and investment start-ups; unfortunately, these are often the most difficult businesses to locate information about. In the United States, the SEC requires companies that are raising less than $1 million to file a Form D. To inquire whether a company has filed Form D, call the SEC's Office of Investor Education and Advocacy at 202-551-8090 or send an e-mail to publicinfo@ sec.gov. Also check with the province's or state's securities regulator. For contact information for provincial and state regulators, you may call the North American Securities Administrators Association at 202-737-0900 or visit its Web site at www.nasaa.org/QuickLinks/ContactYourRegulator.cfm.

And if something does sound too good to be true, check out and possibly report your concerns to Internet fraud-fighting organization sites. In addition to the SEC's Web site, check out the National Association of Securities Dealers Regulation Web site (www.nasdr.com) and the National Consumers League's Fraud Information Center (www.fraud.org; 800-876-7060).

Unfortunately, here in Canada, we are now only starting discussions about having a national body overseeing the securities industry. Worse, our regulatory system is a patchwork, with a mix of federal and provincial bodies overseeing different aspects of the financial services and securities industries.

A good starting place for digging up information is the Ontario Securities Commission Web site at www.osc.gov.on.ca, as well as the regulators of the other provinces.

The best investment Web sites

Although you can live without the Internet and not suffer any financial or educational consequences, the quality of what's on the Internet is gradually improving, and a handful of sites are setting a high standard.

In addition to the consumer advocacy sites that we recommend earlier in this chapter, here are our top picks for investing sites worthy of your online time:

- **CorporateInformation.com** is owned and operated by Wright Investors' Services, which, in addition to managing money for affluent individuals, also publishes comprehensive reports on thousands of companies around the globe. Those wanting to do Web-based stock research will also enjoy the many links to other Internet investing information and research sites. This site also provides plenty of current business news.

- **CXO Advisory**'s excellent Web site (www.cxoadvisory.com) was created and is run by Steve LeCompte. In addition to tracking macroeconomic measures (such as corporate earnings, inflation rates, and so on) that affect stock prices, CXO Advisory also tracks the performance of numerous gurus' and pundits' stock market calls. For example, you can see how accurate prominent radio talk show hosts, television commentators, magazine and online columnists, and others have been with their public stock market predictions.

What we especially like about this site is that LeCompte isn't selling anything that would create a conflict of interest. He's a superb and detail-oriented analyst who enjoys doing and providing interesting stock market research. The more we've used his site, the more we've enjoyed it (comics included from his daughter) and found it useful.

✔ **Globeinvestor.com** covers most publicly traded stocks in both Canada and the United States. It's easy to get a quick snapshot of a company's stock, including a chart of its historical prices going back five years. You can also access quarterly and annual financial results, sift through the press releases archive, and search current news from *The Globe and Mail*. Like other good sites, globeinvestor.com makes intelligent use of technology by allowing you to search out stocks according to the price and company financial information you specify. If you're looking for undervalued stocks, for instance, you can search for stocks trading below a certain price/earnings level, or stocks whose prices dropped by 60 percent in the last year but that have started to recover. As well, you can sift companies according to how they're growing in terms of profits, sales, and earnings.

✔ **Globefund.com**, a companion site to GlobeInvestor, is a straightforward and easy-to-navigate site for researching and screening funds. You can chart funds, compare them with others, look up ratings, and sift the Canadian fund world for those funds that meet your needs. In addition to profiles of funds and fund companies, you can look up data from the *Globe*'s 15-year fund review. This is an excellent resource, because looking at a fund's year-by-year performance for a decade and a half can offer you lots of insights into a fund's behaviours and up and down markets.

✔ **Morningstar** is the behemoth of the mutual fund data business, with a Web site (`www.morningstar.ca`) that provides information and tools for mutual fund and stock research. In addition to providing more data on funds and stocks than you could ever possibly digest, this site includes short, insightful articles that are useful to more educated investors.

✔ **The St. Louis Federal Reserve** (`www.research.stlouisfed.org`) is the place to be for those who enjoy analyzing economic data. In addition to sometimes heady articles such as "Pandemic Economics: The 1918 Influenza and Its Modern-Day Implications," this site provides a treasure trove of current economic data along with graphs. The long-term graphs are particularly useful in providing folks with the often missing long-term perspective in our daily diet of news.

Look who's talking

If you're at a cocktail party and you receive investing information and advice from someone you've just met, check him out to determine how much credence you should give to his words. And no matter how wise he seems, you shouldn't judge him on the basis of just one conversation.

In the online world, you need to do the same, but you may have greater difficulty determining who's doing the talking and why. On some Internet sites, visitors may post comments and opinions on message boards (the online equivalent of a big bulletin board).

As the National Association of Securities Dealers (NASD) says on its Web site, "In most instances, there is simply no way to uncover someone's true identity. Are you getting information from a broker, short seller, corporate insider, amateur investor, or stock touter?" You have to use a little induction and a lot of intuition. Start by discounting any advice from online posters who are totally anonymous. Pseudonyms are common online, and some salespeople try to hide their true identities.

Among the more popular message boards on the Internet are those where people debate and discuss the prospects for individual stocks. The postings play fast and loose with the facts. "Investors need to understand that, although they may be reading honest conversations, they could just as easily be looking at the work of a corporate insider, stock promoter, or short seller using an alias to deceive the unsuspecting or to manipulate the market," says the NASD Regulation unit.

For example, we had to laugh the other day when we saw a headline online that screamed "U.S. Dollar at Record Low." The article only mentioned the euro, and it never pointed out that the euro only came into existence in 1999! In fact, when you compare the U.S. dollar to a broad basket of other currencies represented by our trading partners, the U.S. dollar is still more than double the value it was a generation ago. Anyone can see this fact for themselves by examining the *trade weighted exchange index* (TWEXBMTH) on the St. Louis Fed site. (According to the site, the index is "a weighted average of the foreign exchange value of the U.S. dollar against the currencies of a broad group of major U.S. trading partners. Broad currency index includes the Euro Area, Canada, Japan, Mexico, China, United Kingdom, Taiwan, Korea, Singapore, Hong Kong, Malaysia, Brazil, Switzerland, Thailand, Philippines, Australia, Indonesia, India, Israel, Saudi Arabia, Russia, Sweden, Argentina, Venezuela, Chile, and Colombia.")

✔ **Sedar.com** is an excellent one-stop shop for the many different documents that publicly traded Canadian companies and mutual funds must file. The information at Sedar (which stands for System for Electronic Document Analysis and Retrieval) is made available by the Canadian Securities Administrators (CSA) and the Canadian Depository for Securities (CDS).

If you're researching individual companies, you can find via this Web site all the corporate reports — annual reports and the like — that we discuss in Chapter 6. (Alternatively, of course, you may call the individual companies that interest you and have them mail you the desired material.) All the files are in PDF format, meaning they each have to open in their own window, and scrolling can be a chore.

✔ **U.S. Securities and Exchange Commission (SEC)** holds the annual and quarterly reports for all U.S. publicly held companies at its Web site (www.sec.gov).

The SEC site isn't pretty, and searching the Electronic Data Gathering, Analysis, and Retrieval system (EDGAR) database can be challenging, especially for the novice investor. But if you're tenacious, you may find something that's hard to come by on the Web these days: cold, hard facts and no spin.

Online investing geniuses?

Nowhere will you find more self-proclaimed investing geniuses than online. Here are some important perspectives and lessons to keep in mind as you surf the Web:

✔ **Beware of promises of easy riches.** To deter investors from mutual funds, one Web site says of its stock picking, "We hope to have put you in position to nearly double the S&P 500 . . . it'll demand little research per year, and present you little, if any, long-term risk." If investing were that easy, we'd all be rich! And as any professional money manager knows first-hand, successfully managing a portfolio of individual stocks takes time, not just a few hours per year.

✔ **Beware of bloated performance claims.** Not surprisingly, many online investing pundits hype claimed returns from their investment recommendations. If you can't independently verify a performance claim, don't believe it. Also, keep in mind that even if performance numbers are indeed accurate, calculated returns often overlook trading commissions and taxes (which can be especially high for sites that advocate selling investments after holding them for less than one year).

✔ **Successful investing doesn't require following the market closely.** Buying and holding index or other quality mutual funds for many years doesn't take much review time — perhaps as little as an hour once per year to read the fund's annual report. The daily and even minute-by-minute tracking of stock prices on many sites causes investors to lose sight of the long term and the big picture (although it draws more visitors to the site, which satisfies advertisers and enriches the site owners).

The bottom line? Be skeptical of financial prognosticators, online or off. Like politicians, they're out to make themselves look as good as possible, taking credit when things go well and blaming external forces when they don't. For an independent assessment of a supposed guru's investment picks, check out CXO Advisory, discussed earlier in this chapter, and *Hulbert's Financial Digest*. See Chapter 17 for more about investment newsletters.

Part VI
The Part of Tens

The 5th Wave — By Rich Tennant

"Sell."

In this part . . .

The Part of Tens contains shorter chapters, each including about ten items on important investing topics that don't quite fit elsewhere in the book. The topics in this part cover the psychological issues to overcome to be a successful investor, what you need to know when you're considering selling an investment, and advice for investing during a down market.

Chapter 20

Ten Investing Obstacles to Conquer

*J*ust as with raising children or in one's career, "success" with personal investing is in the eye of the beholder. In our work as financial instructors and writers, we've come to define successful investors as people who, with a modest commitment of time, develop an investment plan to accomplish financial and personal goals and earn returns commensurate with the risk they're willing to accept.

In this chapter, we point out ten common obstacles that may keep you from fully realizing your financial goals, and we share tips and advice for overcoming those obstacles on the road to investing success.

Trusting Authority

Some investors assume that an adviser is competent and ethical if she has a lofty title (financial consultant, vice president, and so on), dresses well, and works in a snazzy office. Such accessories are often indicators of salespeople — not objective advisers — who recommend investments that will earn them big commissions that come out of your investment dollars.

Additionally, if you put too much trust in an adviser, you may not research and monitor your investments as carefully as you should. Figuring that Mr. Vice President is an expert, some investors go along without ever questioning his advice or watching what's going on with their investments.

You should also question authority elsewhere in the investment business. Too many investors blindly follow analysts' stock recommendations without considering the many conflicts of interest that such investment dealer employees have. Investment dealer analysts are often cheerleaders for buying various companies' stocks because their firms are courting the business of new stock and bond issuance of the same companies. And just because a big-name accounting firm has blessed a company's financial statements (Nortel) or a company's CEO says everything is fine (Bear Stearns) doesn't make a firm's financial statements accurate or its conditions sound.

You can't possibly evaluate the competence and agenda of someone you hire until you understand the lay of the land. You can't possibly know for sure that an analyst's report or a professional service firm's recommendation or approval of a company is worth the paper it's printed upon. Read good publications (see Part V) on the topic to master the jargon and figure out how to evaluate investments. Seek independent second opinions before you act on someone's recommendations. If you're in the market for a investment adviser, be sure to read Chapter 9.

Getting Swept Up by Euphoria

Feeling strength and safety in numbers, some investors are lured into buying hot stocks and sectors (for example, industries like technology, health care, biotechnology, retail, and so on) after major price increases. Psychologically, it's reassuring to buy into something that's going up and gaining accolades. The obvious danger with this practice is buying into investments selling at inflated prices that too soon deflate.

In North American stock markets, by the late 1990s investors were getting spoiled with gains year after year in excess of the historic average annual return of 9 to 10 percent. Numerous surveys conducted during this period showed that many investors expected to earn returns in the range of 15 to 20 percent annually, nearly double the historic average. As always happens, though, after a period of excessively high returns such as those of the 1990s — which were fuelled by the tech bubble — returns were below average in the subsequent period beginning in 2000 (and were quite negative in the early 2000s). During the market slump in the early 2000s, real estate–related stocks continued to do well; some folks mistakenly believed that the housing sector was immune to setbacks and were surprised by the slump in that sector in the late 2000s.

For many years, Tony has written a column for *The Globe and Mail*'s "Report on Business" about the investing approach, philosophy, and experiences of Canadians. Called "Me and My Money," the column looks at how different people — from homemakers to bus drivers to engineers — decide what to invest in, and why.

He also asks them to pick one great investment move, and one really bad mistake. As to what led to their "worst move," many investors blame it on the same general error: "I didn't know anything about it, but everybody was saying it was going to go higher!" And what did they have to say about their best investment move? Typically, it's an investment they understood, had reasonable expectations for, and invested in for the long term!

Develop an overall allocation among various investments (especially diversi-fied mutual funds), and don't make knee-jerk decisions to change your alloca-tion based on what the latest hot sectors are. If anything, de-emphasize or avoid stocks and sectors that are at the top of the performance charts. Think back to the last time you went bargain shopping for a consumer item — you looked for value, not high prices. See Chapter 5 to find out how to spot good values in the financial markets and speculative bubbles to avoid.

Being Overconfident

As we discuss in Part V, newsletters, books, and even some financial peri-odicals lead investors to believe that you can be the next Peter Cundill or Warren Buffett if you follow a simple stock-picking system. The advent of the Internet and online trading capabilities has spawned a whole new generation of short-term (sometimes even same-day) traders.

In our work, we've come across plenty of people who lost a lot of money after they had an early winner and had attributed that early success to their investing genius. These folks usually wake up to the fact that no one is blessed with supernatural ability to pick winning investments only after great and humbling losses.

If you have the speculative bug, earmark a small portion of your portfolio (no more than 10 to 20 percent) for more aggressive investments. See Chapter 5 for more information on questions to help you decide whether you or some-one you know has a gambling problem.

Giving Up When Things Look Bleak

Inexperienced or nervous investors may be tempted to bail out when it appears that an investment isn't always profitable and enjoyable. Some inves-tors dump falling investments precisely at the times when they should be doing the reverse — buying more. Whenever the stock market drops more than a few percentage points in a short period, it attracts a lot of attention, which then leads to concern, anxiety, and in some cases, panic. Corrections in excess of 10 percent, such as happened throughout 2007, 2008, and 2009, lead to all sorts of hand wringing and gloom-and-doom talk.

Investing always involves uncertainty. Many people forget this, especially during good economic times. We find that investors are more likely to feel more comfortable with riskier investments, such as stocks, when they recognize that all investments carry uncertainty and risk — just in different forms.

History has repeatedly proved that continuing to buy stocks during down markets increases your long-term returns. The worst thing you can do in a slumping market is to throw in the towel.

Unfortunately, the short-term focus that the media so often takes causes some investors to worry that their investments are in shambles during the inevitable bumps in the road. As we discuss in Part V, the media are often to blame because they hype short-term events and blow those events out of proportion to captivate viewers and listeners. Leading up to the huge collapse of the stock market in the fall of 2008, for example, you would have been hard-pressed to find any warning signs of the coming collapse in the papers or on business television. And when the markets plummeted, headlines and TV reporters couldn't get enough of telling readers and viewers how bad things had become due to the credit crisis.

History has shown that financial markets recover; recovery is just a question of time. If you invest for the long term, then the last six weeks — or even the last couple of years — is a short period. Plus, countless studies demonstrate that no one can predict the future, so you gain little from trying to base your investment plans on predictions. In fact, you can lose more money by trying to time the markets.

Larger-than-normal market declines hold a significant danger for investors: They may encourage decision making that's based on emotion rather than logic. Just ask anyone who sold *after* the stock market collapsed in 1987 — the stock markets dropped over 30 percent in a matter of weeks in the fall of that year. Since then, even with the significant drop in 2008 of over 40 percent — stock markets have still risen threefold!

Investors who can't withstand the volatility of riskier growth-oriented investments, such as stocks, may be better off not investing in such vehicles to begin with. Examining your returns over longer periods helps you keep the proper perspective. If a short-term downdraft in your investments depresses you, avoid tracking your investment values closely. Also, consider investing in highly diversified, less-volatile funds that hold stocks worldwide as well as bonds (see Chapter 8).

Refusing to Accept a Loss

Although some investors realize that they can't withstand losses, and then sell at the first signs of trouble, other investors find that selling a losing investment is so painful and unpleasant that they continue to hold a poorly performing investment, despite the investment's poor future prospects. Psychological research backs this up — people find the pain of accepting a given loss twice as intense as the pleasure of accepting a gain of equal magnitude.

Analyze your lagging investments to identify why they perform poorly. If a given investment is down because similar ones are also in decline, hold on to it. However, if something is inherently wrong with the investment — such as high fees or poor management — make taking the loss more palatable by remembering two things:

 ✔ If your investment is not in an RRSP or other tax-protected plan, you can use the loss to offset the tax you would otherwise have to pay on profits you've made on other investments.

 ✔ Consider the "opportunity cost" of continuing to keep your money in a lousy investment — that is, what returns can you get in the future if you switch to a "better" investment?

Overmonitoring Your Investments

The investment world seems so risky and fraught with pitfalls that some people believe that closely watching an investment can help alert them to impending danger. "The constant tracking is not unlike the attempt to relieve anxiety by fingering worry beads. Yet paradoxically, it can increase emotional distress because it requires a constant state of vigilance," says psychologist Dr. Paul Minsky.

In our work, we see that investors who are the most anxious about their investments and most likely to make impulsive trading decisions are the ones who watch their holdings too closely, especially those who monitor prices daily. The proliferation of Internet sites and stock market cable television programs offering up-to-the-minute quotations gives these investors even more temptation to overmonitor investments.

Restrict your "diet" of financial information and advice. Quality is far more important than quantity. Watching the daily price gyrations of investments is akin to eating too much junk food — doing so may satisfy your short-term cravings but at the cost of your long-term health. Remember that the goal of the minute-by-minute market "updates" is not to help you make more money, but to help media companies sell more advertising. If you invest in diversified mutual funds (see Chapter 8), you really don't need to examine your fund's performance more than once or twice per year. An ideal time to review your funds is when you receive their annual or semi-annual reports. Although many investors track their funds daily or weekly, far fewer read their annual reports. Reading these reports can help you keep a long-term perspective and gain some understanding of why your funds perform as they do and how they compare to major market averages.

Being Unclear about Your Goals

Investing is more complicated than simply setting your financial goals (see Chapter 3) and choosing solid investments to help you achieve them. Awareness and understanding of the less tangible issues can maximize your chances for investing success.

In addition to considering your goals in a traditional sense (such as when you want to retire and how much of your kids' university costs you want to pay), before you invest, you should also consider what you want and don't want to get from the investment process. Do you treat investing as a hobby or simply as another one of life's tasks, such as maintaining your home? Do you enjoy the intellectual challenge of picking your own stocks? Don't just ponder these questions on your own; discuss them with family members, too — after all, you're all going to have to live with your decisions and investment results.

Ignoring Your Real Financial Problems

We know plenty of high-income earners, including more than a few who earn six figures annually, who have little to invest. Some of these people have high-interest debt outstanding on credit cards and auto loans, yet they spend endless hours researching and tracking investments.

We also know many people who built significant personal wealth despite having modest-paying jobs. The difference: the ability to live within their means.

If you don't earn a high income, you may be tempted to think that you can't save. Even if you are a high-income earner, you may think that you can hit an investment home run to accomplish your goals or that you can save more if you can bump up your income. This way of thinking justifies spending most of what you earn and saving little now. Investing is far more exciting than examining your spending and making cutbacks. If you need help coming up with more money to invest, see the latest edition of our book *Personal Finance For Canadians For Dummies* (published by Wiley).

Overemphasizing Certain Risks

Saving money is only half the battle. The other half is making your money grow. Over long time periods, earning just a few percent more makes a big difference in the size of your nest egg. Earning inflation-beating returns is easy to do if you're willing to invest in stocks, real estate, and small businesses. Figure 20-1 shows you how much more money you'll have in 25 years if you can earn investment returns that are greater than the rate of inflation (which has been averaging about 3 percent).

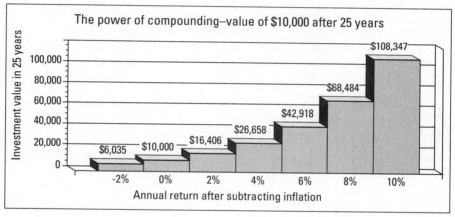

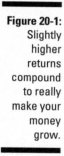

Figure 20-1: Slightly higher returns compound to really make your money grow.

The power of compounding—value of $10,000 after 25 years

As we discuss in Chapter 2, ownership investments (stocks, real estate, and small business) have historically generated returns greater than the inflation rate by 6 percent or more, while lending investments (savings accounts and bonds) tend to generate returns of only 1 to 2 percent above inflation. However, some investors keep too much of their money in lending investments out of fear of holding an investment that can fall greatly in value. Although ownership investments can plunge in value, you need to keep in mind that inflation and taxes eat away at your lending investment balances.

Believing in Gurus

Stock market declines, like earthquakes, bring all sorts of prognosticators, soothsayers, and self-anointed gurus out of the woodwork, particularly among those in the investment community, such as newsletter writers, who have something to sell. The words may vary, but the underlying message doesn't: "If you had been following my sage advice, you'd be much better off now."

People spend far too much of their precious time and money in pursuit of a guru who can tell them when and what to buy and sell. Peter Lynch, the former manager of the Fidelity Magellan Fund, amassed one of the best long-term stock market investing track records. His stock-picking ability allowed him to beat the market averages by just a few percent per year. However, even he says that you can't time the markets, and he acknowledges knowing many pundits who have correctly predicted the future course of the stock market "once in a row"!

Clearly, in the world of investing, the most successful investors earn much better returns than the worst ones. But what may surprise you is that you can end up much closer to the top of the investing performance heap than the bottom if you follow some relatively simple rules, such as regularly saving and investing in low-cost growth investments. In fact, by doing so you can beat many of the full-time investment professionals.

Chapter 21

Ten Things to Consider When You're Selling an Investment

You can and should hold good investments for years and decades. Each year, people sell trillions of dollars' worth of investments. Our experience speaking with people about their investments suggests that too many people sell for the wrong reasons and hold on to investments that they should sell. In this chapter, we highlight important issues to consider when you contemplate selling your investments.

Remembering Your Preferences and Goals

If your life has changed since the last time you took a good look at your investment portfolio (or you've inherited investments), your current portfolio may no longer make sense for you. We generally recommend that you review your holdings once a year. Don't make quick decisions about selling — take your time and be sure that you understand tax and other ramifications before you sell.

The time it takes you to manage your portfolio, for example, is a vital matter if you're starved for time or weary of managing time-consuming investments. Leo, for example, loved to research, track, and trade individual stocks — until his daughter was born. Then Leo realized how many hours his hobby was taking away from his family, and that realization put his priorities into perspective. Leo now invests in time-friendly mutual funds and doesn't follow them like a hawk.

In contrast, Mary loves investing in real estate because she enjoys the challenge of researching, selecting, and managing her properties. She works in a job where she has to put up with lots of controlling, stressed-out bosses. For Mary, real estate isn't just a profitable investment; it's also a way of expressing herself and growing personally.

Maintaining Balance in Your Portfolio

A good reason to sell an investment is to allow you to better diversify your portfolio. Suppose that before reading this book, you purchased a restaurant stock every time you read about one, or even just ate in one in which you'd enjoyed the cooking! Now your portfolio resembles several bad strip malls, and restaurant stocks comprise 80 percent of your holdings. Or maybe, through your job, you've accumulated such a hefty chunk of stock in your employer that this one stock now overwhelms the rest of your investments.

It's time for you to diversify. Sell off some of the holdings you have too much of and invest the proceeds in solid investments, such as those that we recommend in this book. If you think your employer's stock is going to be a superior investment, holding a big chunk is your gamble. At a minimum, review Chapter 6 to see how to evaluate a particular stock. But remember to consider the consequences if you're wrong about your employer's stock.

Conservative investors often keep too much of their money in bank accounts, GICs, and the like. Read Chapter 3 to come up with an overall investment strategy that fits with the rest of your personal financial situation.

Deciding Which Investments Are Keepers

Often, people are tempted to sell an investment for the wrong reasons. One natural human tendency is to want to sell investments that have declined in value. Some people fear a further fall, and they don't want to be affiliated with a loser, especially when money is involved. We think this reaction resembles the phenomenon of piling into the lifeboats when a ship springs a leak.

Step back, take some deep breaths, and examine the merits of the investment you're considering selling. If an investment is otherwise still sound, why bail out when prices are down and a sale is going on? What are you going to do with the money? If anything, you should be contemplating buying more of such an investment. Don't make a decision to sell based on your current emotional response, especially to recent news events. If bad news has recently hit, it's already old news. Don't base your investment holdings on such transitory events.

Use the criteria for finding good investments in this book to evaluate the worthiness of your current holdings. If an investment is fundamentally sound, don't sell it.

A better reason to sell an investment is that it comes with high fees relative to comparable investments. For example, if you own a bond mutual fund that is socking it to you with fees of 2 percent per year or more, check out Chapter 8 to discover high-performing, lower-cost funds.

Tuning In to the Tax Consequences

When you sell investments that you hold outside a tax-sheltered retirement plan, such as a Registered Retirement Savings Plan (RRSP), taxes should be one factor in your decision. (See Chapter 3 to find out about tax rates that apply to the sale of an investment as well as to the distributions that investments make.) If the investments are inside a retirement plan or other account or plan that's sheltered from taxation, taxes aren't an issue unless you're withdrawing funds from the plan.

Just because you pay tax on a profit from selling an investment that's not inside a tax-sheltered plan or account doesn't mean that you should avoid selling. With real estate you live in, you can often avoid paying taxes on the profit you make (see Chapters 10 and 11). With stocks and mutual funds, things get a little more complex.

Figuring Out What Shares Cost

If you're selling stock, your capital gain is simply the difference between what you receive less what you paid when you bought the investment, along with any fees or commission. The purchase cost, plus any extra fees you incur when buying and selling it, is called the *adjusted cost base.* If you've bought shares in the same company at different times — and at different prices — you'll need to do a little math to calculate your adjusted cost base. Each time you make another purchase of the same investment, you have to add together your total number of shares or units and divide them by your total cost to that point to come up with an average.

Say you bought 1,000 shares of Bombardier for $5 a share including any commissions. Now suppose the stock rose to $6 and you bought another 1,000 at $6 a share including associated costs. You would now own 2,000 shares for a total cost of $11,000. Here's how to determine your adjusted cost base:

$$\frac{(\text{Initial purchase} + \text{commissions/fees})}{\text{Total number of shares/units}} + (\text{Subsequent purchase price} + \text{commissions/fees})$$

Or, to apply it to the example:

$$\frac{\$5,000 + \$6,000}{2,000} = \$5.50$$

Selling Investments with Hefty Profits

Of course, no one likes to pay taxes, but if an investment you own has appreciated in value, someday you'll have to pay tax when you sell it. Capital gains tax applies when you sell an investment at a higher price than you paid for it. As we explain in Chapter 3, your capital gains tax rate is different from the tax rate you pay on ordinary income (such as from employment earnings or interest on bank savings accounts).

Odds are, the longer you've held securities such as stocks, the greater the capital gains you'll have, because stocks tend to appreciate over time. If all your assets have appreciated greatly, you may resist selling to avoid taxes. However, if you need money for a major purchase, sell what you need and pay the tax. Even if you're in the highest marginal tax bracket, your tax rate on those profits is only about 23 percent, so you'll have lots left. Before you sell, however, do some rough figuring to make sure that you'll have enough money left to accomplish what you want.

If you hold a number of assets, in order to diversify and meet your other financial goals, give preference to selling your largest holdings with the smallest capital gains. If you have some securities that have profits and some that have losses, you can sell some of each to offset the profits with the losses.

Cutting Your (Securities) Losses

Perhaps you own some turkeys in your portfolio. If you need to raise cash for some particular reason, you may consider selling some securities at a loss. You can use these losses to offset gains you've made — or will make in the future — on the sale of other securities.

Your actual loss when it comes to the tax department is the difference between what you paid for the investment — the adjusted cost base — and what you received when you sold it, after deducting commissions and other fees involved in selling.

Just as you take half of any capital gain before calculating any taxes due, you can use only one-half of your loss to offset these taxable capital gains. However, if you can't use some or all of your allowable capital losses in a given year, it's not wasted. In general, you can't use capital losses to reduce ordinary income. But you can apply a capital loss against taxable capital gains you had in any of the three prior years. You can also carry the allowable capital loss forward indefinitely, and use it to offset taxable capital gains in any future year. The current amount of allowable capital losses that you have yet to apply against taxable capital gains is known as your *net capital losses.*

If you own a security that has ceased trading and appears worthless (or you've made a loan that hasn't been repaid), you can likely deduct this loss. Peruse the latest edition of *Tax Tips For Canadians for Dummies* (Wiley) for more information on what losses are deductible and how to claim these losses on your annual tax return.

Selling Investments with Unknown Costs

You may not know what some investments originally cost you or the person who bought them and later gave them to you. If you can't find that original statement, start by calling the firm where the investment was purchased. Whether it's an investment dealer or mutual fund company, the company should be able to send you copies of old account statements, although you may have to pay a small fee for this service.

Also, increasing numbers of investment firms, especially mutual fund companies, can tell you upon the sale of an investment what its original cost was. The cost generally calculated is the average cost for the shares you purchased. See *Tax Tips For Canadians For Dummies* for more ideas of what to do when original records aren't available for other assets, such as real estate.

Recognizing Dealer Differences

If you're selling securities such as stocks and bonds, you need to know that some dealers charge more — in some cases, lots more — to sell. Even if the securities you want to sell currently reside at a high-cost investment dealer, you can transfer them to a discount dealer. See Chapter 9 to read about the different types of investment dealers and how to select the best one for your situation.

Finding a Trustworthy Financial Adviser

You aren't stupid. Before you picked up this book, you may have considered yourself an investing dummy. We didn't, and we still don't, but hopefully you feel less like a dummy after reading this book. If you delegate your investment decision making to an adviser, you're likely to be disappointed.

Few financial advisers offer objective and knowledgeable advice. Unfortunately, if you're grappling with a selling decision, finding a competent and impartial financial adviser to help with the decision is about as difficult as finding a politician who doesn't accept special-interest money. Most financial consultants work on commission, which can cloud their judgment. And among the minority of fee-based advisers, a good number manage money, which creates other conflicts of interest. The more money you give them to invest and manage, the more money these advisers make. If you need advice about whether to sell some investments, consider turning to a tax or financial adviser who works on an hourly basis.

Chapter 22

Ten Tips for Investing in a Down Market

In This Chapter

▶ Keeping a level head amid the doom and gloom

▶ Identifying and fixing flaws in your portfolio

▶ Understanding why value stocks have less downside risk

*U*nless there's a lot of other breaking news, sharp drops in the stock market make headlines — stock market gyrations are great media fodder. Every day the market environment is different, and new stocks are plunging and rising. And now, with more individuals holding stocks through company and personal retirement plans, the media has a captive, concerned audience. In this chapter, we discuss how to maximize your chances for investing success when stocks take a turn for the worse.

Don't Panic

No one enjoys turning on the car radio, clicking the television set on, or logging on to the Internet and getting this news: "Stocks plunge. The Toronto Stock Exchange plummeted 800 points today."

Don't panic — it's just one day's events. Just because a home burned to the ground recently in your town and the news is being broadcast over all the local media, you probably wouldn't start living on the street out of fear of being at home during a fire. But you might take some sensible precautions, such as installing smoke alarms and repairing any malfunctioning appliances that might cause a fire, to ensure that your home isn't likely to become the next fire department statistic. Likewise, don't shun stocks, which produce terrific long-term returns, just because of the down periods. As we discuss in Chapter 2, risk and return go hand in hand. If you want wealth-building investments that provide superior long-term returns, you must be willing to accept risk (that is, volatility and down periods).

Although other wealth-building investments, such as real estate and small businesses, go through significant declines, you generally see few headlines on their daily price movements. A good reason for this is that no one reports on the pricing of real estate and small businesses minute by minute every business day, as is done with stock prices.

Keep Your Portfolio's Perspective in Mind

If you follow our advice, your portfolio will consist of diversified stock holdings, including some international stocks, preferably through mutual funds, along with some bonds.

Consider the perspective of one investor during the summer of 2002 when the stock market was dropping precipitously. "I just saw that the S&P 500 is now down 28 percent so far this year, and the NASDAQ is down 34 percent," he commented, with the not unusual follow-up question: "Should I sell?"

He was quite surprised to find that, after some number crunching, *his* portfolio of stocks and bonds was down just 8 percent for the year. Now, mind you, we're not trying to minimize or trivialize the fact that this investor had lost money so far that year. However, he overlooked the fact that the bonds in his portfolio had actually increased in value, as had some of his stock funds that were invested in value-oriented stocks. Please see Chapter 8 for tips on how to build a diversified mutual fund portfolio.

View Major Declines as Sales

Unlike retail stores, which experience bigger-than-normal crowds when prices are reduced, fewer investors, especially individual investors, want to buy stocks after they've suffered a sharp decline. When stock prices decline, don't get swept up in the pessimism. View declines as the financial markets having a sale on stocks. Stocks usually bottom when pessimism reaches a peak. The reason: Those who were motivated to sell have done so, and the major selling has exhausted itself.

Now, we're not saying you should randomly buy just any stock after a decline. For example, as we discuss in Part II, we're not advocates of buying individual stocks, especially a collection of stocks focused in the same industry (such as technology or auto manufacturing). When technology stocks started declining in 2000, some investors made the mistake of buying more of them after prices dropped 10 or 20 percent. Unfortunately, what such "buy on the dip" investors didn't realize was that the technology stocks that they were buying were still grossly overpriced when measured by price/earnings ratios and other valuation measures (see Chapter 5).

You're best off buying stocks gradually over time through well-managed, diversified mutual funds (see Chapter 8). When the broad stock market suffers a substantial decline and stocks are at reduced prices — on sale — you can step up your buying.

Identify Your Portfolio's Problems

Stock market declines can be effective at quickly exposing problems with your portfolio. For example, when technology stocks tumbled in the early 2000s, we started getting questions from investors who had loaded up on these stocks and wanted to know what they should do with their holdings. Many of these investors kept thinking about how much more their technology stocks were worth at their peak before the decline set in.

Our advice was to acknowledge the huge risk these investors were clearly taking by putting so many eggs in one basket. We also highlighted the dangers of chasing after a hot sector, and pointed out that what is a hot sector today often becomes tomorrow's laggard.

In addition to poorly diversified portfolios, a declining stock market can also expose the high fees you may be paying on your investments. Fewer investors care about getting whacked with fees amounting to, say, 2 percent annually when they're making 20 percent year after year. But after a few years of low or negative returns, such high fees become quite painful and more obvious.

Avoid Growth Stocks If You Get Queasy Easily

In a sustained stock market slide *(bear market),* the stocks that get clobbered the most tend to be the ones that were most overpriced from the period of the previous market rise *(bull market).* Like fads such as hula hoops, pet rocks, and Cabbage Patch dolls, in each bull market, particular types of growth stocks, such as Internet companies or biotechnology companies, can be especially hot.

Predicting the duration and magnitude of a bear market is nearly impossible. Consequently, wouldn't it make sense to focus your stock investing on those stocks that produce solid long-term returns and that tend to decline less in a major market decline? So-called value stocks tend to be among the safer types of stocks to hold during a bear market. Value stocks generally have less downside risk because they typically pay higher dividends and have relatively greater underlying asset values in comparison to their stock valuations.

As has happened in some past bear markets, numerous value-oriented stocks actually appreciated during the bear market in the early 2000s. Please see Chapter 8 for our discussion of the different types of stocks and mutual funds that practice value stock investing.

Tune Out Negative, Hyped Media

When the stock market is crumbling, such as the huge declines seen in late 2008 and early 2009, subjecting yourself to a daily diet of bad news and conflicting opinions about what to do next makes most investors do the wrong things. When major stock markets are really getting clobbered, it's not unusual to find people saying something along these lines: "It seems that the civilized world as we know it is coming to an end. We have all this tension and conflict in the Middle East, there's a war in Afghanistan, no one can believe company financial statements, the market keeps falling, and stocks are just too risky to hold. All I keep hearing is bad news when I turn on my television or go online. Shouldn't I just sell my stocks and buy something else?"

If you find yourself saying something similar, as a friend of Tony's did when the markets cratered in 2008, our advice is simple: Stop watching and focusing on bad news. Just like a steady diet of junk food is bad for your physical health, a continuous stream of negative, hyped news is bad for your financial health. In our observation, dwelling on bad news doesn't do such great things for people's emotional health, either.

Conflict is always occurring somewhere in the world. The business world will always have unethical and corrupt company executives. Holding stocks always carries risk. That's why those who see the glass as half full and who see the positive and not just the negative build wealth by holding stocks, real estate, and small business over the long term.

Ignore Large Point Declines — Consider the Percentages

It drives us crazy when the news media show a one-day chart of a major stock market index, such as the Toronto Stock Exchange Composite, on a day when the index drops a large number of points. In recent years, 200- and 300-point drops in the TSX happened fairly frequently.

Look at the percentage decline in an index rather than at a point decline. Although 200 to 300 points sounds like a horrendous drop, such a drop amounts to a move of about 2 to 3 percent. No one likes losing that portion of their wealth invested in stocks in one day, but the percentage of change sounds less horrifying than the point change.

Don't Believe You Need a Rich Dad to Be a Successful Investor

A young man wrote to Eric about an interview that he had read about the *Rich Dad, Poor Dad* series, by author Robert Kiyosaki. In the interview, Kiyosaki said that the rich are different from the rest of us because "They teach their children how to be rich. . . . These get-rich techniques include investing with leverage . . . and staying away from mutual funds . . . which are way too risky."

The young man came from a humble background and had been salting money away in mutual funds through his company's retirement plan. But he thought that he might be doomed to a lifetime of poverty after reading what the *Rich Dad* guru had to say. Here's what we say.

We've known plenty of people over the years who came from non-wealthy families who built substantial wealth by living within their means and by investing in the three wealth-building assets that we focus on in this book: stocks, real estate, and small business.

With regard to mutual funds and retirement savings plans, in addition to his saying that they are way too risky, Kiyosaki also says, "Those vehicles are only good for about 20 percent of the population, people making $100,000 or more." We couldn't disagree more. In fact, our experience is that mutual funds are tailor-made for non-wealthy people who don't have the assets to properly create a diversified portfolio themselves.

Kiyosaki also says that he doesn't like mutual funds because "Mutual funds have got no insurance from a stock market crash. To me, that's sad, and I am concerned." As we discuss in Parts I and II of this book, the best way to reduce the risk of investing in stocks is to diversify your holdings, not only in a variety of stocks, but also in other investments that don't move in tandem with the stock market.

Kiyosaki claims that he invests with the benefit of insurance when investing in real estate. He says, "My banker requires me to have insurance from catastrophic losses." This is a nonsensical comparison because such an insurance policy would cover losses from say, a fire, but not a decline in market value of the real estate due to overall market conditions. Interestingly, Kiyosaki followers got clobbered by shunning stocks, which rose sharply in the mid-2000s, and piling into real estate, which levelled off and then dropped sharply in most areas.

(Re) Read Chapters 4 and 5

When the going gets tough in the stock market, you can easily lose perspective. Even if you've already read them, please go back and read Chapters 4 and 5 again. These chapters explain how the stock market works and what influences stock prices in the short term versus the longer term. Be sure that you have the long-term perspective that you need to succeed with stock investing and that you really understand how the financial markets work.

Talk to People Who Care about You

Life's challenging events can be humbling and sometimes depressing. Holding an investment that's dropped a lot in value — whether it's a stock, mutual fund, real estate, or small business — is one such event. But you don't have to carry the burden yourself. Talk about your feelings with someone who understands and cares about you. Be clear about and communicate what you're seeking — empathy, good listening, a sounding board, or advice.

Index

• C •